CW00375829

The Longman Companion to
The European Union since 1945

Longman Companions to History

General Editors: Chris Cook and John Stevenson

Now available

The Longman Companion to

The European Union since 1945

Alasdair Blair

LONGMAN
London and New York

Pearson Education Limited
Edinburgh Gate
Harlow, Essex CM20 2JE, England
and Associated Companies throughout the world.

*Published in the United States of America
by Addison Wesley Longman, New York.*

© Pearson Education Limited 1999

The right of Alasdair Blair to be identified
as author of this Work has been asserted by him
in accordance with the Copyright,
Designs and Patents Act 1988.

All rights reserved; no part of this publication may be
reproduced, stored in any retrieval system, or transmitted
in any form or by any means, electronic, mechanical,
photocopying, recording, or otherwise, without either the
prior written permission of the Publishers or a licence
permitting restricted copying in the United Kingdom issued
by the Copyright Licensing Agency Ltd,
90 Tottenham Court Road, London W1P 9HE.

First published 1999

ISBN 0–582–36885–5 CSD
ISBN 0–582–36884–7 PPR

Visit Addison Wesley Longman on the world wide web at
http://www.awl-he.com

British Library Cataloguing in Publication Data

A catalogue entry for this title is available from the British Library

Library of Congress Cataloging-in-Publication Data

Blair, Alasdair, 1971–
    The Longman companion to the European Union since 1945 /
Alasdair Blair.
        p.   cm. — (Longman companions to history)
    Includes bibliographical references and index.
    ISBN 0–582–36885–5 (hardbound). — ISBN 0–582–36884–7 (pbk.)
    1. European federation.   2. Europe—Politics and government—
1945–   I. Title.   II. Series.
JN15.B59   1999
341.242′2—dc21   98–51662
                                                                   CIP

Set by 35 in 9½/12 pt New Baskerville
Produced by Addison Wesley Longman Singapore (Pte) Ltd.,
Printed in Singapore

Contents

List of Maps

Diagram

Preface

This book examines the development of the European Union from the Paris and Rome Treaties to the recent Amsterdam reforms. The provisions of those Treaties have sprouted numerous policy-making and decision-making procedures embracing a plethora of subjects, while it is testament to the European Union's importance that there has been a vast expansion in the number of texts which analyse the subject. This companion is a further contribution to the field, although not being an exhaustive survey. Rather, it aims to provide reliable analysis to students, academics and the wider public of the main policies which encompass the European Union. In doing so it is clearly not an original piece of research, but instead draws heavily on the works of others, especially reference books such as *Keesings Contemporary Archives* and *The Dictionary of National Biography*.

The categories which the book covers have been selected to provide easily accessible information. Wherever possible this has been cross-referenced with other entries, while a detailed subject index has been provided. This should ensure that readers are able to access information pertinent to the subject they are interested in. Bibliographical information is provided at the end of the book.

The construction of the book owes much to the kind encouragement of the series editors, Dr Chris Cook and Dr John Stevenson, while the staff at Longman, in particular Hilary Shaw, have helped to bring the project to fruition. Staff and students at the Universities of Leicester and North London have both stimulated my interest and helped to refine my thoughts on European politics. I would particularly like to thank Geoff Berridge, Christopher Goldsmith, Jennifer Hutchinson, Simon Kear, Renie Lewis, Philip Lynch, Mark Maynard, Jan Melissen, Jörg Monar, Sandy Pearson, Wyn Rees, Jane Savage, Timothy Stanton, Paul Trickett and John Young.

Alasdair Blair
30 November 1998

List of Abbreviations

ACP	African, Caribbean and Pacific Countries
Benelux	Benelux Economic Union (Belgium, the Netherlands and Luxembourg)
BIS	Bank for International Settlements
BoE	Bank of England
BSE	Bovine spongiform encephalopathy
CAP	Common Agricultural Policy
CBI	Confederation of British Industry
CCP	Common Commercial Policy
CCT	Common Customs Tariff: tariff on goods entering the EC
CDU	Christian Democratic Union
CEC	Commission of the European Communities
CEEC	Central and Eastern European Countries
CEN	European Committee for Standardisation: standards body including EC and EFTA states
CENELEC	European Committee for Electrotechnical Standardisation
CEP	Common Energy Policy
CERN	European Organisation for Nuclear Research
CET	Common External Tariff
CFP	Common Fisheries Policy
CFSP	Common Foreign and Security Policy
CJD	Creutzfeldt-Jakob disease
CJHA	Common action on Justice and Home Affairs
CM	Common Market
CMEA	Council for Mutual Economic Assistance
CMU	Capital Market Union
COMECON	Council for Mutual Economic Assistance
COMETT	Community Action Programme for Education and Training for Technology: EU high-technology cooperation
Copenur	Standing Committee on Uranium Enrichment
CoR	The Committee of the Regions
COREPER	Committee of Permanent Representatives: Member States' Ambassadors to the EC: COREPER I consists

	of Deputy Permanent Representatives, while COREPER II consists of Permanent Representatives
COREU	Telex Network among EPC 'correspondents Européens' (European correspondents)
COST	Committee on European Cooperation in the field of Scientific and Technical Research
CPE	Centrally Planned Economies
CSCE	Conference on Security and Cooperation in Europe
CSF	Community support framework
CU	Customs Union
DG	Directorate General: name for departments within the Commission
DI	Direct Investment
EAEC	European Atomic Energy Community (Euratom)
EAGGF	European Agricultural Guidance and Guarantee Fund
EBRD	European Bank for Reconstruction and Development
EC	European Community
ECA	European Court of Auditors
ECB	European Central Bank (Eurofed)
ECE	European Commission for Europe
ECHR	European Court of Human Rights
ECJ	European Court of Justice
EcoFin	Council of Economic and Finance Ministers
ECOSOC	Economic and Social Committee
ECPE	European Centre for Public Enterprises
ECSC	European Coal and Steel Community
ECU	European Currency Unit
EDC	European Defence Community
EDF	European Development Fund
EDIE	European Direct Investment in Europe
EDIUS	European Direct Investment in the USA
EEA	European Economic Area
EEC	European Economic Community
EEIG	European Economic Interest Grouping: legal framework for EC joint ventures
EES	European Economic Space: original term for EU–EFTA negotiations
EFTA	European Free Trade Association
EIB	European Investment Bank
ELDR	Group of the Liberal Democratic and Reformist Party
EMCF	European Monetary Cooperation Fund
EMI	European Monetary Institute
EMS	European Monetary System
EMU	Economic and Monetary Union

EMUA	European Monetary Unit of Account
EP	European Parliament
EPC	European Political Community/Cooperation
EPP	European People's Party
EPU	European Political Union
ERA	Group of the European Radical Alliance
ERASMUS	European Community Action Scheme for the Mobility of University Students
ERDF	European Regional Development Fund
ERM	Exchange Rate Mechanism
ESA	European Space Agency
ESC	Economic and Social Committee
ESCB	European System of Central Banks
ESF	European Social Fund
ESPRIT	European Strategic Programme for Research and Development in Information Technology
ETUC	European Trade Union Confederation
EU	Economic Union
EUA	European unit of account, the forerunner of the ECU
EUI	European University Institute
EUL/NGL	Confederal Group of the European United Left/ Nordic Green Left
Euratom	European Atomic Energy Community
EUREKA	European Research Coordination Agency
Eurostat	Statistical Office of the European Communities
EUROGROUP	Acronym used for the informal Group of NATO European Defence Ministers
FCMA	Free Capital Movement Area
FEU	Full Economic Union
FLMZ	Free Labour Movement Zone
FNU	Netherlands Federation of Trade Unions
FOREX	Foreign exchange
FRG	Federal Republic of Germany
FRY	Federal Republic of Yugoslavia
FTA	Free Trade Area
GATT	General Agreement on Tariffs and Trade
GDP	Gross domestic product
GFCF	Gross fixed capital formation
GNP	Gross national product
IAEA	International Atomic Energy Authority
IBRD	International Bank for Reconstruction and Development (World Bank)
IEA	International Energy Authority

I-Edn	Group of Independents for a Europe of Nations
IEPG	Independent European Programme Group
IGC	Intergovernmental conference
ILO	International Labour Organisation
IMF	International Monetary Fund
IMP	Integrated Mediterranean Programmes
IoD	Institute of Directors
JET	Joint European Torus
JHA	Justice and home affairs
JRC	Joint Research Centre
LDC	Less developed country
LEC	Labour exporting country
LIC	Labour importing country
LMU	Labour Market Union
MCA	Monetary Compensatory Amounts
MEP	Member of the European Parliament
MFN	Most Favoured Nation
MU	Monetary Union
NACC	North Atlantic Cooperation Council
NATO	North Atlantic Treaty Organisation
NCI	New Community Instrument
NIC	Newly industrialised countries
NTB	Non-Tariff Barriers
OCA	Optimum Currency Area
OCTs	Overseas Countries and Territories
OECD	Organisation for Economic Cooperation and Development
OEEC	Organisation for European Economic Cooperation
OIEC	Organisation for International Economic Cooperation
OPEC	Organisation of Petroleum Exporting Countries
OSCE	Organisation for Security and Cooperation in Europe
PermRep	Permanent Representation
PES	Group of the Party of European Socialists
PHARE	Poland and Hungary Assistance for Economic Reconstruction Programme – now covers all of Eastern and Central Europe
PPS	Purchasing power standard
QMV	Qualified Majority Voting
QR	Quantitative Restrictions
R & D	Research and development
RACE	Research and Development in Advanced Communications Technology in Europe
RPR	Rally for the Republic (French Political Party)

RS	Bosnian Serb Republic, later renamed 'Republika Srpska'
SEA	Single European Act
SHAPE	Supreme Headquarters Allied Powers Europe
SME	Small and medium-sized enterprises
SOEC	Statistical Office of the European Communities
TAC	Total allowable catch
TACIS	Technical Assistance to the Commonwealth of Independent States and Georgia
TEMPUS	Trans-European Mobility Programme for University Studies
TEU	Treaty on European Union
TREVI	*Terrorisme, Radicalisme, Extrémisme, Violence Internationale*
UDF	Union for French Democracy
UFE	Union for Europe Group
UN	United Nations
UNCTAD	United Nations Conference on Trade and Development
UNICE	Union of Industries of the European Community
USA	United States of America
UN	United Nations
VAT	Value Added Tax
VER	Voluntary Export Restraint
WEU	Western European Union
WTO	World Trade Organisation

Countries

A	Austria
B	Belgium
D	Federal Republic of Germany
DK	Denmark
E	Spain
F	France
FIN	Finland
GR	Greece
I	Italy
IRL	Ireland
L	Luxembourg
NL	The Netherlands
P	Portugal
S	Sweden
UK	United Kingdom
EUR 9	European Union excluding Greece, Spain and Portugal

EUR 10	European Union excluding Spain and Portugal
EUR 12	European Union excluding Austria, Finland and Sweden
EUR 15	European Union, 15 Member States

Currencies

BFR	Belgian franc
CAD	Canadian dollar
DKR	Danish krone
DM	Deutschmark
DR	Greek drachma
ECU	European currency unit
ESC	Portuguese escudo
FF	French franc
HFL	Dutch guilder
IRL	Irish pound (punt)
LFR	Luxembourg franc
LIT	Italian lira
OS	Austrian schilling
PTA	Spanish peseta
SFR	Swiss franc
UKL	Pound sterling
USD	US dollar
YEN	Japanese yen

For Katherine

SECTION I

Overview

1951   Belgium, the Federal Republic of Germany (FRG), France, Italy, Luxembourg and the Netherlands formed the European Coal and Steel Community (ECSC).

1957   The European Economic Community and the European Atomic Energy Community (Euratom) were founded. The European Parliament (EP) comprised 142 members delegated by their national parliaments.

1967   The Merger Treaty established a single executive for the ECSC, the EEC and Euratom. The European Community denoted the coming together of the institutions of the three organisations.

1973   The accession of Denmark, Ireland and the United Kingdom. The EP increased in size to 198 members.

1979   The EP was elected by direct universal suffrage for the first time, with a total number of 410 members meeting at the Palais de l'Europe in Strasbourg in July.

1981   Greece joined the EC. The membership of the EP increased to 434.

1984   The second EP elections by direct universal suffrage.

1986   Spain and Portugal joined the EC. The EP increased to 518 members. The Single European Act established a single market, introduced legislative cooperation between the EP and the Council and brought the system of political cooperation in the field of foreign policy.

1989   The third EP elections by direct universal suffrage.

1991   The Treaty on European Union was negotiated at the Maastricht European Council, conferring important new powers on the EP, including co-decision on legislation and the appointment of a European Ombudsman.

1993   The Treaty on European Union came into force, establishing a three-pillar structure, including a common foreign and security policy (CFSP), the establishment of cooperation in the field of justice and home affairs (JHA) and provisions for the creation of an Economic and Monetary Union with a single European currency.

1994   The fourth EP elections by direct universal suffrage. The number of members increased to 567 to take account of German unification.

1995   The accession of Austria, Finland and Sweden. Membership of the EP increased to 626.

1997   The Treaty of Amsterdam was agreed to by Member States at the Amsterdam European Council of 17 June 1997. This included the placing of employment and citizens' rights at the heart of the Union; providing Europe with a stronger voice in world affairs; making the institutional structure of the Union more efficient with a view to future enlargement; and eliminating any remaining obstacles to the freedom of movement.

Primary areas of competence: agriculture, competition, consumer protection, culture, education, environment, fisheries, overseas development, regional policy, single market, trade and transport. Intergovernmental cooperation for CFSP and JHA.

Council of Ministers: comprises a representative of each state (15 Ministers) who meet in Brussels and Luxembourg with the purpose of analysing and adopting EU legislation.

Court of Auditors: comprises 15 members (one from each state) and is based in Luxembourg. Its primary task is to monitor the EU's finances.

Court of Justice: comprises 15 judges (one from each state) and is based in Luxembourg. Its primary task is to ensure that the Treaties are applied.

European Council: meetings of Heads of State and Government which take place at least twice a year, providing the EU with political direction.

European Commission: there are 20 European Commissioners, of which two come from France, the FRG, Italy, Spain and the UK. Other Member States only have one European Commissioner. The European Commission proposes legislation and policy and is responsible for reviewing its implementation.

European Parliament: direct elections take place every five years, the first of which was in 1979. The EP scrutinises EU legislation, approves the appointment of the European Commission, approves international agreements, questions the Presidency of the Council and decides the annual budget.

Legislative process:

1. The European Commission puts forward a proposal (draft directive).
2. The EP must be consulted on proposals. It gives its opinions and suggests amendments (after one or more readings).
3. Other bodies are consulted, including the Economic and Social Committee and the Committee of the Regions.
4. The Council of Ministers adopts the new law, having examined the proposal with representatives of its governments. In certain circumstances the Council of Ministers adopts the law jointly with the EP. Some decisions are made by unanimity, others by qualified majority voting (QMV).

SECTION II

Chronology

Overview

From Rome to Amsterdam and six to 15, the European Union has undergone a process of near constant change and adaptation. Readers of this companion are witness to a European continent that does not bear the division and difficulties which the early post-war years experienced. In that period Europe became a focal point for wider global tensions, with Winston Churchill rightly noting in March 1946 the creation of an Iron Curtain across Europe. Some five decades later, those countries of Eastern Europe are applicant members of the EU and all that remains of the Iron Curtain are souvenirs. In the intervening period, the then European Economic Community and its predecessor organisations, such as the European Coal and Steel Community, demonstrated a willingness in its Member States to carve out a peaceful and prosperous future. The events which span the period are detailed in this chronology, from the UK's initial decision not to participate in the construction of the European project, to its unsuccessful attempts to gain entry in the 1960s. These episodes of history provide information not just about developments within Europe, but detail the views and attitudes of European and non-European countries to wider issues.

Of external factors, it was as clear in the 1960s as it is today that a special bond exists between the UK and the USA. While de Gaulle may have used that relationship as a basis for vetoing the UK's application to join the Community, the USA has nevertheless been a constant supporter of greater European integration. It rightly considered that an alliance of European nations would foster an environment of peace and security and believed that the UK would be a key member of such an organisation. That London joined at a later stage obviously influenced its position within Europe, where it has often been perceived to be awkward, adopting an Atlanticist perspective. But the UK has, of course, been instrumental to the success of the present EU and was a primary supporter of the single market programme and before that helped to establish the European Regional Development Fund. Today, its political and security resources are often called upon to assist in solving the many problems that face the EU and the world in general. As with many world issues, it is the USA which has the ability to reach across the globe and this has been instrumental behind London's reluctance to support fully the creation of a European defence identity in the face of weakening NATO.

It is, however, in other areas that the EU has made its greatest impact on world affairs. This clearly includes the present issue of Economic and Monetary Union, which is one of the most significant issues that the EU has ever tackled. Although a single currency is not yet a reality, its creation will, of course, have a great impact not just on EU members but also on the global economy. Within the EU, a single currency will bring obvious benefits for consumers and industry through the abolition of currency exchange transactions. In addition, it is likely that the lower interest rates of continental Europe will spread to countries such as the UK. But this project also brings with it the problem of acceptance, especially among sceptical audiences such as those in the UK. Elsewhere, an often unrecognised crucial aspect of the EU's history has been its external relations. This has included providing assistance to the developing world, with trade and association agreements, ensuring that the EU is not a fortress. European consumers can readily see the advantages of these agreements through the products available to them, while trade agreements, for example in the form of the General Agreement on Tariffs and Trade, demonstrate the benefit of European rather than domestic bargaining. But it is important to note that such benefits are not just for the domestic audience. The whole point of creating a network of alliances is to increase stability and prosperity throughout the world. These and numerous other issues are traced in this chronology, while further detailed and specific information can be found in the next section, embracing points of crisis in the history of the EU.

1.   Cold War, 1945–49

1945
26 June.   The United Nations Charter was signed in San Francisco.
27 July.   Victory for the Labour Party in the UK general election.
6 August.   Explosion of Hiroshima atomic bomb.

1946
16 March.   Winston Churchill's 'Iron Curtain' speech at Fulton, Missouri.
19 September.   Winston Churchill urged Franco-German reconciliation within a United States of Europe in a speech at Zürich.

1947
4 March.   Treaty of Dunkirk. France and the UK signed a 50-year Treaty of Alliance and Mutual Assistance at Dunkirk.
12 March.   President Truman said that 'it must be the policy of the United States to support free peoples who are resisting attempted subjugation by armed minorities or by outside pressure' (Truman Doctrine), and requested financial aid to Greece and Turkey.
17 March.   Benelux Treaty came into force, an agreement comprising Belgium, Luxembourg and the Netherlands.
5 June.   The US Secretary of State, General George Marshall, announced a plan for the economic rehabilitation of Europe which motivated the

European Recovery Programme and helped form the Organisation for European Economic Cooperation (OEEC).

5 October. The Soviet Union and its allies' rejection of Marshall aid resulted in the formation of Cominform.

23 October. The General Agreement on Tariffs and Trade (GATT) was signed after a prolonged 23-nation conference which resulted in the setting up of a permanent secretariat in Geneva. A set of rules governing the conduct of international trade was established, and 123 bilateral treaties were made during the first round of negotiations.

1948

January. Belgium, Luxembourg and the Netherlands established a customs union.

22 January. The UK Foreign Secretary, Ernest Bevin, proposed a form of Western Union in a House of Commons speech.

17 March. Brussels Treaty was signed by Belgium, France, Luxembourg, the Netherlands and the UK. Constituting a 50-year alliance against attack in Europe, it provided for economic, social and cultural collaboration and collective self-defence. It was the forerunner of the North Atlantic Treaty Organisation (NATO).

3 April. President Truman signed the Foreign Assistance Act, making the Marshall Plan law.

16 April. The OEEC was formed out of the Committee for European Economic Cooperation. It had been formerly set up by 16 countries to assess their requirements in goods and foreign exchanges between 1948 and 1952. The members of the OEEC were Austria, Benelux, Denmark, France, the FRG, Greece, Iceland, Ireland, Italy, Norway, Portugal, Sweden, Switzerland, Turkey and the UK.

7–11 May. The International Committee of the Movement for European Unity held a European Congress in The Hague.

24 June. The Berlin blockade by the Soviet Union began.

6 July. Start of talks in Washington between the US and the Brussels-Treaty powers on North Atlantic defence.

1 September. Convening of West German Constituent Assembly.

27–28 September. The Defence Ministers of the Brussels-Treaty powers decided to create a Western European Union defence organisation.

October. European Movement established in the wake of the May 1948 Congress of Europe.

25–26 October. The Consultative Council of the Brussels-Treaty powers announced 'complete agreement on the principle of a defensive pact for the North Atlantic and on the next steps to be taken in this action'.

10 December. Start of negotiations in Washington on the drafting of the North Atlantic Treaty between the representatives of Canada, the USA and the Brussels-Treaty powers.

1949

15 March. The negotiating powers of the North Atlantic Treaty asked Denmark, Iceland, Italy, Norway and Portugal to accede.

18 March. Publication of the text of the North Atlantic Treaty.

4 April. NATO was formed for defence purposes by Belgium, Canada, Denmark, France, Iceland, Italy, Luxembourg, the Netherlands, Norway, Portugal, the UK and the USA.

20 April. Start of six-day European Economic Conference in London organised by the European League for Economic Cooperation.

5 May. Statute of the Council of Europe was signed in Strasbourg by the five Brussels-Treaty powers as well as Sweden, Denmark, Ireland, Italy and Norway. They were later joined by Iceland, Greece, Germany and Austria. While the intention was to provide a forum for Western European Parliamentarians, the aim of political unity did not arise, with the Council having been given no real powers, decisions being subjected to a veto.

9 May. Lifting of the Berlin blockade.

10 August. Inaugural session of the Council of Europe in Strasbourg.

24 August. North Atlantic Treaty came into force.

20 September. Constitution of the Federal Republic of Germany (FRG).

6 October. US President Truman signed the Mutual Defence Assistance Act.

2. Ideals and breakdown, 1950–54

1950

9 May. Schuman Plan proposal to put French and German coal and steel industries under one authority. European Defence Community (EDC) plan was presented by French Defence Minister, René Pleven. While it proposed to integrate the FRG into the defence of Western Europe, it was eventually rejected by the French National Assembly in 1954.

11 May. The three Foreign Ministers of the USA, France and the UK – Dean Acheson, Robert Schuman and Ernest Bevin – met in London to discuss the problems of Western defence and the future of the FRG.

27 May. UK government explained to the French government that it could not accept a prior commitment to pool coal and steel resources and set up a common authority.

3 June. The Six issued their first communiqué announcing their intention to go ahead with 'the pooling of the production of coal and steel and the institution of a new high authority'.

20 June. Start of the negotiations between the Six that led to the ECSC Treaty.

25 June. North Korean forces attacked the Republic of South Korea.

1 July. The European Payments Union was established, providing multilateral payments among the OEEC countries and their associated territories.

1 August. Turkey announced that it would make a formal application to join the North Atlantic Treaty.

11 August. The Consultative Assembly of the Council of Europe in Strasbourg adopted a proposal that called for a 'common European army under the authority of a European Minister of Defence'.

24 October. The Pleven Plan was put to the French National Assembly by Prime Minister René Pleven. It envisaged the creation of a supranational army of initially 100,000 men, including West German troops, financed by a common budget and placed under the leadership of a European Minister of Defence who would be responsible to the Council of Ministers and Common Assembly. Members of NATO, with the exception of the FRG, would retain control of those national forces not used as part of the European Army.

28–31 October. The UK refused to join the Pleven Plan because the government believed France was advocating a plan whose only function was to prevent a resurgence of German power.

4 November. The UK ratified the European Convention on Human Rights.

18 December. The Spofford Proposal stressed that the USA would increase its European defence commitment if European NATO powers agreed to establish an integrated European force (including a West German contribution).

19 December. US General Dwight Eisenhower was appointed Supreme Allied Commander Europe (SACEUR) by the North Atlantic Council.

20 December. The Consultative Council of the Brussels-Treaty powers decided to merge the military organisation of the Western Union into NATO.

1951

12 February. UK Prime Minister, Clement Attlee, stated four conditions for a West German contribution to the defence of Europe: (1) the rearmament of NATO countries had to procede that of the FRG; (2) Allied forces had to be significantly strengthened before West German units could be raised; (3) West German units had to be associated with other NATO forces in a manner that did not constitute them being a threat; and (4) there had to be an agreement with the West Germans on the level of their contribution.

15 February. Commencement of the Paris European Army conference. The UK noted its intention not to participate in the EDC by only sending an observer, Sir Oliver Harvey, the Ambassador to Paris. Canada, Denmark, Norway, Portugal and the USA did likewise.

18 April.   The Treaty of Paris, which established the ECSC, was signed by Benelux, France, the FRG and Italy 'to establish, by creating an economic community, the foundation of a wider and deeper community'. The Treaty was to become operational in 1953 and established the first common European authority. The ECSC High Authority was subject to democratic control through an Assembly composed of representatives from the six national parliaments, as well as to rule of law through the Court of Justice.

8 July.   Petersberg negotiations on the FRG's role in the defence of Europe were suspended.

25 October.   Victory for the Conservative Party in the UK general election.

1952

18 February.   Greece and Turkey joined the North Atlantic Treaty.

27 May.   The EDC Treaty was signed in Paris by the Six and a Treaty of Association was signed with the UK on the same day. Member States' representatives of the North Atlantic Treaty signed a Protocol to the Treaty which gave guarantees to EDC members.

25 July.   The ECSC came into operation.

10 August.   First meeting in Luxembourg of the ECSC High Authority; a UK diplomatic representative was appointed to the organisation.

10 September.   The ECSC Common Assembly held its first sitting in Strasbourg.

1953

29 January.   France ratified the EDC Treaty.

10 February.   An ECSC common market for coal, iron ore and scrap was opened.

1 May.   An ECSC common market for steel was opened.

1954

13 April.   Memorandum of UK association with the EDC was published.

30 August.   The French National Assembly rejected the EDC Treaty.

3 October.   The London Treaty included a commitment by the UK to pledge four army divisions to the continent in support of the Western European Union (WEU).

23 October.   Paris Agreements were signed, embodying decisions of the London Conference for amendment of the Brussels Treaty to admit Italy and the FRG, with German membership of NATO. The WEU was formed, consisting of the Six ECSC countries plus the UK.

21 December.   An association agreement between the UK and the ECSC was signed in London by Jean Monnet and Duncan Sandys. This provided for a Council of Association meeting to take place alternatively in London or Luxembourg, the meeting comprising four representatives from each side, with a provision for subsidiary committees.

3. Road to Rome, 1955–60

1955

February. The UK's associate status of the ECSC was ratified in the House of Commons.

5 May. The Federal Republic of Germany was integrated into NATO and the WEU by the Treaties of Paris.

20 May. Benelux countries proposed to other ECSC countries the creation of a European atomic organisation and customs union.

26 May. Victory for the Conservative Party in the UK general election.

2–4 June. A committee was set up under the chairmanship of Paul-Henri Spaak at the Messina Conference of Foreign Ministers of the Six. The committee was to look at ways in which 'a fresh advance towards the building of Europe' could be achieved.

23 September. The Association Agreement between UK and the ECSC entered into force.

1956

29 May. The Spaak Report was approved by Foreign Ministers.

June. Negotiations between the Six with the intention of forming an Economic Community and an Atomic Energy Community were formally opened.

18 July. The European Nuclear Energy Agency (ENEA) was proposed.

26 July. Egypt nationalised the Suez canal.

17 August. The Communist Party was banned in the FRG.

29 September. Franco-German agreements on the Saar.

3 October. UK Chancellor of the Exchequer, Harold Macmillan, announced the government's readiness to join a limited European Free Trade Area (EFTA).

31 October. Franco-British intervention in the Suez canal area.

1957

1 January. Political integration of the Saar with the FRG.

7 February. The UK put forward its proposal for the establishment of EFTA to the OEEC.

25 March. The Treaties of Rome, which established the EEC and European Atomic Energy Community (Euratom), were signed.

29 July. Signing in Berlin of a declaration by the governments of France, the FRG, the UK and the USA which affirmed the identity of their policies regarding the reunification of the FRG and European security.

1958

1 January. The Treaties of Rome came into effect.

7 January. Walter Hallstein was appointed the first President of the European Commission.

1 February.   The ENEA came into effect.

March.   The Monetary Committee was established 'to keep under review the monetary and financial situation of the Member States and of the Community'.

19 March.   First meeting in Strasbourg of the European Parliamentary Assembly.

1 June.   General Charles de Gaulle was invited to head the French government.

3–11 July.   A conference in Stresa established the foundations for the CAP.

21 December.   General Charles de Gaulle was elected President of the French Republic.

27 December.   Ten European countries restored the convertibility of their currencies as defined in Article VIII of the IMF Articles of Agreement. This signalled the demise of the European Payments Union.

29 December.   A 14.8% devaluation of the French franc.

1959

1 January.   The first tariff reductions and quota enlargements in the common market took place.

February.   Benelux states signed a new treaty of economic union to establish the Benelux Economic Union.

4 February.   A cooperation agreement was signed between the UK and Euratom.

May.   First meeting of the Council of Economics and Finance Ministers (EcoFin).

8 June.   Greece requested association with the EEC under Article 238 of the Treaty of Rome.

8 October.   Victory for the Conservative Party in the UK general election.

1960

January.   The Benelux Economic Union formally came into operation.

4 January.   Stockholm Convention, establishing the EFTA, was signed by Austria, Denmark, Norway, Portugal, Sweden, Switzerland and the UK.

13 April.   The UK government announced the end of the Blue Streak Missile programme.

May.   First Directive on the liberalisation of capital movements.

3 May.   EFTA formally came into existence, being subsequently joined by Finland, Iceland and Liechtenstein.

17 May.   The Paris Summit meeting collapsed.

9 June.   The Six rejected early negotiations to join with EFTA.

27 July.   A UK Cabinet reshuffle meant that Lord Home became the Foreign Secretary and Edward Heath became the Lord Privy Seal with special responsibility for Europe.

7 November. In a speech to the UK Council of the European Movement Harold Macmillan called for European economic unity.

1 December. The WEU invited the UK to negotiations for full EEC membership.

14 December. Organisation for Economic Cooperation and Development (OECD) Treaty was signed in Paris, replacing the OEEC with the inclusion of Canada and the USA.

19–20 December. The basic principles governing the CAP were approved by the Council of Ministers.

4. Establishment and progress, 1961–63

1961

1 January. The common market took its first action in establishing a common external tariff.

28–29 January. General de Gaulle and Harold Macmillan had private talks at Rambouillet, at which UK membership of the Community was discussed.

10–11 February. Paris Summit of the Six on the development of the Union with regard to expansion. The communiqué of the meeting expressed a willingness to create agreements with other European countries, especially the UK. The representatives were de Gaulle (France), Adenauer (Federal Republic of Germany), Amintore Fanfani (Italy), Jan de Quay (the Netherlands), Gaston Eyskens (Belgium), and Pierre Werner (Luxembourg).

27 February. Edward Heath told the WEU that the UK was prepared to accept, in principle, the common external tariff.

1 March. France rejected a UK proposal for a European system in which the UK would retain her Commonwealth preference and agricultural arrangements. The French Foreign Minister, Couve de Murville, invited the UK to join the EEC.

11 May. Denmark's Foreign Minister, J.O. Krag, stated that Denmark would apply for membership of the EEC if the UK did.

28 June. The London Declaration stated that the UK would coordinate any EEC accession negotiations with its EFTA partners.

July. The Monnet Committee proposed the creation of a European Union of Monetary Reserves as the first move towards a European currency.

4 July. Ireland announced its intention of joining the EEC.

9 July. The EEC signed an association agreement with Greece known as the Treaty of Athens.

18 July. Bonn Declaration on political union was signed by the Six.

1 August. Austria announced its intention of seeking some form of participation in the EEC. Ireland applied for membership of the EEC.

9 August. The UK sent its formal application to join the EEC.

10 August. Denmark applied for EEC membership.

13 August.   Erection of Berlin Wall.

1 September.   The first regulation regarding the free movement of workers from Member States within the EEC came into effect.

12–14 September.   The Commonwealth Consultative Council met in Accra to discuss the implications of the UK's entry into the EEC.

13 September.   Commonwealth Finance Ministers criticised the UK's decision to join the EEC.

26 September.   The common market Council of Ministers unanimously agreed to open negotiations for the UK's entry.

30 September.   The convention which established the OECD came into force.

10 October.   Edward Heath accepted the Rome Treaty and the political consequences but sought conditions for UK agriculture in a statement in Paris.

12 October.   The UK Conservative Party approved Macmillan's decision to enter the common market.

23 October.   Ireland commenced its negotiations for membership of the EEC.

26 October.   Denmark's negotiations for membership of the EEC began.

2 November.   Publication of the Fouchet Plan Draft Treaty for political union. This was rejected by the Six apart from France.

8 November.   Formal negotiations began in Brussels between the UK and the common market Council of Ministers.

15 December.   The three neutrals, Austria, Sweden and Switzerland, applied for association with the common market.

30 December.   The common market countries postponed the decision on UK agriculture.

1962

14 January.   The Community fixed the basic features of the common agriculture policy, as well as regulations for grains, pigmeat, eggs and poultry, fruit and vegetables.

20 January.   The talks between the UK and the common market were delayed while the Six sought agreement on a common agricultural policy.

9 February.   Spain applied for an association agreement with the EEC.

28 February.   The Norwegian Prime Minister announced that Norway would apply for membership of the EEC.

2 March.   The UK applied for membership of the ECSC.

5 March.   The UK applied for membership of Euratom.

30 March.   The Assembly changed its name to the EP.

17 April.   The Fouchet Plan collapsed at a Foreign Ministers' meeting, primarily because of a lack of agreement over the UK's role.

30 April.   Norway requested negotiations for membership to the common market.

11 May.   Edward Heath put forward the first practical offer on the UK's membership of the common market.

15 May.   The Six agreed to accelerate the establishment of a common market.

28 May.   Portugal announced its desire to join the EEC.

30 May.   In its negotiations to join the common market, the UK made a concession on Commonwealth manufactured goods.

2 June.   Harold Macmillan visited General de Gaulle in Paris.

5 June.   The UK received criticism from Australia, New Zealand and Canada over its handling of the negotiations to enter the common market.

1 July.   The European Agricultural Guidance and Guarantee Fund (EAGGF) began operation.

4 July.   Negotiations with Norway for membership of the EEC began.

6 July.   The Six accepted annual agricultural reviews.

20 July.   Hugh Gaitskell of the Labour Party suggested that a general election should be held if UK terms of entry were not satisfactory.

30 July.   The first regulations implementing the common agriculture policy came into effect.

5 August.   After a long negotiating session no agreement was produced between the UK and the Six. Spaak stated that the UK was unable to accept the Six's proposal and the talks were recessed until October.

19 September.   Conclusion of the London Commonwealth conference, which had commenced on 10 September. The meeting produced a communiqué which agreed to the UK continuing its negotiations to join the common market.

1 November.   Agreement was reached on Greece's associate membership of the EEC.

28 November.   The Gaullist Party won an absolute majority in the French National Assembly.

December.   Second Directive on the liberalisation of capital movements.

5 December.   Dean Acheson stated that the UK 'has lost an empire and not yet found a role' in a speech to the West Point Military Academy in New York.

15 December.   Harold Macmillan had talks with General Charles de Gaulle at Rambouillet over the question of UK membership of the Community.

18–21 December.   Macmillan met with President Kennedy in Nassau. The talks were concerned with the US cancellation of Skybolt, which had been intended as a replacement for the UK Blue Streak missile (which itself had been cancelled). As a consequence, the USA agreed to supply the Polaris missile to the UK. This was later to be used by de Gaulle as a means of vetoing the UK's application to join the EEC because it demonstrated unacceptable close cooperation between London and Washington.

1963

14 January. The day before Edward Heath was due to start one of two scheduled long sessions in Brussels with the Six, President de Gaulle announced that the UK was not yet ready to join the EEC.

22 January. French President Charles de Gaulle and German Chancellor Konrad Adenauer signed the Franco-German Treaty of Friendship and Cooperation.

29 January. The UK's negotiations to join the common market ended.

11 July. EEC agreement to hold regular WEU meetings, including the discussion of economic cooperation issues, between the UK and EEC.

20 July. The Yaoundé Convention was signed, consisting of an association of 18 African states and Madagascar with the EEC for five years.

12 September. Association agreement was signed between Turkey and the EEC.

11 October. Konrad Adenauer resigned as Chancellor of the Federal Republic of Germany. He was succeeded by Ludwig Erhard on 17 October.

23 December. Agreement was reached on the common farm-policy regulations for rice, beef and dairy products to take effect on 1 November 1964.

5. Institutional amalgamation, 1964–66

1964

May. The GATT Kennedy Round of international tariff negotiations opened in Geneva with the states of the Community participating as a single delegation.

8 May. Establishment of the Committee of Governors of the Central Banks of the Member States of the EEC.

1 June. The Yaoundé Convention came into force.

1 July. The Guidance and Guarantee Fund of the CAP began operation.

23 September. The common market Commission banned the Grundig–Consten exclusive sales agreement because it contravened monopoly rules.

October. Third Directive on the liberalisation of capital movements was proposed, though never approved.

15 October. Victory for the Labour Party in the UK general election.

26 October. Announcement of 15% surcharge on UK imports.

1 December. Agreement on Turkey's associate membership took effect.

15 December. The Council adopted the Commission's Plan for common prices for grains.

1965

15 February. Sir Alec Douglas-Home declared himself to be in favour of political, military and economic union with Europe at a Young Conservative rally.

16 February. In the House of Commons the UK Prime Minister stated that it was not practical to join the EEC, but if favourable conditions developed then London would negotiate, but with the condition that UK and Commonwealth interests were satisfied.

31 March. The common market Commission proposed that as from 1 July 1967 all Community countries' import duties and levies should be paid into the Community budget and that the powers of the EP should be increased.

3 April. Conclusion of the merger Treaty to establish a unified Council and Commission of the Communities.

8 April. The Six signed the Treaty merging the Executives of the Community, which enhanced the status of the Commission. While there already existed a single Assembly, single Court of Justice and, in practice, a single Council for the three Communities, there were three different executives served by a separate President.

30 June–1 July. The European Council failed to achieve agreement on the financing of the CAP. This resulted in France boycotting the Community institutions for seven months in opposition to the Commission proposal that all import duties and levies be paid into the Community budget, and the powers of the EP be increased – a period commonly referred to as the 'empty chair' crisis.

3 August. The UK Prime Minister stated in the House of Commons that while some conditions for EEC membership had changed, agriculture was still a problem.

9 September. President Charles de Gaulle announced at a press conference that French military integration within NATO would end by 1969 at the latest.

1966

29 January. The Foreign Ministers of the Six reached a compromise and agreed to resume the full activities of the Community. Commonly referred to as the 'Luxembourg compromise', it settled a dispute which had hampered the Community's activities for seven months.

7 March. President Charles de Gaulle informed US President Johnson of France's intention to cease participation in the integrated military commands of NATO.

10 March. President de Gaulle announced France's intention of withdrawing from the Alliance's integrated military structure and the need to remove Allied military forces and military headquarters from France.

29 March. The French government announced that French force assignments to NATO would end on 1 July 1966 and that Allied military forces and headquarters would have to be removed from France by 1 April 1967.

31 March.   Victory for the Labour Party in the UK general election.

21 April.   The Queen's speech highlighted the UK government's desire to enter the EEC if essential UK and Commonwealth interests were safeguarded.

11 May.   The Council agreed that all tariffs on trade between the Member States should be removed on 1 July 1968 and that the common external tariff should come into effect, therefore completing the Community's customs union. It also agreed on the completion of the common farm policy by the same date.

13 June.   Commonwealth Trade Ministers' Conference in London at which the issue of the UK's relationship with the EEC was discussed.

21 June.   The Belgian Chamber of Representatives approved the transfer of the Supreme Headquarters Allied Powers Europe (SHAPE) to Belgium.

July.   An EEC association agreement was signed with Nigeria.

24 July.   The Council agreed on common prices for beef, milk, sugar, rice, oilseeds and olive oil which would, therefore, enable free trade in agricultural products by 1 July 1968.

14 September.   At a meeting of Commonwealth Prime Ministers, the issue of the UK's position in the EEC was discussed, with the decision that Commonwealth ministers would be kept informed of all proceedings.

26 October.   The UK informed other EFTA countries that it would try to join the EEC.

November.   The Segrè Report on the development of a European capital market was published.

10 November.   The UK Prime Minister, Harold Wilson, announced his plan for a high-level approach to the Six with the intention of applying for membership.

1 December.   Formation of a coalition government in the FRG, including Kurt-Georg Kiesinger as Chancellor (Christian Democrat) and Willy Brandt as Vice-Chancellor and Foreign Minister (Social Democrat).

5 December.   The UK government met with EFTA representatives, resulting in approval of its decision to explore the possibility of membership of the Communities.

14 December.   At a WEU meeting in Paris the West German Foreign Minister, Willy Brandt, made a plea for the UK to join the EEC.

16–17 December.   The UK Prime Minister and Foreign Secretary visited Rome to start their examination of the membership opportunities of the UK joining the Communities.

6.   Claims for expansion, 1967–70

1967

25 January.   The UK application was welcomed without opposition by the Consultative Assembly of the Council of Europe.

8–9 February.   The Council of Ministers accepted the first five-year programme outlining economic development and agreed to introduce in all the six countries a uniform system of value added tax.

3 March.   At EFTA Ministerial talks in Stockholm, the UK promised to consult the members before taking the final decision over membership of the Communities.

21 April.   Military coup in Greece.

28 April.   The UK government met with EFTA government representatives.

2 May.   Harold Wilson announced the UK's decision to apply for membership of the EEC, ECSC and Euratom.

10–11 May.   Denmark, Ireland and the UK submitted formal applications for membership of the EEC, ECSC and Euratom.

15 May.   The end of the Kennedy Round negotiations resulted in an agreement to make major cuts in industrial tariffs.

5 June.   The EEC Council acknowledged the UK's application without any major discussion.

1 July.   The Community Executives (ECSC High Authority, EEC and Euratom Commissions) were merged into a one 14-member Commission with the Belgian Jean Rey as President. The Community introduced free trade for grains, oilseeds and those products whose production costs were essentially dependent on the price of grains, that is pigmeat, eggs and poultry.

10 July.   M. Couve de Murville told the European Council that the UK's membership would transform the Community into an Atlantic Community.

24 July.   Norway formally applied for membership of the Communities.

28 September.   Sir Alec Douglas-Home, in a lecture in Luxembourg, stated that the UK's membership of the Communities was 'an act of faith'.

3 October.   Submission of the Preliminary Opinion of the Commission on the UK's enlargement application.

18 November.   The pound sterling was devalued by 14.3%.

27 November.   At a press conference de Gaulle noted the incompatibility of the EEC with the state of the UK's economy.

29 November.   Harold Wilson refuted de Gaulle's stance against the UK through a 16-point programme.

18–19 December.   The Council reached deadlock over enlargement of the Community after de Gaulle objected to the UK's membership, insisting that negotiations would only resume when there had been an improvement in the UK economy. Nevertheless, the UK kept its application on the table and later advanced it through the WEU.

1968

17 March.   World bankers agreed to a two-tier price system for gold, with an official price of US $35 and a free market for private dealings.

2 April. The European Commission submitted its opinion on transnational arrangements.

26 April. At a WEU Ministerial meeting the UK stressed that it would reject any arrangements that fell short of full membership of the Communities.

1 July. The customs union was completed and the common external tariff operated around the Community, with the Six having removed all the remaining restrictions on the free movement of workers. The Community made the first Kennedy Round tariff cuts.

18–19 July. The Six adopted basic regulations for a common transport policy.

20 July. For the first time the Community applied Article 108 (mutual aid) of the Treaty of Rome and thereby authorised France to impose some quotas so as to overcome balance of payments difficulties.

26 July. The Community signed association agreements with Kenya, Uganda and Tanzania at Arush, Tanzania.

28 July. The single market was introduced for dairy and beef products.

29 July. The Six decided to remove the last remaining restrictions on the free movement of workers and the last national discriminations between workers of the Member States in employment, pay and other conditions.

9 December. The Six adopted a common foreign trade policy for a large section of the Community's imports.

10 December. A radical ten-year agricultural reform programme was announced by the Vice-President of the Commission, Sicco Mansholt. The Six agreed on technological cooperation with other interested European states.

18 December. The Commission put forward guidelines for a common energy policy.

1969

4 February. A two-year extension of cooperation between the UK and Euratom was arranged.

12 February. The Commission urged the Six to coordinate more closely their economic and monetary policies as well as advocating a joint mutual-aid system to help member countries that were in balance of payments difficulties.

25 March. The Six adopted a programme to align legislation on technical standards for food and industrial goods.

25 April. The Commission drafted the 1970–74 Euratom programme urging the Six to let Euratom extend its activities to non-nuclear scientific research.

28 April. The French President, General Charles de Gaulle, resigned and was succeeded in July by Georges Pompidou, there having been a short interim presidency of Poher.

May. The Heads of Government of the Six met in The Hague and decided to widen and deepen the Community.

31 May. The Yaoundé Convention expired.

10 July. The French President Georges Pompidou declared that in principle he did not oppose UK membership.

16 July. The Commission proposed that the activities of the Community should be financed from its own resources by 1974, and that the Six increased the budgetary powers of the EP.

17 July. The Six agreed, in principle, to the short-term mutual-aid system and decided to hold prior consultations on proposed major short-term economic policy measures.

28 July. First Amendment to the IMF Articles of Agreement (creation of special drawing rights).

29 July. The Second Yaoundé Convention was signed.

8 August. The French franc devalued by 11.1%.

1 September. Partial association agreements were signed with Morocco and Tunisia.

24 September. Kenya, Uganda and Tanzania renewed their association agreements with the EEC.

29 September. The Federal Republic of Germany floated the Deutschmark.

2 October. The Commission gave its revised opinion on the UK's application.

15 October. The Commission presented proposals on the harmonisation of national regional policies and called for an interest-rebate fund for, and permanent committee on, regional development.

17 October. France accepted the opinion that negotiations for the UK's membership of the European Communities should begin.

24 October. The Deutschmark was revalued by 9.3%.

1–2 December. At The Hague Summit, the Six agreed to complete, enlarge and strengthen the Community. The Council agreed to finance CAP by giving the Community its own resources from 1978 and strengthening the EP's budgetary powers.

6 December. The Six agreed to reorganise Euratom.

31 December. Ending of the 12-year transitional period for the establishment of the common market, as provided for in the EEC Treaty.

1970

1 January. The common foreign trade policy came into operation.

26 January. The Six agreed on steps to define jointly medium-term economic policy and to create a short-term mutual-aid system.

9 February. The central banks of the Community activated a US $2 billion short-term mutual-aid system.

4 March. The Commission submitted a three-stage plan for full monetary and economic union by 1980 (Werner Plan).

19 March.   A three-year non-preferential agreement with Yugoslavia was signed.

21 March.   The Commission outlined the necessary steps for the achievement of common industrial policy.

June.   1980 was set as the date for the completion of economic and monetary union (EMU).

18 June.   Victory for the Conservative Party in the UK general election.

29 June.   Preferential trade agreement between the Communities and Spain was signed.

30 June.   The opening of negotiations with Denmark, Ireland, Norway and the UK.

1 July.   The Commission was reduced from 14 to nine members, and Franco-Maria Malfatti succeeded Jean Rey as President.

27 July.   The Six agreed to give the European Social Fund more powers to re-train and re-settle workers.

31 July.   The Davignon Report stated the need for twice-yearly Ministerial meetings on political cooperation, bringing into play European Political Cooperation (EPC).

12 August.   Signing in Moscow of a Non-Aggression Treaty between the FRG and the USSR.

1 October.   Preferential trade agreement with Spain and Israel came into effect.

7–8 October.   The Werner Report provided Member States with an outline for Economic and Monetary Union (EMU).

27 October.   The Davignon Report was approved by Member States which therefore initiated the process of European Political Cooperation.

19 November.   Foreign Ministers of the Six met in Munich for the first time in an effort to harmonise views on foreign policy under the auspices of EPC.

7 December.   Signing in Warsaw of a Treaty on the normalisation of relations between the FRG and Poland.

7.   Enlargement I, 1971–73

1971

1 January.   Second Yaoundé and Arusha Conventions came into force. The Community's own revenue system came into effect.

1 February.   The Common Fisheries Policy took effect.

9 February.   The Six launched a three-stage, ten-year plan for full EMU.

22 March.   The European Council decided to set up machinery for medium-term financial assistance. The European Council and Member States' representatives adopted a resolution on the achievement, by stages, of EMU in the EEC.

24 March. The Six took their first steps to modernise farming in accordance with the Mansholt Plan.

1 April. The association agreement with Malta became operational.

May. The Community issued its first joint foreign policy declaration on the Middle East.

10 May. The Dutch guilder was floated.

23 June. Agreement at Ministerial level was reached on the main issues concerning the UK's entry into the EEC.

1 July. The EEC introduced general tariff preferences for 91 developing countries.

15 August. The USA imposed a 10% temporary surcharge on imports and suspended the convertibility of the dollar into gold.

12 September. The European Council decided to give priority to the search for solutions to international monetary problems and to the problem of organising European exchange rates.

17–18 December. The Group of Ten decided on a currency realignment, including a devaluation of the US dollar, at its meeting at the Washington Smithsonian Institute.

1972

22 January. The Treaty of Accession was signed by Denmark, Ireland, Norway and the UK.

21 March. Introduction of the currency 'snake' which formed the exchange rate agreement between Belgium, France, the FRG, Italy and the Netherlands. While Norway, Denmark and the UK joined in May, the latter two countries withdrew from the system in June, although Denmark rejoined in October.

22 March. Sicco Mansholt became President of the Commission.

19 April. The Six signed an agreement to set up the European University Institute in Florence.

23 April. Enlargement of the European Communities to include Denmark, Ireland, Norway and the UK was approved by France in a referendum.

24 April. The Basle Agreement came into force establishing the system for the narrowing of the margins of fluctuation between the currencies of the Community, otherwise known as the snake (margins of 2.25%) in the tunnel (plus or minus 2.25%). The participating countries were Belgium, France, the FRG, Italy, Luxembourg and the Netherlands.

1 May. The pound sterling, Irish pound and the Danish krone joined the snake.

10 May. Yes vote in Irish referendum.

12 May. An association agreement was signed between Mauritius and the EEC.

31 May. The Commission submitted proposals to the Council for a common policy for scientific research and technological development.

23 June.   The UK floated the pound and, along with Ireland, withdrew from the snake.

27 June.   The Danish krone temporarily left the snake.

22 July.   Conclusion of a special relations agreement between the Community and EFTA countries, namely Austria, Iceland, Portugal, Sweden and Switzerland.

26 July.   An IMF Committee on the international monetary system (Committee of the Twenty) was set up.

24–25 September.   Norway withdrew its application to join the Community after a Norwegian referendum showed a majority against entry.

2 October.   Yes vote in Danish referendum on Community membership.

10 October.   The Danish krone rejoined the snake.

19–20 October.   The Paris Summit of the Nine prepared a blueprint for the future development of the Community. It was the very first summit meeting of the Heads of State and Government of the future enlarged Community of the Nine.

27–29 November.   The deputy members of the Committee of the Twenty began their work on the reform of the international monetary system at their meeting in Washington.

18 December.   Trade agreements were signed with Egypt and Lebanon.

21 December.   Signature in East Berlin of the Basic Treaty between the FRG and the German Democratic Republic (GDR).

31 December.   Denmark and the UK left EFTA.

1973

1 January.   Denmark, Ireland and the UK officially joined the Community and the Six became the Nine. Portuguese and other EFTA countries' special relations and preferential trade agreements with Communities came into effect.

6 January.   François-Xavier Ortoli was appointed President of the Commission of the European Communities.

1 February.   Agreement on accession to CAP and on five-year transition period.

13 February.   The Italian lira left the snake.

12 March.   The Deutschmark was revalued by 3% against the EMUA. Announcement by the European Council of a joint float of EEC currencies within 2.25% margins of fluctuation against each other. This agreement did not include the pound sterling, the Irish pound and the lira, which continued to float independently.

14 March.   The Norwegian krone and the Swedish krone became associate members of the snake.

2 April.   A trade agreement was signed between the EEC and Uruguay.

3 April. The European Monetary Cooperation Fund (EMCF or FECOM) was established.

14 May.   Trade agreement between Norway and EEC was signed.

29 June.   The Deutschmark was revalued by 5.5% against the EMUA.

July.   Commencement of negotiations with the countries of the Yaoundé Convention, which had expanded to include Mauritius, and with the 27 countries of the ACP (Africa, Caribbean and Pacific).

1 July.   Denmark took over the Presidency of the European Council for the first time.

3–7 July.   Start of the Helsinki Conference on Security and Cooperation in Europe (CSCE).

17 September.   The Dutch guilder was revalued by 5% against the EMUA.

6–27 October.   In the wake of the Yom Kippur War between Egypt and Israel, Arab oil-producing nations stated that exports of oil would be stopped to certain Western countries. This influenced the decision by the Organisation of Petroleum Exporting Countries (OPEC) to raise oil prices.

5 November.   EC Member States issued a joint statement on the Middle East conflict, including conditions for a peaceful solution.

16 November.   The Norwegian krone was revalued by 5% against the EMUA.

December.   A trade agreement was signed with Brazil and India.

14–15 December.   The Nine agreed to the introduction of a common energy policy at the Copenhagen European Council.

23 December.   OPEC announced the doubling of the price of crude oil sold by the six Persian Gulf members.

8.   Eurosclerosis and enlargement II, 1974–78

1974

17–18 January.   The Committee of Twenty decided to adopt a gradualist approach to the reform of the international monetary system at its Rome meeting.

19 January.   The French franc left the snake.

21 January.   The Council of Ministers introduced the Social Action Programme.

4 March.   Harold Wilson became UK Prime Minister as head of a minority Labour government with James Callaghan as Foreign Secretary.

1 April.   The Labour government presented demands for the UK's renegotiation of accession terms.

25 April.   Outbreak of the Portuguese revolution.

4 June.   At a meeting of the Council of Ministers, James Callaghan gave details of the UK's renegotiation terms.

14 June.   The Committee of Twenty published a plan for reform, including immediate measures and completion of its work.

31 July.   Euro–Arab dialogue opened in Paris.

September.   The FRG completely liberalised capital movements.

14 September.   Community Heads of State and Government, along with with President of the European Commission, met at the Elyseé Palace at the invitation of the French President Valéry Giscard d'Estaing, where they decided to launch the European Council.

10 October.   Victory for the Labour Party in the UK general election.

15 November.   The International Energy Agency was established by the USA, Japan, Canada and other oil-consuming countries, including eight of the Nine. France's refusal to join highlighted the failure of the Nine to act together in the international oil crisis of the previous year.

December.   An association agreement was restored with Greece after a civilian government came to power in July 1974.

9–10 December.   Paris meeting of Heads of State and Government resulted in the institutionalisation of summit meetings through creation of the European Council. The meeting also agreed to the principle of universal direct elections to the EP, as well as to details concerning the creation of the European Regional Development, as agreed at the 1972 Paris and 1973 Copenhagen Summits.

1975

28 February.   The Lomé Convention was signed. It replaced and extended the 1963 and 1969 Yaoundé Conventions and the Arusha Agreement. The Convention was between the EC and the 46 underdeveloped countries in Africa, the Caribbean and Pacific (ACP countries).

March.   The European Unit of Account (EUA) was created as a basket comprising fixed quantities of the currencies of the nine Member States. This replaced the gold-based unit which had been used since the creation of the Community to determine the amounts involved in the CAP and budget.

10–11 March.   Conclusion of the UK's budget renegotiations at the first European Council meeting in Dublin.

17 March.   The UK Cabinet voted 16 to seven in favour of the terms achieved in the wake of the Dublin meeting. The seven Ministers who rejected the terms were Castle, Benn, Foot, Shore, Silkin, Ross and Varley.

18 March.   The European Regional Development Fund was established.

9 April.   The UK House of Commons voted by 398 to 172 in favour of the renegotiated terms, although a majority of Labour MPs were opposed (145 against with 137 in favour).

21 April.   The EUA was introduced in certain areas of Community activity.

11 May.   A trade agreement was signed between the EEC and Israel.

5 June.   The UK referendum on the EC, in which 17.3 million voted yes and 8.4 million voted against the referendum (57.2%–32.8%); 64.55% of the electorate voted.

12 June. Greek application for membership.

10 July. The French franc rejoined the snake.

15 July. A trade agreement was signed between the EEC and Mexico.

22 July. The Treaty amending Certain Financial Provisions of the Treaties, which strengthened the budgetary powers of the EP and established the Court of Auditors, was signed.

1 August. The Final Act of the Conference on Security and Cooperation in Europe (CSCE) was signed in Helsinki by the 35 nations which took part. It initiated the CSCE process which included human rights provisions and confidence-building measures, regular implementation reviews and follow-up meetings.

6 October. Negotiations on a new trade agreement with Spain were broken off.

1–2 December. The Rome European Council decided that elections to the European Parliament should be by direct universal suffrage.

29 December. The Tindemanns Report on political cooperation was presented to Member States, having been called for at the 1974 Paris Summit.

1976

7–8 January. The IMF Interim Committee met in Jamaica and approved, in principle, the Second Amendment to the IMF Articles of Amendment.

20 January. Agreement on resumption of negotiations with Spain on a new trade agreement.

2 February. The Independent European Programme Group was established with the participation of all European members of NATO apart from Iceland, to promote cooperation in research, development and production of defence equipment.

16 February. The Council for Mutual Economic Assistance (Comecon) sought negotiations with the EC, although these turned out not to be fruitful.

15 March. The French franc left the snake.

25–27 April. Collective bilateral trade and aid agreements were signed between the EC and the Maghreb states of Algeria, Morocco and Tunisia.

1 June. A trade cooperation agreement was signed between the EEC and Pakistan.

27 July. Formal opening of negotiations concerning accession of Greece to EC.

17 October. Frankfurt realignment of exchange rates against the EMUA. The Deutschmark was revalued by 2%, the Danish krone was devalued by 4%, and the Norwegian and Swedish krone were devalued by 1%.

30 December. The French constitutional court resolved that direct elections to the EP would not violate the French constitution. This decision came with the provision that the powers of the Parliament were not increased.

1977

1 January. The Nine agreed that all future negotiations with non-Member States for fishing rights within the 200-mile EEC limit were to be the responsibility of the Community and not to be resolved by individual Member States.

18 January. Collective bilateral trade and aid agreements were signed with the Mashreq states of Egypt, Jordan, Lebanon and Syria.

9 March. The European Centre for the Development of Vocational Training (CEDEFOP) was established in Berlin.

28 March. Portuguese application for EC membership.

April. MacDougall Report on the role of federal finance in overcoming regional differences in the Community was published.

1 April. The Swedish krone was devalued by 6%, and the Danish and Norwegian krone were devalued by 3% against the EMUA.

3 May. A trade agreement was signed between the EEC and Lebanon.

21–22 May. Informal meeting of Foreign Ministers of the European Council at Leeds Castle. The decision was taken to give more responsibility to the Committee of Permanent Representatives (COREPER) in an effort to ensure that Ministers were left with more time to deal with the major issues.

1 July. The Court of Auditors started operation.

28 July. Spain applied for EC membership.

28 August. The Swedish krone left the snake. The Danish and Norwegian krone were devalued by 5% against the EMUA.

27 October. Roy Jenkins, speaking at the European University Institute in Florence, called for EMU to be put back at the top of the EEC agenda.

17 November. The European Commission's communication to the European Council on the prospect of economic and monetary union.

1978

13 February. The Norwegian krone was devalued by 8% against the EMUA.

3 April. A trade agreement was signed between the EEC and the People's Republic of China.

7–8 April. At the Copenhagen European Council meeting the FRG Chancellor Schmidt and the French President Giscard d'Estaing discussed the issue of the European Monetary System (EMS) as a new route to EMU in a private meeting with the other Heads of State and Government. The intention was for it to be a fixed exchange rate linking European currencies together, with the advantage for the FRG being that it would reduce speculation against the Deutschmark as its value would be static.

6–7 July. European Council Summit in Bremen approved the Franco-German plan to establish the EMS.

October. James Callaghan told Helmut Schmidt of his domestic political difficulties and that he would not be able to enter the Exchange Rate Mechanism (ERM) of the EMS at the outset.

17 October. The Deutschmark was revalued by 4%, and the Dutch guilder and Belgian franc were both revalued by 2% against the EMUA. Formal accession negotiations were opened with Portugal.

4–5 December. European Council meeting in Brussels adopted a resolution on the establishment of the EMS.

7 December. Multilateral free trade agreement initiated between Spain and EFTA.

12 December. The Norwegian krone left the snake.

18 December. The European Council adopted resolutions concerning the European Currency Unit (ECU) and the EMS.

21 December. The European Council adopted a decision increasing the amounts of medium-term financial assistance.

9.   EMS, enlargement II and budget, 1979–84

1979

1 January. The European Currency Unit (ECU) was devised as a replacement for the European Unit of Account (EUA).

5 February. Accession negotiations with Spain were opened.

9–10 March. The European Council meeting in Paris brought the EMS into operation. The decision had already been taken in Brussels the December before, but had been held up pending agreement on the monetary compensatory amounts applied under the CAP. The four main concepts of the EMS were the ECU, an exchange and information mechanism, credit facilities and transfer payments.

13 March. The EMS began operation (+/−2.25% for all participants except the Italian lira at +/−6%).

3 May. Victory for the Conservative Party in the UK general election.

28 May. An Accession Treaty with Greece was signed in Athens.

7–10 June. First direct elections were held to the EP. In the UK on 7 June the Conservative Party received 60 seats, the Labour Party 17, Others 4, and Liberal Party 0.

21–22 June. The new UK Prime Minister, Margaret Thatcher, requested a reduction in the government's budget contributions at the Strasbourg European Council.

28 June. Tokyo Group of Seven (G7) Summit.

24 September. The Deutschmark was realigned in the EMS by +2%, while the Danish krone was realigned by −2.9%.

October. Margaret Thatcher stated in a speech in Luxembourg her belief that the budget of the EC was 'unjust' and 'politically indefensible'. The UK completely liberalised capital movements.

31 October. The Second Lomé Convention (Lomé II) was signed between the EEC and the 58 ACP states.

20 November. The Council of Ministers endorsed the results of the Tokyo Round of GATT agreements which reduced customs duties.

29–30 November. The Dublin European Council agreed that there should be a complementarity of measures in favour of the UK, while additional projects would be financed by the regional and social funds.

30 November. The Danish krone was realigned in the EMS by −4.76%.

27 December. The Soviet Union invaded Afghanistan.

1980

24 January. Announcement of plan to station Cruise missiles in the UK.

7–8 March. Cooperation agreements were signed between the EEC and the ASEAN nations of Brunei, Indonesia, Malaysia, the Philippines, Singapore and Thailand.

29–30 May. A European Foreign Ministers' meeting resolved the budgetary problem. The eight Member States conceded that it was not equitable to impose an excessive financial burden on a less prosperous country, but refused to set a ceiling on future UK contributions on the basis that the principle of Community financial solidarity must be upheld. The UK's net EEC contributions were cut by two-thirds.

2 June. The UK Cabinet endorsed the EEC budget agreement.

22 June. Venice G7 Summit.

12 September. The Turkish military leadership took over the administration of the country.

1 October. The Labour Party conference voted to pull the UK out of the Community. A Cooperation Agreement commenced between the Community and ASEAN.

15 October. James Callaghan retired as leader of the Labour Party to be replaced by Michael Foot.

1981

1 January. Greece entered the EC. The ECU replaced the EUA in the budget of the EC.

23 February. Attempted coup in Madrid.

23 March. The Italian lira was realigned in the EMS by −6%.

10 May. François Mitterrand was elected the first Socialist President of the French Fifth Republic.

23 June. A commercial and economic agreement was signed between the EEC and India.

7–9 July. Based on an initiative by Altiero Spinelli, the European Parliament decided to establish a committee on institutional affairs which would draft amendments to the existing Treaties.

20 July. Ottawa G7 Summit.

October. Community Foreign Ministers reached agreement on the London Report which strengthened and extended European Political Cooperation.

1 October. The Labour Party conference voted to pull the UK out of the EEC without a referendum.

5 October. The Deutschmark and the Dutch guilder were realigned in the EMS by +5.5%, while the French franc and the Italian lira were realigned by −3%.

18 October. Greek elections to the EP. Andreas Papandreou became the first Socialist Prime Minister of Greece.

21 October. Papandreou entered power in Greece.

6–12 November. A 'Draft European Act' was submitted by the German and Italian governments to other Member States, the European Parliament and the European Commission, commonly referred to as the Genscher–Colombo Plan.

13 December. Imposition of martial law in Poland.

1982

22 February. The Belgian franc was realigned in the EMS by −8.5%, while the Danish krone was realigned by −3%. This was the fifth realignment of the EMS.

23 February. A referendum in Greenland resulted in a majority in favour of withdrawal from the EC.

25 February. A Common Fisheries Policy was established by the Council.

2 April. Argentina invaded the Falklands, surrendering to UK forces on 14 June.

5 June. Versailles G7 Summit.

14 June. The Deutschmark and the Dutch guilder were realigned in the EMS by +4.25%, while the Italian lira was realigned by −2.75% and the French franc by −5.75%.

30 June. Agreement reached on declaration of revised budgetary procedures.

17 September. Fall of Helmut Schmidt's government, with Helmut Kohl succeeding him as Chancellor.

2 December. Felipe Gonzáles became Prime Minister of Spain.

1983

25 January. Agreement of the Common Fisheries Policy after six years of negotiation.

March. The Committee of Governors of EC central banks adopted directives on an agreement between banks and the Bank for International Settlements for an ECU clearing system.

21 March. The Deutschmark was realigned in the EMS by +5.5%, the Dutch guilder by +3.5%, the Danish krone by +2.5%, the Belgian franc by +1.5%, the French franc and Italian lira by −2.5%, and the Irish pound by −3.5%.

9 June.   Victory for the Conservative Party in the UK general election.

19 June.   'Solemn Declaration on European Union' was signed in Stuttgart at the European Council meeting by Heads of State and Government and Foreign Ministers.

17–18 October.   Community agreement on the organisation of fruit, vegetable and olive oil markets.

17 December.   A bilateral trade and aid agreement was signed with Bolivia, Ecuador, Peru and Venezuela, often referred to as the Andean Pact.

1984

1 January.   Establishment of EEC–EFTA free trade area.

14 February.   The EP approved the Draft Treaty on European Union by 237 votes to 31 with 43 abstentions. Six Conservative MEPs opposed.

28 February.   The Council adopted a decision which established a European strategic programme for research and development in information technology (ESPRIT).

13 March.   Signature of agreement on withdrawal of Greenland from the EC.

19–20 March.   Brussels European Council meeting failed to produce a budget settlement.

30 March.   Measures to reform the CAP were approved by the Council of Ministers.

May.   French President, François Mitterrand, supported the idea of a Treaty on European Union in a speech to the EP.

12 June.   Paris meeting of the seven Foreign Ministers of the WEU decide to reactivate the organisation.

14–17 June.   Second set of direct elections to the EP. The Conservative Party won 45 seats, the Labour Party 32, while there were four others.

25–26 June.   At the Fontainebleau European Council meeting an agreement was reached on the annual correction method from 1985 for the UK's budget rebate, as well as an increase in the resources of the Community from January 1986 by raising the VAT percentage from 1% to 1.4%. For 1984 the UK received a compensation lump-sum of 1,000 million ECU and in subsequent years it was to receive two-thirds of the difference between what it paid in VAT and what it received from the Community. Member States also decided to establish an *ad hoc* committee on institutional affairs to examine amendments to the Treaty of Rome, under the chairmanship of the former Irish Foreign Minister, Jim Dooge.

September.   First revision of the ECU weights and inclusion of the Greek drachma.

9 October. A non-preferential cooperation agreement was signed between the EEC and the Yemen Arab Republic.

26–27 October. WEU Foreign and Defence Ministers published the 'Rome Declaration' which demonstrated their decision to increase cooperation within the WEU.

4 December. At the Dublin European Council meeting agreement was reached on budgetary discipline and on reducing wine production.

8 December. The third Lomé Convention was signed between the EC and the 65 ACP countries.

10. Enlargement III and single market, 1985–87

1985

1 January. European passports started to be introduced in Member States.

1 February. Greenland withdrew from the EC.

9 March. The Dooge Committee recommended the convening of an intergovernmental conference to examine the reform of the Treaty of Rome.

11 March. Mikhail Gorbachev was appointed First Secretary of the Communist Party of the Soviet Union.

29 March. Conclusion of enlargement negotiations with Portugal and Spain.

29–30 March. At the European Council meeting in Brussels agreement was reached on the Integrated Mediterranean Programmes.

22 April. WEU Foreign and Defence Ministers met in Bonn to review the reactivation of the organisation, as decided upon at their 1984 meetings in Paris and Rome.

29–30 April. Conclusion of bilateral agreement between Spain and Portugal.

8–9 June. Stresa paper suggested the creation of a secretariat for improving foreign policy coordination.

12 June. Signature of Portugal and Spain's Accession Treaties.

14 June. Schengen agreement. The Federal Republic of Germany, France, Belgium, Luxembourg and the Netherlands agreed on the gradual abolition of frontier controls.

15 June. Lord Cockfield presented his timetable for the internal market.

28–29 June. Milan European Council meeting approved the Commission's White Paper on completing the internal market. The meeting also established an intergovernmental conference to look at numerous issues as well as reform of the Treaty.

22 July. In the EMS the Belgian franc, Danish krone, Deutschmark, French franc, Irish pound and Dutch guilder were realigned by +2%, while the Italian lira was realigned by −6%.

September.   Plaza Agreement between the USA, Japan, the FRG, France and the UK on concerted intervention so as to correct the overvaluation of the dollar.

2–3 December.   At a meeting of Heads of Government of the European Council in Luxembourg it was agreed to complete the internal market by 1992. Proposals for institutional reform were pared down to a minimum, with only a limited extension of majority voting and only a modest extension of the powers of the EP. In exchange, the UK accepted that the objective of a free market by 1992 would require a revision of the Treaty of Rome and was prepared to go along with what appeared to be innocuous statements on eventual European unity and the development of the EMS.

16 December.   Foreign Ministers' agreement on the reforms to the Treaty of Rome.

1986

1 January.   Portugal and Spain joined the EC, thereby enlarging the membership to 12 nations.

17–18 February.   The SEA was signed in Luxembourg by the representatives of the governments of Belgium, France, the FRG, Ireland, Luxembourg, the Netherlands, Portugal, Spain and the UK.

27 February.   Danish referendum approved the Treaty reforms.

28 February.   The SEA was signed in The Hague by representatives of the governments of Denmark, Greece and Italy.

12 March.   In a Spanish referendum organised by Prime Minister Felipe González, voters supported the continuation of Spain's membership of the Atlantic Alliance, but without participating in NATO's integrated military structure.

20 March.   The Centre Right party leader, Jacques Chirac, was elected Prime Minister in France after legislative elections. This meant that the country had a Socialist President, François Mitterrand, and a Conservative Prime Minister – a period referred to as cohabitation.

7 April.   The Deutschmark and Dutch guilder were realigned in the EMS by +3%, the Belgian franc and Danish krone by +1%, and the French franc by −3%.

23 April.   The SEA was given a second reading in the House of Commons and received a majority of 159 with only a handful of Conservative anti-marketeers teaming up with the Labour Party and voting against.

28 April.   Venice meeting of WEU Foreign and Defence Ministers reviewed the revitalisation of the organisation.

May.   The European Commission proposed to advance the deadline for the complete liberalisation of capital movements.

1 May.   The third ACP–EEC Convention came into force.

4 August.   The Irish pound was devalued by 8% in the ERM.

15–20 September.   Ministers of 92 countries agreed to a fresh round of multilateral trade negotiations in Punta del Este in Uruguay.

October.   The ECU clearing system came into operation.

December.   Creation of the Giscard d'Estaing–Schmidt Committee for the Monetary Union of Europe.

31 December.   All the members of the EC, except Ireland, had ratified the SEA.

1987

12 January.   The Deutschmark and the Dutch guilder were realigned in the EMS by +3%, while the Belgian franc was realigned by +2%. This was the eleventh realignment of the EMS.

15 February.   The European Commission presented its view for achieving the objectives contained in the SEA in a document entitled 'The Single Act: A New Frontier for Europe'. This included proposals to double the structural funds, complete the reforms of CAP and to promote cohesion within the Community.

22 February.   Louvre Accord among the Group of Seven countries to stabilise the US dollar.

14 April.   Turkey applied to join the EC.

May.   Italy adopted measures to liberalise capital movements and abolish the non-interest-bearing deposit against foreign investments.

26 May.   A referendum in Ireland allowed the ratification of the SEA to proceed.

8 June.   Venice G7 Summit opened.

11 June.   Victory for the Conservative Party in the UK general election.

19 June.   The Chancellor of the FRG, Helmut Kohl, proposed the formation of a joint Franco-German brigade as the first phase of a joint European force.

29–30 June.   Brussels European Council meeting under the chairmanship of Belgian Premier Wilfied Martens.

1 July.   The SEA came into effect after months of ratification problems in Ireland.

8 July.   Morocco applied to join the EC.

20 August.   WEU experts meeting in The Hague reviewed possible joint actions in the Gulf to protect regional oil shipping lanes.

12 September.   Community Finance Ministers agreed to strengthen the EMS during a meeting in Nyborg, Denmark.

21 September.   France and Italy proposed measures to promote the exchange of information and technical coordination between naval forces operating in the Gulf region for the protection of oil shipping lanes.

26 October.   WEU meeting in The Hague coordinated military activities in the Gulf.

28 October.   Having been formally adopted on 27 October, the Netherlands, acting as President of the WEU, presented the WEU 'Platform on European Security Interests' to the 16 members of the North Atlantic Alliance.
4–5 December.   Copenhagen European Council meeting chaired by Danish (Conservative) Prime Minister Poul Schlutter.

11.   Delorist expansion and reform, 1988–92

1988
January.   The Single Administrative Document (SAD) came into operation. A memorandum from Edouard Balladur summarised the necessary reforms of the EMS for the completion of the internal market.
11–13 February.   Extraordinary Brussels Summit agreed that there would be an increase in structural funds from nearly £5 billion in 1988 to £9.17 billion in 1993. The UK Prime Minister, Margaret Thatcher, accepted a package deal where she achieved tight and binding controls on the rate of increase of CAP expenditure along with the continuation of the Fontainebleau rebate scheme. She did concede on the increase in funds available to the Community and the change in the method of financing the EEC budget, both of which would cost the UK more. Agreement was also reached on the doubling of regional and social funds by 1992.
March.   Publication of the Giscard d'Estaing–Schmidt Committee's proposals for monetary union.
15 June.   Cooperation agreements were signed between the EC and the Cooperation Council for Arab States of the Gulf.
27–28 June.   An agreement was signed between the EC and Comecon that enabled the two organisations to recognise each other. The agreement included Comecon's recognition of the authority of the EC to negotiate on behalf of Member States. European Council meeting in Hanover agreed to a proposal put forward by the President of the European Commission, Jacques Delors, for a new study on EMU. France and the FRG stressed the importance of the emergence of a single European currency as an essential complement to the freeing of the internal market. They argued that the EMS needed to be strengthened through the creation of a European central bank along with steps to establish the ECU as the common currency of the Community.
8 September.   Jacques Delors addressed the Trade Union Congress in Brighton.
20 September.   Speech by Margaret Thatcher to the College of Europe in Bruges. She attacked the Commission for wanting to regulate the internal market as well as for wanting to centralise power in Brussels, and also attacked the idea of common rules for the protection of workers as this regulation would result in an increase in the cost of employment. Her speech especially reflected concerns over federalism.

26 September. Trade, commercial and economic agreements were signed between the EC and Hungary.

24 October. The Council adopted the decision to establish the Court of First Instance.

14 November. Portugal and Spain signed the Treaty of Accession to the WEU.

8 December. A new European Commission was appointed.

1989

12 April. Publication of the Report of the Delors Committee proposing a three-stage process for EMU, namely linking the currencies together, integration between states and the creation of a European central bank. The UK Chancellor of the Exchequer, Nigel Lawson, immediately rejected these proposals and stated that the UK would be publishing its own proposals.

30 May. The Commission adopted the preliminary draft of the Community Charter of Fundamental Social Rights, it being immediately challenged by the UK.

15–18 June. In the third set of elections to the EP Labour received 45 MEPs, Conservative 32 (13 Labour gains), while the Greens received 13% of the vote.

19 June. The Spanish peseta entered the EMS at +/−6%.

26–27 June. At the Madrid meeting of the European Council Margaret Thatcher adopted a more conciliatory tone and made significant progress on the question of UK membership of the ERM by stating the conditions that would be necessary for membership. Her previous stance had been that the UK would join when the time was right. Thatcher accepted the implementation of the first stage of the Delors Report. However, at the meeting she still registered her disapproval of plans that would lead to a monetary union as well as the social policy side of the 1992 programme.

July. The Poland and Hungary Assistance for Economic Restructuring programme (PHARE) was established, and was thereafter extended in 1990 to include other East European states.

14–16 July. Paris Western Economic Summit asked the Commission to coordinate measures to assist economic restructuring in Hungary and Poland.

17 July. Austria applied to join the Community.

September. Collapse of Communist governments in Eastern Europe. Trade and cooperation agreements were concluded between the EEC and Poland.

October. The Report of the Guigou Group identified the main issues that needed to be resolved regarding the attainment of a Treaty on Economic and Monetary Union.

November.   In an address to the EP, François Mitterrand stated that the recent events in Eastern Europe reinforced the need for political unity as a way of creating stability throughout the whole of Europe.

9 November.   Breaching of the Berlin Wall.

19 November.   Extraordinary meeting of the European Council in Paris.

29 November.   The European Commission adopted the work programme for implementing the Social Charter.

December.   A negative opinion was given on Turkey's application to join the EC.

8–9 December.   At the Strasbourg European Council meeting, the UK Prime Minister, Margaret Thatcher, was forced to accept a majority decision to assemble an intergovernmental conference to draw up a Treaty on Monetary Union on the basis of the Delors Report. Eleven Member States (with the exception of the UK) also approved the 'Community Charter of the social basic laws of working people'.

10 December.   End of Communist rule in Czechoslovakia.

15 December.   Council of Finance Ministers' meeting approved the amendments to the second banking directive which allowed providers of financial services the right (in principle) to trade anywhere in the EC as long as they met minimum standards. The Fourth Lomé Convention was signed between the EC and 69 ACP countries.

18 December.   The EC and the USSR signed a ten-year trade and cooperation agreement.

19 December.   Community and EFTA representatives agreed to commence formal negotiations to establish a closer cooperation agreement between both organisations.

21 December.   The Council of Ministers adopted Commission proposals concerning the control of mergers and acquisitions.

1990

8 January.   The first realignment of the EMS took place since January 1987. The Italian lira was devalued by 3.68% against the Deutschmark, while the relative value of all other currencies remained virtually the same. Realignment had been decided on 5 January, taking effect on 8 January and it was the twelfth realignment since the creation of the EMS in March 1979. At the same time the Italian government reduced the margin that the lira was allowed to fluctuate from 6% to 2.25% either side of the central rate. This meant that all the currencies in the ERM would limit fluctuations to 2.25%, except the Spanish peseta which had joined the ERM on 19 June 1989.

15–16 January.   Meeting in Paris of experts from 34 countries along with the EC Commission and European Investment Bank to discuss the formation of a European Bank for Reconstruction and Development (EBRD). It was agreed that the new bank's capital should amount to

70,000 million ECU and that its objective should be to help to reinforce the competitive and private sector.

5 February. An Action Programme for the development of relations between the EC and the countries of Central and Eastern Europe was defined by the Council.

March. The Oslo Declaration was issued by EFTA states' Heads of Government which confirmed their association with the EC.

2 April. Framework Agreement for Trade and Economic Cooperation with Argentina was signed in Luxembourg.

8 April. General elections in Greece.

19 April. Chancellor Kohl and President Mitterrand sent a joint letter to the Irish President of the Council, Charles Haughey, which urged that a second intergovernmental conference be convened which would accelerate the political construction of Europe. It would be in parallel with that of EMU.

27 April. EC Council of Agriculture Ministers reached agreement for the pricing of agricultural produce in the year starting 1 April 1990.

28 April. At an extraordinary meeting of the European Council in Dublin, the decision was taken to ask Foreign Ministers to consider the progress of Political Union that was the result of the Kohl–Mitterrand letter. Margaret Thatcher spoke against the intergovernmental conference that Kohl and Mitterrand wanted.

7 May. Trade and cooperation agreement negotiations began between the EC and Romania having been suspended between 20 December 1989 and March 1990.

8 May. Trade, commercial and economic cooperation agreements were signed between the EC and Bulgaria, Czechoslovakia and the GDR, although the reunification of the FRG meant that the latter was never ratified.

18 May. State Treaty signed between the FRG and the GDR which established a monetary, economic and social union.

29 May. The founding charter of the EBRD was signed in Paris at the Elysee Palace by representatives of 40 countries, the EC Commission and the European Investment Bank.

8 June. The Turnberry NATO Foreign Ministers' meeting issued a 'Message from Turnberry' which noted their determination to grasp the opportunities resulting from the changes in Europe, and to extend friendship and cooperation to the Soviet Union and other European countries.

13 June. The European Commission adopted three proposals for directives on atypical work.

19 June. The Schengen agreement was signed by Belgium, the Netherlands, Luxembourg, France and the FRG. It committed them to the abolition of all controls at internal borders, as well as passport control at airports for flights between the signatory countries.

25–26 June. European Council meeting in Dublin agreed to the establishment of a second intergovernmental conference that would concentrate on the political construction of Europe. The parallel IGCs would take place in Rome on 13–14 December 1990 so as to amend the Treaty of Rome in order to allow the introduction of political union and EMU by 1 January 1993.

29 June. Negotiating directives for agreement with EFTA countries on the establishment of a European Economic Space (EES) were issued by the Council.

1 July. Stage one of EMU formally began. This meant that limited monetary functions and the technical preparations for the Monetary Institute were carried out by the Committee of Central Bank Governors. The German Union Treaty also came into force. German monetary union was established.

4 July. Cyprus applied to join the EC.

6 July. NATO Summit in London produced the London Summit Declaration on a Transformed North Atlantic Alliance. Major steps were announced to bring East–West confrontation to an end, including a fundamental review of NATO strategy and arms control initiatives.

12 July. The Greek government announced its intention to join the ERM in 1993 if fiscal measures had been successfully implemented.

16 July. Malta applied to join the EC.

25 July. The European Commission adopted a proposal for a directive on certain aspects of the adoption of working time.

2 August. Iraq invaded Kuwait.

8 August. The EC adopted measures instituting an embargo on trade with Iraq.

21 August. Jacques Delors made public an EC Commission internal document containing official proposals for EMU that had been prepared in consideration of the forthcoming December IGC in Rome. It recommended that the second stage of progress towards EMU, as previously noted in the 1989 Delors Plan, should commence on 1 January 1993 and the time period should be as short as possible. It also stated that the proposed European Central Bank (ECB), Eurofed, should be independent of national governments as well as EC authorities, and have a democratic responsibility.

27 August. The European Commission specified in a communication the objectives and contents of association agreements to be negotiated with the countries of Central and Eastern Europe.

8 September. The Rome meeting of the EC Council of Finance Ministers failed to reach a consensus on the pace of European integration. Belgium, Denmark, France and Italy supported a fast-track approach, as highlighted in the April 1989 Delors Plan which would result in stage two of EMU starting on 1 January 1993. The Netherlands, the FRG and the UK favoured a slower pace of integration.

12 September. Two-Plus-Four Treaty on the Final Settlement with respect to the FRG.

19 September. The President of the Bundesbank, Karl Otto Pöhl, outlined tight requirements for economic and monetary union which helped to deepen divisions in the West German government over EMU.

3 October. Incorporation of the former GDR into the FRG as three separate Länder. Therefore, the unification of the FRG brought the former GDR into the EC.

5 October. The UK announced that it would join the ERM as of 8 October at a central rate against the Deutschmark of 2.95. The pound was allowed to float at 6% either side of its central parity (same rate as the Spanish peseta). It was expected that the pound would move to the narrower band of 2.25% as soon as possible. Only Portugal and Greece now remained outside the ERM. Pressure from senior Cabinet members Douglas Hurd and John Major had forced Margaret Thatcher to join the ERM. Some commentators thought the value of the pound was set too high, with interest rates maintained at a high level so as to convince people to buy pounds.

8 October. Entry of pound sterling into ERM at +/−6% band.

19 October. Norway tied its currency to the ECU.

22 October. General Affairs Council at which a trade and economic cooperation agreement was signed with Romania.

27–28 October. Extraordinary Summit held in Rome to decide the date for the opening of stage two of Monetary Union before the December IGC began. Eventually 1 January 1994 was the date chosen after a long period of German indecision. The outcome of the vote for the date of stage two was eleven to one and Thatcher, being the only dissenting voice, was annoyed with the result.

29 October. The European Council strengthened the embargo against Iraq.

November. The Conference of Parliaments of the Community or Assizes met in Rome. This was a forum that was promoted by the EP to involve national parliaments in Community discussions. It was attended by 250 parliamentarians of which two-thirds were from national parliaments and one-third MEPs. Karl Otto Pöhl, President of the Bundesbank, criticised the UK government's economic policy in a speech at the London School of Economics.

7 November. The Commission proposed directives to the Council to authorise it to negotiate Association or European Agreements with Czechoslovakia, Hungary and Poland.

13 November. EC central bank Governors agreed draft statutes to the proposed European Central Bank.

19 November. Finance Council met to discuss the Investment Services Directive, though no final decision was reached.

19–21 November.   Paris Summit of Conference on Security and Cooperation in Europe at which 34 Heads of State or Government signed a Charter for a New Europe.

23 November.   Release of the Transatlantic Declaration on EC–USA relations.

26 November.   At the Social Affairs Council, Ministers rejected the legal basis of the proposed Commission directive on part-time work.

27 November.   John Major won the Conservative Party leadership election. Italy became the sixth EC country to sign the Schengen agreement, while Portugal and Spain joined the system as observers.

28 November.   John Major became UK Prime Minister, Margaret Thatcher having resigned. The European Commission issued a review of the Commons Fisheries Policy.

2 December.   First free all-German elections. At the Milan Informal Finance Council, EC central bankers presented Ministers with draft statutes for Eurofed.

5 December.   The European Council adopted a proposal for a directive on European works councils in companies or groups of companies operating Community-wide.

14–15 December.   Rome European Council meeting established a broad framework for negotiations by the intergovernmental conference.

15 December.   Opening of intergovernmental conferences on EMU and political union.

19 December.   At the Employment Council meeting in Brussels, Ministers accepted the proposal to grant part-time and temporary workers the same health and safety conditions as full-time workers. However they blocked other complementary proposals from the Social Action Programme. EC–EFTA Foreign Ministers' meeting in Brussels focused on the establishment of the European Economic Area (EEA).

19–20 December.   Fisheries Council meeting in Brussels reached agreement on 1991 TACs, but postponed a decision on technical conservation matters.

20 December.   Foreign Ministers from the Rio Group of Latin American countries and the EC signed the 'Declaration of Rome' which aimed to develop closer economic and political links.

1991

4 January.   EC Foreign Ministers held an emergency meeting to discuss the Gulf crisis and sought to meet the Iraqi Foreign Minister in Luxembourg.

5 January.   CMEA nations agreed to disband the organisation, with it to be replaced by the Organisation for International Economic Cooperation (OIEC).

8 January.   UK Chancellor, Norman Lamont, announced proposals for a new currency, the Hard ECU, which would be created and managed by a European Monetary Fund. The Hard ECU would float alongside existing currencies in the ERM of the EMS.

14 January. EC Foreign Ministers held an emergency meeting in Brussels to discuss the Gulf crisis and the Soviet attack on a Lithuanian television centre.

17 January. The beginning of hostilities in the Gulf War was signalled by air strikes. John Major created a war Cabinet of himself, Hurd, King, Wakeham and Mayhew. Emergency EC Foreign Ministers and WEU meeting in Paris discussed the outbreak of hostilities in the Gulf.

22 January. Brussels Agriculture Council meeting, at which the Commission presented its proposals for a reform of the CAP.

28 January. The EC agreed a £1.7 billion loan to Greece.

15 February. Czechoslovakia, Hungary and Poland signed the Visegrad Declaration.

16–17 February. EC Troika mission to the Soviet Union discussed EC aid to the Soviet Union and a post-war Middle East policy.

21 February. Czechoslovakia joined the Council of Europe.

24 February. Land hostilities start in the Gulf War, with victory achieved by 28 February.

28 February. End of Gulf War hostilities.

7 March. In a speech at the Institute of Strategic Studies in London, Jacques Delors proposed that the EC went beyond establishing a joint foreign and security policy and commit itself to a common European defence policy.

11 March. At a summit with Helmut Kohl in Bonn, John Major said that the UK would play a role 'at the very heart of Europe' which contrasted with views expressed by Thatcher at Bruges in October 1988 when her desire to impose limits on European integration was made clear.

19 March. In his evidence to the EP's Committee of Economic and Monetary Affairs, the President of the Bundesbank, Karl Otto Pöhl, suggested that there might have to be a two-speed progression towards EMU.

15 April. Inauguration of the European Bank for Reconstruction and Development.

16 May. Start of the civil war in Yugoslavia due to ethnic and political tensions. Karl Otto Pöhl resigned as President of the Bundesbank.

25 June. Croatia and Slovenia declared themselves to be independent of Yugoslavia.

28–29 June. EC Heads of State and Government Summit in Luxembourg took stock of progress on EMU and EPU. The summit discussed a Draft Treaty put forward by Luxembourg but postponed any decisions on contentious issues until the December 1991 EC Summit in Maastricht.

1 July. Sweden applied for membership of the EC. Andorra joined the customs union, but does not participate in any other EC institutions. The Warsaw Treaty Organisation was disbanded.

25 July.   The European Court of Justice overturned a UK Act of Parliament in a dispute over Spanish trawlers fishing in UK waters.

6 August.   Emergency EC Foreign Ministers' meeting in The Hague discussed tensions between Serbia and Croatia.

19 August.   President Gorbachev was overthrown in the USSR.

27 August.   Brussels EC Foreign Ministers' meeting reached agreement on the recognition of the independence of the Baltic Republics, and discussed the Yugoslav crisis.

2 September.   EC-sponsored cease-fire signed in Belgrade.

3 September.   EC Foreign Ministers met in The Hague and Lord Carrington was appointed Chair of the Peace Conference of the former Yugoslavia.

10 October.   The EP voted to increase the number of German MEPs from 81 to 99 in order to take account of unification.

7–8 November.   Rome NATO Ministerial meeting discussed the future relationship between NATO, the EC and the WEU. Rome Declaration on Peace and Cooperation issued.

8 November.   The EC formally imposed sanctions on Yugoslavia.

9–10 December.   The Dutch Prime Minister, Ruud Lubbers, opened the European Council meeting in Maastricht on 9 December. The summit ended with agreement early on 11 December on a framework Treaty on European Union (TEU), incorporating EPU and EMU agreements. It also set a timetable for their implementation and provided for a new security and defence dimension to EC cooperation. The UK Prime Minister, John Major, won an opt-out for the UK from stage three of EMU. The UK also rejected the Social Chapter, which the 11 other members of the Community signed.

16 December.   General Affairs Council at which 'Europe Agreements' were signed with Czechoslovakia, Hungary and Poland.

20 December.   Inaugural meeting of North Atlantic Cooperation Council. Foreign Ministers and representatives from the 16 NATO countries participated, as well as six Central and Eastern European countries and three newly independent Baltic States.

23 December.   Russia succeeded the Soviet Union as a member of the United Nations Security Council.

25 December.   Mikhail Gorbachev resigned as President of the Soviet Union.

1992

14 January.   Egon Klepsch was elected President of the EP. The priorities included supporting peace initiatives in the crumbling Yugoslavia; continuing the progress of the single market programme; attempting to formulate policies for the enlargement of the EC; working out the conclusions of the Maastricht Summit; and stabilising relations with states from the former USSR.

15 January.   The EC recognised the independence of Slovenia and Croatia.
21 January.   The Advocate-General of the European Court of Justice endorsed two charges which had been brought against the UK government as a result of its failure to comply with the EC directive on drinking water purity.
7 February.   The TEU was formally signed at Maastricht by the EC Foreign and Finance Ministers.
12 February.   The European Commission unveiled its budgetary proposals for the years 1993–97, the so-called 'Delors II' package. The Commission presented to the EP its programme of work for 1992. It identified three main areas: completion of the single market; agreement on the Delors II package; and the development of the international role of the Community as well as making decisions on enlargement.
14 February.   Agreement was reached on the altered EC–EFTA accord to establish the European Economic Area (EEA).
18 March.   The Finnish Parliament endorsed the government's proposal to join the Community.
24 March.   Month-long Helsinki CSCE Conference began as part of an attempt to resolve its role in post-Cold War Europe.
6 April.   The Portuguese escudo joined the ERM of the EMS. The escudo was fixed at the central rate of 178.735 escudos to the ECU. This corresponded to its previous national rate in the ECU currency basket. The escudo entered the broad band of the ERM and was allowed to fluctuate at 6% either side of the central rate, like the Spanish peseta and UK sterling.
7 April.   The EP endorsed the TEU by 226 votes to 62, with 31 abstentions. Delors stated in a debate preceding the vote that if there was an expansion in the membership of the Community, then there would have to be at least a corresponding increase in powers.
9 April.   Decision of the French Constitutional Council requiring revision of the French Constitution in conjunction with the ratification of the TEU. Victory for the Conservative Party in the UK general election.
2 May.   The European Economic Area agreement was signed in Portugal.
11 May.   Three Baltic States, and Albania, signed a ten-year trade and cooperation agreement with the EC. The UK rejected the demands of the European Commission to abandon its border controls and insisted on its rights to maintain passport controls.
11–12 May.   Brussels General Affairs Council resulted in the EC recalling its Ambassadors from Belgrade.
12 May.   The Danish Folketing approved the Treaty of Maastricht by 130 votes to 25. Danish ratification was, however, subject to a popular vote under the constitution.
20 May.   Switzerland presented its official application for accession to the EC.

20–21 May. The European Communities (Amendment) Bill passed the second reading debate in the House of Commons by 336 to 92.

22 May. France and the FRG announced the creation of a joint military corps based in Strasbourg so as to provide the EC with its own military capacity. It would comprise two divisions, 35,000 strong.

27 May. The EC decided to re-impose sanctions against Serbia.

2 June. Danish referendum on the TEU resulted in a 'no' vote by 50.7% to 49.3% of votes cast, a margin of only 46,269 votes. The turnout was 82.3%.

4 June. NATO Foreign Ministers at a meeting in Oslo stated their readiness to support peacekeeping activities under the CSCE on a case-by-case basis.

5 June. Albania became a participant of the North Atlantic Co-operation Council and Finland an observer at the Oslo meeting of the NAAC.

18 June. An Irish referendum supported the Maastricht Treaty by 68.7% to 31.3%.

19 June. The Foreign and Defence Ministers of the WEU met in Petersberg, near Bonn, with their opposite numbers from Bulgaria, the Czech and Slovak Federal Republic, Estonia, Hungary, Latvia, Lithuania, Poland and Romania. The Petersberg Declaration stated that the process of integration between the WEU and Central and Eastern European countries would follow the same path taken between those countries and the EU.

23 June. In a meeting at the Congress of Versailles the French National Assembly and the Senate adopted the amendments to the Constitution that allowed the French constitution to ratify the Maastricht Treaty by 592 to 73.

26–27 June. The EU Lisbon Summit concerned itself with events in Yugoslavia and the enlargement of the Community. Jacques Delors was reappointed President of the European Commission until 31 December 1994.

29 June. Political agreement at the Ecofin Council was reached on the principle of the harmonisation of VAT and of excise duty rates.

1 July. Decision of the Spanish Constitutional Court requiring revision of the Constitution with regard to the ratification of the TEU.

2 July. The Chamber of Deputies in Luxembourg voted in favour of the TEU by 51 to six.

9 July. The EP regretted the lack of 'real' consultation on the appointment of the President of the Commission. However, by 276 votes to ten it endorsed the Lisbon Summit's appointment of Jacques Delors.

10 July. At the Helsinki Foreign Ministers' meeting of the WEU the decision was taken to send an air–sea force on a sanctions patrol against Serbia. This was the first WEU action in Europe.

17 July. The Belgian Chamber of Deputies approved the Treaty of Maastricht by 143 votes to 33, with three abstentions. All the major parties voted in favour.

22 July. The Spanish Congress of Deputies (lower House of Parliament) approved a constitutional change to allow ratification of the Maastricht Treaty. The Senate (upper House) approved the amendment on 30 July. This was the first amendment since the adoption of the Constitution in 1978 and it allowed EU citizens to stand in municipal elections. The Constitutional tribunal ruled on 1 July that such a change was necessary and could be approved by a three-fifths majority in both Houses of Parliament.

1 August. The TEU was adopted by the Greek Parliament by 286 votes to eight with all the main parliamentary parties supporting the Treaty and only a few Communists voting against it.

24 August. Luxembourg deposited its instrument of ratification of the Maastricht Treaty.

25 August. International Conference on the former Yugoslavia opened in London. Lord Owen was appointed chairman of the EC-sponsored peace conference after the resignation of Lord Carrington.

4–6 September. Informal meeting of the EC Finance Ministers in Bath. It subsequently emerged that the UK Presidency did not pick up on the suggestion that a realignment of the ERM could be considered.

8 September. The Finnish government, in a joint decision with the Bank of Finland, let the markka float freely and, therefore, abandoned its self-imposed peg to the ECU. This position resulted in an immediate 15% drop in value of the markka.

8–9 September. Sweden raised its marginal intervention rate from 16% to 75%.

14 September. The Belgian franc, Deutschmark, Dutch guilder, Danish krone, Portuguese escudo, French franc, Irish pound, Spanish peseta and UK sterling were realigned in the EMS by +3.5%. The Italian lira was realigned by −3.5%, effectively representing a 7% devaluation of the lira. This was the first major realignment within the EMS since 1987. The Bundesbank cut its Lombard rate from 9.75% to 9.5% and its discount rate from 8.75% to 8.25%. Furthermore, rates were also cut in Austria, Belgium, the Netherlands, Switzerland and Sweden – currencies that were most closely linked with the Deutschmark.

16 September. Pressure on the pound increased and the minimum lending rate was increased from 10% to 12%. Due to the continuing turbulence, it was announced that the base rate would rise further, to 15% the next day. At the close of business in London, the pound stood at DM 2.75. The worsening situation meant that the Chancellor, Norman Lamont, announced that the UK would pull out of the ERM and that the second interest rate increase would not take place. These events were referred to as 'Black Wednesday'.

17 September. The Swedish Central Bank raised the marginal interest rate to 500% in an effort to protect the krona and stop the outflow of capital. The EC's Monetary Committee agreed to the temporary suspension of the Italian lira and UK sterling from the ERM. The peseta was devalued by 5% and the UK cut its base rate to 10%. The TEU was approved by the Italian Senate by 176 votes to 16.

20 September. The TEU was narrowly passed in France by 51.04% to 48.95% in a public referendum.

23 September. The French and German governments intervened heavily on the exchange markets in a successful defence of the French franc. Spain reintroduced foreign exchange controls.

24 September. Ireland and Portugal introduced new foreign exchange controls.

24–25 September. The House of Commons was recalled to debate the sterling crisis with a vote of 322 to 296 in favour of a motion supporting the government's economic policy.

25 September. The German Bundesrat opened its debate on the TEU.

1 October. The UK government, after tense Cabinet discussions, announced its desire to ratify the TEU and to bring the bill back to Parliament in December, or early in the new year.

8 October. The German Bundestag opened its debate on the TEU.

16 October. An extraordinary meeting of the European Council was convened in Birmingham in an attempt to iron out the problems that existed with the ERM. The meeting was also intended as a means of defining a suitable stance for Denmark and the UK so that their governments' position could be made easier through a declaration on subsidiarity. In the end all decisions were deferred to the Edinburgh European Council meeting.

22 October. The TEU was approved by the Belgian Council of the French-speaking Community.

27 October. In Denmark, seven out of eight parliamentary parties reached a 'national compromise' on additions to the Maastricht Treaty on the basis of which they would support a second referendum in 1993. The European Commission produced its influential report on the application of the principle of subsidiarity.

29 October. The Spanish Chamber of Deputies approved the TEU by 314 votes to three, with eight abstentions. The Italian Chamber of Deputies approved the Treaty of Maastricht by 403 votes to 46.

3 November. Greece deposited its instrument of ratification of the Treaty of Maastricht.

4 November. In a debate on the TEU in the House of Commons, the government won the paving debate, allowing the bill to proceed into the committee stage, by 319 votes to 316. While 19 Liberal Democrats voted with the government, 26 Conservatives voted against it, along with Labour MPs. There were seven deliberate Conservative abstentions. Without the

Liberal Democrat votes the government would have lost the vote despite the fact that the government commanded a 21-seat overall majority in the House of Commons. France deposited its instrument of ratification of the TEU. The Belgian Senate approved the TEU by 115 to 26 with one abstention.

5 November. The first EC cooperation agreement with a state of the former Yugoslavia was signed with Slovenia. The Irish government lost a vote of confidence in the Dáil and was forced to resign and call a general election.

12 November. The Netherlands Chamber of Deputies approved the Maastricht Treaty by 137 votes to 13.

17 November. The Portuguese Assembly passed the necessary amendments to the Constitution by 196 votes to 20.

18 November. The Swedish Parliament voted to ratify the European Economic Area agreement between the EC and EFTA states.

19 November. Sweden abandoned the pegging of its currency to the ECU after intense currency speculation.

20 November. Greece joined the WEU.

23 November. The TEU was approved by the Belgian Council of the German-speaking Community. Ireland deposited its instrument of ratification of the Maastricht Treaty. Spanish peseta and Portuguese escudo were realigned in the EMS by −6%.

25 November. The Spanish Senate approved the TEU by 222 votes to zero, with three abstentions. Norway finally applied to join the EC. In the Irish general election the Labour Party held the balance of power in the Dáil.

1 December. At the House of Commons committee stage, MPs started 23 days of debating the bill in committee on the floor of the House. Over 500 amendments to the three-clause bill were proposed.

2 December. The German Bundestag assented to the TEU by 543 votes to 17.

5 December. Italy deposited its instrument of ratification of the TEU.

6 December. The Swiss population voted not to ratify the EEA by 50.3% to 49.7% in a referendum.

10 December. The Portuguese Assembly of the Republic approved the TEU by 200 votes to 21. Belgium deposited its instrument of ratification of the TEU. Following currency speculation, Norway abandoned the pegging of its currency to the ECU.

11–12 December. At the Edinburgh European Council meeting agreement was reached on several important issues, including: Danish opt-outs from the TEU; the clarification of subsidiarity and transparency; the Delors II financial package; and the opening of accession negotiations in early 1993 with Austria, Finland and Sweden, and with Norway later in 1993. The Council also agreed the number of seats for each

Member State in the EP in order to take account of German unification and the prospect of future enlargement. The distribution of seats was as follows (previous numbers in brackets): Belgium 25(24); Denmark 16(16); the FRG 99(81); Greece 25(24); Spain 64(60); France 87(81); Ireland 15(15); Italy 87(81); Luxembourg 6(6); the Netherlands 31(25); Portugal 25(24); the UK 87(81). The agreement reached at Edinburgh saved the process of European integration after it had been stalled since June 1992 due to the Danish 'no' vote in a referendum.

13 December.   Liechtenstein voted in favour of ratifying the European Economic Area agreement in a referendum.

15 December.   The Netherlands Senate approved the TEU *nemine contradicente.*

17 December.   The Council and EP reached agreement on the budget for 1993, which was formally adopted.

18 December.   The German Bundesrat unanimously passed the TEU.

28 December.   The Netherlands deposited its instrument of ratification of the TEU.

31 December.   Spain deposited its instrument of ratification of the TEU.

12.   Enlargement IV and reform, 1993–97

1993

1 January.   The Single European Market came into force, implementing the SEA that had originally been drawn up in 1985 and implemented in mid-1987. This meant that there would be free movement of goods, services, capital and people throughout all the Member States of the EC. Czechoslovakia separated into two new independent states, the Czech Republic and the Slovak Republic.

21 January.   Cooperation agreement signed by NATO and Franco-German Eurocorps.

25 January.   A new Danish government entered office, led by the Social Democrat Poul Nyrup Rasmussen.

1 February.   The EC opened negotiations in Brussels for EFTA states to join the Community. The EC signed a Europe Agreement with Romania. The Irish pound was realigned in the EMS by −10%.

3 February.   The UK government announced a review of its defence cuts and four infantry regiments that were previously threatened with merger were saved.

4 February.   The German Bundesbank unexpectedly lowered its discount and Lombard rates due to pressure on the ERM. The discount rate was reduced from 8.25% (at which it had stood since September 1992) to 8%, while the Lombard rate was reduced from 9.5% to 9%.

16 February.   The new European Commission was sworn into office at Parliament in Luxembourg. Portugal deposited its instrument of ratification of the Maastricht Treaty.

8 March.   The UK government was defeated on a Labour amendment to the Maastricht Bill concerning membership of the Council of Regions. The General Affairs Council meeting in Brussels resulted in the EC signing a Europe Agreement with Bulgaria.

21 March.   The ruling French Socialist Party was defeated by the right-wing RPR–UDF alliance in the first round of legislative elections.

29 March.   In France Edouard Balladur was appointed Prime Minister after the RPR–UDF won the legislative elections.

30 March.   The TEU was approved by the Danish Parliament by 154 votes to 16.

5–6 April.   The General Affairs Council meeting in Luxembourg resulted in the opening of accession negotiations with Norway.

22 April.   The Italian government resigned.

28 April.   It was announced that Carlo Campi would lead a new Italian coalition government.

14 May.   Spanish peseta was realigned in the EMS by −8% and Portuguese escudo by −6.5%.

18 May.   In Denmark, 56.7% voted 'yes' in the second TEU referendum on a turnout of 86.2%. Approval took place after an agreement had been reached allowing Denmark to opt-out of participation in the final stages of EMU and the common defence policy.

20 May.   The House of Commons gave a third reading to the Maastricht Bill and the government secured a majority by 292 votes to 112.

24–27 May.   The European Agriculture Council adopted 1993–94 farm prices.

17 June.   Denmark deposited its instrument of ratification of the TEU.

21–22 June.   Copenhagen European Council meeting produced agreement on the target date of 1 January 1995 for EC membership for Austria, Finland, Norway, and Sweden. The summit was dominated by the situation in Yugoslavia and by attempts to work out a concerted policy for unemployment and recession.

30 June.   Negative opinion given on Malta's application to join the EC. Rejection of Cyprus's application to join the EC.

2 August.   The UK government formally ratified the TEU in Rome. The ERM of the EMS effectively collapsed and agreement was reached to allow currencies to fluctuate within a broad band of 15% either side of their central rates, rather than the 2.25% band for strong currencies or the 6% band for the Spanish and Portuguese currencies.

18 August.   Jacques de Larosière was appointed the new head of the European Bank for Reconstruction and Development.

1 September.   The European Commission implemented the Community Charter of the Fundamental Social Rights of Workers and adopted an opinion on equitable wage.

2 September.   The UK deposited its instrument of ratification of the TEU.

4 October.   The EU signed Europe Agreements with the Czech and Slovak Republics.

11 October.   Andreas Papandreou's Pan-Hellenic Society Movement (PASOK) was returned to power after elections in Greece.

12 October.   The German Constitutional Court found against a challenge that was intended to stop the German President ratifying the TEU. The challenge included the Liberal politician Manfred Brunner, who was also *chef de cabinet* of the European Commission Vice-President Martin Bangemann – until he was sacked. The Federal Republic of Germany deposited its instrument of ratification of the TEU.

18 October.   The nine Schengen states decided to postpone the removal of passport checks at airports from 1 December 1993 to 1 February 1994. This was due to problems with the Schengen information system.

29 October.   At the extraordinary European Council meeting in Brussels, the first steps were taken towards the adoption of a common foreign policy by requesting the Council to define the conditions and procedures for joint action with regard to the situations in Central and Eastern Europe, the Middle East, South Africa, Russia and the former Yugoslavia. Frankfurt was chosen as the seat of the European Central Bank, as well as the European Monetary Institute, which was to be established at the start of stage two of EMU.

1 November.   The EC formally became the European Union (EU) due to the TEU.

8–9 November.   The General Affairs Council in Brussels decided to rename the Council of Ministers the Council of the EU.

17 November.   The Commission of the European Communities decided to call itself the European Commission.

18 November.   The European Commission launched the Green Paper on 'European Social Policy – Options for the Union'.

22 November.   The European Council adopted a series of decisions and regulations on secondary legislation necessary for stage two of economic and monetary union.

23 November.   The Brussels Labour and Social Affairs Council adopted the Organisation of Working Time Directive.

29 November.   The EU Interior and Justice Ministers met for the first time in Brussels as part of the third pillar of the EU (coordinating justice and home affairs) and, therefore, replaced the Trevi Group.

5 December.   The European Commission adopted the White Paper on growth, competitiveness and employment – the challenges and ways forward into the twenty-first century.

6–7 December.   The Brussels General Affairs Council adopted the directive on the right to vote and stand in EP elections. The directive, implementing Article 8b.2 of the amended Treaty of Rome, gave EC nationals residing in other Member States the right to vote, and to stand as candidates in EP elections. The Foreign Affairs Council also agreed on the necessary standards for public access to Council and Commission documents.

10–11 December. The European Council Summit, meeting in Brussels, was primarily concerned with the European Commission's White Paper on growth, competitiveness and employment.

13 December. The European Council adopted three Regulations in preparation for the start of stage two of EMU on 1 January. Alexander Lamfalussy was appointed Chairman of the European Monetary Institute.

16 December. Five EU states announced that they would give full diplomatic recognition to the former Yugoslav Republic of Macedonia, namely Denmark, France, Germany, the Netherlands and the UK.

1994

1 January. Stage two of EMU began and the European Monetary Institute was established in Frankfurt as a precursor to a European Central Bank. Stage one of EMU had come into effect in July 1990. Stage two was implemented according to the timetable which had been set out in the TEU. This was despite the setback suffered by the EMS when the ERM collapsed in August 1993. The agreement establishing the European Economic Area came into force.

10–11 January. Brussels NATO Summit discussed the organisation's future role, and its relationship to countries in Eastern and Central Europe.

16 January. The Italian President dissolved parliament and called a general election for 27 March.

1 February. Association agreements between the EU and Poland and Hungary, which had been signed in December 1991, came into effect.

7 February. EU Foreign Ministers backed the use of NATO air power if necessary to lift the Bosnian Serb siege of Sarajevo.

9 February. NATO agreed to the United Nations (UN) request to authorise air strikes in the former Yugoslavia. A 20 km total exclusion zone was declared around Sarajevo and the Bosnian Serbs were required to withdraw their heavy weapons from the zone or place them under UN control within ten days.

21–22 February. EU Foreign Ministers met in Brussels with their counterparts from Austria, Finland, Norway and Sweden to discuss enlargement negotiations.

1 March. Austria, Finland and Sweden agreed terms to join the EU.

3 March. The House of Lords ruled that certain aspects of UK employment protection legislation relating to statutory redundancy payments and unfair dismissal were in conflict with EU directives of 1975 and 1976. This was because they discriminated against part-time workers.

15 March. There was a breakdown of negotiations in Brussels over the size of the blocking minority due to the UK's reluctance to allow an increase from three countries and 23 votes for a blocking vote to four countries and 27 votes.

26–27 March. Ioannina informal General Affairs Council meeting in Greece. The UK Prime Minister, John Major, told the House of Commons on 29 March that at the meeting a compromise had been reached and that the blocking minority would be increased to 27 votes, but that the existing 23-vote minority could be used to create a delay in the implementation of EU legislation.

28 March. The right-wing Freedom Alliance, comprising Forza Italia, the National Alliance and the Northern League, won the Italian general election. They had a clear majority in the lower house of parliament.

30 March. Conclusion in Brussels of accession negotiations with Austria, Sweden, Finland and Norway.

1 April. Hungary was the first former Communist state to apply for membership of the EU.

8 April. Poland applied for membership of the EU.

8–9 April. Informal meeting of the EU Finance Ministers and Central Bank Governors in Athens. The Central Bank Governors opposed a return to the narrow 2.25% and 6% currency fluctuation bands within the ERM. These bands had been widened to 15% in August 1993 due to the currency speculation in that month.

11 April. NATO planes bombed Bosnian Serb armoured vehicles in a response to the resumption of the shelling of Gorazde.

21 April. Abel Matutes, the Spanish member of the European Commission responsible for Energy and Transport since 1993, stepped down and was replaced by Marcelino Oreja, a former Spanish Foreign Affairs Minister, on 28 April.

22 April. NATO authorised the use of air strikes against Bosnian Serb heavy weapons within the 20 km exclusion zone around Gorazde unless certain conditions were met. These were an immediate cease-fire; the retreat of Bosnian Serb forces by 3 km from the centre of Gorazde; and permission to send in humanitarian convoys and carry out medical evacuations. Furthermore, NATO also authorised the use of air strikes against the Bosnian Serbs in the event of attacks against any UN safe area, or if the Bosnian Serb heavy weapons entered the 20 km exclusion zones around these areas.

26 April. The first meeting of the 'Contact Group' on the former Yugoslavia was held in London. The group comprised representatives of the UK, Russia, France, Germany and the USA. The purpose of the group was to act as a united front to the warring parties. It concentrated on securing a territorial agreement as the first step to a political settlement. As part of this process it produced a map for the various parties to consider.

28 April.   The Italian President asked the leader of the right-wing Freedom Alliance, Silvio Berlusconi, to form a government.

3 May.   The coalition government in the Netherlands lost its Parliamentary majority in a general election, resulting in the resignation of the Prime Minister, Ruud Lubbers.

4 May.   The EP approved agreements providing for Austria, Finland, Norway and Sweden to join the EU.

9 May.   Bulgaria, Estonia, Hungary, Latvia, Lithuania, Poland, Romania, the Czech and Slovak Republics became associate members of the WEU.

11 May.   The new Italian government, led by Silvio Berlusconi, was sworn in. The Vienna Agreement between Bosnians and Croats established the Bosnian/Croat Federation at 58% of Bosnian territory. The agreement divided the Federation into eight cantons and determined the composition of the federal government.

13 May.   Meeting in Geneva of the Foreign Ministers of the UK, France, Russia, the USA, the EU Troika, and the Vice-President of the European Commission, with regard to the situation in former Yugoslavia. The meeting called for a four-month cessation of hostilities and requested negotiations to commence within two weeks, under the aegis of the Contact Group. The basis of the negotiations was to be a territorial division of 51% for the Bosnian Federation and 49% for the Bosnian Serbs.

16 May.   EU Council of Ministers approved the four accession treaties, which also required approval by all 12 EU Member States' parliaments.

12 June.   European elections were held in Belgium, Germany, Spain, France, Italy, Luxembourg and Portugal. In a referendum in Austria, the majority of the population was in favour of accession to the EU.

24 June.   The Prime Ministers of Austria, Finland, Norway and Sweden each signed their country's Treaties of Accession to the EU.

24–25 June.   The Corfu European Council meeting was dominated by the failure of the Heads of State and Government to appoint a President of the European Commission. The UK Prime Minister, John Major, vetoed the candidacy of the Belgian Prime Minister Jean-Luc Dehaene due to his 'interventionist tendencies', while it was also clear that the UK was not prepared to accept a candidate who had emanated from a Franco-German proposal.

12 July.   Ruling by the German Constitutional Court that German forces could take part in armed missions outside the NATO area. The provision was that on each occasion the decision had to be subject to parliamentary approval.

15 July.   An extraordinary meeting of the European Council in Brussels agreed on the selection of Jacques Santer to succeed Jacques Delors as President of the European Commission for a five-year term from January 1995. Santer had been Prime Minister of Luxembourg since 1984. He was a compromise candidate following John Major's veto of the Belgian Prime Minister, Jean-Luc Dehaene, at the Corfu European Council meeting in June.

19 July.   The German Socialist, Klaus Hansch, was elected President of the new EP.

26 July.   Jacques Santer's nomination as President of the European Commission was confirmed by a Council decision.

27 July.   The European Commission adopted the White Paper on European Social Policy.

4 August.   President Milosevic announced the decision to sever political and economic ties with the Bosnian Serbs because of their rejection of the peace plan.

1 September.   The German Christian Democrats (CDU/CSU) published a discussion paper entitled 'Reflections on European Policy'. The document envisaged a core Europe (of all the original members except Italy) that would advance at a faster pace towards European integration. The document suggested that proceeding on the basis of variable geometry was wise as not every state could take every step in unison. Dr Jürgen Trumpf was appointed the Secretary-General of the Council of Ministers.

8 September.   UK, French and American troops withdrew from Berlin after 49 years.

18 September.   In Sweden the Social Democratic Party won the general election without a majority.

19 September.   The meeting of EU Finance and Economy Ministers in Brussels found that the budget deficits of all the EU Member States, except Ireland and Luxembourg, were excessive when judged by the economic convergence criteria set out in the Maastricht Treaty as a prerequisite for EMU.

21 September.   In the Danish general election the Social Democratic-led coalition lost its majority, but retained power with the help of the Socialist and Communist parties.

22 September.   The European Council adopted the directive on the establishment of European Works Councils or procedures in Community-wide undertakings for the purposes of informing and consulting employees. This was the first measure adopted by the 11 Member States under the Social Policy Protocol.

16 October.   A referendum in Finland approved its accession to the EU. The three-party centre-right coalition won a fourth term of office in the German general election. The coalition, led by Chancellor Kohl, had been in power since 1982.

13 November.   A referendum in Sweden approved its accession to the EU.

14 November.   A meeting of the WEU's Defence and Foreign Ministers in Noordwijk approved the appointment of José Cutileiro, a Portuguese diplomat, to succeed Willem van Eekelen as Secretary-General of the WEU.

15 November. The European Monetary Institute Council met for the first time in Frankfurt. Helmut Kohl was re-elected by the Bundestag as German Chancellor by only one vote more than the absolute majority required.

17 November. Albert Reynolds, the Irish Prime Minister, resigned after the Labour Party withdrew from the coalition government.

18 November. At a meeting in Chartres, west of Paris, the French President, François Mitterrand, and the UK Prime Minister, John Major, unveiled plans for a joint military airborne command with a permanent headquarters and multinational staff.

28 November. A referendum in Norway rejected accession to the EU.

28–29 November. The General Affairs Council met in Brussels.

4 December. Austria announced its decision to join the EMS on its accession to the EU, as well as its desire to join the ERM as soon as possible thereafter.

9–10 December. The European Council Summit, meeting in Essen, established the approach for continuing and strengthening the strategy of the White Paper on growth, competitiveness and employment. Special reference was given to measures to combat unemployment and to bring the trans-European networks into operation.

14 December. The EP gave its assent to the Final Act of the Uruguay Round.

22 December. Silvio Berlusconi resigned as Prime Minister of Italy after his coalition government collapsed following an investigation into his business affairs. The Schengen Group reached agreement on the abolition of frontier controls on 26 March 1995.

1995

1 January. Austria, Finland and Sweden joined the EU on the basis of the terms settled in March 1994, and approved in referendum votes in June, October and November respectively. The 12 became the 15, and the EU's population increased from 345 million to 368 million. With regard to voting in the Council of Ministers, Austria and Sweden would have four votes and Finland three, out of a total of 87. A qualified majority therefore required 62 votes (except for decisions on Commission proposals) with at least ten Member States voting in favour. The accession of the three states meant that the EP increased from 567 to 625 members, with 22 from Sweden, 21 from Austria and 16 from Finland.

9 January. The Austrian schilling joined the ERM of the EMS at a central rate of ECU 1 = OS 13.7167.

13 January. Italian President Scalfaro appointed Lamberto Dini Prime Minister-designate of Italy.

17 January. Lamberto Dini's government of technocrats was sworn in in Italy. The new EU Commission President, Jacques Santer, presented the priorities for his Presidency to the EP in Strasbourg.

18 January.   The EP approved by 416 votes to 103 the appointment of the new 20-member Commission with Jacques Santer as President. There were 59 abstentions. The Commission finally took office after it had been sworn in by the European Court of Justice on 24 January.

1 February.   The European Commission elected Manuel Marin and Sir Leon Brittan as its Vice-Presidents.

2 February.   The Bank of England raised the base lending rate by a half a percentage point to 6.75%.

15–16 February.   The 15 EU Foreign Ministers failed to agree on re-newed funding for the African, Caribbean and Pacific states under the Fourth Lomé Convention, which had been signed in 1989 and covered the period 1990–2000.

6 March.   The EU monetary committee agreed to a realignment of the ERM by devaluing the Spanish peseta by 7% and the Portuguese escudo by 3.5%. EU Foreign Ministers and Turkey signed an agreement to introduce a customs union from January 1996.

20–21 March.   Paris Conference on European Stability Pact.

26 March.   The Schengen Convention came into effect. This meant that passport controls at the common internal borders of seven EU Member States were abolished and such controls at external borders were strength-ened. The countries were Belgium, France, Germany, Luxembourg, the Netherlands, Portugal and Spain.

12 April.   The EU signed associate membership agreements with Estonia, Latvia and Lithuania. This meant that existing economic cooperation and free trade agreements were upgraded.

13 April.   Paavo Lipponen became Prime Minister of Finland. He was the head of a five-party coalition government.

23 April.   In the first round of the French Presidential election, Lionel Jospin (Socialist) won 23.2% of the vote, while Jacques Chirac (Gaullist) won 20.1%.

28 April.   Austria became the tenth EU country to sign the Schengen Convention.

3 May.   A UN-brokered cease-fire agreement was signed by Croatia and Croatian Serb representatives.

7 May.   Jacques Chirac was elected President of France.

10 May.   Jacques Santer presented a report by the Commission on the func-tioning of the EU Treaty in light of the 1996 IGC. The Commission report rejected the concept of a Europe 'à la Carte', in which some countries could choose some elements of the Union and reject others. However, Santer accepted that some Member States might need to move at different speeds.

15 May.   At the Lisbon WEU Ministerial meeting, the members agreed to establish in Torrejón, Spain, a permanent WEU base for the reception and examination of satellite photographs, as well as to increase the staffing of the WEU headquarters in Brussels.

17 May. The EP approved by 288 votes to 103 votes, with 76 abstentions, the so-called 'Bourlanges/Martin Report' as part of the preparations for the 1996 IGC. Jacques Chirac succeeded François Mitterrand as President of France, and appointed Alain Juppé Prime Minister.

21 May. In the Belgian general election the four-party coalition government retained power.

2 June. The IGC Reflection Group was launched. The first Ministerial meeting in Messina revealed that a large gulf existed between the UK and the majority of the other Member States over the extent of reform that was desired.

3 June. The UK agreed to send 5,500 troops to Bosnia as part of the new UN rapid intervention force.

9 June. It was announced that the former Swedish Prime Minister, Carl Bildt, would succeed Lord Owen as co-chairman of the International Conference on the Former Yugoslavia.

20 June. NATO requested the permission of the UN for air strikes on Banja Luka airport as a response to Bosnian Serb violations of the No Fly Zone.

22 June. John Major resigned as leader of the Conservative Party and stated that he would stand in the forthcoming leadership contest.

12 July. The UN and EU demanded the withdrawal of Bosnian Serbs from Srebrenica.

21 July. A meeting was held in London of the EU, UN, NATO, Contact Group and other UN troop contributors to discuss a response to Serb attacks on safe areas.

25 July. The International Criminal Tribunal indicted the Bosnian Serbs Karadzic and Mladic for genocide, and Martic for war crimes.

1 August. NATO agreed to use theatre-wide air power as part of an effort to protect the safe areas.

11 August. A European Court of Justice ruling held that rules ending entitlement to invalidity benefit for a woman at the age of 60 did not breach a European directive of equal treatment for men and women in matters concerning social security.

22–23 September. The informal European Council meeting in Majorca was dominated by the issue of the timing and the criteria for EMU. Leaders for the first time stated that certain countries might not be able to comply with the economic convergence criteria as set out in the TEU.

14 November. The European Monetary Institute published a timetable for the introduction of a single currency.

23 November. The Justice and Home Affairs Council, meeting in Brussels, approved a non-binding 'joint-action' setting out a new, harmonised definition of the term 'refugee'. It was more restrictive than the original definition that was contained in the 1951 Geneva Convention relating to the Status of Refugees.

15–16 December.   Madrid European Council meeting at which leaders confirmed that the single European currency was to be introduced from January 1999, in the third and final phase of EMU. They also decided that the currency should be called the 'Euro', and agreed that the inter-governmental conference to review the functioning of the European institutions would be opened on 29 March 1996.

1996

8 January.   Former President François Mitterrand of France died.

22–24 January.   Jacques Santer launched a three-day round-table session in Brussels to publicise the intended EU single currency.

17–18 February.   The USA organised a mini-summit in Rome as part of an effort to reinforce support for the December 1995 peace agreement for Bosnia-Herzegovina. The implementation of the agreement had been placed in jeopardy by a series of events in Bosnia during early February that were primarily related to the issues of war crimes and of territorial transfers in Mostar and Sarajevo.

5 March.   European Court of Justice ruling stated that EU governments must compensate companies and individuals for losses resulting from their failure to implement EU laws correctly.

12 March.   Publication of the UK government White Paper on the IGC: 'A partnership of nations'.

20 March.   It was announced that the UK could face a major health crisis in the form of a possible link between BSE which is found in cattle and the fatal disease found in humans known as Creutzfeldt-Jakob disease (CJD).

25 March.   The EU veterinary committee voted by 14 to one to recommend a total ban, which was immediately implemented, on the export of beef and beef products from the UK. The only dissenter was the UK.

29 March.   Launch of the 1996 IGC in Turin. The IGC process was expected to continue until mid-1997, concluding at the June 1997 Amsterdam Summit.

3 April.   The UK government announced that it would hold a referendum if it decided that the UK should join a European single currency.

21 April.   In the Italian general election the centre-left Olive Tree alliance won a decisive advantage over the right-wing Freedom alliance. Yet, with 284 out of 630 seats in the Chamber of Deputies (and 157 out of 315 elective Senate seats), it was dependent on support from outside the alliance to obtain an overall majority.

7 May.   WEU Ministerial meeting in Birmingham included the Foreign and Defence Ministers from the ten-member WEU, along with their counterparts from the five neutral observer countries – Austria, Denmark, Finland, Ireland and Sweden. The 12 associate or partner countries also attended – Bulgaria, the Czech Republic, Estonia, Hungary, Iceland, Latvia, Lithuania, Norway, Poland, Romania, Slovakia and Turkey.

21 May. The UK adopted a policy of non-cooperation with the EU until a timetable to lift the ban on the export of beef was settled. The government established a Ministerial committee on 22 May, chaired by Prime Minister Major, to oversee the confrontational strategy.

24 May. The UK vetoed a EU bankruptcy convention as part of its policy of non-cooperation.

4 June. The European Commission announced that it would phase out the UK export ban on tallow, gelatine and semen over the following weeks if stricter health controls were imposed (commencing on 11 June). On the same day the UK government put forward to EU Agriculture Ministers its plans for the eradication of BSE from cattle herds, which, despite some additional safety measures, was a reiteration of its existing stance.

5 June. The UK approved the EU–Slovenia association agreement, despite still adopting a policy of non-cooperation. French President Jacques Chirac and German Chancellor Helmut Kohl met in Dijon and reached agreement that the December Franco-German Summit should finalise a 'common security and defence concept'.

10 June. The UK approved EU cooperation talks with Algeria and the allocation of funds to monitor elections in Bosnia, despite a policy of non-cooperation.

17 June. The UK agricultural dispute dominated the Rome Foreign Ministers' meeting which was intended to prepare the agenda for the forthcoming European Council meeting in Florence. EU Transport Ministers meeting in Luxembourg produced agreement by 14 to one (the UK voted against) that future negotiations with the USA on the 'open skies' agreements, relating to the liberalisation of the aviation industry, should be negotiated by the EU as a bloc rather than individual Member States.

21–22 June. The European Council meeting in Florence reached agreement on the first day to end the confrontation between the UK and the other Member States over the EU ban imposed on UK exports of beef and beef products. Thus, the summit was able to deal with the main items on the agenda, which included the analysis of the first three months of the IGC to review the Maastricht TEU.

2 July. The European Commissioner responsible for fisheries suggested that 1997 fish quotas should reduce the quota for North Sea herring by half.

8 July. EU Finance Ministers examined the progress made by Member States towards the EMU convergence criteria, with criticism levied at all countries apart from Denmark, Luxembourg and Sweden. They were acknowledged to have made significant progress in reducing their debt.

12 July. The European Court of Justice rejected an appeal by the UK government to lift the ban on UK beef exports which had been imposed by the European Commission in March 1996. The Court's ruling was based on scientific evidence of a link between BSE in cattle and Creutzfeldt-Jakob disease in humans.

22 July. The European Commissioner with responsibility for agriculture, Franz Fischler, asked EU Agriculture Ministers to ban the spleen, brain and spinal cord of sheep and goats from entering the human food chain.

24 July. EU Member States signed a protocol to the Europol Convention which allowed states to choose to accept the jurisdiction of the European Court of Justice, but did not oblige them to do so.

8 August. Belgium was the first Member State which promised to meet the timetable for the transition towards a single currency that was agreed in Madrid at the December 1995 European Council.

13 August. The European Monetary Institute published a report on the technical aspects of the Target payments system which was to operate from the start of stage three of EMU in January 1999.

28 August. Publication of an article in *Dagens Nyheter* by Sweden's Finance Minister, Erik Asbrink, stating that Sweden would not seek to be part of the first countries to participate in EMU. This was despite the government being confident that it would meet the convergence criteria.

1 September. Franco-German Summit in Bonn between Jacques Chirac and Helmut Kohl.

7–8 September. Foreign Ministers' meeting confirmed that a mini-summit would take place on 5 October to examine progress made in the IGC negotiations, with it having been initially expected to conclude by June 1997.

13 September. Budget austerity measures were approved in Germany as part of efforts to meet the EMU convergence criteria.

16 September. Annual Spanish–Italian Heads of Government meeting in Valencia.

17 September. Agricultural Ministers reached agreement on the request of an increase in the intervention purchasing of beef.

18 September. Presentation of a deficit-cutting budget in line with attempts to conform to the EMU convergence criteria.

20–21 September. Dublin meeting of EU Finance Ministers and Central Bank Governors supported the concept of a stability pact on budgetary discipline.

24 September. Agricultural Ministers proposed the use of 500 million ECU from surplus budget funds to assist farmers affected by the loss of consumer confidence in beef products as a result of the BSE crisis. This was in addition to the 850 million ECU which was approved in June 1996.

26–27 September. Dublin meeting of EU Justice and Home Affairs Ministers signed a convention to facilitate extraditions between Member States where an offence can be punished by a prison sentence in both of the concerned states.

27 September.   The Spanish and Italian governments committed themselves to meeting the EMU convergence criteria with the presentation of tough austerity budgets.

5 October.   Extraordinary Dublin European Council meeting examined the IGC negotiations, at which Member States reaffirmed June 1997 as the deadline for completing all work. The UK Prime Minister, John Major, noted his opposition to 'over-extending' the EU's competence in the field of defence cooperation. He also insisted that any treaty should remove the possibility of allowing health and safety regulations to limit the length of the working week.

14 October.   Transport Ministers rejected proposals for extra EU budget funding for 14 major projects on road, rail and airport infrastructure, as advocated by the President of the European Commission, Jacques Santer. Finland became a member of the EMS. The UK noted its opposition to European Commission proposals to reduce up to 50% the capacity of fishing fleets for certain types of fish.

24 October.   The European Parliament voted by 386 to 35 (15 abstentions) in favour of a 1997 budget totalling 88 billion ECU, which represented an increase of 1% on 1996.

6 November.   A European Monetary Institute report emphasised that the majority of Member States had not fulfilled the necessary convergence criteria conditions to progress to EMU. The report stressed that 'great attention will have to be paid to the substance and not only to the accounting methods used in measuring both deficits and debts', a reference directed towards French and Italian attempts to improve their position in 1997 by one-off measures.

18 November.   Channel Tunnel rail fire.

24 November.   EU Finance Ministers and Central Bank Governors reached agreement on allowing the lira to re-enter the ERM, four years after it was suspended from the system.

12 December.   The European Parliament approved a budget of 89 billion ECU for 1997. This represented a 2.8% increase over 1996 expenditure.

13–14 December.   Dublin European Council meeting reached agreement on a single currency stability pact.

1997

8 January.   The European Commission imposed a quota on rice imports from Member States' overseas territories as part of an effort to protect EU rice producers.

14 January.   The Spanish Christian Democrat, José Maria Gil-Robles, was elected Speaker of the European Parliament, succeeding the German Social Democrat, Klaus Hänsch.

20 January.   Brussels Foreign Ministers' meeting discussed the IGC negotiations. The first discussions on flexible decision-making took place, thereby allowing groups of Member States to pursue greater integration. France and Germany especially advocated a policy which would allow deeper integration among some Member States, with the German Foreign Minister, Klaus Kinkel, stating that 'no Member State should be able to block the way ahead by means of the veto'. This position was, however, opposed by Denmark, Greece, Portugal, Sweden and the UK. The European Commission imposed fines on Germany and Italy for breaching EU legislation, being the first time that it attempted to use its powers to fine Member States via Article 171 of the Treaty on European Union.

18 February.   The Netherlands Foreign Minister, Michel Patijn, published draft proposals on flexible decision-making as part of the IGC negotiations. This would allow groups of Member States to pursue greater integration, with majority voting extended to 25 policy areas, including industry, culture, research and technology and the free movement of people. However, the veto would still apply to sensitive policy areas such as social security, enlargement, future treaty amendments and direct taxation.

18–20 February.   The European Parliament debated a report from a cross-party committee which accused the UK government of fuelling the beef crisis.

19 February.   The European Parliament gave the European Commission nine months to conduct substantial reforms of its food and health policies or it would face a motion to dismiss all 20 European Commissioners.

17–19 March.   Brussels EU Agricultural Ministers' meeting reached agreement that all beef had to be marked with its country of origin. This development was resisted by the UK because the government considered it would affect the sales of beef in the wake of the March 1996 worldwide ban on UK beef exports, which was a response to BSE fears.

25 March.   EU Foreign Ministers met in Rome to commence the 40th anniversary of the Treaty of Rome. At this meeting the Netherlands presented a Draft Treaty for discussion at the June Amsterdam European Council meeting. Certain parts of the draft included the provision for the transfer from national governments to the EU of certain policies such as immigration, asylum and visas.

5–6 April.   Noordwijk meeting of EU Finance Ministers and Central Bank Governors reached agreement on an outline EMU timetable and endorsed the single currency stability pact. The meeting decided that a special EU Council would be held in May 1998 to determine which Member States had met the EMU economic convergence criteria.

1 May.   Labour Party won UK general election, gaining a majority of 179 in the House of Commons. Tony Blair became Prime Minister.

21 May.   The European Commission appointed Carlo Trojan of the Netherlands as its Secretary-General to replace David Williamson, with effect from 1 July 1997.

23 May. EU Heads of State and Government and Foreign Ministers met at Noordwijk to prepare for the June Amsterdam European Council. Greater optimism among Member States was apparent at the summit, primarily because of the change of the government in the UK general election which had resulted in Tony Blair becoming Prime Minister.

16–17 June. Amsterdam European Council meeting finalised the Treaty which had been negotiated during the IGC, while the newly elected UK Labour government accepted the Social Chapter. However, the Treaty did not resolve key institutional questions, including the reform of voting in the Council of Ministers, the extension of majority voting and a condensing of the European Commission. The meeting was particularly noted for the negative position of the German Chancellor, Helmut Kohl, who blocked the extension of majority voting in certain areas and defended both national and regional rights at the expense of new EU-wide powers. A further development of the meeting was the defeat of the Franco-German proposal to integrate the WEU into the EU by the combination of an alliance of the UK, Denmark, Finland, Ireland and Sweden.

16 July. The President of the European Commission, Jacques Santer, presented *Agenda 2000* to the European Parliament in Strasbourg. This represented a package of plans to cover EU enlargement, the budget and the future of the CAP.

18 July. Austria, Germany and Italy agreed to implement the Schengen Convention from 1 April 1998.

17 August. Chancellor Helmut Kohl called for a reduction in Germany's contributions to the EU budget in a television interview.

28 August. Bonn Franco-German Summit attempted to improve relations between both nations which had become strained since the election of Lionel Jospin as French Prime Minister in June. Germany had been concerned about statements by Jospin and his Finance Minister, Dominique Strausshan, that called for a relaxation of the EMU convergence criteria and more expansionist economic policies.

13–14 September. Meeting of EU Finance Ministers in Mondorf, Luxembourg, reached agreement that the bilateral rates for currencies joining EMU would be announced in May 1998. The meeting also emphasised divisions between Member States over contributions to the EU budget, with Germany and the Netherlands calling for a reduction in their net contributions.

25–26 October. EU Foreign Ministers meeting in Mondorf, Luxembourg, discussed prospects of enlargement, but did not reach agreement as to which countries would be invited to participate in accession talks with EU Heads of State and Government at their summit meeting in December 1997.

17 November. Luxembourg EU Finance Ministers' meeting examined French proposals for the creation of an informal new council that would bring together only those EU Member States participating in the single currency stage of EMU. This would therefore allow them to coordinate policies, with the new group likely to exclude Denmark, Greece, Sweden and the UK.

20–21 November.   The extraordinary Luxembourg Summit, devoted to employment, reached agreement on new guidelines for job creation and assistance for the young and long-term unemployed.

9 December.   The European Court of Justice condemned the French government for being reluctant to intervene in a succession of strikes that had blocked roads and prevented the free movement of goods.

12–13 December.   The Luxembourg European Council meeting reached agreement on inviting six countries to start membership talks in March 1998: the Czech Republic, Estonia, Hungary, Poland, Slovenia and Cyprus.

22 December.   The Defence Ministers of Germany, Italy, Spain and the UK signed an agreement for the full production phase of the £42 billion Eurofighter aircraft, the idea for which had been initially conceived in the late 1970s.

13.   Towards a single currency, 1998–99

1998

January.   The EU approved a partial lifting of the 1996 export ban on UK beef, with the proposal only applying to the export of beef products from Northern Ireland. This was because it was the only part of the UK which had a complete computerised tracking system, while it also had fewer recorded cases of BSE than elsewhere in the UK.

12 January.   EU–Japan Summit in Tokyo.

28 January.   European Commission fined Volkswagen ECU 102 million for forcing its authorised dealers in Italy to refuse to sell Volkswagen and Audi cars to foreign buyers, primarily from Germany and Austria. This was the largest fine ever imposed upon a company as part of the European Commission's efforts to remove obstacles to the single European market.

4 February.   The European Commission decided on a list of objectives which the ten applicant countries should achieve by the end of 1998 if they were to qualify for EU membership. Of these, Poland was asked to reduce its external debt and restructure its steel industry, and Slovakia was asked to hold free and fair presidential, legislative and local elections in 1998.

9 February.   155 leading German economists called for an 'orderly postponement' of the plan to introduce the single European currency on 1 January 1999.

27 February.   The 15 EU Member States formally filed their 1997 statistical reports that would form the basis for deciding whether they would be able to participate in the single currency stage of EMU. All countries, except Greece, met the basic economic convergence criteria established by the TEU.

12 March. The London European Conference at Lancaster House brought together present and future EU members to examine means of tackling issues on a pan-European basis, as provided for by the December 1997 Luxembourg European Council. Subjects discussed included drugs and organised crime, economic policy, the environment, foreign policy and security policy (including Kosovo). The conference was attended by the 15 EU Member States, Bulgaria, the Czech Republic, Estonia, Hungary, Latvia, Lithuania, Poland, Romania, Slovenia, Slovakia and Cyprus.

13–14 March. Informal Foreign Ministers' meeting in Edinburgh.

14 March. The Greek drachma rejoined the ERM after it had been devalued by 14%.

16–17 March. The Brussels meeting of EU Agricultural Ministers approved a partial lifting of the 1996 export ban of UK beef. This had previously been approved by the European Commission in January 1998. Eleven of the 15 Member States supported a relaxation of the ban, Belgium and Germany voting against and Luxembourg and Spain abstaining. The easing of export restrictions applied to deboned beef from cattle aged between six and 30 months which had come from herds that were certified to have been BSE free for the last eight years.

18 March. The European Commission published plans for a review of EU spending in line with plans for future enlargement. This included reductions in agricultural subsidies and changes in regional subsidies and structural funds.

20–21 March. Informal Finance Ministers' meeting at York.

25 March. The European Commission recommended that 11 Member States adopt the single currency from 1 January 1999 after having examined the statistical data issued by Member States on 27 February. Austria, Belgium, Finland, France, Germany, Ireland, Italy, Luxembourg, the Netherlands, Portugal and Spain were all considered by the European Commission to have met the convergence criteria. Denmark, Sweden and the UK had previously opted-out of joining the Euro in the first wave and Greece was not considered to have met the required criteria.

8 April. The UK Court of Appeal ruled that Spanish trawlers were able to claim £100 million in compensation from the UK government for the time that they had been banned from fishing in UK waters.

16 April. The Swedish parliament voted in favour of Sweden joining the Schengen agreement that linked nine EU states.

2–3 May. Brussels EMU Council decided that 11 of the 15 EU Member States were deemed to have qualified to adopt the single currency on 1 January 1999, namely Austria, Belgium, Finland, France, Germany, Ireland, Italy, Luxembourg, the Netherlands, Portugal and Spain.

19 May.   EU Finance Ministers decided that duty-free shopping within the EU would be abolished by July 1999.

22 May.   Irish referendum on the Amsterdam Treaty: 62% voted yes.

27 May.   The European Commission agreed to lift the ban on the exportation of beef from Northern Ireland from 1 June 1998. The lifting of the ban in Ulster had been agreed in March 1998 but it was conditional on the inspection of meat plants by EU veterinary experts.

28 May.   Danish referendum on the Amsterdam Treaty: 55.1% to 44.9%.

15–17 May.   Birmingham Group of Eight (G8) Summit.

8 June.   Prior to the June Cardiff European Council, Chancellor Kohl and President Chirac wrote a letter with the aim of settling the summit agenda. Their letter called for increased subsidiarity, including a more decentralised EU that would be closer to its citizens and which would respect political and cultural diversity. Both leaders also complained about the remoteness of the EU institutions.

15–16 June.   Cardiff European Council meeting.

23 June.   150 troops from the Eurocorps flew to Sarajevo from their Strasbourg base in their first operation mission since Helmut Kohl and François Mitterrand created the unit in 1993. The Eurocorps consists of 60,000 troops from five countries.

7 July.   The London and Frankfurt Stock Exchanges laid foundations for a future pan-European stock market after they agreed to a strategic alliance.

8 July.   UK Strategic Defence Review outlined a reduction of £915 million in British defence spending in real terms over a three year period (to £23 billion in 2001–02, or 2.4% of GDP). The main elements of the Review were a 3,300 increase in the regular armed forces, a reduction in the Terrilorial Army from 56,000 to 40,000, the creation of a 15,000 strong rapid reaction force and the building of two new large aircraft carriers, each capable of taking 50 aircraft.

22 July.   The European Commission approved a negotiating mandate for the proposed creation of a free trade area, the world's largest, with the Mercosur nations (Argentina, Brazil, Paraguay and Uruguay) and Chile (an associate member of Mercosur). The European Commission decided to allow Air France (the French state airline) to retain a French Franc 20 billion subsidy which had been annulled by the European Court of Justice in late June 1998.

27–29 July.   UK Cabinet reshuffle resulted in the dismissal of four members of the Cabinet. It was perceived as a means of strengthening the Blairite and pro-European representation of government, as well as curbing the power of Chanceller Brown. The new appointments included Peter Mandelson as President of the Board of Trade and Secretary of State for Trade and Industry, Nick Brown as Minister of Agriculture, Fisheries and Food, Stephen Byers as Chief Secretary to the Treasury and Baroness

Jay of Paddington as Lord Privy Seal, Leader of the House of Lords and Minister for Women. Other members of the Cabinet moved to different posts, of which Alistair Darling was appointed Secretary of State for Social Security, Jack Cunningham was made Chancellor of the Duchy of Lancaster and Minister for the Cabinet Office, Margaret Beckett was appointed President of the Council and Leader of the House of Commons, while Ann Taylor was made the government's Chief Whip. The four departures from the Cabinet were Harriet Harman (Social Security), Gavin Strang (Transport), David Clark (Chancellor of the Duchy of Lancaster) and Lord Richard (Lord Privy Seal and Leader of the House of Lords).

3 August.   A new Dutch Cabinet was inaugurated comprising members of the coalition which had governed since August 1994. This included the leftist Labour Party (PvdA), right-wing People's Party for Freedom and Democracy (VVD) and the centre-left formation Democrats 66 (D66).

27 September.   German election resulted in victory for the Social Democrats (led by Gerhard Schröder), who obtained 298 seats in the Bundestag (252 in 1994). The Christian Democrats/CSU (led by Helmut Kohl) got 245 (294 in 1994), the Greens 47 (49), Liberals 44 (47) and the ex-Communists 35 (30). As for the percentage of votes cast, the Social Democrats obtained 40.9% (36.4% in 1994), the Christian Democrats/CSU 35.2% (41.4%), the Greens 6.7% (7.3%), the Liberals 6.2% (6.9%), the ex-Communists 5.1% (4.4%) and others 6% (3.6%). The significance of the Social Democrat victory was that it meant that the main nations within the EU now had left-of-centre governments, with Spain being the only large EU country to have a Conservative government.

1 October.   EU Working Time Directive entered force in Britain.

20 October.   A two-day meeting of EU farm ministers in Luxembourg signalled a determination to conclude an agreement in early 1999 on widespread agricultural reforms. Numerous difficulties were nevertheless highlighteed, with there being a division among ministers over cuts in guaranteed prices paid to beef, dairy and cereal farmers. Futhermore, a proposal by the UK, Denmark, Italy and Sweden to scrap EU milk quotas after the year 2000 was opposed by other Member States.

20 October.   The House of Lords voted against the UK government's proposals to rank candidates in European elections in closed lists because this would take away the ability of electors to directly choose candidates.

24–25 October.   Portschach (Austria) European Council meeting.

27 October.   Gerhard Schröder took office as Chancellor of Germany.

30 October.   Lord Jenkins delivered his report on the future of Voting Systems in the UK.

2 November.   Meeting in London between Tony Blair and Gerhard Schröder, of which the latter delivered a speech to the Confederation of British Industry. The UK Prime Minister publicly went out of his way prior to the meeting to court the new German Chancellor, which is the first attempt at coordination between centre-left governments in the UK and Germany since the time of James Callaghan and Helmut Schmidt. The discussions centred on Schröder's proposed Anglo-German-French triangle. The most tangible element of the new Anglo-German relationship was the announcement that the UK Trade and Industry Secretary, Peter Mandelson, and his counterpart in Bonn, the chancery minister, Bodo Hombach, would explore possibilities where the relationship between the two countries could be deepened.

2 November. The UK Chancellor of the Exchequer, Gordon Brown, gave a speech to the Confederation of British Industry conference in Birmingham which stressed that the government would publish a 'national changeover plan' in January 1999 to prepare for joining the single currency. This move, which marked an acceleration in the governments preparations for monetary union, was prompted by concerns from business that it is necessary for their preparations to have a clear indication that the UK would join if the conditions were right.

10 November. Commencement of detailed negotiations on EU enlargement with Hungary, Poland, Czech Republic, Slovenia, Estonia and Cyprus. All nations have been preparing their countries policies so that they meet EU regulations in seven areas, namely science and research, telecommunications and information technologies, education and training, culture and audio-visual policy, industrial policy, small and medium-sized undertakings, and common foreign and security policy. But while these areas have produced little differences, more crucial topics will be discussed in 1999, including agriculture, property purchase rights, environmental costs and the control of borders with non-EU countries further east.

11 November. German Chancellor Gerhard Schröder stressed in his inaugural speech to Parliament that Bonn would use its Presidency of the EU in 1999 to 'drive forward European integration'.

25 November. First meeting of the German cabinet to be held in Berlin since 1945.

30 November. UK and Spain issued a joint initiative on employment which emphasised the need to liberalise labour markets. The joint declaration was timed ahead of the Vienna European council meeting. Jacques Chirac and Gerhard Schröder met in Potsdam for a Franco-German summit. They agreed that France, Germany and Britain should coordinate more closely on the EU's defence policy.

1 December. France and Germany advanced the idea of majority voting in EU tax policy. This was opposed by Britain, Sweden and Luxembourg.

14 December 1998. In an article in *The Times*, Tony Blair called for a 'sense of balance' in the debate over the future of Europe. His call for restraint followed a difficult EU summit in Vienna, at which other Member

States stressed that the UK's £2 billion budget rebate should be subject to renegotiation.

16 December 1998.   The US, backed by the UK, launched military strikes against Iraq. President Clinton gave the order for operation Desert Fox shortly before the US Congress was to make a decision on impeachment. The decision to strike at Iraq therefore resulted in some commentators suggesting that it was an attempt to take public attention away from President Clinton's domestic difficulties. But irrespective of such concerns, the attack was prompted by the difficulties which United Nations weapons inspectors encountered in carrying out their tasks within Iraq. They were seemingly hampered by attempts by the government of Iraq to hide their weapons of mass destruction. Tension between UN weapon inspectors and the government of Iraq have been a particularly notable feature of 1998. In early January the Iraqi leader, Saddam Hussein, threatened to halt all UN weapons inspections within Iraq, while the UN Special Commission on Iraqi Arms (Unscom) suspended its inspection of new sites within Iraq in August after Baghdad's decision to halt all cooperation. The head of Unscom, Richard Butler, published a report on 16 December 1998 which was critical of Iraqi cooperation, thereby prompting the withdrawal of all UN inspectors from Iraq on that day and the subsequent commencement of military activity. UK forces joined in the attack on 17 December, with targets being of a military nature. Attacks by US and UK forces consisted of bombing raids from aircraft and cruise missiles launched from US warships in the Gulf region. Although the UK's involvement was backed by all sides of the domestic political spectrum, the absence of other European forces prompted some criticism. Predictably, Russia was critical of the attacks (as it was initially in 1990–91) and recalled for 'consultation' its Ambassadors in Washington and London.

Europe in Crisis:
Detailed Chronologies

Overview

As the title of this section implies, it details key periods in the history of the EU when it has been faced with great pressures. There have been many such occasions, but the intention here is to focus on three distinct periods. The first is the crisis which engulfed the Community in the 1960s, initially with de Gaulle's rejection of the UK's application for membership and subsequently France's abstention from Community activities in 1965. The rejection of the UK's application for membership clearly influenced the proceedings of the rest of the decade. At that time it was evident that London's application was a serious one. Many commentators have different views on the nature of the application and the reasons which motivated it, but it is hard not to notice that barely one week after de Gaulle's January 1963 announcement that the UK was not ready to join the Community, France and Germany signed a Treaty of Friendship. The effect of these events was to cast France as the dominant force within the Community (initially), being able to determine the failure and then success of the next two applications. In the meantime, the influence of Paris on European affairs was demonstrated by its decision to boycott Community procedures in the mid-1960s. It was specifically opposed to European Commission proposals relating to the financing of the CAP, the introduction of own resources, the extension of budgetary powers to the EP and especially the introduction of majority voting into the Council of Ministers. That action eventually produced what is referred to as the Luxembourg compromise, which essentially provided Member States with a veto over matters of vital national interest. An effect was that policies such as the introduction of own resources were delayed until 1970. The nature of 'vital' and 'national' was fully exploited by Member States in the following years.

After the excitement and turbulence of the 1960s, the 1970s witnessed a period of sluggish progress within the Community, often shaped by a rather lacklustre Commission. Indeed, it was not until the early 1990s that the affairs of the then European Union were fully thrown into turmoil. In early February 1992 Member States had just finished initialling the Treaty on European Union. But barely before the ink was dry, it was evident that the Treaty would prove to be a major challenge for the EU. The specific difficulty was the necessity of national ratification, which was highlighted by the failure of the Danish electorate to pass the Treaty in a June referendum. That decision lit the touchpaper in other Member States, most notably the UK, where Euro-sceptic MPs harassed a Conservative government that had been recently returned to power with a depleted majority. In France, President Mitterrand decided to hold a referendum on the subject of the Treaty, partly so as to provide momentum to the process of national ratification, but also as a test of his popularity. Clearly he did not envisage the less than one per cent margin of victory in the September referendum.

In conjunction with these events, Member States were preparing themselves for Economic Monetary Union, as noted in the Treaty on European Union. For some years the Exchange Rate Mechanism of the European Monetary System had become more rigid, influenced by a conscious decision to avoid realignments. Yet, this was what many national economies required in the summer of 1992. The effect was that currency speculators were able to wage war against national currencies, which eventually pushed sterling and the lira out of the ERM in September 1992. The effect of sterling's departure from the ERM was to increase Euro-sceptic pressures within the UK. Voices from within and outwith the Conservative government pressurised for a more abrasive line towards Brussels. The opportunity for Ministerial tough talking came in the form of the 1996 intergovernmental conference, during which the UK adopted a far more negative position than it had in 1990–91.

Yet, it was the failure of the government's own domestic regulation of the beef industry which caused real tension with Brussels, more so than the drive towards monetary union. In the 1980s there had been an outbreak of bovine spongiform encephalopathy (BSE) in cattle and while the then Minister of Agriculture, John Gummer, attempted to convince the public that meat was safe, the EU veterinary committee decided in March 1996 to recommend and implement a total ban on the export of beef and beef products from the UK. That decision had been influenced by the earlier announcement of a possible link between BSE and the fatal disease found in humans known as Creutzfeld-Jacob disease (CJD). Inevitably, London was the only dissenter to the ban and one month later introduced a policy of non-cooperation with the EU until the ban was lifted. This was widely regarded to be a tactical blunder, possibly influenced by Cabinet pressure on Prime Minister Major.

1.   De Gaulle and the Common Market

1960
4 January.   The Convention of Stockholm, which established the European Free Trade Association, was signed by Austria, Denmark, Norway, Portugal, Sweden, Switzerland and the UK.
9 June.   The Six rejected early negotiations to join with EFTA.
27 July.   A UK Cabinet reshuffle meant that Lord Home became the Foreign Secretary and Edward Heath became the Lord Privy Seal with special responsibility for Europe.
7 November.   In a speech to the UK Council of the European Movement, Harold Macmillan called for European economic unity.

1 December. The WEU invited the UK to negotiations for full EEC membership.

1961

28–29 January. General de Gaulle and Harold Macmillan had private talks at Rambouillet.

10–11 February. Paris Summit of the Six on the development of the Union with regard to expansion. The communiqué of the meeting expressed a willingness to create agreements with other European countries, especially the UK. The representatives were de Gaulle (France), Adenauer (Federal Republic of Germany), Amintore Fanfani (Italy), Jan de Quay (the Netherlands), Gaston Eyskens (Belgium), and Pierre Werner (Luxembourg).

27 February. Edward Heath told the WEU that the UK was prepared to accept, in principle, the common external tariff.

1 March. France rejected a UK proposal for a European system in which the UK would retain her Commonwealth preference and agricultural arrangements. The French Foreign Minister, Couve de Murville, invited the UK to join the EEC.

11 May. Denmark's Foreign Minister, J.O. Krag, stated that Denmark would apply for membership of the EEC if the UK did.

13 June. Senior UK Ministers began visits to the Commonwealth to discuss the Common Market.

28 June. The London Declaration stated that the UK would coordinate any EEC accession negotiations with its EFTA partners.

4 July. Ireland announced its intention of joining the EEC.

9 July. The EEC signed an association agreement with Greece known as the Treaty of Athens.

31 July. Harold Macmillan announced in the House of Commons that the UK would apply to join the EEC and would seek conditions for the Commonwealth, agriculture and EFTA.

1 August. Austria announced its intention of seeking some form of participation in the EEC. Ireland applied for membership of the EEC.

3 August. The House of Commons supported the decision of the government to seek negotiations with the aim of membership of the EEC.

9 August. The UK sent its formal application to join the EEC.

10 August. Denmark applied for EEC membership.

5 September. The UK Trade Union Congress supported the government's decision to open negotiations with a view to joining the EEC.

12–14 September. The Commonwealth Consultative Council met in Accra to discuss the implications of the UK's entry into the EEC for the Commonwealth.

13 September. The Commonwealth Finance Ministers criticised the UK decision to join the EEC.

26 September.   The Common Market Council of Ministers unanimously agreed to open negotiations for the UK's entry.

10 October.   In a statement in Paris, Edward Heath accepted the Rome Treaty and the political consequences but sought conditions for UK agriculture.

12 October.   The Conservative Party approved Harold Macmillan's decision to enter the Common Market.

23 October.   Ireland commenced its negotiations for membership of the EEC.

26 October.   Danish negotiations for membership of the EEC began.

8 November.   Formal negotiations began in Brussels between the UK and the Common Market Council of Ministers.

15 December.   The three neutrals, Austria, Sweden and Switzerland, applied for association with the Common Market.

30 December.   The Common Market countries postponed the decision on UK agriculture.

1962

14 January.   The Community fixed the basic features of the common agriculture policy, as well as regulations for grains, pigmeat, eggs and poultry, fruit and vegetables.

20 January.   The talks between the UK and the Common Market were delayed while the Six sought agreement on a common agricultural policy.

9 February.   Spain applied for an association agreement with the EEC.

28 February.   The Norwegian Prime Minister announced that Norway would be applying for membership of the EEC.

2 March.   The UK applied for membership of the ECSC.

5 March.   The UK applied for membership of Euratom.

30 March.   The Assembly changed its name to the European Parliament.

30 April.   Norway requested negotiations for membership to the Common Market.

11 May.   Edward Heath put forward the first practical offer on the UK's membership of the Common Market.

28 May.   Portugal announced its desire of joining the EEC.

30 May.   In its negotiations to join the Common Market, the UK made a concession on Commonwealth manufactured goods.

2 June.   Harold Macmillan visited General de Gaulle in Paris.

4 June.   The Beaverbrook press announced it would oppose the Conservatives over the Common Market issue in a general election.

5 June.   The UK received criticism from Australia, New Zealand and Canada over its handling of the negotiations to enter the Common Market.

4 July.   Negotiations with Norway for membership of the EEC began.

6 July.   The Six accepted annual agricultural reviews.

13 July.   Sweeping changes took place in the UK Cabinet.

20 July. Hugh Gaitskell suggested a general election if the terms of entry were not satisfactory.

30 July. The first regulations implementing the common agriculture policy came into effect.

31 July. Forty Conservative MPs signed a motion that urged the government to stand firm over Europe.

5 August. After a long negotiating session, no agreement was reached between the UK and the Six. Spaak stated that the UK was unable to accept the Six's proposal and the talks were recessed until October.

19 September. Conclusion of the Commonwealth Conference in London, which had started on 10 September. Commonwealth Prime Ministers signed a communiqué that agreed to the UK continuing its negotiations to join the Common Market.

21 September. Harold Macmillan, in a television speech, stated that the UK could be harmed if it did not join the Common Market and this, therefore, meant that entry was of major political importance.

24 October. Memorandum from the European Commission on the Community's action programme during the second stage of the Common Market.

26 October. Differences over agricultural policies created a deadlock in Brussels.

1 November. Agreement was reached on Greece's associate membership of EEC.

28 November. The Gaullists won an absolute majority in the French National Assembly.

3 December. Hugh Gaitskell attacked the Brussels' terms in a speech in Paris.

5 December. Dean Acheson stated that the UK 'has lost an empire and not yet found a role' in a speech to the West Point Military Academy in New York.

15 December. Harold Macmillan met with General de Gaulle for talks at Rambouillet.

18–21 December. Harold Macmillan met with President Kennedy in Nassau. The talks were concerned with the US cancellation of Skybolt which was to be a replacement for the UK Blue Streak missile which itself had been cancelled. The USA agreed to supply the Polaris missile to the UK as a replacement for the Skybolt missile.

1963

14 January. President de Gaulle announced that the UK was not yet ready to join the EEC. This was the day before Edward Heath was due to start one of two scheduled long sessions in Brussels with the Six.

22 January. De Gaulle and Adenauer signed the Franco-German Treaty of Friendship and Cooperation.

29 January. The UK's negotiations to join the Common Market ended.
11 July. EEC agreement to hold regular WEU meetings, including the discussion of economic cooperation issues, between the UK and the EEC.

1965

1 January. France took over Presidency of the European Council for a period of six months.
31 March. The Common Market Commission proposed that as from 1 July 1967 all Community countries' import duties and levies should be paid into the Community budget and that the powers of the European Parliament should be increased.
3 April. Conclusion of the Treaty to establish a unified Council and Commission of the Communities.
8 April. The Six signed the Treaty merging the Executives of the Community. This enhanced the status of the Commission. There were already, for the three Communities, a single Assembly, a single Court of Justice and, in practice, a single Council, but there were three different Executives each with a President.
1 July. The European Council failed to achieve agreement on the financing of the CAP. This resulted in France boycotting the Community institutions for seven months in opposition to the Commission proposal that all import duties and levies be paid into the Community budget, and the powers of the European Parliament be increased. De Gaulle withdrew the French permanent representative from Brussels. It became known as the 'empty chair' crisis.

1966

1 January. Luxembourg took over from Italy the Presidency of the European Council.
17 January. The Six Foreign Ministers agreed to resume full Community activity.
29 January. The Foreign Ministers of the Six reached a compromise and agreed to resume the full activities of the Community. In settling the seven-month dispute, the Luxembourg compromise allowed for decisions that the Treaties of Rome perceived to be subjected to majority voting within the Council of Ministers to be delayed until a unanimous agreement was achieved. Each nation was provided with a veto over key policy decisions. This was to have a profound effect on the Community over the next two decades when it essentially limited major policy advancements.

2. The crises of 1992 and 1993

1992

7 February. The Treaty on European Union was formally signed at Maastricht by the EC Foreign and Finance Ministers.

6 April.   The Portuguese escudo joined the ERM of the EMS. The escudo was fixed at the central rate of 178.735 escudos to the ECU. This corresponded to its previous national rate in the ECU currency basket. The escudo entered the broad band of the ERM and was allowed to fluctuate at 6% either side of the central rate, like the Spanish peseta and UK sterling.

9 April.   Decision of the French Constitutional Council requiring revision of the French constitution in conjunction with the ratification of the Maastricht Treaty.

7 May.   First reading of the European Communities Act in the House of Commons.

12 May.   The Danish Folketing approved the Treaty of Maastricht by 130 votes to 25. Danish ratification was, however, subject to a popular vote under the constitution.

20–21 May.   The European Communities (Amendment) Bill passed the second reading debate in the House of Commons by 336 to 92.

2 June.   Danish referendum on Maastricht Treaty resulted in a 'no' vote by 50.7% to 49.3% of votes cast, a margin of only 46,269 votes. The turnout was 82.3%.

3 June.   More than 100 Conservative MPs signed a House of Commons motion which called for a fresh start in Europe. The Prime Minister promised a further debate on the bill to ratify the Maastricht Treaty before the committee stage began.

4 June.   John Major defended the Maastricht Treaty in a debate in the House of Commons by stating that 'the ratification and implementation of the treaty is in our national interest'.

8 June.   In the House of Commons, Douglas Hurd stated that it was important to allay fears that the Maastricht Treaty would result in centralising the Community. He therefore advocated a separate interpretation of the Treaty.

18 June.   An Irish referendum supported the Maastricht Treaty by 68.7% to 31.3%. Opponents concentrated their arguments on the common defence provision as was the case in the previous SEA referendum.

23 June.   In a meeting at the Congress of Versailles, the French National Assembly and the Senate adopted the amendments to the Constitution that allowed the French constitution to ratify the Maastricht Treaty by 592 to 73.

29 June.   John Major reported to the House of Commons on the European Council meeting in Lisbon and also defended the Maastricht Treaty and dismissed calls for a referendum.

1 July.   Decision of the Spanish Constitutional Court requiring revision of the constitution with regard to the ratification of the Maastricht Treaty.

2 July.   The Chamber of Deputies in Luxembourg voted in favour of the Maastricht Treaty by 51 to six. The Luxembourg constitution was also amended by the Chamber of Deputies with regard to provisions on

EMU and on EU citizens' right of vote and to stand in local elections. However, the large percentage of EU citizens in the Luxembourg population meant that a compromise was necessary. Therefore, EU citizens who had lived in Luxembourg for ten years and who spoke the languages of Luxembourg were allowed to stand as town councillors, but not as mayor or aldermen.

17 July. The Belgian Chamber of Deputies approved the Maastricht Treaty by 143 votes to 33, with three abstentions. All the major parties voted in favour.

22 July. The Spanish Congress of Deputies (lower House of Parliament) approved a constitutional change to allow ratification. The Senate (upper House) approved the amendment on 30 July. This was the first amendment since the adoption of the Constitution in 1978 and it allowed EU citizens to stand in municipal elections. The Constitutional tribunal ruled on 1 July that such a change was necessary and could be approved by a three-fifths majority in both Houses of Parliament.

1 August. The Maastricht Treaty was adopted by the Greek Parliament by 286 votes to eight with all the main parliamentary parties supporting it and only a few Communists voting against it.

24 August. Luxembourg deposited its instrument of ratification of the Maastricht Treaty.

26 August. The Chancellor of the Exchequer, Norman Lamont, announced that despite the turbulence of the foreign exchange rates, the government would stay in the ERM.

4–6 September. Informal meeting of the EC Finance Ministers in Bath. It subsequently emerged that the UK Presidency did not pick up on the suggestion that a realignment of the ERM could be considered.

8 September. The Finnish government, in a joint decision with the Bank of Finland, let the markka float freely and therefore abandoned its self-imposed peg to the ECU. This position resulted in an immediate 15% drop in the value of the markka.

8–9 September. Sweden raised its marginal intervention rate from 16% to 75%.

14 September. The Belgian franc, Deutschmark, Dutch guilder, Danish krone, Portuguese escudo, French franc, Irish pound, Spanish peseta and UK sterling were realigned in the EMS by +3.5%. The Italian lira was realigned by −3.5%, which effectively represented a 7% devaluation of the lira. This was the first major realignment within the EMS since 1987. The Bundesbank cut its Lombard rate from 9.75% to 9.5% and its discount rate from 8.75% to 8.25%. Rates were also cut in Austria, Belgium, the Netherlands. Switzerland and Sweden – currencies that were most closely linked with the Deutschmark.

16 September. Pressure on the pound increased and the minimum lending rate was increased from 10% to 12%. Due to the continuing turbulence, it was announced that the base rate would rise further, to 15% the next day. At the close of business in London, the pound stood at DM 2.75. The worsening situation meant that the Chancellor, Norman Lamont, announced that the UK would pull out of the ERM and that the second interest rate increase would not take place. These events were referred to as 'Black Wednesday'.

17 September.   The Swedish Central Bank raised the marginal interest rate to 500% in an effort to protect the krona and stop the outflow of capital. The EC's Monetary Committee agreed to the temporary suspension of the Italian lira and UK sterling from the ERM. The peseta was devalued by 5% and the UK cut its base rate to 10%. The Maastricht Treaty was approved by the Italian Senate by 176 votes to 16.

20 September.   The Maastricht Treaty was narrowly passed in France by 51.04% of valid votes cast (13,162,992 votes) to 48.95% (12,623,582 votes) in a public referendum – a difference of 539,410 votes. These were the official results announced on 23 September by the Constitutional Council and differed slightly from the earlier version distributed by the Interior Ministry. The turnout was 69.7% of a total electorate of 38,305,534, with 909,377 null or void votes. Mitterrand used the referendum as a public endorsement of his Presidency and his policy on Europe. In reality, the Treaty could have been easily ratified in Parliament, but Mitterrand also wanted to use the referendum as a means of dividing the right-wing opposition who were bitterly divided over Maastricht.

22 September.   UK interest rates (base rate) were cut from 10% to 9%.

23 September.   The French and German governments intervened heavily on the exchange markets in a successful defence of the French franc. Spain reintroduced foreign exchange controls.

24 September.   Ireland and Portugal introduced new foreign exchange controls.

24–25 September.   The House of Commons was recalled to debate the sterling crisis with a vote of 322 to 296 in favour of a motion supporting the government's economic policy.

25 September.   The German Bundesrat opened its debate on the Maastricht Treaty.

1 October.   The UK government, after tense Cabinet discussions, announced its desire to ratify the Maastricht Treaty and to bring the bill back to Parliament in December, or early in the new year.

8 October.   The German Bundestag opened its debate on the Maastricht Treaty.

16 October.   An extraordinary meeting of the European Council was convened in Birmingham in an attempt to iron out the problems that existed with the ERM. The meeting was also intended as a means of defining a suitable stance for Denmark and the UK so that their governments' position could be made easier through a declaration on subsidiarity. In the end all decisions were deferred to the Edinburgh European Summit.

22 October.   The Maastricht Treaty was approved by the Belgian Council of the French-speaking Community.

27 October.   In Denmark, seven out of eight parliamentary parties reached a 'national compromise' on additions to the Maastricht Treaty, on the basis of which they would support a second referendum in 1993.

29 October.   The Spanish Chamber of Deputies approved the Maastricht Treaty by 314 votes to three, with eight abstentions. The Italian Chamber of Deputies approved the Maastricht Treaty by 403 votes to 46.

3 November.   Greece deposited its instrument of ratification of the Maastricht Treaty.

4 November.   In a debate on the Maastricht Treaty in the House of Commons, the government won the paving debate, allowing the bill to proceed into the committee stage, by 319 votes to 316. While 19 Liberal Democrats voted with the government, 26 Conservatives voted against, along with Labour MPs. There were seven deliberate Conservative abstentions. Without the Liberal Democrat votes the government would have lost the vote despite the fact that the government commanded a 21-seat overall majority in the House of Commons. France deposited its instrument of ratification of the Maastricht Treaty. The Belgian Senate approved the Maastricht Treaty by 115 to 26 with one abstention.

5 November.   The UK Prime Minister said that the European Communities Bill would not receive its third reading until after the second Danish referendum in May 1993.

12 November.   The Netherlands' Chamber of Deputies approved the Maastricht Treaty by 137 votes to 13.

23 November.   The Maastricht Treaty was approved by the Belgian Council of the German-speaking Community. Ireland deposited its instrument of ratification of the Maastricht Treaty. The Spanish peseta and Portuguese escudo were realigned in the EMS by −6%.

25 November.   The Spanish Senate approved the Maastricht Treaty by 222 votes to zero, with three abstentions.

1 December.   At the House of Commons committee stage, MPs started 23 days of debating the bill in committee on the floor of the House. Over 500 amendments to the three-clause bill were proposed.

2 December.   The German Bundestag assented to the Maastricht Treaty by 543 votes to 17.

5 December.   Italy deposited its instrument of ratification of the Maastricht Treaty.

10 December.   The Portuguese Assembly of the Republic approved the Maastricht Treaty by 200 votes to 21. Belgium deposited its instrument of ratification of the Maastricht Treaty. Following currency speculation, Norway abandoned the pegging of its currency to the ECU.

11–12 December.   At the Edinburgh European Council Summit, agreement was reached on several important issues, including: Danish opt-outs from the Maastricht Treaty; the clarification of subsidiarity and transparency; the Delors II financial package; and the opening of accession negotiations in early 1993 with Austria, Finland and Sweden, and with Norway later in 1993. The Council also agreed the number of seats for each Member State in the European Parliament in order to take account of German unification and the prospect of future enlargement. The distribution of seats was as follows (previous numbers in brackets): Belgium 25(24); Denmark 16(16); Germany 99(81); Greece 25(24); Spain 64(60); France 87(81); Ireland 15(15); Italy 87(81); Luxembourg 6(6); the Netherlands 31(25); Portugal 25(24); the United Kingdom 87(81). The agreement reached at Edinburgh saved the process of European integration after it had been stalled since June 1992 due to the Danish 'no' vote in a referendum.

15 December.   The Netherlands Senate approved the Maastricht Treaty *nemine contradicente.*

28 December.   The Netherlands deposited its instrument of ratification of the Maastricht Treaty.

31 December.   Spain deposited its instrument of ratification of the Maastricht Treaty.

1993

1 February.   The Irish pound was realigned in the EMS by −10%.

4 February.   The German Bundesbank unexpectedly lowered its discount and Lombard rates due to pressure on the ERM. The discount rate was reduced from 8.25% (at which it had stood since September 1992) to 8%, while the Lombard rate was reduced from 9.5% to 9%.

15 February.   Douglas Hurd (the Foreign Secretary) announced that fresh legal advice had suggested that parliamentary defeat over the Labour amendment (number 27) to the Social Chapter would not stop the UK ratifying the Treaty. This information contradicted earlier statements given by the Minister of State at the Foreign Office, Tristan Garel-Jones.

8 March.   The UK government was defeated on a Labour amendment to the Maastricht Bill concerning membership of the Council of Regions by 314 votes to 292 despite the fact it had a majority in the House of Commons of 20 seats.

22 March.   The House of Commons rejected a call for a referendum on the Maastricht Treaty, while the committee stage was finally completed after 163 hours of debate.

30 March.   The Maastricht Treaty was approved by the Danish Parliament by 154 votes to 16.

14 May.   The Spanish peseta was realigned in the EMS by −8% and Portuguese escudo by −6.5%.

18 May.   In Denmark, 56.7% voted 'yes' in the second Maastricht referendum. The turnout was 86.2%.

20 May.   The House of Commons gave a third reading to the Maastricht Treaty Bill and the government secured a majority by 292 votes to 112.

24 May.   The first reading in the House of Lords, of the European Communities Bill.

7–8 June.   The second reading in the House of Lords, with agreement reached without division.

9 June.   In his resignation speech, Norman Lamont revealed that John Major rejected his earlier proposal to withdraw sterling from the ERM. He criticised Major for giving 'the impression of being in office but not in power'.

17 June.   Denmark deposited its instrument of ratification of the Maastricht Treaty.

22 June.   The European Communities Bill reached the committee stage in the House of Lords. It was the first of six days in committee which ended without any amendment being passed.

12 July.   The report stage of the European Communities Bill in the House of Lords – the first of three days spent on report.

20 July.   The third reading of the European Communities (Amendment) Bill in the House of Lords was secured by 141 votes to 29. This, therefore, completed the parliamentary stages of the bill and it received royal assent that evening.

2 August.   The UK government formally ratified the Maastricht Treaty in Rome. The ERM of the EMS effectively collapsed and agreement was reached on allowing currencies to fluctuate within a broad band of 15% either side of their central rates, rather than the 2.25% band for strong currencies or the 6% for the Spanish and Portuguese currencies.

2 September.   The UK deposited its instrument of ratification of the Maastricht Treaty.

12 October.   Germany deposited its instrument of ratification of the Maastricht Treaty.

1 November.   The European Community formally became the European Union due to the Maastricht Treaty.

3.   Mad Cows and Englishmen

1996

20 March.   It was announced that the UK could face a major health crisis in the form of a possible link between BSE which is found in cattle, and the fatal disease found in humans known as Creutzfeldt-Jakob disease (CJD).

25 March.   The EU veterinary committee voted by 14 to one to recommend a total ban (with immediate effect) on the export of beef and beef products from the UK. The only dissenter was the UK.

21 May. The UK adopted a policy of non-cooperation with the EU until a timetable to lift the ban on the export of beef was settled. The government established a Ministerial committee on 22 May, chaired by Prime Minister Major, to oversee the confrontational strategy.

24 May. The UK vetoed a EU bankruptcy convention as part of its policy of non-cooperation.

4 June. The European Commission announced that it would phase out the UK export ban on tallow, gelatine and semen over the following weeks if stricter health controls were imposed (commencing on 11 June). On the same day the UK government put forward to EU Agriculture Ministers its plans for the eradication of BSE from cattle herds, which, despite some additional safety measures, was a reiteration of its existing stance.

5 June. The UK approved the EU–Slovenia association agreement, despite still adopting a policy of non-cooperation.

10 June. The UK approved EU cooperation talks with Algeria and the allocation of funds to monitor elections in Bosnia, despite a policy of non-cooperation.

17 June. The UK agricultural dispute dominated the Rome Foreign Ministers' meeting which was intended to prepare the agenda for the forthcoming Florence European Council meeting.

21–22 June. On the first day of the European Council meeting at Florence agreement was reached by Foreign Ministers on ending the confrontation between the UK and the other Member States over the EU-imposed ban on UK exports of beef and beef products. As a result the summit was able to deal with the main items on the agenda, which included the analysis of the first three months of the IGC to review the Maastricht TEU.

12 July. The European Court of Justice rejected an appeal by the UK government to lift the ban on UK beef exports which had been imposed by the European Commission in March 1996. The Court's ruling was based on scientific evidence of a link between BSE in cattle and Creutzfeldt-Jakob disease in humans.

22 July. The European Commissioner with responsibility for agriculture, Franz Fischler, asked EU Agriculture Ministers to ban the spleen, brain and spinal cord of sheep and goats from entering the human food chain.

17 September. Agricultural Ministers reached agreement on the request of an increase in the intervention purchasing of beef.

24 September. Agricultural Ministers proposed the use of 500 million ECU from surplus budget funds to assist farmers affected by the loss of consumer confidence in beef products as a result of the BSE crisis. This was in addition to the 850 million ECU which was approved in June 1996.

1997

17–19 March. Brussels EU Agricultural Ministers meeting reached agreement that all beef had to be marked with its country of origin. This development was resisted by the UK because the government considered it would affect the sales of beef in the wake of the March 1996 worldwide ban on UK beef exports, which was a response to BSE fears.

1 May. The Labour Party won the UK general election. Tony Blair was appointed Prime Minister.

1998

January. The EU approved a partial lifting of the 1996 export ban on UK beef, with the proposal only applying to the export of beef products from Northern Ireland. This was because it was the only part of the UK which had a complete computerised tracking system, while it also had fower recorded cases of BSE than elsewhere in the UK.

16–17 March. The Brussels meeting of EU Agricultural Ministers approved a partial lifting of the 1996 export ban of UK beef. This had previously been approved by the European Commission in January 1998. Eleven of the 15 Member States supported a relaxation of the ban, Belgium and Germany voting against and Luxembourg and Spain abstaining. The easing of export restrictions applied to deboned beef from cattle aged between six and 30 months which had come from herds that were certified to have been BSE-free for the last eight years.

27 May. The European Commission agreed to lift the ban on the exportation of beef from Northern Ireland from 1 June 1998. The lifting of the ban in Ulster had been agreed in March 1998 but was conditional on the inspection of meat plants by EU veterinary experts.

12 November. At the BSE inquiry in London, it was announced that John Major and his Cabinet blocked a proposal for an independent public inquiry into the BSE epidemic just before the announcement in March 1996 that the disease was linked to the deaths of young people.

23 November. Britain won a 32-month battle to life a worldwide ban on the export of beef when 10 member states voted to lift the ban at an EU Agriculture Ministers meeting in Brussels. Only Germany's Karl-Heinz Funke voted against. The vote meant that Britain would be able to export boneless beef from cattle born after August 1996 and over six months old.

SECTION IV

European Institutional Development

1.   European Commission

Based in Brussels, there are 20 European Commissioners: two from France, Germany, Italy, Spain and the UK, and one from each of the other ten Member States. All serve a five-year term of office (current term from 1995 to 2000), and are served by a bureaucracy of some 15,000 staff, of which one-fifth work in translation and interpretation services. Meetings of European Commissioners take place once a week, with policy ranging from adopting proposals to finalising policy papers. While the President of the European Commission is chosen by Heads of State or Government after consultation with the European Parliament (EP), other members are solely nominated by Member States. The European Commission has to be approved by the EP before members can take office. If a vote of censure is made by the EP, then the European Commission is required to resign *en bloc*. This power has yet to be used.

Structure

The European Commission is divided into 26 Directorates-General (DGs) with an additional 15 or so specialised services. A DG is headed by a director-general, who in turn reports to an individual European Commissioner responsible for that area of work. Each Commissioner is served by a group of officials known as a Cabinet, whose purpose is to provide advice on policy initiatives. The Cabinet comprises a large proportion of nationals from the European Commissioner's own country. Heads of Cabinet meet every week with the primary purpose of clearing issues prior to, or after, meetings of the European Commission.

Initiation

The European Commission's primary role is in initiating legislation. The EP needs a proposal from the Commission before it can pass legislation. The European Commission puts forward a proposal which is then targeted by interest groups (including national governments, industry, trade unions, special interest groups and technical experts) which wish to influence the motion so that it represents their views. In this context, the European Commission attempts to reflect what is best for the Union as a whole, rather than specific interests. After a legislative proposal has been made to the Council and the EP, it is important that full cooperation takes place between these three bodies to ensure a smooth law-making process. The European Commission does not have an exclusive right of initiative in the two areas of intergovernmental cooperation which are covered by the Treaty on European Union (TEU), namely common foreign and security policy (CFSP) and justice and home affairs (JHA). It is, however, able to submit proposals in a similar manner as national governments, while it also participates in discussions at all levels. The European Commission often provides the impulse towards wider integration, for example the launching of the strategy which resulted in the completion of the single market by 1993 and the drive towards economic and monetary union (Delors Report). Individual European Commissioners are crucial to this process, providing political leadership to direct policy initiatives. They have often served in national governments and therefore bring added experience to their post.

General powers

Apart from its powers of initiation, the European Commission plays a significant part in upholding European Union (EU) laws, sustaining and managing agricultural and regional development policies and preserving the integrity of the single market. It also plays a major role in furthering research and technological development initiatives, and in developing cooperation with the countries of Central and Eastern Europe, Africa, the Caribbean and Pacific. Broader responsibilities include ensuring compliance among Member States by monitoring the implementation of legislation. If obligations are broken, then the European Commission can take legal proceedings at the Court of Justice. Scrutiny of national governments also covers central government subsidies to industry and types of state aid. Individual firms can be fined for violating Treaty law (although they have the right to appeal to the Court of Justice). A crucial task is managing the annual budget of the Union, which is dominated by spending on agricultural policy and structural funds. The latter are designed to eliminate disparities between rich and poor areas. As the central executive of the Union, the European Commission plays an important part in international negotiations, particularly those relating to trade (GATT). Over 100 countries have agreements with the Union, such as the Lomé Convention.

Presidents of the High Authority and European Commission

High Authority of the European Coal and Steel Community

August 1952–June 1955	Jean Monnet (F)
June 1955–January 1958	Rene Mayer (F)
January 1958–September 1959	Paul Finet (F)
September 1959–October 1963	Piero Malvestiti (I)
	Resigned May 1963

June 1963–July 1963	Albert Coppe (B)
October 1963–July 1967	Rinaldo Del Bo (I)
	Resigned March 1967
March 1967–June 1967	Albert Coppe (B)

Commission of the European Atomic Energy Community (Euratom)

January 1958–January 1959	Louis Armand (F)
	Enrico Medi (I) President from
	September 1958
February 1959–January 1962	Etienne Hirsch (F)
January 1962–July 1967	Pierre Chatenet (F)

Commission of the European Economic Community

January 1958–January 1962	Walter Hallstein (D)
January 1962–July 1967	Walter Hallstein (D)

Presidents of the Commission of the European Communities

July 1967–July 1970	Jean Rey (B) (14 members)
July 1970–March 1972	Franco Maria Malfatti (I)
	Resigned (9 members)
March 1972–January 1973	Sicco Mansholt (NL) (9 members)
January 1973–January 1977	Francois-Xavier Ortoli (F)
	(13 members)
January 1977–January 1981	Roy Jenkins (UK) (13 members)
January 1981–January 1985	Gaston Thorn (L) (14 members)
January 1985–December 1985	Jacques Delors (F) (14 members)
January 1986–January 1989	Jacqus Delors (F) (17 members)
January 1989–January 1993	Jacques Delors (F) (17 members)
January 1993–January 1995	Jacques Delors (F) (17 members)
January 1995–January 2000	Jacques Santer (L) (20 members)

European Commissioners, 1995–2000

1. **President Jacques Santer** (L): Secretariat-General, Legal Service, Security Office, Forward Studies Unit, Inspectorate-General, Joint Interpreting and Conference Service (JICS), Spokesman's Service, Monetary matters (with Yves-Thibault de Silguy), CFSP and human rights (with Hans van den Broek), Institutional questions and inter-governmental conference (with Marcelino Oreja).

2. **Vice-President Sir Leon Brittan** (UK): External relations with North America, Australia, New Zealand, Japan, China, Korea, Hong Kong, Macao and Taiwan, Common commercial policy relations with the OECD and WTO.
3. **Vice-President Manuel Marín** (E): External relations with southern Mediterranean countries, the Middle East, Latin America and Asia (except Japan, China, Korea, Hong Kong, Macao and Taiwan), including development aid.
4. **Martin Bangemann** (D): Industrial affairs, Information and telecommunications technologies.
5. **Karel van Miert** (B): Competition.
6. **Hans van den Broek** (NL): External relations with the countries of Central and Eastern Europe (CEECs), the former Soviet Union, Mongolia, Turkey, Cyprus, Malta and other European countries, CFSP and human rights (in agreement with the President), External missions.
7. **João de deus Pinheiro** (P): External relations with African, Caribbean and Pacific countries and South Africa, including development aid, Lomé Convention.
8. **Pádraig Flynn** (IRL): Employment and social affairs, Relations with the Economic and Social Committee.
9. **Marcelino Oreja** (E): Relations with the EP, Relations with the Member States (transparency, communication and information), Culture and audio-visual policy, Office for Official Publications, Institutional matters and preparation for the 1996 intergovernmental conference (in agreement with the President).
10. **Anita Gradin** (S): Immigration, home affairs and justice, Relations with the Ombudsman, Financial control, Fraud prevention.
11. **Édith Cresson** (F): Science, research and development, Joint Research Centre, Human resources, education, training and youth.
12. **Ritt Bjerregaard** (DK): Environment, Nuclear safety.
13. **Monika Wulf-Mathies** (D): Regional policies, Relations with the Committee of the Regions, Cohesion Fund (in agreement with Neil Kinnock and Ritt Bjerregaard).
14. **Neil Kinnock** (UK): Transport (including trans-European networks).
15. **Mario Monti** (I): Internal market, Financial services and financial integration, Customs, Taxation.
16. **Franz Fischler** (A): Agriculture and rural development.
17. **Emma Bonino** (I): Fisheries, Consumer policy, European Community Humanitarian Office (ECHO).
18. **Yves-Thibault de Silguy** (F): Economic and financial affairs, Monetary matters (in agreement with the President), Credit and investments, Statistical Office.
19. **Erkki Liikanen** (FIN): Budget, Personnel and administration, Translation and in-house computer services.

20. **Christos Papoutsis** (GR): Energy and Euratom Supply Agency, Small business, Tourism.

Directorates-General of the European Commission

DG I	External Relations: Commercial Policy and Relations with North America, the Far East, Australia and New Zealand
DG IA	External Political Relations: Europe and New Independent States, External Policy and Common Security
DG II	Economic and Financial Affairs
DG III	Industry
DG IV	Competition
DG V	Employment, Industrial Relations and Social Affairs
DG VI	Agriculture
DG VII	Transport
DG VIII	Development
DG IX	Personnel and Administration
DG X	Information, Communication, Culture, Audio-visual
DG XI	Environment, Nuclear Safety and Civil Protection
DG XII	Science, Research and Development
DG XIII	Telecommunications, Information Market and Exploitation of Research
DG XIV	Fisheries
DG XV	Internal Market and Financial Services
DG XVI	Regional Policies and Cohesion
DG XVII	Energy
DG XVIII	Credit and Investments
DG XIX	Budgets
DG XX	Financial Control
DG XXI	Customs and Indirect Taxation
DG XXII	Education, Training and Youth
DG XXIII	Enterprise Policy, Distributive Trades, Tourism and Cooperative Services
DG XXIV	Consumer Policy

2. European Parliament (formally 'European Assembly')

The European Parliament (EP) provides democratic legitimacy to the EU, having been given greater powers in the 1986 Single European Act (SEA) through the cooperation procedure, the 1992 Treaty on European

Union (TEU) through the co-decision procedure and having had these granted to a wider policy area in the 1997 Treaty of Amsterdam. It is fully involved in adopting Community legislation and the budget, and in supervising the activities of the European Commission and the Council. Members of the EP (MEPs) represent interests of the citizen via the Committee on Petitions and by appointing the European Ombudsman. The EP has the power of veto over agreements made between the EU and other countries and to the enlargement of the EU. It has to be consulted by the European Commission and the Council of Ministers on most proposals and policy initiatives. The EP adopts the Union's budget each year (usually in December), with the signature of the President bringing it into effect, and it exercises democratic supervision over all Community activities and can set up committees of inquiry. The EP meets every month for a plenary session in Strasbourg. The agenda is drawn up by a bureau comprising the President and 12 Vice-Presidents. In addition to plenary sessions, working sessions or committee meetings are held in Brussels.

European Parliament and the European Commission

The TEU provided the EP with an important role in appointing the President and members of the European Commission, with the latter having to be approved by the EP in a vote of investiture. This is in addition to the EP's ability to censure the European Commission with a 'motion of censure', forcing it to resign. MEPs can put written or oral questions to the European Commission, while members of the European Commission take part in parliamentary committee meetings.

European Parliament and the Council

The EP's influence over the Council expanded with the introduction of the co-decision procedure in the TEU, thereby providing a legislative balance. Each Council President-in-office presents the work programme of that Member State to the EP at the beginning of each Presidency, while the fruits of that programme are discussed at the end. Council Ministers also attend the plenary sessions of the EP, whese MEPs can put oral or written questions to them.

The Presidents of the Common Assembly of the ECSC (1952–58)

1952–1954	Paul Henri Spaak
1954	Alcide De Gasperi
1954–1956	Giuseppe Pella
1956–1958	Hans Furler

The Presidents of the European Parliament (1958–79)

1958–1960	Robert Schuman
1960–1962	Hans Furler
1962–1964	Gaetano Martino
1964–1965	Jean Duvieusart
1965–1966	Victor Leemans
1966–1969	Alain Poher
1969–1971	Mario Scelba
1971–1973	Walter Behrendt
1973–1975	Cornelissss Berkouwer
1975–1977	Georges Spénale
1977–1979	Emilio Colombo

The Presidents of the European Parliament from 1979 (direct elections)

1979–1982	Simone Veil (ELDR, F)
1982–1984	Piet Dankert (PES, NL)
1984–1987	Pierre Pflimlin (EPP, F)
1987–1989	Sir Henry Plumb (Conservative, UK) Conservative MEPs were in the former European Democrats group during the Presidency of Lord Plumb. In 1992 they followed their former European Democrats group partners and joined the EPP group.
1989–1992	Enrique Baron Crespo (PES, E)
1992–1994	Egon Klepsch (EPP, D)
1994–1997	Klaus Hänsch (PES, D)
1997–1999	José Maris Giles Robles (EPP, E)

The Presidency and the Bureau

The Bureau is responsible for all the activities of the EP. It consists of the President and 14 Vice-Presidents and also includes five quaestors responsible for administrative and financial matters directly affecting members (in a consultative capacity). All of its members are elected for a two-and-a-half-year period.

Vice-Presidents

Nicole Fontaine (EPP, F), Nicole Péry (PES, F), David Martin (PES, UK), Georgios Anastassopoulos (EPP, GR), Antoni Gutiérrez Díaz (EUL/NGL, E), Ursula Schleicher (EPP, D), Renzo Imbeni (PES, I), Magdalene Hoff (PES, D), Josep Verde I Aldea (PES, E), Paraskevas Avgerinos (PES, GR),

Luis Marinho (PES, P), António Capucho (EPP, P), Bertel Haarder (ELDR, DK), Guido Podestà (UFE, I).

Quaestors

Richard Balfe (PES, UK), Sérgio Ribeiro (EUL/NGL, P), Otto Bardong (EPP, D), Pertti Paasio (PES, FIN), Mark Killilea (UFE, IRL).

The Committees of the European Parliament

Members are divided up into 20 standing committees, each of which specialises in a particular field. The EP can additionally set up sub-committees to deal with specific problems, or committees of inquiry.

1. Committee on Foreign Affairs, Security and Defence Policy
2. Committee on Agriculture and Rural Development
3. Committee on Budgets
4. Committee on Economic and Monetary Affairs and Industrial Policy
5. Committee on Research, Technological Development and Energy
6. Committee on External Economic Relations
7. Committee on Legal Affairs and Citizens' Rights
8. Committee on Social Affairs and Employment
9. Committee on Regional Policy
10. Committee on Transport and Tourism
11. Committee on the Environment, Public Health and Consumer Protection
12. Committee on Culture, Youth, Education and the Media
13. Committee on Development and Cooperation
14. Committee on Civil Liberties and Internal Affairs
15. Committee on Budgetary Control
16. Committee on Institutional Affairs
17. Committee on Fisheries
18. Committee on the Rules of Procedure, the Verification of Credentials and Immunities
19. Committee on Women's Rights
20. Committee on Petitions

Members of the European Parliament

The first democratic elections to the EP took place in 1979, with members sitting in political rather than national groups. There are currently eight political groups plus some 'non-attached' members. Elections are held every five years in Member States. The last general EP election was held between 9 and 12 June 1994. The next election is in June 1999.

Austria, Finland and Sweden elected MEPs before 1999 because they had not joined the EU in 1994, with MEPs appointed by national parliaments until specific EP elections. There are currently 626 MEPs:

- 99 elected in Germany;
- 87 each in France, Italy, the UK;
- 64 in Spain;
- 31 in the Netherlands;
- 25 each in Belgium, Greece, Portugal;
- 22 in Sweden;
- 21 in Austria;
- 16 each in Denmark and Finland;
- 15 in Ireland;
- 6 in Luxembourg.

Political Groups in the European Parliament

They represent the various political tendencies within the EP, of which a minimum of 29 members from one Member State is required to form a group, or 23 if they come from two Member States, 18 if they come from three Member States and 14 if they come from four or more Member States. The chairman of each group takes part in the Conference of Presidents and has the additional task of explaining the group's position on issues under discussion at plenary sessions. The eight political groups in the 1994–99 Parliament are:

Group	Chairmen
1. Group of the Party of European Socialists (PES)	Pauline Green (UK)
2. Group of the European People's Party (EPP)	Wilfried Martens (B)
3. Union for Europe Group (UFE)	Jean-Claude Pasty (F) & Claudio Azzolini (I)
4. Group of the Liberal Democratic and Reformist Party (ELDR)	Gijs de Vries (NL)
5. Confederal Group of the European United Left/Nordic Green Left (EUL/NGL)	Alonso Puerta (E)
6. Green Group in the European Parliament (Green)	Magda Aelvoet (B) & Claudio Roth (D)
7. Group of the European Radical Alliance (ERA)	Catherine Lalumière (F)
8. Group of Independents for a Europe of Nations (I-EdN)	Jens-Peter Bonde (DK)

Legislative power

There has been a gradual expansion in the EP's legislative role since the Treaty of Rome gave the European Commission the ability to propose and the Council to decide after having consulted the EP. If the obligation to consult is not met, then a Community law becomes null and void. The EP and Council now equally share the power of decision in a large number of areas. The EP can request the European Commission to take a particular initiative that it views to be important. The EP additionally examines the European Commission's annual work programme. Four possible legislative procedures exist for the EP to exercise power.

1.   Consultation procedure (single reading)

The EP's opinion has be obtained before a legislative proposal from the European Commission is adopted by the Council. While such an opinion is intended to influence the decision of the Council, the latter is not bound by it. As a procedure it is particularly applicable to the Common Agricultural Policy.

Procedure is as follows:

1.   European Commission proposal.
2.   Opinion of the EP.
3.   The proposal is adopted by the Council by QMV or unanimity.

Applies to the following Articles: Citizenship (8b), Agriculture (43(2,3)), Cohesion (130b), CFSP consultation (J(7) 1st sentence), JHA consultation (K(6) 2nd para), Excessive deficit protocol revision (104c(14)), Appointment of EMI President (109f(1)), Start of third stage of EMU (109j(2)).

2.   Cooperation procedure

Introduced in the SEA (Article 189c), it provided the EP with a greater say in the legislative process, European Commission proposals being subjected to a 'double reading'. This procedure allows the EP to reject the proposal at the second reading if the opinion it delivered at its first reading is not sufficiently taken into account in the Council's common position. To overturn rejection it is necessary for the Council to obtain a unanimous decision, which is difficult to achieve. The Council therefore has to seek conciliation with the EP to ensure its proposal is not rejected. This procedure embraces the European Regional Development Fund (ERDF), research, the environment, and cooperation and development.

Procedure is as follows:

1. European Commission proposal.
2. Opinion of the EP.
3. Common position of Council by QMV.
4. Communication of common position to EP.
5. The EP can either approve the common position by a qualified majority within three months, or express no opinion within three months. The effect is for the Council to adopt the act. But if the EP proposes amendments to the common position by an absolute majority within three months, or rejects the common position by an absolute majority of its members, then the EP forwards the result to the Council and European Commission.
6. The European Commission has one month to reconsider its proposal and submit a re-examined proposal and its view on the EP's amendments which the former did not accept.
7. The council, acting by QMV, shall adopt the proposal which has been re-examined by the Commission. Unanimity is necessary for the Council to amend the proposal as re-examined by the Commission.
8. In the situation noted in points 5, 6 and 7, the Council is required to act within a three-month period. If no decision is taken within this period, the Commission proposal is considered to have been adopted.
9. On a technical point, the three-month period can be extended by one month by common accord between the Commission and the Council.

Applies to the following Articles: Social policy (2), Social fund (125), Economic and social cohesion: implementing decisions (130e), Rules for multilateral surveillance procedure (103(5)), Measures of harmonisation with regard to circulation of coins (105a(2)).

3. Co-decision procedure

Introduced by the TEU (Article 189b), this three-reading procedure provides the EP with the power to adopt instruments jointly, as a last resort, with the Council. The EP shares decision-making powers with the Council, the EP being able to prevent the proposal being adopted if the Council does not take into account the EP's views in its common position. If the proposal is rejected by the EP, then it cannot be adopted by the Council, but to prevent this happening a Conciliation Committee comprising members of the EP, Council and the European Commission is convened. Its purpose is to obtain a compromise prior to the EP's third reading. However, if an agreement is still not obtained, then the EP can reject the proposal outrightly.

Procedure is as follows:

1. European Commission proposal.
2. Opinion of the EP.
3. Common position of Council by QMV. This does not apply for culture and research and development because, as multi-annual framework programmes, they require unanimity.
4. If the EP adopts the common position within three months, or gives no opinion within three months, then the Council adopts the act. But if the EP states by QMV to reject the common position and informs the Council, then the three-month period is extended by two months. If, by an absolute majority of its members, the EP proposes an amendment to a common position within three months, then it is forwarded to the European Commission and Council.
5. An opinion is then provided on the EP's amendments by the European Commission and Council.
6. If the Council adopts the EP's amendments within three months by QMV, or by a unanimity vote where the European Commission's opinion is unfavourable, then the act is adopted. But if the Council does not adopt the act, then the Conciliation Committee is convened. Composed of an equal number of Council and EP representatives, agreement by QMV of Council members and a majority vote of EP members is necessary.
7. If the Conciliation Committee approves the joint text within six weeks, then the EP and Council must adopt it within six weeks or the proposal fails. If the Committee does not agree, then the proposal is considered not to have been adopted, unless the Council confirms its original common position within six weeks, or the EP does not veto by an absolute majority of its members within six weeks of confirmation by the Council.
8. On a technical point, the three-month and six-week periods can be extended respectively by two months or two weeks by means of a common agreement between the Council and EP. Furthermore, the European Commission can alter its proposal as long as the Council has not adopted the act (Article 189a (2)).

Applies to the following Articles: Free movement of workers (49), Free movement of establishment: implementation programme (54(2)), Free movement of establishment: treatment of foreign nationals (56(2)), Self-employed persons (57(1)), Internal market (100a), Internal market: inventory (100b), Education (128), Culture (unanimity) (128), Public health (129), Consumer protection (129a), Guidelines: trans-European networks (129d), Research: multi-annual framework programme (unanimity) (130I(1)), Environment: general action programmes (130s(3) 1st para).

4. The assent procedure

The assent of the EP is required for decisions regarding the accession of new Member States, association agreements with third countries, the conclusion of international agreements, a uniform procedure for elections to the EP, the right of residence for Union citizens, the organisation and goals of the structural funds and the cohesion funds and the tasks and powers of the European Central Bank.

Procedure is as follows: The Council must obtain Parliament's assent by an absolute majority of its members before important decisions can be taken. The Parliament can accept or reject a proposal, but cannot amend it. The EP's assent will also be required in the case of sanctions to be imposed on a Member State for a persistent breach of fundamental rights (new article F.1 of Amsterdam Treaty).

3. European Council of Ministers and the European Council

The Council of the EU, normally known as the Council of Ministers, represents Member State governments. It is where they legislate for the Union, set its political objectives, coordinate national policies and resolve differences between themselves and other institutions. Comprising Ministers of the 15 Member States, it incorporates both supranational and intergovernmental concepts because some decisions can be made by QMV (the votes of a Member State are weighted and cast in a block), and others by unanimity (particularly on major policy decisions). The Council is composed of Member State Ministers and comprises those responsible for specific areas of policy, depending on the matter under discussion. There are in excess of 25 different types of Council meeting. At the apex of these is General Affairs (comprising Foreign Ministers) and Economy and Finance (EcoFin), while others include Agriculture. Meetings generally take place every month (August is a holiday month), while some, such as Transport, Environment and Industry, meet two to four times a year. Meetings usually take place in Brussels, except in April, June and October when all Council meetings take place in Luxembourg. Additional meetings take place within the nation which has the Presidency of the Union.

Presidency

The Council of Ministers and the European Council have a rotating Presidency. Each Member State is in the chair for a period of six months

(January until June, July until December). The Presidency has rotated since 1 July 1995 in the following sequence: Spain, Italy, Ireland, the Netherlands, Luxembourg, the UK, Austria, Germany, Finland, Portugal, France, Sweden, Belgium, Spain, Denmark and Greece. The Presidency's role is particularly important as it is responsible for arranging and presiding over all meetings, at which it must find acceptable compromises and solutions to problems. In this connection it is important to ensure that continuity and consistency are maintained in the decision-taking process. The Presidency is assisted in its work by the Friends of the Presidency group, which comprises a representative from every permanent representation and is chaired by the official whose nation holds the Presidency. This group assists policy development by providing a clearing ground for topics, thereby ensuring that more senior staff, such as the permanent representative or government Ministers, are not burdened with unnecessary work. In this context, its work is similar to the Antici group which assists permanent representative meetings throughout the year by providing a clearing ground for policies.

1991	Luxembourg, the Netherlands
1992	Portugal, the UK
1993	Denmark, Belgium
1994	Greece, Germany
1995	France, Spain
1996	Italy, Ireland
1997	The Netherlands, Luxembourg
1998	The UK, Austria
1999	Germany, Finland
2000	Portugal, France
2001	Sweden, Belgium
2002	Spain, Denmark

Structure

Every Member State has a national delegation in Brussels known as a permanent representation which is headed by permanent representatives who are usually senior diplomats. As a group they comprise a committee (COREPER II) that meets weekly with the primary task of preparing the Ministerial sessions and resolving more routine problems. COREPER II focuses on topics not covered in European Councils and the General Affairs, Budget, Development, EcoFin, and Justice and Home Affairs Councils. By contrast, deputy permanent representatives (COREPER I) have particular responsibility for specialist Councils, including Consumers, Energy, Environment, Fisheries, Industry, Internal Market, Social Affairs, Telecommunications and Transport. Their work is in turn prepared by various working groups, working parties and committees, including the Budget Committee, Committee on Cultural Affairs, Education Committee, Energy Committee, Special Committee on Agriculture, Standing Committee on Employment, Select Committee on Cooperation Agreements between Member States and Third Countries, Scientific and Technical Research Committee (CREST) and Standing Committee on Uranium Enrichment (Copenur). They comprise staff either from the permanent representation or experts visiting from national capitals. To assist the work of national officials, the Secretariat-General provides advice at all levels, giving such assistance as legal support to committees and Council meetings. Its head, the Secretary-General, is appointed unanimously by the Council.

Decision-making

The 1992 TEU based the activities of the Union on three 'pillars', establishing that decisions should essentially be taken either by unanimity or qualified majority voting (QMV). Within pillars two (CFSP) and three (JHA) the Council acts as both the promoter of initiatives and the decision-maker. Decisions by unanimity are the norm, apart for the implementation of joint actions which can be decided by QMV. By contrast, pillar one covers a wider range of Community policies, of which culture, industry, regional and social funds, taxation and the framework programme for research and technology development are subject to unanimity decision-making. Here, the method of decision-making follows a different process, starting with a European Commission proposal. After it has been examined by the EP and other experts, the Council can either adopt it, amend it or ignore it. The TEU did, however, slightly amend this process through a co-decision procedure. This meant that both the Council and the EP have responsibility for adopting a wide range of legislation, including consumer affairs, education, health, the internal market and trans-European networks. The vast majority of legislation, including agriculture, environment, fisheries, internal market, and transport, is decided by QMV:

- 10 votes each for France, Germany, Italy and UK;
- 8 votes for Spain;
- 5 votes each for Belgium, Greece, the Netherlands, Portugal;
- 4 votes each for Austria and Sweden;
- 3 votes each for Denmark, Finland and Ireland;
- 2 votes for Luxembourg.

When a European Commission proposal is involved, at least 62 votes must be cast in favour. Elsewhere, a QMV is valid if 62 out of the 87 votes are in favour of it, but these must be cast by at least ten Member

States. In practice, however, the Council attempts to obtain consensus before a decision is taken, to ensure that only a minority percentage of legislation adopted is the subject of negative votes and abstentions.

Pillar structure

EUROPEAN COUNCIL
Heads of State and Government and
Ministers of Foreign Affairs
Provides an overall guidance and coordination of policy

FIRST PILLAR	SECOND PILLAR	THIRD PILLAR
COMMON POLICIES & ACTIONS i.e. CAP, Common Commercial Policy, Environment, Cooperation and Development, Social Policy. *Economic and Monetary Union. Citizenship of the Union.*	*COMMON FOREIGN & SECURITY POLICY Common Defence (WEU).*	*JUSTICE AND HOME AFFAIRS* i.e. Asylum Policy, Immigration, Control on External Borders, European Police Office.
Cooperation and Co-decision with the European Parliament.	National Parliaments.	National Parliaments.
European Court of Justice has judicial control.	National Courts.	National Courts.

Legislation

All of the legislation made by the Community, as well as common positions dispatched by the Council to the EP, are published in the official languages of the Community in the *Official Journal*. Greater efforts have additionally been made by the Council to make its work more accessible to citizens. This process of transparency has meant that all legislative votes are automatically made public, journalists have been provided with wider briefings and background notes, and detailed press releases are assembled by the Press Service after Council meetings. The actual adoption of legislation by the Council (or by the Council and the EP through the co-decision procedure) takes various forms:

1. Regulations, which are applied directly with no need for national measures in the implementation process.
2. Directives, binding Member States to the achievement of objectives, but giving national authorities the ability to choose the method and form to be used.

3. Decisions, acting as binding measures to those to whom they are addressed, which can be served to all or any Member State, to individuals or to undertakings.
4. Recommendations and opinions, which are not binding.

European Council

Since 1974 Heads of State or Government have met at least twice a year in the form of the European Council or 'European Summit', whose membership also includes the President of the European Commission, with the President of the EP invited to make a presentation at the opening session. Its existence was, however, only legally recognised in the SEA. By then it had become a significant part of the Community, playing a major role by providing motivation for development, giving political direction, establishing priorities and resolving disputes. After each of its meetings, the European Council submits a report to the EP, also taking the form of an annual report assessing the progress achieved by the Union.

European Summits

Copenhagen	14–15 December 1973
Paris	9–10 December 1974
Dublin	10–11 March 1975
Rome	1–2 December 1975
Brussels	13–15 June 1976
The Hague	29–30 November 1976
Rome	25–26 March 1977
London	29–30 June 1977
Brussels	5–6 December 1977
Copenhagen	7–8 April 1978
Bremen	6–7 July 1978
Brussels	4–5 December 1978
Paris	12–13 March 1979
Strasbourg	21–22 June 1979
Dublin	29–30 November 1979
Luxembourg	27–28 April 1980
Venice	12–13 June 1980
Luxembourg	1–2 December 1980
Maastricht	23–24 March 1981
Luxembourg	29–30 June 1981
London	26–27 November 1981
Brussels	29–30 March 1982
Brussels	28–29 June 1982
Copenhagen	3–4 December 1982

Brussels	21–23 March 1983
Stuttgart	17–19 June 1983
Athens	4–6 December 1983
Brussels	19–20 March 1984
Fontainebleau	14–17 June 1984
Dublin	3–4 December 1984
Brussels	29–30 March 1985
Milan	28–29 June 1985
Luxembourg	2–3 December 1985
The Hague	26–27 June 1986
London	5–6 December 1986
Copenhagen	4–5 December 1987
Brussels	23–24 June 1987
Hanover	27–28 June 1988
Rhodes	2–3 December 1988
Madrid	26–27 June 1989
Strasbourg	8–9 December 1989
Dublin I	28 April 1990
Dublin II	25–26 June 1990
Rome I	27–28 October 1990
Rome II	14–15 December 1990
Luxembourg	28–29 June 1991
Maastricht	9–10 December 1991
Lisbon	26–27 June 1992
Birmingham	16 October 1992
Edinburgh	11–12 December 1992
Copenhagen	20–22 June 1993
Brussels	29 October 1993
Brussels	10–11 December 1993
Corfu	24–25 June 1994
Brussels	15 July 1994
Essen	9–10 December 1994
Cannes	26–27 June 1995
Majorca	22–23 September 1995
Madrid	15–16 December 1995
Florence	21–22 June 1996
Dublin	5 October 1996
Dublin	13–14 December 1996
Noordwijk	23 May 1997
Amsterdam	16–17 June 1997
Luxembourg	12–13 December 1997
Cardiff	15–16 June 1998
Portschach	24–25 October 1998
Vienna	11–12 December 1998

4. European Court of Justice and the Court of First Instance

Established in 1952 and based in Luxembourg, the Court of Justice comprises 15 judges and nine Advocates General who help the Court by making preliminary recommendations that are almost invariably followed. The Court of First Instance comprises just 15 judges with there being no permanent Advocates General (the duties of Advocate General are performed in a limited number of cases by one of the judges). Until 1 September 1989 the Court of Justice worked alone. Thereafter a Court of First Instance was attached to it with the aim of dealing with most of the actions brought by individuals and companies against decisions of the Community, institutions and agencies (judgments can be liable to an appeal taken before the Court of Justice, but only on a point of law). Thus, the Court of Justice has concentrated its activities on its fundamental task of ensuring a uniform interpretation of Community law, that is deciding on cases brought by Member States, Community institutions and by individuals and companies. It accordingly interprets the Treaties or secondary EU legislation when disputes arise, but does not have any jurisdiction over the courts and laws of Member States. The rulings that the Court makes are directly applicable to all Member States concerned, though an appeal may be brought to the Court of Justice. The decisions of the Court have made Community law a reality for the citizens of Europe, resulting in important constitutional and economic consequences.

Organisation

Members of both Courts are appointed by common accord of the governments of Member States for a renewable six-year term. The President of the Court of Justice is elected from, and by, the judges for a three-year term. He/she is responsible for directing the work of the Court and presiding over hearings and deliberations. The President of the Court of First Instance is elected in a similar manner, although there are no Advocates General. The Court of Justice may sit in plenary session or in chambers of three or five judges. It sits in plenary session when it so decides or if requested by a Member State or an EU institution which is a party to the proceedings. For its part, the Court of First Instance sits in chambers of three or five judges, and may sit in plenary session for certain important cases.

Role

The Court of Justice is responsible for maintaining a balance between the respective powers of the Community institutions, the powers transferred to the Community and those retained by Member States. An important contribution of the Court has been establishing the direct effect of Community law in Member States and the primacy of Community law over national law. This has ensured European citizens are able to challenge a national law if it is contrary to Community law. Thus, the principle of a Community law has become a reality, a factor particularly important to the free movement of goods, the creation of a common market and the removal of barriers protecting national markets. For example, the 1979 Cassis de Dijon judgment ensured that it was possible for European consumers to purchase in their own country any food product from another Community country.

Cases

Two types of case can generally be brought before the Court of Justice:

1. **Direct actions.**   Can be brought directly before the Court by the European Commission, other Community institutions or a Member State. Cases brought by individuals or companies challenging the legality of a Community act are brought directly before the Court of First Instance. If an appeal is lodged against a Court of First Instance decision, it is dealt with by the Court of Justice according to a procedure similar to that of other direct actions.
2. **Preliminary rulings.**   Can be requested by courts or tribunals in Member States when they need a decision on a question of Community law to be able to give a judgment. The Court of Justice is not a court of appeal from the decisions of national courts and can only rule on matters of Community law. Having given its decision, the national court is bound to apply the principles of Community law as laid down by the Court in deciding the case before it.

In a direct action, the language of the case is chosen by the applicant whereas in preliminary rulings the Court of Justice uses the same language as the national court which referred the case. Thus, any of the Community's languages may be used. Written exchanges are an important part of the Court's procedures, both for pleadings and for the submission of observations. After the end of the written phase, cases are argued orally in open court.

Composition of the Court of Justice in order of their entry into office

1. **Giuseppe Federico Mancini.**   Judge at the Court of Justice since 7 October 1988.

2. **José Carlos de Carvalho Moitinho de Almeida.** Judge at the Court of Justice since 31 January 1986.
3. **Gil Carlos Rodríguez Iglesias.** Judge at the Court of Justice since 31 January 1986; President of the Court of Justice since 7 October 1994.
4. **Francis Jacobs QC.** Advocate General at the Court of Justice since 7 October 1988.
5. **Paul J.G. Kapteyn.** Judge at the Court of Justice since 29 March 1990.
6. **Claus Christian Gulmann.** Advocate General at the Court of Justice from 7 October 1991 to 6 October 1994; Judge at the Court of Justice since 7 October 1994.
7. **John Loyola Murray.** Judge at the Court of Justice since 7 October 1991.
8. **David Alexander Ogilvy Edward.** Judge at the Court of First Instance from 25 September 1989 to 9 March 1992; Judge at the Court of Justice since 10 March 1992.
9. **Antonio Mario La Pergola.** Judge at the Court of Justice from 7 October 1994 to 31 December 1994; Advocate General at the Court of Justice since 1 January 1995.
10. **Georges Cosmas.** Advocate General at the Court of Justice since 7 October 1994.
11. **Jean-Pierre Puissochet.** Judge at the Court of Justice since 7 October 1994.
12. **Philippe Léger.** Advocate General at the Court of Justice since 7 October 1994.
13. **Günter Hirsch.** Judge at the Court of Justice since 7 October 1994.
14. **Peter Jann.** Judge at the Court of Justice since 19 January 1995.
15. **Hans Ragnemalm.** Judge at the Court of Justice since 19 January 1995.
16. **Leif Sevón.** Judge at the Court of Justice since 19 January 1995.
17. **Nial Fennelly.** Advocate General at the Court of Justice since 19 January 1995.
18. **Dámaso Ruiz-Jarabo Colomer.** Advocate General at the Court of Justice since 19 January 1995.
19. **Melchior Wathelet.** Judge at the Court of Justice since 19 September 1995.
20. **Romain Schintgen.** Judge at the Court of First Instance from 1 September 1989 to 11 July 1996; Judge at the Court of Justice since 12 July 1996.
21. **Krateros M. Ioannou.** Judge at the Court of Justice since 7 October 1997.
22. **Siegbert Alber.** Advocate General at the Court of Justice since 7 October 1997.

23. **Jean Mischo.** Advocate General at the Court of Justice since 19 December 1997.
24. **Antonio Saggio.** Judge at the Court of First Instance from 1 September 1989 to 17 September 1995; President of the Court of First Instance from 18 September 1995 to 4 March 1998; Advocate General at the Court of Justice since 5 March 1998.
25. **Roger Grass.** Legal Secretary to the President of the Court of Justice; Registrar at the Court of Justice since 10 February 1994.

5.   The Court of Auditors

Based in Luxembourg and established on 22 July 1975 by the Brussels Treaty, it aims to check whether the accounts of all EU institutions are in accordance with current legislation and jurisdiction. Its creation coincided with the extension of the EP's powers in the field of budgetary control and the financing of the EU budget through own resources. It was therefore important and necessary to create an independent organisation to audit the Community's finances, which became a reality when the Court became operational in October 1977. Its authority was subsequently strengthened when it was promoted to the rank of an Institution on 1 November 1993 when the Treaty on European Union (TEU) came into force. The Court of Auditors is composed of 15 members (one from each Member State) who are appointed by a unanimous decision of the Council after consulting the EP for a (renewable) term of six years. Members come from those who belong or have belonged to external audit bodies in their respective Member States, or who are particularly qualified to carry out the duties of office. The President of the European Court of Auditors is elected by colleagues for a three-year term (with the possibility of re-election), his/her role being to ensure the smooth running of the Court's departments and the pursuit of correct procedures. Since 18 January 1996 the President has been Dr Bernhard Friedmann. The total number of staff employed by the Court is approximately 500.

General powers

The Court is essentially a guarantor that certain administrative and accounting principles are adhered to in the Union. Its reports serve as a means of applying pressure on institutions to ensure proper management takes place, thereby reassuring public opinion that money is being spent responsibly. This has meant that all bodies and institutions which have access to EU finances are scrutinised by the Court of Auditors. It specifically audits the general budget of the Union, Community loans and borrowings, the expenditure and revenue entered in the ECSC budget, the revenue and expenditure of the European Development Funds, the Euratom Supply Agency, the European Centre for the Development of Vocational Training, the European Foundation for the Improvement of Living and Working Conditions, the Joint European Torus research undertaking, the European Schools and other bodies, including the new satellite agencies. Accordingly, the local, regional and national administrations that administer Community funds need to be able to satisfy the Court's scrutiny. When discrepancies are identified by the Court, it then highlights the action to be taken by the pertinent administrations and other bodies, while equally illustrating those points which have allowed problems to occur. The Court can make its views known at any time by issuing reports on specific areas of budget management. These are published in the *Official Journal.* In this context, the Court carries out its control and consultative functions autonomously and independently. Views, as well as the correspondence from the particular institution concerned, are published in its annual report. This is adopted annually in November, having been subjected to examination by the EP on a recommendation of the Council when it is considering whether or not to give a discharge to the European Commission for its management of the budget.

6.   The Economic and Social Committee

Based in Brussels, the ESC was established by the 1957 Treaties of Rome with the aim of involving economic and social interest groups in the establishment of the common market and of providing institutional machinery for briefing the European Commission and the Council of Ministers on EU issues. It comprises 222 members, representing employers, employees and other groups such as consumers and farmers. Members are appointed by the Council after having been nominated by national governments. They serve for a renewable four-year term of office and belong to one of three groups: employers (group 1), workers (group 2), and various interests (group 3). Membership is proportionally distributed among Member States:

- 24 members each for Germany, France, Italy and the UK;
- 21 members for Spain;
- 12 members each for Belgium, Greece, the Netherlands, Portugal, Austria and Sweden;

- 9 members each for Denmark, Ireland and Finland;
- 6 members for Luxembourg.

The primary task of members is to issue opinions on matters referred to the ESC by the European Commission and the Council. Being optional in some cases, in certain other cases it is mandatory for the European Commission and the Council to consult the ESC, while it may also adopt opinions on its own initiative. These roles were reinforced by the SEA (1986) and the TEU (1992), especially new policies such as environmental and regional policy. This process was continued by the draft Amsterdam Treaty (1997) which providing for the ESC to be consulted by the EP.

Organisation – Presidency and bureau

A bureau is elected by the ESC every two years, comprising 36 members (12 per group), a President and two Vice-Presidents chosen from each of the three groups in rotation. The main task of the bureau is to organise and coordinate the work of the ESC's various bodies, establishing policy guidelines. In addition, the responsibilities of the bureau and the President embrace joint briefs (relations with EFTA, CEEC, ACP countries, Latin American and other third countries, and the Citizens' Europe). The responsibilities of the President include the functioning of the Committee's business and external representation with other bodies, a task assisted by the Vice-Presidents, deputising in the event of absence. In carrying out these duties, the Committee is serviced by a secretariat-general, which is headed by a secretary-general reporting to the President.

Sections. There are nine sections within the ESC: Economic, Financial and Monetary Questions; External Relations, Trade and Development Policy; Social, Family, Educational and Cultural Affairs; Protection of the Environment, Public Health and Consumer Affairs; Agriculture and Fisheries; Regional Development and Town and Country Planning; Industry, Commerce, Crafts and Services; Transport and Communications; Energy, Nuclear Questions and Research.

Study groups. The opinions of particular sections are prepared by study groups, normally comprising 12 members (including a rapporteur who may be assisted by experts, usually totalling four).

Sub-committees. A temporary sub-committee can be set up by the ESC for the purpose of dealing with particular issues; it is organised on a similar basis to the sections.

Plenary session. The full Committee generally meets in plenary session ten times a year, at which opinions are adopted by a simple majority on the basis of section opinions. These are then advanced to the institutions, and published in the *Official Journal of the European Communities*.

7.   The Committee of the Regions

Based in Brussels, it is a new advisory body established by the TEU comprising 222 members. It represents local and regional authorities, which have been elected by the citizens, and therefore is the European body which most closely reflects the interests of the people. Since its first plenary session in March 1994, the Committee, which holds five plenary sessions a year in Brussels, has evolved as a strong guardian of the principle of subsidiarity. It has adopted over 80 opinions dealing with such subjects as drought problems in southern Europe, urban and land-use policy, the structural and cohesion funds, the development of trans-European transport, energy and telecommunications networks, and the information society. Members serve for four years. The first four-year term of office was appointed by the Council on 26 January 1994. The President, First Vice-President and Bureau are elected from among the members for a two-year term. Membership is proportionally distributed among Member States:

- 24 members each for France, Germany, Italy and the UK;
- 21 members for Spain;
- 12 members each for Austria, Belgium, Greece, the Netherlands, Portugal and Sweden;
- 9 members each for Denmark, Finland and Ireland;
- 6 members for Luxembourg.

Work

While the EU Treaty specifies that the Council or the European Commission must consult the Committee on issues relating to culture (Title IX, Article 128), economic and social cohesion (Title XIV, Article 130b: progress report; Article 130d: Structural Funds; and Article 130e: European Regional Development Fund), education and youth (Title VIII, Chapter 3, Article 126), public health (Title X, Article 129), trans-European networks (Title XII, Article 129d), it can give its opinion on other policy areas affecting cities and regions, including agriculture and environmental protection. The work of the Committee is structured around eight standing Commissions and four Sub-Commissions, and has also established a Special Commission on Institutional Affairs that is responsible for contributing to the debate on the reform of the EU institutions. The work of the Committee of the Regions is organised by the Bureau, which is elected for a two-year term.

1. Regional Development, Economic Development, Local and Regional Finances
   Sub-Commission: Local and regional finances

2. Spatial Planning (agriculture, hunting, fisheries, marine environment and upland areas)
   Sub-Commission: Tourism, rural areas
3. Transport and Communications Networks
   Sub-Commission: Telecommunications
4. Citizen's Europe, Research, Culture, Youth and Consumers
   Sub-Commission: Youth and sports
5. Urban Policies
6. Land-use Planning, Environment, Energy
7. Education, Training
8. Economic and Social Cohesion, Social Policy, Public Health

Members of the Bureau for the second two-year period (1996–98)

1. **Federal Republic of Germany:** Manfred Dammeyer (Vice-President), Erwin Teufel, Gerhard Gebauer
2. **Austria:** Franz Romeder, Christof Zernatto (Vice-President)
3. **Belgium:** Luc van den Brande (Vice-President), Robert Collignon
4. **Denmark:** Knud Andersen (Vice-President), Søren Andersen
5. **Spain:** Manuel Fraga Iribarne, Juan José Lucas Giménez (Vice-President), Juan Carlos Rodriguez Ibarra
6. **Finland:** Markku Kauppinen, Risto Koivisto (Vice-President)
7. **France:** Jean-Louis Joseph, Jean-Jacques Weber (Vice-President)
8. **Greece:** Konstantinos Kosmopoulos, Thrassyvoulos Lazaridis (Vice-President)
9. **Ireland:** Betty Coffey, Tony Mckenna (Vice-President)
10. **Italy:** Enzo Bianco, Vannino Chiti (Vice-President), Domenico Ricchiuti
11. **Luxembourg:** Léon Bollendorff, Carlo Meintz (Vice-President)
12. **The Netherlands:** Philip Houben, Jan Terlouw (Vice-President)
13. **Portugal:** Fernando Gomes (Vice-President), Alberto João Jardim
14. **Sweden:** Roger Kaliff (Vice-President), Joakim Ollén
15. **The UK:** Lord Peter Bowness, Charles Gray (Vice-President), Lord Graham Tope

8. The European Investment Bank

Based in Luxembourg and established in 1957 by the Treaty of Rome, it raises funds on the capital markets to finance investments that contribute to the development of the Union. Projects need to fulfil certain objectives before the EIB will grant loans. These objectives include:

- strengthening economic progress in the less favoured regions;
- improving trans-European networks in telecommunications, transport and energy transfer;
- enhancing industry's world competitiveness and its integration at a European level, and supporting small and medium-sized enterprises;
- protecting the environment and quality of life, safeguarding the EU's architectural heritage and promoting urban development;
- achieving secure energy supplies.

General powers

Funding of regional development projects by the EIB often takes place in tandem with grants from the EU's structural funds and cohesion fund, a process which ensures the need for a close collaboration with the European Commission so as to establish complementarity. The EIB has been particularly active in providing finance for trans-European networks (TENs) in transport and telecommunications and energy, projects which require large amounts of investment. To provide guarantees for TENs, as well as for small and medium-sized enterprises, the EIB, in collaboration with the European Commission and the banking sector, established the European Investment Fund (EIF).

In addition to funding projects within the borders of the Union, the EIB also grants loans to undertakings outside the Union, including:

- the countries of Central and Eastern Europe;
- the signatories to the Lomé Convention, and the Republic of South Africa;
- fostering cross-border infrastructure and environmental projects as well as developing the productive private sector in Mediterranean non-member countries;
- assisting the Middle East peace process, notably in the Lebanon, Gaza and the West Bank;
- financing projects of mutual interest, including technology transfer, joint ventures and environmental protection in Asian and Latin American countries which have signed cooperation agreements with the EU.

9. European Ombudsman

The current Ombudsman, Jacob Söderman, was elected by the EP in 1995, and has responsibility for investigating complaints regarding maladministration (including administrative irregularities, discrimination and abuse of power) by institutions and bodies of the Community, although his office is not able to deal with complaints embracing national, regional or local administrations of Member States.

10.   The European Monetary Institute and the European Central Bank

Based in Frankfurt, the European Monetary Institute coordinates the monetary policy of the central banks of the Member States within the European System of Central Banks (ESCB). It is involved in the preparation of the third stage of Economic and Monetary Union when a European single currency will be introduced. It is intended that this stage will start no later than 1999, and at the start of the third stage the EMI will be renamed the European Central Bank. The director of the EMI is Alexandre Lamfalussy (Belgium).

Council of the EMI

1.	Antonio Fazio	Banca d'Italia
2.	Pierre Jaans	Institut Monétaire Luxembourgeois
3.	Maurice O'Connell	Central Bank of Ireland
4.	Urban Bäckström	Sveriges Riksbank
5.	António José Fernandes de Sousa	Banco de Portugal
6.	Alfons Verplaetse	Banque Nationale de Belgique
7.	Jean-Claude Trichet	Banque de France
8.	Nout Wellink	De Nederlandsche Bank
9.	Lucas Papademos	Bank of Greece
10.	Klaus Liebscher	Oesterreichische Nationalbank
11.	Edward George	Bank of England
12.	Hans Tietmeyer	Deutsche Bundesbank
13.	Sirkka Hämäläinen	Suomen Pankki
14.	Willem Duisenberg	President of the EMI
15.	Luis Ángel Rojo	Banco de España
16.	Bodil Nyboe Andersen	Danmarks Nationalbank

SECTION V

Major Community Policies

1. Agricultural Policy

Treaty basis

Articles 38–47 of the Treaty on European Union.

Institutional dynamics

While the European Commission is responsible for formulating and initiating policy proposals, the Council of Ministers is the decision-making body and establishes the primary policy guidelines for the common agricultural policy (CAP). The European Parliament (EP) has to give its opinion on legislative proposals before the Council of Ministers can take its decision. National Ministers are assisted by the Special Committee for Agriculture (SCA), comprising senior agricultural officials from Member States. The day-to-day functioning of the CAP is the responsibility of the European Commission, a duty in which it is assisted by the Management Committees for the different sectors. They are made up of the relevant experts from the national Ministries and chaired by the European Commission, which also seeks to ensure obligations are fulfilled by national agencies.

Overview

The CAP is the most important Common Policy in the institutional system of the EU and was essentially the forerunner of the single market. The general orientations of the CAP were introduced in January 1962, being based upon the principles of market unity, Community preference and financial solidarity. Article 39 of the Treaty of Rome stressed that the CAP had five objectives, each of which recognised the need to take account of the structural and natural disparities between agricultural regions, namely to increase productivity; to ensure a fair standard of living for the agricultural Community; to stabilise markets; to assure food supplies; and to provide consumers with food at reasonable prices.

History

The CAP was established as a means of rectifying the deficit in food production within Europe through supporting internal prices and incomes. This policy was conducted either via intervention and/or border protection and made a significant contribution to the Community's economic growth. But the system included problems which became particularly apparent as the Community established a surplus for most of its agricultural products. The first of these was the increasing of output beyond the market's need via the guaranteeing of prices through intervention and production aids. Indeed, the agricultural production of the Community increased by 2% per annum between 1973 and 1988, while internal consumption increased by only 0.5% per annum. A consequence was the creation of large surpluses within certain product areas, most notably butter and wine, with a consequence of depressing market prices. Secondly, the very success of the CAP caused tension with the Community's trading partners as subsidised exports affected the market. Finally, the desire to produce more food brought with it environmental damage to certain regions. The effect of these factors was the need to reform the CAP in tune with the demands and pressures within the Community during the 1990s.

Reform

A meeting of the EU Council of Agriculture Ministers in June 1992 decided to reform the CAP by adopting four broad policies, the first of which involved reducing EU prices in the arable and beef sectors over a three-year period to levels closer to those of the world market. This was deemed to ensure the competitiveness of Community agricultural production. Secondly, farmers received compensatory payments for reductions in EU support prices to ensure their viability. Thirdly, payment of compensation for cereals and other arable crops was to be dependent on the withdrawal of land from production (set-aside), with payments in the beef sector to be established through a maximum stocking rate per hectare determined by individual or regional ceilings. Finally, reform of the CAP included policies such as agri-environment, afforestation and early retirement measures. Of these, the former is concerned with granting aid to encourage farmers to protect the environment, the landscape and natural resources. Afforestation refers to the development of farm forestry as a means of providing an alternative use for agricultural land, while early retirement measures are optional (agri-environmental and agri-forestry measures are compulsory), allowing the granting of aid to farmers and farm workers who are at least 55 years of age and wish to stop working prior to the normal retirement age. Reform of the CAP had the additional advantage of enabling the EU to comply with the obligations established by the General Agreement on Tariffs and Trade (GATT) Uruguay Round, signed on 15 April 1994. This involved a 20% reduction in domestic support for agriculture over a six-year period, a reduction of 36% in budget spending on export subsidies and a 21% cut in the quantity of subsidised exports. Future reform will be influenced by the publication in December 1998 of a Court of Auditors report which is likely to put greater pressure on placing limits on EU spending.

EU farm budget

The European Agricultural Guidance and Guarantee Fund (EAGGF) has been the largest single item in the Community budget, the resources of which are jointly provided by Member States. It comprises two parts, of which the Guarantee Section finances Community expenditure under the policy on prices and markets, including CAP reform, compensatory payments and the accompanying measures. By far the greater part of EAGGF expenditure goes on the Guarantee Section (90% in 1995), of which half is spent on direct payments to farmers. By contrast, the far smaller Guidance Section (10% in 1995) contains the Community resources allocated to the structures policy, including aids for the modernisation of holdings, the installation of young farmers, aids for processing, marketing and diversification. This component also finances rural development actions along with the European Regional Fund and European Social Fund. Such measures are planned and executed in a decentralised manner in cooperation with individual Member States or regions, while the principle of co-financing is applicable. In addition to national financial contributions to the Community budget and revenues from customs duties, the CAP plays a major role in the provision of revenues through duties on farm trade and sugar levies. The total expenditure on agriculture is decided by the Council of Ministers and the EP under the general budgetary procedure, of which the overall proportion of the EU budget devoted to agriculture has been on a downward trend with it representing less than 50% of total spending.

2. The European Union's Budget

Treaty basis

Title II, Articles 199–209 of the Treaty on European Union.

Institutional dynamics

The European Commission proposes the annual budget to the Council and the EP and manages expenditure once the budget is approved (DG XX controls revenue and expenditure). The EP approves the EU's budget each year and is able to suggest changes and amendments to the European Commission's original proposals and to the positions taken by the Council. However, the Council has the final say on agricultural spending and costs arising from international agreements. By contrast, the EP has the last say on expenditure relating to cooperation with third countries, environmental projects, education, social and regional programmes, and food and humanitarian aid. Expenditure is scrutinised by the EP's Committee on Budgetary Control. This ensures that money is not wasted, while it also helps to prevent fraud.

Overview

Despite the budget of the EU being over 80 billion ECU, it is a small amount in terms of Member States' wealth, representing just over 1% of their combined gross domestic product (GDP). The budget is, however, a contentious issue and has sparked many conflicts within the Community. It is proposed every year by the European Commission, but has to be adopted by the Council, and ultimately by the EP. An inter-institutional agreement between the Council, the EP and the European Commission in 1988 (revised in 1993) helped to reduce tension over budgetary issues by establishing the budget size and spending ceilings for main policy areas within a seven-year framework.

Policy areas

The budget allocates funds for policies relating to agriculture and fisheries, structural funds for the regions and employment measures, and the cohesion fund for the poorest Member States. Internal policy areas include research and technological development programmes; measures to promote the internal market; energy and telecommunications networks; environmental protection; cooperation in the fields of justice and home affairs; culture; trans-frontier educational initiatives and exchanges; and schemes to help young people. External policy areas include aid to other countries, such as development aid or technical assistance; reconstruction aid or emergency assistance; joint actions under the common foreign and security policy; refugee funding; and protecting human rights.

Spending priorities

Of the areas which comprise the budget, the Common Agricultural Policy (CAP) has witnessed a decline in its proportion of total EU spending, having declined from 68% in 1985 to less than 50% today (although still being a dominant share). The decline in the importance of agriculture has, however, been matched by an increase in the proportion of the budget allocated to the structural funds which finance regional and social policies designed to raise employment levels and reduce wealth disparities between EU regions. At present the structural funds comprise approximately one-third of the budget, compared to one-sixth in 1988, and is accordingly the second most important spending category. Other important spending priorities include research and external action, while about 5% of the budget is spent on the administrative running costs of Community institutions and bodies.

Financing

The budget is financed by the EU's four own resources, comprising agricultural and sugar levies, customs duties, VAT resources and GNP resources. Levies are charged on agricultural products which emanate from non-member countries, while sugar levies are imposed on sugar companies either to cover outlay on market support (manufacture levies) or to manage disposal (storage levies). Customs duties are Common Customs Tariff duties and other duties established in respect of trade with non-member countries. VAT own resources come from the application of a standard rate (1% in 1999) to the VAT base which is settled in a uniform style for all Member States. Additional income comes from the GNP-based resources which provide the revenue required to cover the difference between planned expenditure and the amount obtained by traditional resources and VAT receipts (contributions are made in proportion to the GNP of a Member State). Finally, the EU's own resources are formed by a fixed ceiling of a percentage of total Community GNP (1.27% in 1999).

Scrutiny

The EU's budget is checked by the Court of Auditors to ensure money is spent for its designated purpose, thereby guaranteeing financial accountability. This scrutiny extends to all the institutions of the EU, while local, regional and national administrations that manage EU funds also have to satisfy the objectives of the Court, which therefore plays an important role in reducing fraud.

3. Social Policy

Treaty basis

Articles 2, 3, 39, 48–51, 100–102, 117–127, 130a–e and 235, plus Protocol (No. 14) of the EU.

Institutional dynamics

The European Commission is responsible for initiating all legislative proposals, managing the European Social Fund (ESF) and other programmes that aim to achieve social policy objectives. The Directorate-General for

Employment, Industrial Relations and Social Affairs (DG V) has primary responsibility for administering policy, while the Council of Ministers adopts social policy legislation in partnership with the European Parliament (EP). Unanimity is necessary for decisions on migrant workers, aspects of employment law and co-determination, for setting the rules, tasks and objectives of the structural funds, and for specific actions outside the structural funds. By contrast, qualified majority voting (QMV) is applicable to proposals affecting the working environment, equal opportunities, worker information and consultation and the integration of persons excluded from the labour market. The EP is responsible for approving alterations to the tasks and objectives of the structural funds, with the co-decision procedure providing it with the ability to block proposals on equal opportunities, improving the working environment, the integration of persons excluded from the labour market and worker information and consultation. Some areas are subject to the cooperation procedure, including health and safety legislation, thereby providing the EP with the ability to amend, but crucially its desires can be overruled by a unanimous Council vote.

Overview

EU employment policy is promoted through the ESF, which is one of the four structural funds. Recent action priorities have included attempts to combat labour market exclusion and long-term unemployment, while emphasis on education and training has been especially directed towards youth unemployment. Social policy covers a myriad of topics, including social security and welfare issues, collective bargaining and industrial relations, and individual rights of workers. Recent emphasis on social policy can be traced to the period after the SEA when there was considerable concern that the single market should not worsen social disparities, while the concern of some countries that 'social dumping' would occur produced increased support for labour market regulation.

History

Social responsibility initially arose in the provisions of the Treaty of Rome, but these were limited in practice (Articles 117–127). While the Treaty considered social policy to be a mechanism for correcting market distortions (free movement of workers), it also set up the ESF. By 1972 political support for the extension of Community social policy led to the first in a series of Social Action Programmes which were intended to provide a coherent plan of action for a four-year period. Nevertheless, limited progress took place in the 1970s (extension of the ESF and action on sex discrimination). This was changed when the SEA extended social policy, promoting labour–management dialogue between 'social partners'. Article 118A of the SEA provided for QMV on proposals to encourage improvements in the working environment, health and safety of workers and the harmonisation of conditions in these areas. Article 118B of the SEA stressed the normalisation of a corporatist policy network, whereby the 'dialogue between management and labour at the European level could, if the two sides consider desirable, lead to relations based on agreement'.

The Social Charter

The European Commission and some Member States looked towards a 'social dimension' of the single market when Heads of State and Government stressed the social dimensions relevant for the 1992 programme at the June 1988 Hanover European Council. It culminated in the Social Charter at the December 1989 Strasbourg European Council. This was a non-binding 'solemn declaration' covering 12 categories of fundamental social rights of workers, namely: freedom of movement; employment and remuneration; social protection; freedom of association and collective bargaining; vocational training; equal treatment for men and women; information, consultation and protection in the workplace; protection of children and adolescents; protection of elderly persons; and protection of disabled persons. However, the UK did not sign, with the government's position reflecting an ideological rift between liberal capitalism and the free market and social welfare and intervention. The President of the European Commission, Jacques Delors, was of the latter school and subsequently championed a social dimension to the Community. The majority of Member States shared this vision, which was followed by a Social Action Programme of 47 measures (27 of which were in the form of directives or other binding measures). Delays took place in the implementation of some measures, such as the UK derogation on the working time directive.

Reform

The TEU created a confused situation after 11 Member States (not the UK) signed the Social Protocol and Agreement on Social Policy (the Social Chapter). This allowed them to implement measures using EC procedures, but crucially outside the *acquis communitaire*. Under the Social Chapter some areas were subject to QMV vote (excluding the UK), namely: health and safety of workers; working conditions; information/consultation; sex equality; and integration of persons excluded from the labour market. Other topics were subject to unanimity (excluding the UK), including: social security/social protection of workers; protection of workers after termination of employment; representation and co–determination; employment conditions of non-EC nationals and subsidies for job creation. Those areas which were excluded from the Agreement included wages, the right of association and the right to strike/lockout.

The TEU also formalised dialogue with 'social partners' whereby consultation with management and labour, and opinions or recommendations from the two sides, is required before proposals are submitted to the Council. The social partners are additionally able to choose to negotiate an agreement to implement the proposal to be adopted as a Council decision at their request. The first EU directive to pass under the new procedures established by the TEU was the European Works Council Directive which was adopted by the Council in September 1994. It required works councils to be established in companies employing in excess of 1,000 people and with establishments in at least two Member States. In a similar development on 29 March 1996, the Social Affairs Council adopted the directive on parental leave via the same procedures. Its significance, however, was that it was the first time legislation had been adopted by Ministers on the basis of a collective agreement proposed by the social partners to the Council. More recently, the victory for Labour in the May 1997 UK general election witnessed a change in UK social policy when the government accepted the Social Chapter at the June 1997 Amsterdam European Council. Moreover, the Amsterdam Treaty included a new Employment Chapter which promised a coordinated social policy strategy that was closer to the priorities of the UK than France.

Changes

The 1993 White Paper of 'Growth, Competitiveness and Employment' and the 1994 Social Policy White Paper marked a new focus on balancing high levels of social protection with European competitiveness. The 1993 White Paper acknowledged that high rates of unemployment on the continent were partly due to labour market rigidities which were not present in nations such as Japan and the USA. It proposed a 'social pact' where productivity gains produced by a limited deregulation of the labour market are used to fund job-creation and training opportunities. This emphasis on job creation, flexibility, reduced non-wage labour costs, structural reforms of social security and taxation systems signalled a decline in Community activism, with attention directed towards consolidation rather than new initiatives. There was therefore a gradual move away from traditional social welfarism to the dual goals of protection and flexibility. This strategy was further emphasised in the 1995–97 Social Action Programme which looked to consolidation rather than to new initiatives. Indeed, while the November 1997 Jobs Summit set broad guidelines for national employment policies, particular focus was attached to enterprise, employability, adaptability and equal opportunities.

Chronology

30 May 1989.   The European Commission adopted the preliminary draft of the Community Charter of Fundamental Social Rights.

29 November 1989.   The European Commission adopted the work programme for implementing the Social Charter.

8–9 December 1989.   The Strasbourg European Council resulted in the approval by all Member States (except the UK) of the 'Community Charter of the social basic laws of working people'.

9–10 December 1991.   The UK rejected the Social Chapter at the Maastricht European Council.

23 November 1993.   The Brussels Labour and Social Affairs Council adopted the Organisation of Working Time Directive.

1 September 1993.   The European Commission implemented the Community Charter of the Fundamental Social Rights of Workers and adopted an opinion on an equitable wage.

22 September 1994.   The European Council adopted the directive on the establishment of European Works' Councils or procedures in Community-wide undertakings for the purposes of informing and consulting employees. This was the first measure adopted by the 11 Member States under the Social Policy Protocol.

11 August 1995.   A European Court of Justice ruling held that rules ending entitlement to invalidity benefit for a woman at the age of 60 did not breach a European directive of equal treatment for men and women in matters concerning social security.

17 June 1997.   The Treaty of Amsterdam included a new employment chapter and the UK signed up to the Social Chapter.

4.   Economic and Monetary Policy

Treaty basis

Articles 3a (2–3), 67–73, 102a, 103, 103a, 104, 104a, 104b, 104c, 105–109m of the EC Treaty, plus Protocols 4 and 5 of the Treaty on European Union.

Institutional dynamics

While macro-economic policy guidelines are set by the European Council, it is the Council of Economic and Finance Ministers that drafts policy guidelines, coordinates macro-economic policies and adopts legis-lative instruments. Those legislative (and policy) initiatives are proposed by the European Commission, which has the additional task of monitoring the economic performance of Member States (for example, regarding the convergence criteria for Economic and Monetary Union (EMU)), while under the excessive deficit procedure it suggests macro-economic policy guidelines and recommendations. The European Commission also plays a global role through its participation in meetings of the Group of Eight leading industrial countries. By contrast, the European Parliament's role is somewhat distanced, including the issuing of reports and recommenda-tions on economic policy. However, the assent of the EP is necessary for the European Central Bank (ECB) to have a role in the supervision of credit institutions, as well as for any amendments to be made to the statutes of the ECB and the European System of Central Banks (ESCB).

Overview

The EU's goal of the attainment of EMU by 1999 represented a further development in the attempt to create a stable currency system, as evid-enced by the establishment of the European Monetary System (EMS) in 1979. But the management of monetary policy was not a central aim of the Treaty of Rome, with the coordination of monetary policy not producing any significant developments and Member States pursuing individual priorities. This changed with the introduction of the ERM of the EMS and the move towards the creation of a single currency through the 1989 Delors Report and the subsequent TEU.

Liberalisation of financial services

This is a key aspect of monetary policy which had previously been ham-pered by exchange controls regulating capital imports and exports, while the existence of different regulatory frameworks within Member States proved to be a barrier to the provision of services such as banking and insurance across national borders. This was an issue which particularly concerned the UK and proved to be a significant motivation behind it supporting the single market, the consequence of which has been three broad strategies pursued by the EU in liberalising financial services:

1. The removal of exchange controls.
2. The harmonisation of essential regulations and the acceptance of mutual recognition of other national regulations. Banks are there-fore able to operate across national borders, while scrutiny of their activities rests with authorities in the home country.
3. The harmonisation of tax rates.

However, while there has been a deregulation of financial services and the removal of exchange controls, little progress has been achieved in the field of harmonising tax rates. One reason why the European Commission's efforts have been diminished in this area is because tax rates are central to the national interest, while decisions by the Council on tax rates have to be taken unanimously.

Multilateral surveillance

The TEU regards the economic policies of Member States to be an issue of common concern, with the Council of Ministers playing a coordinating role. Multilateral surveillance flows from the European Commission, establishing a set of guidelines for Member States' economic policies. The guidelines act as a basis for a draft to be adopted by the Council of Finance Ministers. This in turn influences European Council conclusions that act as a basis for the recommendations adopted by the Council. To ensure that each Member State pursues a consistent policy, the Council of Finance Ministers performs a monitoring role, which can result in the Council highlighting ineffective policies.

The Exchange Rate Mechanism

This is a parity grid with currencies given a central value in relation to the ECU. Prior to 1993 Member States were not allowed to let their currencies diverge from the central valuation by more than 2.25% (Italy, Spain and the UK had 6% bands). Member States must intervene, by means of interest rates and intervention on FOREX markets, if their currency hits the three-quarters level of the fluctuation margin.

Chronology of the EMS

1979–83.   ERM was the 'crawling peg' of stable but adjustable exchange rates, there being eight realignments as currencies found a settled parity.
1983–87.   This was the most successful period of the system as Member States viewed the ERM as the instrument of domestic monetary discipline. Weaker states gained anti-inflationary credibility by tying monetary policies to those of the Bundesbank, with the Deutschmark becoming the anchor currency. This resulted in a minimisation of exchange rate fluctuations and lower inflation rates. There were only four realignments in this period.
1987–93.   The 1987 Basle–Nyborg agreement on closer coordination of monetary policy set an informal rule that realignments were to be avoided. This represented a political desire to move towards EMU. The ERM therefore became a quasi-fixed exchange rate system. But, the ERM

consequently lost its flexibility, causing asymmetry, while the removal of exchange rate controls meant it became harder to resist currency speculation. Turbulence within the ERM was also caused by German unification, which influenced high interest rates across the Community during a recession. But there was no broad realignment of the ERM, with the UK refusing to devalue. In this context, the Bundesbank became concerned about ERM rigidity and focused on the domestic economy. In September 1992 the lira and sterling were forced out of the ERM as speculators attacked currencies, while the peseta, escudo and punt were devalued in 1992–93.

1993–96. Pressure on the French franc led to the August 1993 decision to widen ERM bands by 15% for all but the Deutschmark and Dutch guilder. There was therefore a retreat to hard floating, but by 1994 many Member States were informally operating in narrow bands, although 15% bands were accepted as 'normal' for EMU purposes. The lira was readmitted in November 1996, while the peseta and escudo were devalued in 1995.

1996–. There was agreement at the Dublin Summit on ERM2 from 1999 for Member States not in the first wave of EMU ('pre-ins'), although membership will be voluntary. Central rates will be set in relation to the Euro, with wide normal bands but narrower bands for Member States closer to the EMU convergence criteria.

Economic and Monetary Union

The TEU prescribed a three-stage route to EMU:

1. Stage one started on 1 July 1990, involving the completion of the single market.
2. Stage two started on 1 January 1994, involving the creation of the European Monetary Institute (EMI) to administer the EMS, coordinate national monetary policy and monitor progress towards convergence. The independent EMI was provided with a commitment to price stability. It will be replaced in stage three by the ECB.
3. Stage three involves the irrevocable locking of exchange rates and the adoption of a single currency, with the ESCB and ECB to be responsible for monetary policy. Although the Treaty made provision for stage three to start on 1 January 1997 or 1998 if the Council decided (by QMV) that a majority of Member States met the 'convergence criteria', this proved impossible due to a lack of convergence among Member States' economies, as illustrated by the 1995 Cannes European Council's decision to rule out a 1997 start. Therefore, EMU commenced on 1 January 1999, as provided for in the Treaty.

Convergence criteria

Article 109j and Protocol 6 of the TEU established four convergence criteria for EMU:

1. A high degree of price stability, with an average rate of inflation of not more than 1.5% higher than that of the three best-performing Member States.
2. A sustainable financial position, including a budget deficit of not more than 3% of GDP and a public debt ratio not exceeding 60% of GDP.
3. Currency stability, with participation in the narrow bands of the ERM for two years without severe tension or devaluation.
4. Interest rate convergence, of which Member States should have an average nominal long-term interest rate not more than 2% higher than that of the three best-performing Member States.

The Treaty therefore provided some flexibility in deciding which Member States met the criteria. For instance, Member States could be accepted if they made 'progress' towards meeting budgetary targets and the Council took account of 'exceptional and temporary circumstances'. The actual process of EMU commenced on 1 January 1999, at which point exchange rates became conversion rates. Thereafter a four-year transition period provides for the maintenance of national currencies, although as units of the Euro. While financial markets started using the single currency in 1999, new coins and notes will not be in circulation until 2002. To ensure that Member States participating in the single currency adhere to strict economic guidelines, a Stability and Growth Pact was established for Euro-zone states. This provided the Council with the ability to impose sanctions on Member States with excessive deficits (above 3%) unless they were in recession (an annual GDP fall of at least 0.75%), while sanctions can take the form of non-interest bearing loans, followed by fines of 0.2% of GDP and one-tenth of excess deficit over the 3% reference value.

Chronology of EMU

27–28 June 1988. The Hanover European Council agreed to a proposal put forward by Jacques Delors for a new study on EMU, which was published on 12 April 1989.

26–27 June 1989. The UK established conditions at the Madrid European Council which would allow it to join the ERM. The UK joined the ERM on 8 October 1990 at a central rate against the Deutschmark of 2.95, with the pound being allowed to float at 6% either side of its central parity (the same rate as the Spanish peseta).

8–9 December 1989.   Agreement was reached at the Strasbourg European Council to assemble an intergovernmental conference to draw up a Treaty on Monetary Union on the basis of the Delors Report.

1 July 1990.   Stage one of EMU formally began. The Committee of Central Bank Governors was able to carry out the technical preparations for the Monetary Institute.

27–28 October 1990.   Agreement was reached at the Rome European Council that stage two of EMU would commence on 1 January 1994.

9–10 December 1991.   Agreement was reached at the Maastricht European Council on a Treaty on European Union, incorporating EPU and EMU agreements. It thereby established a timetable for their implementation. The agreement stressed that a single currency would be introduced by 1 January 1999 at the latest. The UK obtained an opt-out from the third stage of EMU.

16–17 September 1992.   UK interest rates were increased to 15% in an inadequate effort to combat financial speculation, resulting in it pulling out of the ERM, with the second interest rate rise cancelled. The EC's Monetary Committee also agreed to the temporary suspension of the Italian lira, and the Spanish peseta was devalued by 5%.

2 August 1993.   The ERM of the EMS effectively collapsed. Agreement was reached to allow currencies to fluctuate within a broad band of 15% either side of their central rates, rather than the 2.25% band for strong currencies or 6% for Spanish and Portuguese currencies.

1 January 1994.   Stage two of EMU began. The European Monetary Institute was established in Frankfurt as a precursor to a European Central Bank.

15–16 December 1995.   The Madrid European Council confirmed that the single European currency would be introduced from January 1999. The currency would be called the Euro.

13 December 1996.   The Dublin European Council reached agreement on the legal status of the Euro and currency discipline – the Stability and Growth Pact. Financial penalties would apply to all Member States running a GDP deficit (negative growth) of up to 0.75%; EU Finance Ministers would be able to exercise discretion in applying penalties if a Member State's GDP falls between 0.75% and 2%; Member States which run an excessive deficit would automatically be exempt from penalties if GDP was at least 2% over one year, or in the event of a natural disaster.

5–6 April 1997.   The Noordwijk Finance Ministers' meeting established agreement on an outline timetable for EMU, and endorsement of the single currency stability pact. Agreement was reached that a special European Council would be held in May 1998 with the task of deciding which countries met the economic criteria for joining EMU. Central Bank Governors had pushed for the decision on EMU eligibility to be taken at an earlier stage, which would allow more time for southern

European states, such as Italy and Spain, to make the criteria. Thus, there would be only eight months for those countries which did not meet the criteria to prepare for the launch of a single currency on 1 January 1999.

27 February 1998. Member States filed their 1997 statistical reports to decide whether they would be able to participate in the single currency. All, except Greece, met the convergence criteria, although a strict application meant that only Finland, France, Luxembourg and the UK met the debt criteria. Belgium and Italy registered debt in excess of twice the level required (the target was no more than 60% of GDP). The TEU provided flexibility by referring to a 'reference value' of 60% of GDP which should be achieved 'unless the ratio was sufficiently diminishing and approaching the reference value at a satisfactory pace'. Some countries imposed significant changes in economic policy: Italy imposed a special one-off Euro tax and Germany discounted large amounts of hospital debt from its budget deficit.

25 March 1998. The European Commission recommended that 11 Member States adopt the single currency from 1 January 1999: Austria, Belgium, Finland, France, Germany, Ireland, Italy, Luxembourg, the Netherlands, Portugal and Spain. Denmark, Sweden and the UK opted-out of joining the Euro in the first wave, and Greece was not considered to have met the required criteria. A further report by the European Monetary Institute stressed that Belgium and Italy had not made sufficient progress in reducing their debt ratios.

2–3 May 1998. The Brussels EMU Council decided that 11 of the 15 EU Member States were deemed to have qualified to adopt the single currency on 1 January 1999, namely Austria, Belgium, Finland, France, Germany, Ireland, Italy, Luxembourg, the Netherlands, Portugal and Spain.

5. Single Market Policy

Treaty basis

Treaty of Rome (European Community Treaty) fundamental provisions: Preamble and Articles 2 (part of Community objectives) and 3 (among Community policies and actions), Article 7a (definition), Articles 8a, 48 ff. (free movement of persons), 30 ff. (free movement of goods), 59 ff. (freedom to provide services), and 52 ff. (freedom of establishment), Articles 67–73b ff. (free movement of capital). Main legal bases for secondary legislation relating to these five freedoms: Articles 8a, 54(2), 57(2), 66, 73c, 75, 99, 100, 100a, 100b and 100c.

Institutional dynamics

All draft legislation is proposed by the European Commission, which has the additional task of monitoring and coordinating the implementation of EU legislation within Member States, and can also enforce policy through the European Court of Justice. The European Parliament (EP) shares with the Council the ability to amend and reject legislative proposals made by the European Commission in certain policy areas. Thus, the Council of Ministers legislates with the EP on the basis of the European Commission's proposals, with decisions being able to be taken by qualified majority voting (QMV) in certain areas, though in others, such as taxation, unanimity is required.

Overview

The single market emerged from the publication of the European Commission's White Paper on completing the internal market in 1985, under the authorship of UK Commissioner Lord Cockfield. The White Paper listed 282 items of European legislation which would result in the harmonisation of national laws, being based upon the four freedoms of people, goods, services and capital. The single market allows EU citizens to live, work and study in another Member State, while partnerships and alliances have been created not just between companies across national borders, but also between universities. The direct benefit to companies of the single market is that they are able to obtain lower transport costs through the abolition of formalities on the free movement of goods at national border crossings. Such benefits extend beyond the areas covered by the harmonisation of national laws as the principle of mutual recognition ensures that Member States have to recognise each other's national rules and regulations.

Reform

The European Commission has recently placed a great deal of emphasis on the single market because while the overwhelming majority (90%) of measures have been implemented at the national level, there has been particularly slow progress with regard to the rules on the open and competitive procurement of goods and services by public authorities and utilities. The difficulties associated with making the single market work principally relate to differences between Member States over the application of EU laws, thereby creating barriers to trade. As a response, the European Commission has increased its focus on streamlining the legislative framework, ensuring national implementation of legislation, providing increased consumer protection in the realm of consumer disputes, while improving the environmental and social aspects of the single market. These areas are especially relevant to the concept of citizenship. Finally, emphasis has been attached to ensure that the single market is able to adapt to future changes to the EU, notably regarding enlargement, trans-European networks and the utilisation of information technology.

SECTION VI

Europe and the Wider World

1. Common Foreign and Security Policy

Treaty basis

Titles I and V (Articles J.1 to J.11) of the Treaty on European Union (TEU).

Institutional dynamics

The placement of CFSP in pillar two of the TEU meant cooperation followed an intergovernmental structure and is accordingly different from other external policies, such as external economic relations. The European Council and the Council of Ministers have overall control, with the former defining the principles and general guidelines for CFSP, while all decisions are taken in the latter on a unanimous basis, apart from certain aspects of joint actions. Member States' Political Directors examine international developments covered by CFSP in meetings of the Political Committee. They also produce policy recommendations and opinions on their own initiative or at the request of the Council. The European Commission is 'fully associated' in all negotiations, has the ability to make proposals, and has a right of initiative (but not the sole right of initiative). The European Commission's CFSP position is coordinated by Directorate-General IA, though all external relations services are involved. The European Parliament can only be consulted by the Presidency and has no direct powers. A special colloquium is held four times a year by the European Parliament's Committee on Foreign Affairs, Security and Defence Policy and the Presidency. The European Parliament's bureau also meets with the chairman of the Political Committee, who is the Political Director of the Member State holding the Presidency.

Objectives

1. To safeguard the common values, fundamental interests and independence of the Union.
2. To strengthen the security of the Union and its Member States in all ways.
3. To preserve peace and strengthen international security, in accordance with the principles of the United Nations Charter as well as the principles of the Helsinki Final Act and the objectives of the Paris Charter.
4. To promote international cooperation.
5. To develop and consolidate democracy and the rule of law and respect for human rights.

Overview

The objective of 'the implementation of a common foreign and security policy including the eventual framing of a common defence policy' was established in the TEU that was negotiated in December 1991 at the Maastricht European Council, signed in February 1992 and came into force in November 1993. This represented a significant development on the process of European Political Cooperation (EPC) which was launched in 1970 and resulted in Member States consulting each other on external political relations. EPC was specifically expanded upon by the creation of 'joint actions' and 'common positions', which represented a significant attempt to create a united identity in the international environment.

Common positions

The creation of a common position must result in Member States adopting a national policy in line with its objectives. Examples include a broad framework approach for the EU's relations with Burundi, Rwanda and Ukraine.

Joint actions

This commits a Member State to adopt policies that reflect a common position. Examples include the administration of the town of Mostar in the former Yugoslavia with policing supplied by the Western European Union, the creation of a convoy of humanitarian aid in Bosnia-Herzegovina, and sending observers to parliamentary elections in Russia, South Africa and the Middle East. A joint action produced the 1994 Stability Pact for Central Europe.

2.   Development Policy

Treaty basis

Articles 43, 113 (trade), 130u–y (development cooperation), 238 (association agreements) of the Treaty establishing the European Community, as amended by the Treaty on European Union.

Institutional dynamics

International aid and development agreements are adopted by the Council of Ministers (in some cases by qualified majority) and generally require the assent of the European Parliament. The European Commission proposes legislation and policy initiatives, negotiates international agreements, manages policies and programmes, and participates in the decision-making of the ACP–EU Council of Ministers and the Committee of Ambassadors. The Lomé Convention and some specific programmes are managed by DG VIII, while the Mediterranean countries, Latin America and Asia are the responsibility of DG IA and I, with humanitarian aid being coordinated by the European Community Humanitarian Office (ECHO). The EU's overseas aid budget is some £2.7 billion (1998), of which the UK contributes £530 million.

Overview

The European Commission's European Office for Emergency Humanitarian Aid (ECHO) was established in 1992 to provide emergency humanitarian aid such as food and medicine. It supplies free assistance to all countries outside the EU suffering from conflicts or disasters, with aid being directly targeted at people in distress. In this context, over 80% of the humanitarian projects are carried out in partnership with specialised organisations like the United Nations, assisting such countries as Afghanistan, Armenia, Azerbaijan, Tajikistan and the former Yugoslavia. The EU and its Member States play an important role in providing aid and development to the 'South' or 'Third World', amounting to some 4 billion ECU a year. EU aid and development takes two forms: (1) regional agreements; and (2) action throughout the world, including financial and technical aid, trade agreements with Asian and Latin American countries, and the system of generalised tariff preferences. The EU's role also extends to providing a market for the exports of developing countries (of which the 70 African, Caribbean and Pacific (ACP) countries obtain preferential terms of access), while also attempting to ensure the provision of democratic government and the erosion of poverty in the countries with which it has a relationship. Contacts have expanded from the 18 countries with which the Community co-operated in the 1960s, whose members almost exclusively came from the former colonies of Belgium, France, the Netherlands and Italy. The accession of the UK in 1973 and Portugal and Spain in 1986 clearly widened the number of links with former colonies, of which the Lomé Convention embraces some 70 ACP countries. Recent funding for the ACP states has come from the European Investment Bank, which granted 406 million ECU in loans in 1994, of which 199 million ECU came from budgetary resources. This covered projects such as the restoration of an oil pipeline between Mombassa and Nairobi in Kenya.

The Lomé Convention

This is the most important regional agreement, the first of which was signed in 1975 and the latest, Lomé IV, came into existence in 1991 for a ten-year period with a mid-term review having taken place in 1995. The Convention provides the 70 ACP states with free access to EU markets for industrial products, while ensuring they receive stable export earnings from products such as coffee and rubber. The Convention also covers the European Development Fund, the Centre for Industrial Development, a Technical Centre for Agricultural and Rural Cooperation, and contains a reference to human rights. A total of 12 billion ECU was devoted to the fourth Lomé Convention from 1990 to 1995, focusing on financing programmes rather than individual projects, and with particular attention directed to agriculture and rural development. A total of 14.6 billion ECU has been made available for the period between 1995 and 2000, accounting for some 55% of all EU aid, and being financed by Member States' contributions to the European Development Fund. This review placed emphasis on developing the competitiveness and trade of the ACP nations and maintaining democracy, the rule of law and good governance.

The 70 ACP states

Angola, Antigua and Barbuda, Bahamas, Barbados, Belize, Benin, Botswana, Burkina Faso, Burundi, Cameroon, Cape Verde, Central African Republic, Chad, Comoros, Congo, Côte d'Ivoire, Djibouti, Dominica, Dominican Republic, Equatorial Guinea, Eritrea, Ethiopia, Fiji, Gabon, Gambia, Ghana, Grenada, Guinea, Guinea-Bissau, Guyana, Haiti, Jamaica, Kenya, Kiribati, Lesotho, Liberia, Madagascar, Malawi, Mali, Mauritania, Mauritius, Mozambique, Namibia, Niger, Nigeria, Papua New Guinea, Rwanda, St Kitts and Nevis, St Lucia, St Vincent and the Grenadines, São Tomé and Príncipe, Senegal, Seychelles, Sierra Leone, Solomon Islands, Somalia, Sudan, Surinam, Swaziland, Tanzania, Togo, Tonga, Trinidad and Tobago, Tuvalu, Uganda, Vanuatu, Western Samoa, Zaire, Zambia, Zimbabwe.

Central and Eastern Europe

The EU has played a crucial role in this area since turbulence in Eastern Europe commenced in 1989. Finance is provided by the European Bank for Reconstruction and Development (EBRD) for infrastructural and industrial projects. The EU has been particularly concerned with:

- granting customs preferences to the countries concerned;
- association treaties with Central and East European countries – Europe Agreements;
- providing loan and credit mechanisms;
- aid and cooperation programmes such as PHARE and TACIS which finance technical assistance projects.

The PHARE programme embraces: Albania, Bulgaria, the Czech Republic, Estonia, Hungary, Latvia, Lithuania, Poland, Romania, Slovakia, Slovenia. The programme has provided upwards of 25% aid of the total cost for direct investment in infrastructure and public sector undertakings, while assistance has also been given to restructure agriculture and banking and insurance industries. The European Investment Bank provides finance to any country covered by the PHARE programme, with funds having been mainly aimed towards the rehabilitation of major communications infrastructure systems or the restructuring of undertakings. By contrast, the TACIS programme provides technical assistance for economic reforms in the countries of the former Soviet Union (Armenia, Azerbaijan, Belarus, Georgia, Kazakhstan, Kyrgyzstan, Moldova, Russia, Tajikistan, Turkmenistan, Ukraine and Uzbekistan) and Mongolia, being primarily concerned with providing foundations for the transition to democracy and a market economy.

Both the PHARE and TACIS programmes encourage exchanges between universities and schools (TEMPUS) and promote joint ventures (JOPP). The TEMPUS programme has been primarily based on the ERASMUS, COMETT and Lingua programmes, and has concentrated in assisting students of applied economics, agriculture and agricultural economics, applied science, technology and engineering, business management, environmental protection, and modern European languages. The aim of JOPP is to establish joint ventures between EU economic interests and those based in Central and Eastern Europe (the countries eligible under the PHARE programme).

Europe and the Mediterranean

The Mediterranean countries are the EU's third-largest trading partner, after EFTA and the USA. Their importance has been illustrated since 1991 by the replacement of individual bilateral agreements with an overall 'new Mediterranean policy', which covers a region with over 210 million people from the Maghreb (Algeria, Morocco and Tunisia), Mashreq (Egypt, Jordan, Lebanon, Syria and the Palestinian territories), Israel, Cyprus, Malta and Turkey. The new Mediterranean programme aims, in the first instance, to strengthen cohesion and develop economic ties between the EU and the Mediterranean countries, and secondly to promote cooperation between these countries and their regional integration. In addition, the European Commission has proposed the creation of a Euro–Mediterranean free trade area by the year 2010, covering between 30 and 40 countries with a population of between 600 and 800 million, with the possible subsequent development of a Euro–Mediterranean Economic Area.

The three primary elements of the EU's policy with these countries are:

1. The promotion of trade to ensure free access for manufactured goods from these countries to the European market and the liberalisation for agricultural imports.
2. Increased cooperation in such sectors as agriculture, industry, research, the environment, fisheries, energy, and the support for democracy and human rights.
3. Financial support in the form of grants from the EU European Investment Bank (EIB), including some 607 million ECU in 1994, of which 210 million ECU went to the horizontal financial component for interregional cooperation operations and environmental projects.

The main instruments of the new Mediterranean policy are financial protocols and cooperation involving all Mediterranean countries, referred to as horizontal cooperation. Financial protocols determine EU contributions made to capital investment projects. The fourth Financial Protocol was signed in 1992. Worth some 2,375 million ECU, it was signed with eight Mediterranean countries: Algeria, Egypt, Israel, Jordan, Lebanon, Morocco, Syria and Tunisia. Its primary objectives were the development of the agricultural sector, support for small businesses and the protection of the environment, with DG IA of the European Commission having the responsibility for administering the programmes. In contrast to such bilateral initiatives, horizontal cooperation represents EU funding for projects covering several European and Mediterranean countries. This embraces the environment, the development of Mediterranean firms (including partnerships with European Union firms) and regional operations for transport, energy or telecommunications. Emphasis has also been attached to decentralised programmes, including MED-Invest (development of small businesses), MED-URBS (cooperation between local authorities), MED-Campus (cooperation between universities), MED-Avicenne (research) and MED-Media (media cooperation).

EU partnership and development aid in Latin America and Asia

EU involvement in Latin America and Asia has been strengthened by the consolidation of the rule of law in Latin America and the economic boom in Asia, although the latter has encountered economic difficulties since 1996. The overall situation has, however, resulted in some 21 Asian countries benefiting from EU programmes, namely: Afghanistan, Bangladesh, Bhutan, Brunei, Burma, Cambodia, China, India, Indonesia, Laos, Macao, Malaysia, Maldives, Mongolia (eligible only for the TACIS programme since 1993), Nepal, Pakistan, Philippines, Singapore, Sri

Lanka, Thailand, Vietnam. The 18 Latin American countries that benefit from EU programmes are: Argentina, Bolivia, Brazil, Chile, Colombia, Costa Rica, Cuba, Ecuador, El Salvador, Guatemala, Honduras, Mexico, Nicaragua, Panama, Paraguay, Peru, Uruguay, Venezuela.

For both regions, the EU attaches emphasis to the development of the least-advanced countries and the promotion of European investment, especially in the more developed countries. This takes the form of advancing trade, economic cooperation, political dialogue, technical assistance, sectoral actions such as an energy programme with ASEAN, cooperation between universities and exchanges on entrepreneurship, food aid for the poorest countries and access to humanitarian aid funds.

On 9 November 1998 Mexico and the European Union commenced week-long trade negotiations with the aim of forging the first free trade agreement between Europe and a Latin American country. The main bargaining over the scale and speed of cutting 14,000 tariffs is not expected to start until 1999. The EU is Mexico's second largest trading partner after the US, although two-way trade has declined since Mexico entered NAFTA.

SECTION VII

Summits

1.   Bremen: 6–7 July 1978

International issues: International trade, relations with developing countries, Africa, Middle East, Lebanon.
Community policies: EMS, ECU, common market, economic policy, employment, energy, Mediterranean agriculture.
Overview: The main item on the agenda of the eleventh meeting of the European Council, chaired by Helmut Schmidt, was a joint Franco-German proposal to create a system of closer monetary cooperation between Member States which would lead to a 'zone of monetary stability in Europe', the introduction of the European Currency Unit (ECU) as the monetary unit of the Community, with the new arrangement being termed the European Monetary System (EMS). The meeting concluded that such a zone was a 'highly desirable objective'. The Council 'agreed to instruct the Finance Ministers at their meeting on July 24, 1978, to formulate the necessary guidelines for the competent Community bodies to elaborate by Oct. 31, 1978, the provisions necessary for the functioning of such a scheme'. This was to be done with the view to decisions being taken and commitments being made at the Brussels European Council in December 1978.

2.   Brussels: 4–5 December 1978

Institutional issues: The meeting appointed three eminent individuals to examine ways of making the institutions of the EU more effective and progress towards European Union. This became commonly known as the Committee of the Three Wise Men.
Community policies: EMS, ECU, Tripartite conference, convergence of economic policies, salaries for Members of the European Parliament.
Overview: In the wake of the July 1978 Bremen European Council, proposals relating to the EMS were examined by Finance Ministers and other Community bodies. The Brussels meeting resulted in the adoption of a resolution which stated that the EMS would be established from 1 January 1979. Only six of the nine Member States agreed to participate from the outset in all aspects of the system: Belgium, Denmark, France, Germany, Luxembourg and the Netherlands. The UK noted that it was not willing to participate in the ERM, but expressed a wish to participate in other aspects. Both Ireland and Italy adopted a reserved position after they were unsuccessful in obtaining sufficient commitments of intra-Community transfer resources which would allow them to take part in the ERM. The European Council appointed a three-man committee to produce a report on possible revisions to the institutional structure of the Community, especially with regard to the future accession of Greece, Portugal and Spain. The committee, which had been proposed

by President Giscard d'Estaing of France, consisted of Edmund Dell (former UK Secretary for Trade), Barend Biesheuvel (Prime Minister of the Netherlands, 1971–73) and Robert Marjolin (Vice-President of the European Commission, 1958–67).

3.   Paris: 12–13 March 1979

Community policies: Employment policy, energy, economic and social cohesion, ERM.

Overview: The communiqué of the meeting noted that 'all the conditions had now been met for the implementation of the exchange mechanism of the European monetary system as defined at the previous meeting of the Council on Dec. 4–5, 1978'. It accordingly 'resolved to implement it from Tuesday, March 13, 1979, as soon as the exchange markets opened'. This decision applied to eight of the nine Member States: Belgium, Denmark, France, Germany, Ireland, Italy, Luxembourg and the Netherlands. The UK Prime Minister, James Callaghan, noted that sterling would not participate.

4.   Strasbourg: 21–22 June 1979

Institutional issues: EP elections.

International issues: Japan and Indochina.

Community policies: EMS, energy, employment, convergence of economic policies, budget and budgetary correcting mechanism, own resources.

Overview: The 14th meeting of the European Council took place shortly after the completion of the first direct elections to the European Parliament on 7–10 June 1979. The Strasbourg meeting noted the progress made within the EMS and emphasised that there should be a greater convergence of the economies of Member States. In this connection, the new UK Prime Minister, Margaret Thatcher, stressed that efforts should be made to reduce the UK's net contribution to the Community budget. The UK Treasury estimated that this would amount to £1,000 million in 1979 and £1,200 million in 1980.

5.   Dublin: 29–30 November 1979

Institutional issues: Committee of Wise Men.

International issues: Iran, Kampuchea, Afghanistan, Middle East.

Community policies: Economic and social cohesion, energy, EMS, budget and budgetary correcting mechanism.

Overview: The UK's claims for a reduction in its budget contribution to the Community were discussed at the 15th meeting of the European Council, being based on proposals presented by the European Commission. However, the UK government rejected all formulas which were presented because they contained no financial guarantees beyond 1980. An agreement was, however, subsequently obtained at the Brussels Foreign Ministers' meeting on 29–30 May 1980.

6.   Stuttgart: 17–19 June 1983

Institutional issues: European Political Cooperation, enlargement, European Union (solemn declaration).
International issues: Poland, CSCE, UNCTAD VI, Central America, Middle East.
Community policies: Agriculture, environment, iron and steel industry, transport, internal market, employment, new technologies (ESPRIT), Integrated Mediterranean Programmes (IMPs), own resources, budgetary discipline, compensation for the UK.
Overview: The 26th meeting of the European Council resulted in Member States agreeing a comprehensive working programme of negotiations on the future of the Community. This revolved around the issue of financial resources, with attention given to the possible restructuring of the CAP. Agreement was also achieved on the question of the UK budgetary dispute, it being decided to include 750,000,000 ECUs in the 1984 draft budget for the purpose of the 1983 UK rebate. More significantly, Heads of State and Government signed a 'solemn declaration on European Union' which outlined possibilities for increased cooperation and development within and between the Council, the European Parliament, the European Commission and the Court of Justice.

7.   Fontainebleau: 25–26 June 1984

Institutional issues: Creation of Ad hoc Committee on Institutional Affairs (Dooge Committee).
Community policies: Fisheries, monetary compensatory amounts, wine market, social action programme, transport, VAT, budgetary and financial discipline, own resources, the UK's contribution to the budget, creation of Ad hoc Committee on a People's Europe (Adonnino Committee).
Overview: The 29th meeting of the European Council produced agreement on a 1984 budgetary rebate for the UK, thereby ensuring that focus could be switched to other Community policy areas. Thus, agreements were adopted on budgetary and financial discipline and the structural funds. Regarding the settlement of the UK budget dispute, Member States noted that '. . . the following arrangement is adopted: (i) for 1984, a lump sum of 1,000 million ECU is fixed; (ii) from 1985 the "gap" . . . [is] corrected annually at 66%'. Otherwise, the European Council decided to establish an ad hoc committee on Institutional Affairs

to make suggestions to improve the functioning of European cooperation within the Community.

8.   Milan: 28–29 June 1985

Institutional issues: Adoption of Dooge Committee report, intergovern-
mental conference on amending the Treaties.
International issues: Japan, COMECON, famine in Africa.
Community policies: VAT, investment, employment, EMS, industrial
strategy, technological cooperation (EUREKA), internal market (White
Paper), ECU.
Overview: The 32nd European Council focused on the reform of the
European Communities, with negotiations having been concluded in
March 1985 on the accession of Portugal and Spain. Particular attention
was directed towards improving the method of decision-making within
the Community. This resulted in the six original members of the Community, plus Ireland, voting in favour of an intergovernmental conference
on reform. By contrast, Denmark, Greece and the UK opposed the vote,
but agreed to attend the conference which was scheduled to commence
on 9 September 1985.

9.   Luxembourg: 2–3 December 1985

Institutional issues: Single European Act, EEC Commission (management
and implementing powers), European Parliament (cooperation procedure),
European Political Cooperation.
International issues: GATT.
Community policies: Integrated Mediterranean Programmes, EMS,
health (programme of action against cancer), internal market (measures for progressive establishment of), EMU, research and technological
development, environment, social policy, economic and social cohesion.
Overview: The 33rd European Council meeting reached agreement
on a document to revise the Treaty of Rome, although subject to further
approval by Foreign Ministers on 16 December 1985. This thereby concluded the intergovernmental conference negotiations which had commenced on 9 September 1985. The areas of reform included the setting
of a deadline of 31 December 1992 for the establishment of an internal
market; the further development of economic and social cohesion; the
introduction of the cooperation procedure for the decision-making of
the European Parliament; and the improvement of policy areas within
the social field, including the working environment regarding the health
and safety of workers. Moreover, reference was made to 'the objective of
the progressive achievement of economic and monetary union', an area
which had been originally opposed by Germany and the UK.

10. Hanover: 27–28 June 1988

Institutional issues: SEA (inter-institutional agreement), Presidency of the EEC Commission.

Community policies: Completion of the internal market, declaration on the environment, EMU Committee of Experts, social affairs – labour/employment/training, free movement of persons.

Overview: Member States confirmed the objective of the progressive realisation of EMU and decided to examine at the June 1989 Madrid European Council the means to achieve it. A committee chaired by the President of the European Commission, Jacques Delors, was entrusted with the task of examining and proposing stages towards EMU. Member States agreed that their Central Bank Governors would participate in the committee in a personal capacity, while it would also include a further member of the European Commission and three specialists. The committee was set the objective of compiling its report before the Madrid European Council meeting.

11. Madrid: 26–27 June 1989

Institutional issues: Implementation of the SEA, conference on amending the Treaties of Rome (EMU).

International issues: CSCE, declarations on Middle East, Cyprus, Latin America, declaration on China, EFTA, Eastern Europe, Poland, Hungary, USA, the Uruguay Round (GATT), the European Guarantee Fund (EGF) – creation of a fund for operations to reduce the payment and level of the foreign debt of heavily indebted countries: Latin America, North Africa, Far East and Eastern Europe.

Community policies: Completion of the internal market, new ACP–EEC convention, EMU, Community Charter of Fundamental Social Rights, economic and social cohesion, social affairs – labour/employment/training, free movement of persons.

Overview: The European Council reached agreement on four main issues, the first of which was a reassertion of the desire to achieve EMU, which was to be placed in the perspective of completing the Internal Market and the context of economic and social cohesion. Secondly, the meeting examined the Delors Report on EMU and noted that its objectives would have to take into consideration the principle of parallelism between economic and monetary issues. Thirdly, agreement was reached that the first stage of EMU would commence on 1 July 1990. Finally, the European Council asked the EcoFin and General Affairs Councils, the European Commission, the Committee of Central Bank Governors and the Monetary Committee to adopt the necessary provisions to allow the first stage of EMU to commence. These bodies were additionally entrusted with the task of conducting the preparatory work regarding the construction of an intergovernmental conference to examine the further development of EMU.

12.   Strasbourg: 8–9 December 1989

Institutional issues: Implementation of the SEA, intergovernmental conference on amending the Treaties of Rome (EMU).

International issues: EFTA, declaration on Central and Eastern Europe, creation of EBRD.

Community policies: Completion of the internal market, research framework programme for 1990–94, adoption of Community Charter of Fundamental Social Rights, new ACP–EEC convention, economic and social cohesion, EMU, report from the coordinators' group on the free movement of persons.

Overview: Member States also declared the EC to be the 'cornerstone of a new European architecture . . . at this time of profound and rapid change' in Central and Eastern Europe, which included the first joint declaration on German reunification. The President of the European Council confirmed that a majority (not the UK) existed for convening an intergovernmental conference to examine EMU, as provided for in Article 236 of the Treaty. The UK appeared to adopt a less isolationist position at Strasbourg, although the government opposed the calling of the IGC and the agreement by the other 11 Member States on the Community Charter of the Fundamental Social Rights of Workers.

13.   Dublin: 28 April 1990

Institutional issues: Intergovernmental conference on amending the Treaties of Rome (EMU).

International issues: EBRD, Central and Eastern Europe, CSCE, Cyprus, the USA, EFTA.

Community policies: EMU, external relations.

Overview: The European Council reached agreement that the Community would establish an EMU in stages and in accordance with the principles of economic and social cohesion. It noted that the intergovernmental conference would open in December 1990 and that its work should be convened rapidly to provide the opportunity for Member States to ratify the final agreement by the end of 1992. The European Council additionally agreed to a declaration on German reunification.

14.   Dublin: 25–26 June 1990

Institutional issues: Report on progress of SEA, renewal of Commission's mandate, seat of the institutions, intergovernmental conferences on amending the Treaties of Rome (EMU and Political Union).

International issues: Central and Eastern Europe, CSCE, the USSR, declaration on South Africa, declaration on Middle East, declaration on Cyprus, GATT Uruguay Round, declaration on the non-proliferation treaty. **Community policies:** Internal market, framework programme for research for 1990–94, EMU, external relations, free movement of persons, the social dimension.

Overview: The European Council paid principal attention to emphasising that the first stage of EMU, which commenced on 1 July 1990, should be used as a means of ensuring convergence in Member States' economic performance, to propel cohesion and to further the usage of the ECU. The meeting also agreed to establish a second intergovernmental conference which would examine Political Union and run in parallel to the negotiations on EMU.

15. Rome: 27–28 October 1990

Institutional issues: IGCs on EPU and EMU.
Community issues: EMU.
International issues: Relations with the Soviet Union and the countries of Central and Eastern Europe, the Gulf crisis.

Overview: Eleven Member States (not the UK) agreed at the European Council that the intergovernmental conference negotiations on EMU would be primarily directed towards the attainment of two objectives. The first concerned Economic Union and involved an open market system combining growth and price stability, employment and environmental protection. Policies would be aimed at obtaining sustainable financial and budgetary conditions and to economic and social cohesion, thereby requiring a strengthening of the Community's institutions. The second aspect concerned Monetary Union and was directed towards the creation of a new monetary institution, consisting of Member States' central banks, which would have responsibility for monetary policy. The meeting further reached agreement that the second stage of EMU would commence on 1 January 1994. This would take place after the completion of the single market and the ratification of the Treaty. The UK expressed reservations at certain points on the IGC on Political Union, including an extension of the Council's powers, an extension of the European Parliament's powers, the definition of citizenship and development of a security policy. This was because the UK government did not want to pre-empt the debate in the IGC on these points.

16. Rome: 14–15 December 1990

Institutional issues: Political Union, intergovernmental conference on amending the Treaties of Rome (EMU and Political Union).

International issues: Declaration on South Africa, declaration on the Gulf crisis, declaration on the Middle East, Central and Eastern Europe, EFTA, drugs, GATT, the USA, the Mediterranean countries.
Community policies: Internal market, EMU, transport, social dimension, free movement of persons.
Overview: The European Council established a broad framework for the negotiations on the parallel IGCs on EMU and Political Union, which were formally opened by the Council on 15 December. One week before the summit, Chancellor Kohl of Germany and President Mitterrand of France addressed a joint open letter to their Community colleagues that contained proposals for Political Union, especially in the field of foreign and defence policy. Regarding discussions on EMU, the European Commission had already established a Draft Treaty, although the UK government declared that it would advance its own proposals in January 1991. On Political Union, the key issues surrounded the strengthening of the European Parliament's powers and the introduction of a concept of citizenship. With respect to the Gulf crisis, the Community and its Member States declared their commitment to the full implementation of the UN Security Council resolutions.

17.   Maastricht: 9–10 December 1991

Institutional issues: Treaty on European Union.
Overview: The European Council reached agreement on the Draft Treaty on European Union based on the texts concerning Political Union and Economic and Monetary Union. The UK obtained an opt-out from the third stage of EMU, which established a deadline of 1999 for the introduction of a single currency. Equally, the UK did not commit itself to the objectives provided for in the 1989 Social Charter. It was therefore decided to annex to the Treaty a Protocol on social policy that committed the Community's institutions to take and implement the decisions of the 11 Member States. The TEU agreement provided for intergovernmental cooperation in the fields of common foreign and security policy and justice and home affairs. This meant that the European Commission, the European Parliament and the Court of Justice had no direct role in these policy areas, thereby ensuring national control. A chapter on citizenship was introduced to the Treaty while Article 3b emphasised the principle of subsidiarity. A further development was the granting of increased powers to the European Parliament through the co-decision procedure.

18.   Edinburgh: 11–12 December 1992

Institutional issues: Ratification of TEU, subsidiarity, openness and transparency, enlargement.

Community policies: Future financing of the Community – Delors package.

Overview: The European Council meeting solved the TEU ratification crisis which had begun with the 'no' vote in the Danish referendum of June 1992. Regarding the Danish problem, Member States approved a clear definition of subsidiarity whereby 'it aims at decisions within the European Union being taken as closely as possible to the citizen'. Denmark was granted exemption from citizenship of the Union, the introduction of a single European currency, defence policy cooperation, and cooperation on justice and home affairs. The European Council also produced agreement on the future financing of the Community, known as the 'Delors package'. A major part of this was an agreement to increase support to southern members of the Community, a development particularly advocated by Spain.

19. Corfu: 24–25 June 1994

Institutional issues: Preparation for the IGC, enlargement.
International issues: Partnership accords with Russia and Ukraine.
Community policies: Appointment of the President of the European Commission.

Overview: The European Council meeting was dominated by the failure of Member States to agree on the appointment of the President of the European Commission for a five-year term of office from 1 January 1995. This meant that an emergency summit was scheduled for 15 July 1994 to resolve the dispute. That the dispute arose was because the UK Prime Minister, John Major, blocked the candidacy of the Belgian Prime Minister, Jean-Luc Dehaene, complaining that his appointment had arisen from a Franco-German proposal and was not representative of the wishes of the wider Member States. Major used his veto despite the withdrawal of Dehaene's main competitor, the Dutch Prime Minister, Ruud Lubbers, and of the other candidate, the UK European Commissioner, Sir Leon Brittan. Clearly, this episode represented an attempt by Major to check the Franco-German entente and was also a means of obtaining support from a hostile Parliamentary Party which was increasingly Euro-sceptic. But despite the lack of progress on this issue, the European Council reached agreement on partnership accords with Russia and Ukraine, with a central element of the latter being assistance with the closure of the remaining nuclear reactors at Chernobyl. An additional feature of the meeting was enlargement, with the Prime Ministers of Austria, Finland, Norway and Sweden signing their country's treaties of accession to the EU on 24 June. The European Council also approved 11 trans-European transport links.

20.   Brussels: 15 July 1994

Community policies: Election of the President of the European Commission.

Overview: The extraordinary European Council reached agreement on the election of the Luxembourg Prime Minister, Jacques Santer, as President of the Commission from January 1995, thereby succeeding Jacques Delors. Santer's election was a compromise after the UK Prime Minister, John Major, vetoed the candidacy of the Belgian Prime Minister, Jean-Luc Dehaene, at the Corfu European Council in June.

21.   Florence: 21–22 June 1996

Institutional issues: Analysis of the first three months of the IGC to revise the TEU.

Community policies: Export of British beef, EMU, European Commission President Jacques Santer's confidence pact on measures to promote employment and infrastructure development, Europol.

Overview: The UK adopted a policy of non-cooperation in May 1996 after the EU implemented a ban on UK beef exports in March 1996 as a result of the BSE crisis – the UK used its veto on more than 70 occasions over a four-week period. A compromise was reached at the Florence European Council whereby a more extensive slaughter programme was required than the UK's initial plan of 11 June. This meant that 147,000 rather than 80,000 cattle would have to be killed. However, no dates were set for when UK exports of beef and cattle could resume. It was agreed that animals over 30 months old would be destroyed at the end of their working lives, while the UK would have to report every two weeks to the European Commission, introduce procedures for identifying cattle and recording their movements, introduce legislation to ensure the removal from farms and feed mills of all meal and bone meal, and introduce improvements in the handling of carcasses. The agreement of these procedures on the first day of the European Council meeting meant that the beef crisis did not dominate the summit meeting. It also helped to appease the UK government, which hoped that a ban on the export of beef would be lifted by the end of November 1996. The European Council subsequently examined EMU, with participants reaffirming their intention to progress to the third stage by the start of 1999. Agreement was reached at the summit on the creation of the Europol police intelligence agency, although the UK retained the right to opt-out over the European Court of Justice's ability to have jurisdiction over the management and use of data gathered by the agency in work conducted on combating crime and drug trafficking.

22.   Amsterdam: 16–17 June 1997

Institutional issues: Amsterdam Treaty, completion of the IGC to revise the TEU.

Overview: The most significant aspect of the agreement was the inclusion of a chapter on employment in the Treaty. This was primarily a response to French demands. It was also agreed that the Social Chapter would be integrated into the Treaty following the UK's decision to sign; that judicial and police cooperation should remain matters for national governments (although Europol was provided with an operational role); that immigration, civil and judicial cooperation, visa policy, political asylum and the harmonisation of divorce laws would become common policies; that there would be a guarantee of free movement of persons throughout the EU (although Ireland and the UK retained national border controls); and that there would be a common foreign and security policy, with common strategies defined by unanimous decisions, and with the secretary general of the Council to represent EU foreign policy to the outside world rather than a politician from a Member State. Further agreement was reached on the stability pact to enforce budgetary discipline on the participating states after the introduction of the single currency, while the European Parliament was provided with more powers and a simplified co-decision procedure. However, Member States failed to resolve important institutional issues in advance of future EU expansion, there being agreement in principle that the European Commission should only have 20 members after enlargement, with one member per state.

23.   Luxembourg: 12–13 December 1997

Institutional issues: Enlargement.

Overview: EU leaders invited six countries to commence membership talks in early 1998. On 13 December the summit issued formal invitations to the Czech Republic, Estonia, Hungary, Poland, Slovenia and Cyprus to open negotiation in March 1998 with a view to obtaining entry early in the next century. European leaders also reached agreement that admission talks with the five other Eastern European applicant nations (Bulgaria, Latvia, Lithuania, Romania and Slovakia) would continue, although it was made clear that these nations would not take part in the first wave of enlargement. The exclusion of Turkey from both groups, in tandem with the decision to pursue the application of Cyprus, prompted deep concern from Turkey. But the decision to pursue such a course of action was validated by the Luxembourg Prime Minister (and Council President), Jean-Claude Juncker, who stressed that human rights abuses were not a feature of the other applicant nations.

24.   Cardiff: 15–16 June 1998

Institutional issues: Enlargement.

International issues: Declaration on Kosovo condemned the indiscriminate violence by the Federal Republic of Yugoslavia and the Serbian security forces. Noting that the crisis affects the stability of the region, the Council called for (among other points) a halt to all operations by the security forces which affect the civilian population in Kosovo and to allow the return of refugees to their homes. Finance Ministers supported the Russian government's economic reforms and examined the economic difficulties affecting Asian countries. The EU committed its support to South Africa's programme of economic reform, with President Mandela attending the meeting. The meeting expressed its deep concern over India and Pakistan's nuclear tests.

Overview: The meeting, which was the first chaired by Prime Minister Tony Blair, examined the EU strategy for economic reform so as to promote growth, prosperity and social inclusion. Central to this was the concept of lifelong learning, the need to improve job prospects among the young, long-term and unemployed and women. Such a strategy obviously reflected Tony Blair's own domestic agenda, centred around the New Deal. The meeting additionally emphasised the necessity of transparency to ensure the Union is identifiable for its citizens. The meeting also noted the need for the EU to promote environmental integration and to combat organised crime and trade in drugs (Justice and Home Affairs). The external relations of the EU were also taken into account. One of the first issues to be discussed at the Council meeting was Economic and Monetary Union, particularly the decision taken on 3 May 1998 which confirmed that 11 Member States had met the necessary conditions to join a single currency. In sum, the meeting which marked the end of the new Labour government's first Presidency of the EU was a solid stock-taking exercise. This was because the summit agenda was dominated by the forthcoming legislative elections in Germany. This meant that all substantial decisions were tacitly postponed until after the September 1998 poll. A notable feature of the meeting was how domestic politics in Germany shaped Kohl's position; he demanded a reduction in Germany's net contribution to the EU budget (so as to revive his electoral campaign). Such a stance was vehemently opposed by France. A particular feature of the meeting was that EU leaders failed to break the deadlock over relations with Turkey and its candidacy for membership of the Union. This was despite US pressure on Greek Prime Minister Kostas Simitis to lift Greece's block on Turkey's attempt to join the EU.

25. Portschach (Austria): 24–25 October 1998

Community policies: Stimulation of economic growth and job creation.
Overview: This European Council was the first summit in 16 years that was not attended by the former German Chancellor, Helmut Kohl. In his place was Gerhard Schröder (who attended the meeting as Chancellor elect and therefore a guest), while the meeting was also represented by a new Italian government led by Massimo D'Alema. Discussion centred on combating unfair taxation, the establishment of minimum social standards and the coordination of economic policies. The agenda was clearly influenced by the fact that 11 of the 15 Member States were now led by social democratic governments. While the importance attached to job creation reflected the views of all Member States, UK Prime Minister Tony Blair was less happy about the use of public spending to increase employment levels. The UK government also dismissed plans for a European income tax which were launched by the head of the European Parliament, José María Gil-Robles. The European Council was also the first to be chaired by the new members (Austria, Finland and Sweden). Priorities of the Austrian Presidency included questions of enlargement, the single currency, employment, the environment and transport. The problems in Kosovo did, however, mean that time was taken away from other priorities, while European business was also put on hold until the German elections had been held.

26. Vienna: 11–12 December 1998

Community policies: EU budget, economic reform and employment policies.
Overview: The European Council, chaired by the Austrian Chancellor, Viktor Klima, took place in the Hofburg Palace, home to the Habsburg dynasty. The summit was dominated by debate concerning the EU budget. At the summit a meeting was held with the Heads of State or Government and the Ministers of Foreign Affairs of Cyprus and the Central and Eastern European countries participating in the accession process. A notable feature of the European Council was the award given to Helmut Kohl, the former Federal Chancellor of Germany, of the title 'Honorary Citizen of Europe'. The European Council was conspicuous for the lack of agreement on reforming the EU budget, with Germany having demanded a reduction in its contribution, while Britain considered that it should not have its budget rebate reduced (as negotiated by Margaret Thatcher at the June 1984 Fontainebleau European Council meeting). Debates over the budget are, of course, particularly sensitive, with southern Member States, such as Greece, Portugal and Spain, being concerned that spending cuts would be especially harmful for them.

Nevertheless, the European Union is committed to a target of March 1999 to complete a revamp of the £60 billion a year budget. Outside the budget debate, there was broad support for the initiative of France and Britain to develop a more coherent European common foreign and security policy. The European Council also reached agreement on the 'Vienna Strategy for Europe', building upon the broad debate on the future development of the EU initiated at the Cardiff European Council and further developed at the Portschach meeting. The strategy attached importance to four objectives, of which the first was concerned with promoting employment, economic growth and stability. The second was concerned with improving security and the quality of life while the third examined reforming the Union's policies and institutions. The final point was concerned with promoting stability and prosperity throughout Europe and in the world. Emphasis on employment reflected the more interventionist and left-wing approach of the majority of Member States.

SECTION VIII

Member States

1. Austria

Population: 8.05m (1995)
Capital: Vienna.
Monetary Unit: 1 Schilling = 100 Grischen.
Next general election: 1999.
Head of State: Thomas Klestil (July 1992).
Political structure: The Republic of Austria was founded in 1919 and re-established in May 1955 after the Second World War. It is a democratic federal state divided into nine provinces: Burgenland, Carinthia, Lower Austria, Upper Austria, Salzburg, Styria, Tyrol, Voralberg and Vienna. Austria has a bicameral Parliament: the Bundesrat is composed of representatives of provincial assemblies and the Nationalrat is elected by universal suffrage. The Federal President is elected for a six-year term by universal suffrage and is not able to serve for more than two terms in office. The duties of the President are primarily ceremonial, although they include the appointment of the Federal Chancellor, the Head of Government.
Community history: Austria joined the EU in 1995 along with Finland and Sweden and has been an active member, joining the ERM on 9 January 1995. Four months later it became the 10th Member State to sign the Schengen Convention on 28 April, with implementation from 1 April 1998. In March 1998 it was one of 11 Member States to be named by the European Commission to have met the EMU convergence criteria, with the Brussels EMU Council of 2–3 May having deemed it able to adopt the single currency from 1 January 1999.

	Federal Chancellor	Foreign Minister	EC/EU Representative
1995			M. Scheich
May 1995		W. Schüssel	
Jan. 1997	V. Klima		

2. Belgium

Population: 10.14m (1996)
Capital: Brussels.
Monetary Unit: 1 Belgian Franc = 100 centimes.
Next general election: 1999 (held every four years).
Head of State: Albert II succeeded on 9 August 1993.
Political structure: A constitutional monarchy with a bicameral Parliament: both the House of Representatives and the Senate are elected by

proportional representation. While executive power belongs to the King and the Cabinet, the King in practice does not use his ability to veto legislation and control and dismiss the Cabinet. Belgium is linguistically divided between Flemish-speaking Flanders in the north and French-speaking Wallonia in the south.

Community history: Belgium has traditionally been perceived to be a strong supporter of European integration, of which Paul-Henri Spaak helped establish the Benelux, the 1948 Congress of Europe, the Council of Europe (where he was elected the Assembly's first President), and proved to be a key figure in the 1955 Messina Conference that led to the 1957 Treaties of Rome. Some years later, the Belgian Prime Minister, Leo Tindemans, was the author of the 1975 Tindemans Report which aimed to propel the Community out of a period of slow growth. During the 1980s Belgium was a consistent advocate of greater integration, especially in the 1985 IGC which led to the SEA. Thereafter, it was one of the maximalist Member States during the 1990–91 IGCs which resulted in the TEU, campaigning for a European defence identity and greater powers for the European Parliament.

	Prime Minister	Foreign Minister	EC/EU Representative
Apr. 1954	A. van Acker	P.-H. Spaak	
May 1957		V. Larock	
June 1958	G. Eyskens	P. Wigny	
Apr. 1961	T. Lefevre	P.-H. Spaak	
July 1965	P. Harmel		
Mar. 1966	P. van den Boeynants	P. Harmel	
June 1968	G. Eyskens		
Jan. 1973	E. Le Burton	R. van Elslande	
Apr. 1974	L. Tindemans		
June 1977		H. Simonet	
Oct. 1978	V. Boeynants		
Apr. 1979	W. Martens		
May 1980		C.F. Nothomb	
1980			P. Noterdame
Apr. 1981	M. Eyskens		
Dec. 1981	W. Martens	L. Tindemans	
1987			P. de Schoutheete de Tervarent
June 1989		M. Eyskens	
Mar. 1992	J.-L. Dehaene	W. Claes	
			F. van Daele
June 1995		E. Derycke	

3. Denmark

Population: 5.3m (1996)
Capital: Copenhagen.
Monetary Unit: 1 Danish Krone = 100 øre.
Next general election: By September 2002.
Head of State: HM Queen Margrethe II.
Political structure: A constitutional monarchy with a single-chamber Parliament. The Folketing is elected by universal and proportional suffrage. The Queen exercises executive power through her Ministers, though in reality has no political power.
Community history: Denmark joined the Community in 1973 along with Ireland and the UK, sharing with the latter a sceptical attitude towards European integration. Its decision to pursue membership was forced by the position of the UK in the 1960s when accession to the Community became a British policy objective. Since joining the Community, Denmark has been especially wary of strengthening the power of the European Parliament against a dilution of the Folketing's authority. However, membership has been beneficial, not least through the common agricultural policy and single market. Nevertheless, during the 1990–91 IGC Denmark was against providing the Community with a defence dimension, while its ratification of the Treaty on European Union proved a difficult issue when the electorate cast a no vote in the May 1992 referendum, although that was later changed to a yes vote.

		Prime Minister	Foreign Minister	EC/EU Representative
Dec.	1973	P. Hartling	O. Guldberg	
Feb.	1975	A. Jørgensen	K.B. Andersen	
Aug.	1978		H. Christophersen	
Oct.	1979		K. Olesen	
	1980			G. Riberholdt
Sept.	1982	P. Schlüter	U. Ellemann-Jensen	
	1984			J.E. Larsen
	1989			J. Rytter
	1992			G. Riberholdt
Jan.	1993		N.H. Petersen	
Jan.	1994	P. Rasmussen		
	1995			P.S. Christoffersen
Mar.	1998	P. Rasmussen	N.H. Petersen	

4. Finland

Population: 5.12m (1995)
Capital: Helsinki.

Monetary Unit: 1 Markka or Finmark = 100 penni.
Next general election: 1999.
Head of State: President of the Republic Martti Ahtisaari (elected 1 March 1994).
Political structure: A republic with a single chamber Parliament (Eduskunta). The President is elected by direct popular vote (two rounds if necessary) and holds executive power. This includes the appointment of a Cabinet led by a Prime Minister, although it has to enjoy the confidence of the Eduskunta.
Community history: Finland joined the Community on 1 January 1995 along with Austria and Sweden. It joined the EMS on 14 October 1996 and was considered by the European Commission in March 1998 to have met the single currency convergence criteria for it to be able to adopt the single currency from 1 January 1999, as later decided by the Brussels EMU Council of 2–3 May 1998.

	Prime Minister	Foreign Minister	EC/EU Representative
1995			A. Satuli
Feb. 1995	P. Lipponen	T. Halonen	

5.   France

Population: 58m (1995)
Capital: Paris.
Monetary Unit: 1 French Franc = 100 centimes.
Next general election: 2002
Head of State: Jacques Chirac (elected 7 May 1995)
Political structure: The Constitution of the Fifth Republic came into effect in 1958. The President is elected by universal suffrage for a seven-year period and holds executive power, with the Prime Minister heading the Council of Ministers. Legislative power is placed in the hands of the National Parliament, which comprises two chambers: the National Assembly and the Senate.
Community history: France played a significant role in the shaping of European politics in the post-war period, Robert Schuman being the instigator of the Community while Jean Monnet helped shape its development. During the early years of the Community France essentially regulated the pace of integration, being insistent on the inclusion of the CAP. This emphasised the French perception of integration as an economic goal, which was further demonstrated by the 1965 'empty chair' crisis when de Gaulle refused to accept decision-making on a

QMV basis. That episode illustrated the ability of de Gaulle to influence events – he was instrumental in refusing to allow the UK to become a member. His replacement by Georges Pompidou in 1969 marked a transition in this policy, with Denmark, Ireland and the UK becoming members in 1973. During the 1980s, France, under the leadership of Mitterrand, was especially influential within the Community, when it supported greater European integration. Mitterrand was important to the single market programme, the SEA, and was the principal motivator behind the 1990–91 IGC on EMU – the setting of a timetable of 1999 for the introduction of a single currency was his main objective at the December 1991 Maastricht European Council. A particular feature of this period was the strong alliance he developed with the German Chancellor, Helmut Kohl.

	Prime Minister	Foreign Minister	EC/EU Representative
Sept. 1944	Gen C. de Gaulle	G. Bidault	
Jan. 1946	F. Gouin		
June 1946	G. Bidault		
Dec. 1946	L. Blum	L. Blum	
Nov. 1947	P. Ramadier	G. Bidault	
Sept. 1947	R. Schuman		
Sept. 1948	H. Queuille		
Oct. 1949	G. Bidault		
July 1950	H. Queuille		
July 1950	R. Pleven		
Mar. 1951	H. Queuille		
Aug. 1951	R. Pleven		
Jan. 1952	E. Faure		
Mar. 1952	A. Pinay		
Jan. 1953	R. Mayer	G. Bidault	
June 1953	J. Laniel		
June 1954	P. Mendès-France	P. Mendès-France	
Feb. 1955	E. Faure	A. Pinay	
Jan. 1956	G. Molet	C. Pineau	
Nov. 1957	F. Gaillard		
Jan. 1959	M. Debré	M. Couve de Murville	
Apr. 1962	G. Pompidou		
July 1968	M. Couve de Murville	M. Debré	
June 1969	J. Chaban-Delmas	M. Schuman	
July 1972	P. Messmer		
Apr. 1973		M. Jobert	

		Prime Minister	Foreign Minister	EC/EU Representative
May	1974	J. Chirac	J. Sauvagnargues	
Aug.	1976	R. Barre	L. de Guiringaud	
Nov.	1978		J. François-Poncet	
	1980			L. de La Barre de Nanteuil
May	1981	P. Mauroy	C. Cheysson	
	1982			J. Leprette
July	1984	L. Fabius		
Dec.	1984	R. Dumas		
Mar.	1986	J. Chirac	J.B. Raimond	
	1987			F. Scheer
	1988			P. Louët
May	1988	M. Rocard	R. Dumas	
	1989			J. Vidal
	1991	E. Cresson		
Apr.	1992	P. Bérégovoy		
	1992			F. Scheer
Mar.	1993	E. Balladur	A. Juppé	
Nov.	1995	A. Juppé	H. de Charette	
				P. de Boissieu
June	1997	L. Jospin	H. Vedrine	

		President
	1947	V. Auriol
	1954	R. Coty
Jan.	1959	C. de Gaulle
Apr.	1969	A. Poher
June	1969	G. Pompidou
Apr.	1974	A. Poher
May	1974	V.G. d'Estaing
May	1981	F. Mitterrand
May	1995	J. Chirac

6.   Federal Republic of Germany

Population: 81.54m (1995)
Capital: Berlin (parliament and government is still in Bonn).
Monetary Unit: 1 Deutschemark = 100 Deutsche Pfennig.
Next general election: 2002.
Head of State: Dr Roman Herzog.

Political structure: The constitution (Basic Law) was established in 1949, the country today being divided into 16 Länder. Each Land has its own constitution, parliament and government and is able to legislate on matters that are not devolved to the federal government, namely local and cultural policy, education and police. The Federal Parliament comprises the Bundestag which is elected by universal suffrage, and the Bundesrat which consists of representatives of the Länder governments. The powers of the President are limited. The government is headed by the Chancellor who is elected by a majority vote in the Bundestag.

Community history: Just as France was instrumental to the establishment of the European Community, the FRG has been its most important member since 1957. It has consistently been a strong supporter of European integration, not least because such a process was perceived as a means of tying the nation into the Community. This was a view adopted by the first post-war Chancellor of Germany, Konrad Adenauer, and was more recently emphasised by Helmut Kohl upon reunification in 1990. During that period, the FRG established a close relationship with France, illustrated by the 1963 Treaty of Friendship signed by Adenauer and de Gaulle. Thereafter, Helmut Schmidt and Valéry Giscard d'Estaing cemented the Franco-German axis, which was further strengthened by Helmut Kohl and François Mitterrand. By contrast, Willy Brandt's tenure between 1969 and 1974 witnessed a significant change of policy with the pursuit of *Ostpolitik.* This referred to a series of agreements negotiated between the FRG and the states of Eastern Europe, of which the most significant was with the German Democratic Republic. The European Commission named Germany as one of the 11 Member States that met the single currency convergence criteria in March 1998, as confirmed by the Brussels EMU Council of 2–3 May 1998. The recent election as Chancellor of the Social Democrat Gerhard Schröder marked a new development in German coalition politics, with there now being an alliance between the Social Democrats and the Green Party. The leader of the latter, Joschka Fischer, has been appointed Foreign Minister and Environment Minister. Other key appointments include Oskar Lafontaine as Finance Minister, who plans to adopt a Keynesian programme of economic reform to increase consumption as a means of reducing unemployment of four million in 1998. It is anticipated that this strategy would be backed-up by greater economic and social policy coordination within the EU. A significant aspect in the appointment of the new government was that it was the first time in the republic's 49-year history that a government changed through the ballot box rather than through a reshuffling of coalition parties between elections. The government has a 21-seat majority in Parliament. Key policies of the government include a shutdown of nuclear power stations. The new government has a more pragmatic approach to Europe than its predecessor and this may provoke a strengthening in the Anglo-German alliance as well as the development of an Anglo-German-French triangle, as proposed by Schröder and reiterated during a meeting with Tony Blair in London on 2 November 1998. There are, nevertheless, strong elements of continuity between Kohl and Schröder: the incoming and outgoing governments cooperated on policy over Kosovo.

	Federal Chancellor	Foreign Minister	EC/EU Representative
Sept. 1949	K. Adenauer		
Mar. 1951		K. Adenauer	
June 1955		H. von Brentano	
Nov. 1961		G. Schröder	
Oct. 1963	L. Erhard		
Dec. 1966	K. Kiesinger	W. Brandt	
Oct. 1969	W. Brandt	W. Scheel	
May 1974	H. Schmidt	H.-D. Genscher	
1980			G. Poensgen
Oct. 1982	H. Kohl		
1985			W. Ungerer
1989			J. Trumpf
1993			D. von Kyaw
Apr. 1993		K. Klinkel	
Oct. 1998	G. Schröder	J. Fischer	

7. Greece

Population: 10.4m (1994)
Capital: Athens.
Monetary Unit: 1 Drachma = 100 Lepta.
Next general election: October 2000.
Head of State: Constantinos Stephanopoulos.
Political structure: A presidential parliamentary republic, the constitution of which was established in June 1975. The Parliament elects the President, who in turn appoints the government in line with absolute parliamentary majority. While the government holds executive power, the unicameral Parliament holds legislative power.
Community history: Having applied for membership of the Community in the mid-1970s after the collapse of the military regime, it did not obtain accession until 1981. That time lapse was caused by the European Commission's perception that the Greek economy was initially not strong enough to join, a problem that continued into the 1980s. Throughout the 1980s the Greek Socialist government of Andreas Papandreou proved

to be a constant disruptive voice to the future development of the Community, particularly in the field of European Political Cooperation. Indeed, the UK's acceptance of an extension of QMV in the SEA was motivated by a concern that Greece would be able to veto the development of the single market if unanimity voting procedures were maintained. However, the return to power of a Conservative government in late the 1980s brought with it an attempt to construct a more positive relationship with the Community, although Greece continued to prevent the Community developing better relations with Turkey. Such a stance was motivated by a dispute over Cyprus, where a Turkish-backed government controlled the Northern section of the island. A primary feature of Greece's membership of the Community has been its weak economy, highlighted in March 1998 when the European Commission did not include it as one of the 11 Member States which met the single currency convergence criteria. This was confirmed by the decision of the Brussels EMU Council of 2–3 May 1998.

	Prime Minister	Foreign Minister	EC/EU Representative
May 1980	G. Rallis	K. Mitsotakis	
Oct. 1981	A. Papandreou	I. Charlambopoulos	
1982			N. Dimadis
1985			A. Zafiriou
1986			C. Lyberopoulos
1988			T. Pangalos
July 1989	T. Tzannetakis		
Nov. 1989	X. Zolotas	A. Samaras	
May 1990	C. Mitsotakis		
1991			A. Vayenas
1992			L. Evangelidis
1993			A. Zaphiriou
Feb. 1993		M. Papaconstantinou	
Oct. 1993	A. Papandreou	K. Papoulias	
Jan. 1996	C. Simitris	T. Pangalos	
			P. Vassilakis

8. Ireland

Population: 3.62m (1996)
Capital: Dublin.
Monetary Unit: Punt (Irish pound).
Next general election: Before 2002 (the lifetime of the Dáil is not more than five years).

Head of State: Mary McAleese (1997).
Political structure: The constitution was established in 1937. Ireland is a Republic with a bicameral Parliament: the Dáil and the Senate. Executive power rests with the government despite the President being elected by universal suffrage.
Community history: Ireland's decision to join the Community was clearly motivated by the UK's conclusion that membership was advantageous. Both countries joined along with Denmark in 1973, after which the Irish economy underwent a period of remarkable growth, especially in the 1980s and 1990s. Membership immediately proved beneficial to the Irish agricultural community via the CAP, although the manufacturing sector benefited less, being troubled by high unemployment. However, the advent of the single market brought with it fresh opportunity for a highly educated English-speaking nation which proved attractive to inward investment. In broader terms, Community membership also allowed Ireland to pursue a more independent foreign policy that was not dominated by the UK, while ensuring that Anglo-Irish relations, especially regarding the dispute over Northern Ireland, could be set in a multilateral context. Ireland was named in March 1998 by the European Commission as one of the 11 Member States which met the convergence criteria for the adoption of a single currency, which was further confirmed by the Brussels EMU Council of 2–3 May 1998.

	Prime Minister	Foreign Minister	EC/EU Representative
Mar. 1973	L. Cosgrave	G. Fitzgerald	
July 1977	J. Lynch	M. O'Kennedy	
Dec. 1979	C. Haughey	B. Lenihan	
1980			B. Dillon
June 1981	G. Fitzgerald	J. Dooge	
Mar. 1982	C. Haughey	G. Collins	
Dec. 1982	G. Fitzgerald	P. Barry	
1982			A. O'Rourke
1986			J.F. Campbell
Mar. 1987	C. Haughey	B. Lenihan	
July 1989		G. Collins	
Mar. 1992	A. Reynolds	D. Andrews	
1992			P. MacKernan
Jan. 1993		D. Spring	
Jan. 1994	A. Reynolds		
Nov. 1994	J. Bruton		
June 1997	B. Ahern	D. Andrews	D. O'Leary

9. Italy

Population: 57.2m (1995)
Capital: Rome.
Monetary Unit: Lira.
Next general election: 2001.
Head of State: Signor Oscar Luigi Scalfaro (May 1992).
Political structure: The constitution was established in 1948, providing the Italian Republic with a bicameral Parliament (the Senate and the Chamber of Deputies). Prior to 1993 both Houses of Parliament were elected by proportional representation. Thereafter 75% (232) of the 315 elected seats in the Senate were elected by a first-past-the-post system, with the remaining elected by proportional representation. In the Chamber of Deputies, 75% (472) of the seats were elected on a first-past-the-post basis and 25% (158) by proportional representation. The President is elected for a seven-year term by an electoral college consisting of both Houses of Parliament and 58 regional representatives, and has the constitutional right to intervene in some legislative, executive and judicial matters. The Prime Minister, who heads the government, is appointed by the President.
Community history: Italy's position as a founder member of the Community had an immediate impact on the economic and political aspects of the nation. Access to wider Community markets resulted in a greater focus on competitiveness, from which the northern industrial sector benefited while the more rural southern sector continued to have economic difficulties. Membership also proved to be a valuable means of providing Italian politicians and civil servants with contact with less corrupt Member States, thereby helping to create a less corrupt government bureaucracy. In broader terms, Italy has consistently advocated a stronger European Commission and European Parliament, although the latter has been motivated by domestic political weakness. In a similar context, Italian membership of the ERM helped to stabilise the lira throughout the 1980s, although the nation suffered during the 1992–93 European currency crisis. In a similar manner, the drive towards monetary union provided a further means of injecting some stability into the Italian economy. This resulted in it meeting the European Commission's recommendation on the EMU convergence criteria in March 1998, which was later decided by the Brussels EMU Council of 2–3 May 1998. This was despite Italy having a debt more than twice the requirement of 60% of GDP.

	Prime Minister	Foreign Minister	EC/EU Representative
May 1957	A. Zoli	G. Pella	
June 1958	A. Fanfani	A. Fanfani	

	Prime Minister	Foreign Minister	EC/EU Representative
Feb. 1959	A. Segni		
Mar. 1960	F. Tambroni	A. Segni	
July 1960	A. Fanfani		
May 1962		A. Piccione	
June 1963	G. Leone		
Dec. 1963	A. Moro	G. Saragat	
Mar. 1965		A. Fanfani	
June 1968	G. Leone	G. Medici	
Dec. 1968	M. Rumor	P. Nenni	
Aug. 1969		A. Moro	
Aug. 1970	E. Colombo		
Feb. 1972	G. Andreotti		
June 1972		G. Medici	
July 1973	M. Rumor	A. Moro	
Nov. 1974	A. Moro	M. Rumor	
July 1976	G. Andreotti	A. Forlani	
Aug. 1979	F. Cossiga	F.M. Malfatti	
1980			E. Plaja
Jan. 1980		A. Ruffini	
Apr. 1980		E. Colombo	
Oct. 1980	A. Forlani		
June 1981	G. Spadolini		
Dec. 1982	A. Fanfani		
1982			R. Ruggiero
Aug. 1983	B. Craxi	G. Andreotti	
1984			P. Calamia
Apr. 1987	A. Fanfani		
July 1987	G. Goria		
Apr. 1988	C. de Mita		
July 1989	G. Andreotti	G. de Michelis	
1989			F. Di Roberto
June 1992	G. Amato		
Mar. 1993		E. Colombo	
Nov. 1993	C. Ciampi	B. Andreatta	
1993			E. Perlot
May 1994	S. Berlusconi		
Jan. 1995	L. Dini	S. Agnelli	
May 1996	R. Prodi	L. Dini	
1996			L.G.C. Garofoli
Oct. 1998	M. D'Alema		

10. Luxembourg

Population: 412,800 (1996)
Capital: Luxembourg.
Monetary Unit: 1 Luxembourg Franc = 100 centimes. The Belgian Franc is also legal tender.
Next general election: 1999.
Head of State: Jean Grand Duke of Luxembourg.
Political structure: A constitutional hereditary monarchy. The Head of State exercises executive power via a Council of Ministers led by the Prime Minister. The latter is chosen by the Head of State, although he/she has to have the support of the Chamber of Deputies. Luxembourg also has a Senate which comprises 21 members appointed by the Head of State, acting as the supreme administrative tribunal and having certain legislative functions, although the Chamber of Deputies has the primary legislative authority.
Community history: A founder member and the smallest nation in the Community, Luxembourg has advocated greater European integration. Its own international profile has been increased through membership, while the location of numerous Community institutions within Luxembourg has resulted in nearly one-quarter of its working population being employed in Community work. But while it has campaigned for the extension of QMV in the Council of Ministers and for a stronger European Parliament, it has been a pragmatic member when it has held the Presidency of the Community. It successfully chaired the 1985 IGC which produced the SEA and imparted a realistic negotiating position during its chairing of the first six months of the 1991 IGC which resulted in the TEU. A pragmatic position during the latter contrasted with the position of the Netherlands, which advocated a maximalist position. It was one of the 11 Member States considered by the European Commission in March 1998 to have met the convergence criteria requirements for the adoption of the single currency, as later decided by the Brussels EMU Council of 2–3 May 1998.

	Prime Minister	Foreign Minister	EC/EU Representative
Jan. 1958	P. Frieden	J. Bech	
Feb. 1959	P. Werner	E. Schauss	
July 1964		P. Werner	
Dec. 1967		P. Gregoire	
Jan. 1969		G. Thorn	
June 1974	G. Thorn	G. Thorn	
July 1979	P. Werner		

	Prime Minister	Foreign Minister	EC/EU Representative
1980			J. Dondelinger
Nov. 1980		C. Flesch	
July 1984	J. Santer	J.F. Poos	
1984			J. Weyland
1992			J.-J. Kasel
Jan. 1995	J.-C. Juncker		

11.   The Netherlands

Population: 15.42m (1995)
Capital: Amsterdam.
Monetary Unit: 1 Guilder or Florin = 100 cents.
Next general election: 2002.
Head of State: HM Queen Beatrix.
Political structure: The constitution was established in 1814, revised in 1815 and modernised in 1983. It is a constitutional monarchy with a bicameral Parliament. The Provincial Councils, which are directly elected, choose the First Chamber of the States General. The Second Chamber is elected by universal suffrage. Although executive power is in the hands of the Cabinet, the Queen has the power to dissolve the Parliament.
Community history: The Netherlands was a founder Member State of the Community and has proved to be a strong supporter of European integration, a position equally reflected by its Benelux partners. Within the Community it has been a consistent supporter of greater powers for the European Parliament and an extension of QMV within the Council of Ministers. In that context, its desire not to have intergovernmental cooperation meant that, upon taking over the Presidency during the 1991 IGC, it rejected the Luxembourg proposal for a pillar structure. That had envisaged JHA and CFSP operating as intergovernmental policies. The Netherlands attempted to incorporate JHA and CFSP into a single pillar so that they would be subjected to influence from all the institutions of the Community. However, that strategy failed, which meant that the Dutch government had to adopt a pillar structure as represented in the TEU. Despite having an integrationist position on institutional policies, the Dutch government has been a strong supporter of NATO and therefore has tended to adopt a similar position to the UK on foreign and defence policy. It was one of the 11 Member States which met the single currency convergence criteria requirements in March 1998, as later decided by the Brussels EMU Council of 2–3 May 1998.

	Prime Minister	Foreign Minister	EC/EU Representative
Aug. 1948	W. Drees	D.U. Stikker	
Sept. 1952		J. Beyan/J. Luns	
Dec. 1958	L. Beel	J. Luns	
May 1959	J.E. de Quay		
July 1963	V.G.M. Marijnen		
Apr. 1965	J. Cals		
Nov. 1966	J. Zijlatra		
Apr. 1967	P. de Jong		
July 1971	B. Biesheuvel	W. Schmelzer	
May 1973	J. den Uyl	M. van der Stoel	
Dec. 1977	A. van Agt	C. van der Klaauw	
1980			M.H.J.Ch. Rutten
Sept. 1981		M. van der Stoel	
May 1982		A. van Agt	
Nov. 1982	R. Lubbers	H. van den Broek	
1986			P.C. Nieman
1992			B.R. Bot
Aug. 1994	W. Kok	H. van Mierlo	
Aug. 1998	W. Kok	H. van Mierlo	

12. Portugal

Population: 9.9m (1994)
Capital: Lisbon.
Monetary Unit: 1 Escudo = 100 centavos.
Next general election: 1999.
Head of State: Jorge Sampaio (January 1996).
Political structure: The constitution was established in 1976. The President of the Republic is elected by universal suffrage and in turn appoints the government which is responsible for the policy of the state. The Assembly of the Republic is charged with legislative power.
Community history: Portugal entered the Community in 1986 along with Spain, having been isolated from the mainstream of post-war European politics through an undemocratic government. However, the removal of the right-wing authoritarian government in the mid-1970s paved the way for Community membership, which was also perceived to be a means of bolstering the democratic basis of government. Upon accession to the Community, Portugal has tended to side with the UK on a great majority of topics, including the European Parliament and foreign and defence policy. But despite this position, it is in favour of the single currency and

was named in March 1998 by the European Commission as having met the convergence criteria, as later decided by the Brussels EMU Council of 2–3 May 1998.

	Prime Minister	Foreign Minister	EC/EU Representative
Nov. 1985	A. Silva	P.P. de Miranda	
1986			L. Mathias
Aug. 1987		J. de Deus Pinhero	
1989			C.A.S. Simöes Coelho
1991			J.C. Paulouro das Neves
Oct. 1995	A. Guterres	J. Gama	
			V. da Cunha Valente

13. Spain

Population: 40.46m (1995)
Capital: Madrid.
Monetary Unit: 1 Peseta = 100 céntimos.
Next general election: 2000.
Head of State: King Juan Carlos I (1975).
Political structure: Spain is a parliamentary monarchy, the government being headed by a President or Prime Minister who is appointed by the King, after his investiture by the Congress of Deputies. Internal and foreign policies are directed by the government. The Cortes Generales (Spanish Parliament) represents the Spanish people, comprising two houses: the Congress of Deputies and the Senate.
Community history: Spain's accession to the Community in 1986, along with Portugal, marked the end of numerous failed attempts. Just as with Portugal, Spain had suffered from an undemocratic and authoritarian government, led by Francisci Franco, between 1939 and 1975. Since accession Spain has proved to be a strong supporter for greater European integration, contrasting with the more pragmatic attitude adopted by Portugal. In this context, Spain supported a greater foreign and defence policy and campaigned for the introduction of citizenship during the 1991 IGC. Spain has also benefited from the introduction of the cohesion fund. In March 1998 the European Commission named it as having met the single currency convergence criteria requirements, which was later decided by the Brussels EMU Council of 2–3 May 1998.

	Prime Minister	Foreign Minister	EC/EU Representative
Dec. 1982	F. González Márquez	F. Morán	
July 1985		F. Fernández Ordóñez	
1986			C. Westendorp y Cabeza
1991			C.B. García-Villamil
Mar. 1996	J.M. Aznar López	A. Matutes Juan	
			J.E. Cavengt

14. Sweden

Population: 8.84m (1996)
Capital: Stockholm.
Monetary Unit: 1 Krona = 100 öre.
Next general election: 2002.
Head of State: HM King Carl XVI Gustaf (1973).
Political structure: Sweden has a constitutional monarchy with a unicameral Parliament that is elected by universal suffrage. The Cabinet is charged with executive power and is responsible to Parliament. The King only has a representative role, having no political power.
Community history: Sweden joined the Community in January 1995 along with Austria and Finland, but unlike Austria and Finland, it holds a more sceptical attitude towards the EU. In August 1996 its Finance Minister, Erik Asbrink, declared that Sweden would not seek to be part of the first countries to participate in EMU. This was despite the government being confident that it would meet the convergence criteria, which it duly did when the European Commission published its March 1998 report on the countries which met the convergence criteria. A more sceptical attitude was further highlighted in January 1997 when it opposed proposals being discussed within the IGC on flexible decision-making, which would allow groups of Member States to pursue greater integration. Sweden's position was equally shared by Denmark, Greece, Portugal and the UK.

	Prime Minister	Foreign Minister	EC/EU Representative
Mar. 1986	I. Carlsson	S. Andersson	
1995			F. Belfrage
Feb. 1997	G. Persson	L. Hjelm-Wallen	
Oct. 1998	G. Persson	A. Lindh	

15.   The United Kingdom

Population: 58.78m (1996)
Capital: London.
Monetary Unit: 1 Pound Sterling = 100 pence.
Next general election: 2002.
Head of State: HM Queen Elizabeth II (1952).
Political structure: The UK has a constitutional monarchy with a bicam-
eral Parliament. While the House of Commons is elected by universal
suffrage, the House of Lords comprises hereditary and appointed peers.
The Cabinet, which is headed by the Prime Minister, has executive power.
The powers of the Queen are nominal, including those of appointing the
Cabinet, summoning and dissolving Parliament and giving her assent
to bills.
Community history: The UK's accession to the Community in 1973,
along with Denmark and Ireland, was the third attempt at membership.
The UK had suffered from economic decline in the post-war period and
this brought with it a reduction in its global influence. Membership of
the Community was supposed to mark a commitment to Europe, but
instead the UK has consistently been an awkward member. This was
emphasised as early as 1974 when it sought a renegotiation of its terms
of membership, and continued through the 1980s with a claim for a
reduction in its budgetary contribution. The UK has shown little enthusiasm for greater integration, particularly in the field of monetary and
social affairs. Other Member States have also shared the UK's scepticism
to certain policies, notably Denmark and Portugal. The present Prime
Minister, Tony Blair, has attempted to cultivate warmer relations with
the leaders of the other EU Member States, in particular Germany. This
is somewhat similar to John Major's attempt to place Britain at the
'heart of Europe'. Links between Britain and Germany were emphasised
when Gordon Brown, the Chancellor, and Oskar Lafontaine, his German opposite number met on 9 November 1998. Indeed, at a meeting
of 11 Socialist EU Finance Ministers in Brussels on 22 November 1998,
Chancellor Brown gave his backing to a common statement setting objectives for cooperation on economic policies after the launch of the
Euro on 1 January 1999. This reflects the growing strength and confidence of the Left since the election of the German Socialist government
in September 1998.

	Prime Minister	**Foreign Minister**	**EC/EU Representative**
July 1945	C. Attlee	E. Bevin	
Mar. 1951		H. Morrison	

		Prime Minister	Foreign Minister	EC/EU Representative
Oct.	1951	Sir W. Churchill	Sir A. Eden	
Apr.	1955	Sir A. Eden	H. Macmillan	
Dec.	1955		S. Lloyd	
Jan.	1957	H. Macmillan		
July	1960		Lord Home	
Oct.	1963	Sir A. Douglas-Home	R. Butler	
Oct.	1964	H. Wilson	P. Gordon Walker	
Jan.	1965		M. Stewart	
Aug.	1966		G. Brown	
Mar.	1968		M. Stewart	
June	1970	E. Heath	Sir A. Douglas-Home	
Jan.	1973			Sir M. Palliser
Mar.	1974	H. Wilson	J. Callaghan	
July	1975			Sir D. Maitland
Apr.	1976	J. Callaghan	A. Crosland	
Feb.	1977		D. Owen	
May	1979	M. Thatcher	Lord Carrington	Sir M. Butler
Apr.	1982		F. Pym	
June	1983		Sir G. Howe	
Oct.	1985			Sir D. Hannay
July	1989		J. Major	
Oct.	1989		D. Hurd	
Sept.	1990			Sir J. Kerr
Nov.	1990	J. Major		
	1995		M. Rifkind	
	1995			Sir S. Wall
May	1997	A. Blair	R. Cook	

SECTION IX

Britain and Europe

Chronology

1. A part of, but not in, Europe, 1945–58

1945
27 July. In the UK general election, the Labour Party received 48% of the vote (393 seats), the Conservative Party 39.6% (213 seats), the Liberal Party 9% (12 seats), and others 1.4% (22 seats).

1947
4 March. Treaty of Dunkirk. France and the UK pledged mutual support against future German aggression.

1950
27 May. The UK government explained to France that it could not accept a prior commitment to pool coal and steel resources and set up a common authority.

1951
15 February. At the European Army conference in Paris, the UK noted its intention not to be a participant in the European Defence Community (EDC) by only sending an observer, Sir Oliver Harvey – the UK Ambassador to France.
25 October. In the UK general the election 81.9% of the electorate voted: 625 MPs were elected. The Conservative Party won 320 seats, the Labour Party 295, the Liberal Party six MPs, and others four, including the Speaker.

1952
27 May. The EDC Treaty was signed by the Six and a Treaty of Association was signed with the UK.
10 August. First meeting in Luxembourg of the ECSC High Authority. A UK diplomatic representative was appointed to it.

1954
3 October. The London Treaty, by which the Churchill government pledged four divisions to the Continent in support of the Western European Union (WEU), was signed.

21 December.   An association agreement between the UK and the ECSC was signed in London by Monnet and Sandys. This agreement provided for a Council of Association, meeting alternately in London or Luxembourg, made up of four representatives from each side, with a provision for subsidiary committees.

1955
26 May.   UK general election. 630 MPs elected. 76.8% of electorate voted. The Conservative Party won 344 seats, the Labour Party 277, the Liberal Party 6, and others three, which included the Speaker.

23 September.   The Association Agreement between UK and the ECSC entered into force, having been ratified in the House of Commons in February.

1956
3 October.   The UK Chancellor of the Exchequer, Harold Macmillan, announced the government's readiness to join a limited European Free Trade Area.

1957
7 February.   The UK put forward its proposal to the OEEC for the establishment of EFTA.

25 March.   The Treaties of Rome, which established the European Economic Community (EEC) and the European Atomic Energy Community (Euratom), were signed.

1958
1 January.   The Treaties of Rome came into effect.

2.   Thinking of Europe, 1959–70

1959
4 February.   A cooperation agreement was signed between the UK and Euratom.

8 October.   In the UK general election 78.7% of electorate voted: 630 MPs were elected. The Conservative Party won 363 seats, the Labour Party 258, the Liberal Party six, and others two, which included the Speaker.

1960
4 January.   The Convention of Stockholm, establishing the European Free Trade Association, was signed by Austria, Denmark, Norway, Portugal, Sweden, Switzerland and the UK.

7 November.   In a speech to the UK Council of the European Movement, Harold Macmillan called for European economic unity.

1 December.   The WEU invited the UK to negotiations for full EEC membership.

1961
27 February.   Edward Heath told the WEU that the UK was prepared to accept, in principle, the common external tariff.
1 March.   France rejected a UK proposal for a European system in which the UK would retain her Commonwealth preference and agricultural arrangements. The French Foreign Minister, Couve de Murville, invited the UK to join the EEC.
28 June.   The London Declaration stated that the UK would coordinate any EEC accession negotiations with her EFTA partners.
31 July.   Macmillan announced in the House of Commons that the UK would apply to join the EEC and would seek conditions for the Commonwealth, agriculture and EFTA.
3 August.   The House of Commons supported the decision of the government to seek negotiations with the aim of membership of the EEC.
9 August.   The UK sent its formal application to join the EEC.
5 September.   The UK Trade Union Congress supported the government's decision to open negotiations with a view to joining the EEC.
12–14 September.   The Commonwealth Consultative Council met in Accra to discuss the implications of the UK's entry into the EEC for the Commonwealth.
13 September.   Commonwealth Finance Ministers criticised the UK decision to join the EEC.
26 September.   The Common Market Council of Ministers unanimously agreed to open negotiations for the UK's entry.
10 October.   In a statement in Paris, Edward Heath accepted the Treaties of Rome and the political consequences but sought conditions for UK agriculture.
12 October.   The Conservative Party approved Macmillan's decision to enter the EEC.
8 November.   Formal negotiations began in Brussels between the UK and the EEC.

1962
20 January.   The talks between the UK and the Common Market were delayed while the Six sought agreement on a common agricultural policy.
2 March.   The UK applied for membership of the ECSC.
5 March.   The UK applied for membership of Euratom.
11 May.   Edward Heath put forward the first practical offer on the UK's membership of the Common Market.
30 May.   In its negotiations to join the Common Market, the UK made a concession on Commonwealth manufactured goods.

4 June.   The Beaverbrook press announced it would oppose the Conservative Party over the Common Market issue in a general election.

5 June.   The UK received criticism from Australia, New Zealand and Canada over its handling of the negotiations to enter the Common Market.

20 July.   Hugh Gaitskell suggested a general election if the terms of entry were not satisfactory.

31 July.   Forty Conservative MPs signed a motion urging the government to stand firm over Europe.

10–19 September.   At the Commonwealth Conference in London, Commonwealth Prime Ministers signed a communiqué that agreed to the UK continuing its negotiations to join the Common Market.

21 September.   Harold Macmillan, in a television speech, stated that the UK could be harmed if it did not join the Common Market and this, therefore, meant that entry was of major political importance.

3 December.   Hugh Gaitskell attacked the Brussels' terms in a speech in Paris.

5 December.   Dean Acheson stated that the UK 'has lost an empire and not yet found a role' in a speech to the West Point Military Academy in New York.

18–21 December.   Harold Macmillan met with President Kennedy in Nassau. The talks were concerned with the US cancellation of Skybolt, which was to be a replacement for the UK Blue Streak missile which itself had been cancelled. The USA agreed to supply the Polaris missile to the UK as a replacement for the Skybolt missile.

1963

14 January.   President de Gaulle announced that the UK was not yet ready to join the EEC.

29 January.   The UK's negotiations to join the Common Market ended.

1964

15 October.   In the UK general election 77.1% of the electorate voted. The Labour Party won the election and Harold Wilson formed a government with a majority of five. The Labour Party won 317 seats, the Conservative Party 303, the Liberal Party nine, and others one, which accounted for the Speaker.

1965

16 February.   In the House of Commons, the Prime Minister stated that it was not practical to join the EEC, but if favourable conditions developed, then the UK would negotiate, but with the condition that UK and Commonwealth interests were satisfied.

3 August.   In the House of Commons, the Prime Minister stated that while some conditions had changed, agriculture was still a problem.

9 November.   The Queen's speech highlighted the fact that the government would continue to work for cooperation in Europe as well as for the establishment of a greater European market.

1966

31 March.   In the UK general election the Labour Party increased its majority. 75.8% of the electorate voted and 630 MPs were elected. The Labour Party won 363 seats, the Conservative Party 253, the Liberal Party 12, and others two, which included the Speaker. The Chancellor of the Duchy of Lancaster, George Thomson, was given special responsibility for Europe.

21 April.   The Queen's speech highlighted the fact that the government would be prepared to enter the EEC if essential UK and Commonwealth interests were safeguarded.

14 September.   At a meeting of Commonwealth Prime Ministers, it was decided that Commonwealth Ministers would be kept informed of the UK's negotiations to join the EEC.

26 October.   The UK informed other EFTA countries that it would try to join the EEC.

10 November.   The UK Prime Minister, Harold Wilson, announced his plan for a high-level approach to the Six, with the intention of applying for membership.

5 December.   The UK government met with EFTA government representatives who approved of the decision of the UK government to explore the possibility of membership of the Communities.

14 December.   At a WEU meeting in Paris, the West German Foreign Minister, Willy Brandt, made a plea for the UK to join the EEC.

16–17 December.   The UK Prime Minister and Foreign Secretary visited Rome to start their examination of possible membership opportunities of the Communities.

22 December.   The Confederation of British Industry (CBI) stated that it was in favour of the UK applying to join the EEC.

1967

25 January.   The UK application was welcomed without opposition by the Consultative Assembly of the Council of Europe.

3 March.   At EFTA Ministerial talks in Stockholm, the UK promised to consult the members of EFTA before taking the final decision over membership of the Communities.

2 May.   Harold Wilson announced the government's decision to apply for membership of the EEC, the ECSC and Euratom.

8–10 May.   House of Commons debate on membership of the European Communities. On 8 May the Prime Minister moved the motion 'That this House approves the statement in the Command Paper, Membership of the European Communities'. The motion was carried on 10 May by

488 votes to 62 (34 Labour MPs, 26 Conservatives, one Liberal and one Plaid Cymru).

10 May. The UK Trade Union Congress Economic Committee announced its support for UK entry of the Communities.

10–11 May. Denmark, Ireland and the UK submitted formal applications for membership of the EEC, the ECSC and Euratom.

16 May. At a press conference, de Gaulle discussed the problems of the UK's application.

17 May. The UK Prime Minister stated that while he 'won't take no for an answer' he was not prepared for the negotiations to continue indefinitely.

5 June. The EEC Council acknowledged the UK's application without any major discussion.

10 July. M. Couve de Murville told the European Council that the UK's membership would transform the Community into an Atlantic Community.

28 September. Sir Alec Douglas-Home, in a lecture in Luxembourg, stated that the UK's membership of the Communities was 'an act of faith'.

3 October. Submission of the Preliminary Opinion of the Commission on the UK's enlargement application.

5 October. At the Labour Party Conference a vote of 2–1 was given in support of the initiative of the government to join the Communities.

24 October. M. Couve de Murville stated that France had 'no objection in principle' to UK membership of the Communities.

13 November. In his Guildhall speech, the Prime Minister stated seven proposals for the realisation of European economic and technological union.

18 November. The pound sterling was devalued by 14.3%.

27 November. At a press conference, de Gaulle noted the incompatibility of the EEC with the state of the UK's economy.

29 November. Harold Wilson refuted de Gaulle's stance against the UK through a 16-point programme.

18–19 December. The Council reached deadlock over enlargement of the Community after de Gaulle objected to the UK's membership. France insisted that resumption must be conditional on an improvement in the UK economy. The application stayed on the table and it was later put forward through the WEU.

1969

4 February. A two-year extension of cooperation between the UK and Euratom was agreed.

28 April. General de Gaulle resigned and was succeeded in July by Georges Pompidou.

10 July. Georges Pompidou declared that in principle he did not oppose UK membership.

2 October. The Commission gave its Revised Opinion on the UK's application.

1970

10 February. A UK White Paper on the benefits of membership of the EEC was published.

19–21 May. Edward Heath met Georges Pompidou in Paris.

18 June. The Conservative Party won the UK general election and Edward Heath became Prime Minister. 71.5% of the electorate voted. and 630 MPs were elected. The Conservative Party won 330 seats, the Labour Party 287, the Liberal Party six, the Scottish National Party one, and others six, which included the Speaker.

30 June. Opening of negotiations with Denmark, Ireland, Norway and the UK.

3. Into Europe, 1971–73

1971

20–21 January. House of Commons debate on the progress of the EEC negotiations.

23 June. Agreement at Ministerial level was reached on the main issues of the UK's entry into the EEC.

7 July. The UK White Paper recommending entry was published.

21–28 October. The House of Commons voted to join the EEC on the terms secured by 356 to 244, a majority of 112. It was the longest Parliamentary debate since the Second World War. The government's motion was 'That this House approves Her Majesty's Government's decision of principle to join the European Communities which have been negotiated'.

26–28 October. The House of Lords held a three-day debate on an identical motion as that of 21–28 October 1971, which was approved by 451 votes to 58, a majority of 393.

1972

22 January. The Treaty of Accession was signed by Denmark, Ireland, Norway, and the UK.

23 April. Enlargement of the European Communities to include Denmark, Ireland, Norway and the UK was approved in a referendum in France.

1 May. The pound sterling joined the snake.

23 June. The UK floated the pound.

17 October. In the UK, the European Communities Act received royal assent.

31 December. The UK left EFTA.

1973

1 January. Denmark, Ireland and the UK officially joined the Community and the Six became the Nine.

4.   The rocky road, 1974–84

1974

28 February.   After a UK general election Labour entered power. 77.9% of the electorate voted and 635 MPs were elected. The Labour Party won 301 seats, the Conservative Party 296, the Liberal Party 14, the Scottish National Party seven, Plaid Cymru two, and others 15, which included the Speaker.

4 March.   Harold Wilson became Prime Minister as head of a minority government with James Callaghan as Foreign Secretary.

1 April.   The Labour government presented demands for UK's renegotiation of accession terms.

4 June.   At a meeting of the Council of Ministers, James Callaghan gave details of the UK's renegotiation terms.

10 October.   In the UK general election 72.5% of the electorate voted and 635 MPs were elected. The Labour Party won 319 seats, the Conservative Party 276, the Liberal Party 13, the Scottish National Party 11, Plaid Cymru three, and others 13, which included the Speaker.

1975

10–11 March.   Conclusion of the UK's renegotiations at the first European Council meeting in Dublin.

17 March.   The UK Cabinet voted 16 to seven in favour of the terms achieved in the wake of the Dublin meeting. The seven Ministers who rejected the terms were Castle, Benn, Foot, Shore, Silkin, Ross and Varley.

18 March.   Harold Wilson told the House of Commons that the UK government had decided to recommend that the population vote to stay in the EEC.

9 April.   The House of Commons voted by 398 to 172 in favour of the renegotiated terms. A majority of Labour MPs opposed the terms, 145 against with 137 in favour.

5 June.   In the UK referendum on the European Community 17.3 million voted yes and 8.4 million voted against (57.2%–32.8%). 64.55% of the electorate voted.

1979

3 May.   Margaret Thatcher was elected Prime Minister in the UK general election. 75.1% of the electorate voted and 635 MPs were elected. The Conservative Party won 339 seats, the Labour Party 268, the Liberal Party 11, the Scottish National Party two, Plaid Cymru two, and others 13, which included the Speaker.

7–10 June.   First direct elections to the European Parliament. In the UK on 7 June the Conservative Party received 60 seats, the Labour Party 17, others four, and the Liberal Party none.

21–22 June.   At the Strasbourg European Council meeting Mrs Thatcher requested a reduction in the UK's budget contributions.

29–30 November.   The European Council meeting in Dublin agreed that there should be a complementary of measures in favour of the UK. Additional projects were to be financed by the Regional and Social Funds.

1980

29–30 May.   A European Foreign Ministers' meeting resolved the budgetary problem. The eight Member States conceded that it was not equitable to impose an excessive financial burden on a less prosperous country, but refused to set a ceiling on future UK contributions on the basis that the principle of Community financial solidarity must be upheld. The UK's net EEC contributions were cut by two-thirds.

2 June.   The UK Cabinet endorsed the EEC budget agreement.

1 October.   The Labour Party Conference voted to pull the UK out of the Community.

10 October.   At the Conservative Party Conference at Brighton Mrs Thatcher announced that 'The lady's not for turning'.

1981

1 October.   The Labour Party Conference voted to pull the UK out of the EEC without a referendum.

1983

9 June.   In the UK general election 71.8% of the electorate voted and 650 MPs were elected. The Conservative Party won 396 seats, the Labour Party 209, the Alliance 23 (the Liberal Party 17 and the Social Democratic Party six), the Scottish National Party two, Plaid Cymru two, and others 18, which included the Speaker.

1984

14 June.   The second set of direct elections to the European Parliament. The Conservative Party won 45 seats, the Labour Party 32, and others four.

25–26 June.   At the Fontainebleau European Council meeting an agreement was reached on the annual correction method from 1985 for the UK's rebate, as well as an increase in the resources of the Community from January 1986, by raising the VAT percentage from 1% to 1.4%. For 1984 the UK received a compensation lump-sum of 1,000 million ECU and in subsequent years it was to receive two-thirds of the difference between what it paid in VAT and what it received from the Community.

5.   Terms of engagement, 1986–88

1986

21 May.   Sir Geoffrey Howe outlined the UK's agenda for its Presidency of the EC. He wanted progress to be made in the freeing of the internal market, specifically the liberalisation of transport, the deregulation of air fares and the opening of routes to competition. He also attempted to lift the burdens on business, especially small and medium-sized business, and to introduce flexibility into the labour market.

1 July.   The UK took over the Presidency of the European Community.

3 November.   In the UK, the European Communities (Amendment) Bill, giving effect to those provisions of the SEA which relate to the EC, passed its final stage in the House of Lords.

7 November.   The European Communities (Amendment) Bill received royal assent in the UK.

19 November.   The SEA was ratified by the UK. This was one of the first ratifications to take place. By the end of 1986 11 of the 12 Member States had ratified the SEA.

1987

11 June.   In the UK general election 74.5% of the electorate voted and 650 MPs were elected. The Conservative Party received 375 seats, the Labour Party 229, the Alliance 22 (the Liberal Party 17 and the Social Democratic Party five), the Scottish National Party three, Plaid Cymru three, and others 18, which included the Speaker. The Conservative majority was 102.

1988

11–13 February.   The extraordinary Brussels Summit agreed that there would be an increase in structural funds from nearly £5 billion in 1988 to £9.17 billion in 1993. Prime Minister Thatcher accepted a package deal where she achieved tight and binding controls on the rate of increase of CAP expenditure, along with the continuation of the Fontainebleau rebate scheme. She did concede on the increase in funds available to the Community and the change in the method of financing the EC budget. Both of these would cost the UK more. She also agreed to the doubling of regional and social funds by 1992.

20 September.   In a speech by Margaret Thatcher to the College of Europe in Bruges, she attacked the Commission for wanting to regulate the internal market as well as for wanting to centralise power in Brussels. She also attacked the idea of common rules for the protection of workers as this regulation would result in an increase in the cost of employment.

6.   In the slow lane, 1989–90

1989

30 May.   The Commission adopted the preliminary draft of the Community Charter of Fundamental Social Rights. The proposals were immediately attacked by Lord Young, the Secretary of State for Industry, before they were published. Furthermore, Norman Fowler, the Employment Secretary, also noted his opposition to certain aspects of the proposals.

26–27 June.   At the Madrid meeting of the European Council Mrs Thatcher adopted a more conciliatory tone and made significant progress on the question of UK membership of the ERM by stating the conditions that would be necessary for membership. Her previous stance had been that the UK would join when the time was right. Mrs Thatcher accepted the implementation of the first stage of the Delors Report. However, at the meeting she still registered her disapproval of plans that would lead to a monetary union as well as the social policy side of the 1992 programme.

26 October.   Nigel Lawson resigned as Chancellor of the Exchequer. John Major became Chancellor and Douglas Hurd became Foreign Secretary.

5 December.   Mrs Thatcher defeated Sir Anthony Meyer in a leadership contest by 314 votes to 24, with 31 abstentions.

8–9 December.   At the European Council meeting in Strasbourg Margaret Thatcher was forced to accept a majority decision to assemble an intergovernmental conference to draw up a Treaty on Monetary Union on the basis of the Delors Report. Eleven member states (with the exception of the UK) also approved the *Community Charter of the Social Basic Laws of Working People*. Thatcher was forced to moderate her position because of a revolt in the Conservative Party.

1990

14 July.   Nicholas Ridley resigned from the Cabinet due to a remark that the ERM was a German attempt to dominate Europe. His resignation weakened Thatcher in the face of Hurd and Major. Peter Lilley moved to Trade and Industry to replace Ridley.

5 August.   In a speech in Aspen, Colorado, Mrs Thatcher called for a 'European Magna Carta' to be agreed at the forthcoming Paris CSCE Summit. She also noted the need for the Community to ensure that Eastern European states are able to join the Community.

5 October.   The UK announced that it would join the ERM as of 8 October at a central rate against the Deutschmark of 2.95. The pound was allowed to float at 6% either side of its central parity (the same rate as the Spanish peseta). It was expected that the pound would move to the narrower band of 2.25% as soon as possible. Pressure from Hurd and Major had forced Thatcher to join the ERM.

8 October.   The entry of pound sterling to the ERM at +/−6% band.

23 October.   The House of Commons debated the UK's accession to the ERM.

27–28 October.   An extraordinary summit was held in Rome to decide the date for the opening of stage two of Monetary Union before the

December IGC began. Eventually 1 January 1994 was the date chosen after a long period of German indecision. The outcome of the vote for the date of stage two was 11 to one, and Thatcher was annoyed that the UK was the only dissenter.

1 November. Sir Geoffrey Howe resigned his posts of Deputy Prime Minister and Leader of the House of Commons which he had held since July 1989. His resignation was the result of the comments regarding the future of the European Community that Mrs Thatcher had made on her return from the Rome Summit in October. He was the last survivor from her original Cabinet in 1979. His resignation speech was given in the House of Commons on 13 November.

13 November. In his resignation speech in Parliament Sir Geoffrey Howe condemned the way Mrs Thatcher had dealt with the other members of the European Community, and blamed her for the rise in inflation due to her resistance to join the ERM. His speech galvanised Mrs Thatcher's opponents and obviously had an impact on Michael Heseltine's decision to oppose her in the annual leadership contest.

20 November. Voting took place in the Conservative Party leadership election. Margaret Thatcher received 204 votes, Michael Heseltine received 152 votes, and there were 16 abstentions. Due to the complex election formula, Margaret Thatcher needed at least 187 votes plus a 56-vote lead over her opponent to win. She was four votes short of victory.

22 November. Margaret Thatcher resigned as leader of the Conservative Party.

Declared supporters in the Conservative Party leadership election, November 1990

For Michael Heseltine

1. Julian Amery
2. Spencer Batiste
3. Anthony Beaumont-Dark
4. William Benyon
5. Sir Antony Buck
6. John Carlisle
7. Lord Carrington
8. Paul Channon
9. Derek Conway
10. Patrick Cormack
11. Julian Critchley
12. Quentin Davies
13. Tim Devlin
14. Den Dover
15. Sir Peter Emery
16. David Evans
17. Keith Hampson
18. Alan Haselhurst
19. Christopher Hawkins
20. Jerry Hayes
21. Sir Barney Hayhoe
22. Kenneth Hind
23. Sir Geoffrey Howe
24. David Howell
25. David Hunt
26. Sir Ian Gilmour
27. Sir Philip Goodhart
28. Ian Grist
29. Dame Jill Knight
30. Michael Knowles

31. David Knox
32. Michael Latham
33. Nigel Lawson
34. John Lee
35. Edward Leigh
36. Sir Neil Macfarlane
37. Tony Marlow
38. Michael Mates
39. Michael Morris
40. Sir Charles Morrison
41. Anthony Nelson
42. David Nicholson
43. Emma Nicholson
44. James Pawsey
45. Elizabeth Peacock
46. Barry Porter
47. William Powell
48. Sir David Price
49. Lord Prior

50. Keith Raffan
51. Lord Rippon
52. Sir Wyn Roberts
53. Peter Rost
54. Lord St John of Fawsley
55. Nicholas Soames
56. Robin Squire
57. Ivor Stanbrook
58. Sir Peter Tapsell
59. Peter Temple-Morris
60. Patrick Thompson
61. Malcolm Thornton
62. David Trippier
63. Peter Walker
64. Sir Dennis Walters
65. Charles Wardle
66. Kenneth Warren
67. Bowen Wells
68. Jerry Wiggin

For Douglas Hurd

1. Tony Baldry
2. Henry Bellingham
3. Peter Bottomley
4. Virginia Bottomley
5. Julian Brazier
6. Peter Brooke
7. Nicholas Budgen
8. Kenneth Carlisle
9. Mathew Carrington
10. Lynda Chalker
11. Kenneth Clarke
12. Michael Fallon
13. Tristan Garel-Jones
14. Jeremy Hanley
15. David Heathcoat-Amory
16. Douglas Hogg
17. Lord Home
18. Sir Peter Hordern
19. Alan Howarth

20. Andrew Hunter
21. Robert Key
22. Tom King
23. Andrew Mackay
24. Richard Needham
25. Stevan Norris
26. Chris Patten
27. John Patten
28. Timothy Raison
29. Malcolm Rifkind
30. Nicholas Scott
31. Sir Giles Shaw
32. Ian Taylor
33. Peter Viggers
34. William Waldergrave
35. Sir John Wheeler
36. Lord Whitelaw
37. Ann Widdecombe
38. Tim Yeo

For John Major

1. Jonathan Aitken
2. James Arbuthnot

3. Jeffrey Archer
4. Jacques Arnold

5.	Robert Atkins	32.	Sir Nichols Lyell
6.	Nicholas Bennett	33.	John MacGregor
7.	Andrew Bowden	34.	David Maclean
8.	Graham Bright	35.	John Maples
9.	Alan Clark	36.	David Martin
10.	Anthony Coombs	37.	Francis Maude
11.	David Davis	38.	David Mellor
12.	Lord James Douglas-Hamilton	39.	Andrew Mitchell
13.	Tony Favell	40.	John Moore
14.	Barry Field	41.	Malcolm Moss
15.	Michael Forsyth	42.	Gerry Neale
16.	Eric Forth	43.	Michael Nenbert
17.	Ceceil Franks	44.	Tony Newton
18.	Roger Freeman	45.	Michael Portillo
19.	John Gummer	46.	Angela Rumbold
20.	William Hague	47.	Richard Ryder
21.	Archie Hamilton	48.	Gillian Shephard
22.	Robert Hayward	49.	Andrew Stewart
23.	Terence Higgins	50.	Norman Tebbit
24.	Michael Howard	51.	Margaret Thatcher
25.	Robert Hughes	52.	Peter Thurnham
26.	Michael Jack	53.	David Waddington
27.	Robert Jackson	54.	John Wakeham
28.	Roger King	55.	Bill Walker
29.	Norman Lamont	56.	John Watts
30.	Ian Lang	57.	Ann Winterton
31.	Peter Lilley	58.	Nicholas Winterton

27 November.   John Major won the Conservative Party leadership election gaining 185 votes which was just short of the 187 that was required for an outright victory. His opponents, Michael Heseltine and Douglas Hurd, conceded.

28 November.   Margaret Thatcher resigned as Prime Minister. John Major became Prime Minister, Norman Lamont became Chancellor of the Exchequer, Chris Patten became Party Chairman and Michael Heseltine moved to Environment. The Labour Party agreed to back the UK's eventual entry into EMU.

6.   Positive tones, 1991

1991

6 January.   Thatcher accepted the Presidency of the Bruges Group.

8 January.   The Chancellor, Norman Lamont, announced proposals for a new currency, the Hard ECU, which would be created and managed by a European Monetary Fund. The Hard ECU would float alongside existing currencies in the ERM of the EMS. The proposals had previously been promised by John Major at the December 1990 European Council meeting and were based on outline proposals that Major had made when he was Chancellor, in June 1990.

11 March.   At a summit with Helmut Kohl in Bonn, John Major said that the UK would play a role 'at the very heart of Europe', which contrasted with views expressed by Thatcher at Bruges in October 1988, when she highlighted her desire to impose limits on European integration.

12 March.   Thatcher was elected President of a new pressure group called the Conservative Way Forward.

11 June.   A leaked memo from the Bruges Group to the *Evening Standard*, criticising the government's policy on Europe, resulted in protests from all sides of the Conservative Party.

25 July.   The European Court of Justice overturned a UK Act of Parliament in a dispute over Spanish trawlers fishing in UK waters.

4 October.   An Anglo-Italian paper on the future of European defence was published. It proposed that while the WEU should be the defence arm of the EC, NATO would remain the primary guarantee of European security.

28 October.   The UK secured the right to keep the pound sterling if it so wished.

8 November.   The Euro-sceptic Bill Cash was to be replaced as Chairman of the Conservative backbench European Affairs Committee by Sir Norman Fowler.

11 November.   In his Mansion House speech, John Major highlighted his willingness to do a deal on European economic and political union at the forthcoming European Council meeting in Maastricht.

13 November.   Sir Norman Fowler unseated William Cash to become the Chairman of the backbench Conservative Party committee on Europe.

18 November.   The UK published the White Paper, *Competing for Quality*, which highlighted certain government services where competitive tendering was being considered.

20 November.   John Major spelt out the UK's position on Europe in a speech during the debate on the European Community in the House of Commons.

9–10 December.   The Dutch Prime Minister, Ruud Lubbers, opened the European Council meeting in Maastricht on 9 December. The summit ended with agreement, early on 11 December, on a framework treaty for European Union, incorporating EPU and EMU agreements. It also set a timetable for their implementation and provided for a new security and defence dimension to EC cooperation. John Major won an opt-out for the UK from stage three of European Monetary Union. The UK also rejected the Social Chapter, which the other 11 members of the Community signed.

18–19 December. In a two-day debate in the House of Commons, on the Maastricht Treaty, seven Conservative MPs voted against the government while 20 other MPs abstained.

7.   Hostage to fortune, 1992–96

1992

21 January. The Advocate General of the European Court of Justice endorsed two charges which had been brought against the UK government as a result of its failure to comply with the EC directive on drinking water purity.

9 April. On polling day, the Conservative Party won the election with a majority of 21 seats (it had stood at 88 when Parliament was dissolved in March) in the House of Commons with 336 seats and 41.9% of the vote as against Labour's 270 seats and 34.4% of the vote: 33,551,000 valid votes were cast, which was 76.7% of the electorate. The new Parliament contained 60 women (44 in the outgoing Parliament) and 140 new MPs. On winning, John Major promised a 'classless society'. During the election the issue of Europe had not surfaced, although all three main parties were officially pro-Europe in their manifestos.

6 May. The new UK Parliament was opened with the Queen's speech, which included a bill to implement the Maastricht Treaty.

7 May. First reading of the European Communities Act.

10 May. Chris Patten was replaced by Sir Norman Fowler as Chairman of the Conservative Party.

11 May. The UK rejected the demands of the European Commission to abandon its border controls and insisted on its rights to maintain passport controls.

20–21 May. The European Communities (Amendment) Bill passed the second reading debate in the House of Commons by 336 to 92. The Liberal Democrats (except one) voted with the government, the Labour Party abstained (officially) and 22 Conservative MPs voted against. An opposition motion declining to give the Bill a second reading, because it allowed the UK to opt-out of the Social Chapter, was defeated by 360 votes to 261, with 61 Labour MPs voting against it.

21 May. In the House of Commons, the Foreign Secretary, Douglas Hurd, gave a speech on the Maastricht Treaty during the second reading debate of the European Communities (Amendment) Bill.

3 June. More than 100 Conservative MPs signed a House of Commons motion which called for a fresh start in Europe. The Prime Minister promised a further debate on the Bill to ratify the Maastricht Treaty before the committee stage began.

4 June. John Major defended the Maastricht Treaty in a debate in the House of Commons by stating that 'the ratification and implementation of the treaty is in our national interest'.

8 June. In the House of Commons, Douglas Hurd stated that it was important to allay fears that the Maastricht Treaty would result in centralising the Community. He therefore advocated a separate interpretation of the Treaty.

28 June. In an interview with David Frost, Margaret Thatcher referred to the Maastricht Treaty as being 'a treaty too far' and criticised John Major for re-appointing Jacques Delors.

29 June. John Major reported to the House of Commons on the European Council meeting in Lisbon and at the same time defended the Maastricht Treaty and dismissed calls for a referendum.

1 July. The UK assumed the Presidency of the European Council.

2 July. Lady Thatcher repeated her call for a referendum on Europe in her maiden speech in the House of Lords.

26 August. The Chancellor of the Exchequer, Norman Lamont, announced that despite the turbulence of the foreign exchange rates the government will stay in the ERM.

16 September. Pressure on the pound increased and the minimum lending rate was increased from 10% to 12%. Due to the continuing turbulence, it was announced that the base rate would rise to 15% the next day. At the close of business in London the pound stering stood at DM 2.75. The worsening situation meant that the Chancellor, Norman Lamont, announced that the UK would pull out of the ERM and that the second interest rate increase would not take place. These events were referred to as 'Black Wednesday'.

17 September. The EC's Monetary Committee agreed to the temporary suspension of the Italian lira and UK sterling from the ERM. The peseta was devalued by 5% and the UK cut its base rate to 10%. The Maastricht Treaty was approved by the Italian Senate by 176 votes to 16.

22 September. UK interest rates (base rate) were cut from 10% to 9%.

24–25 September. The House of Commons was recalled to debate the sterling crisis with a vote of 322 to 296 in favour of a motion supporting the government's economic policy.

1 October. The UK government, after tense Cabinet discussions, announced its desire to ratify the Maastricht Treaty and bring the European Communities (Amendment) Bill back to Parliament in December, or early in the new year.

8 October. In an article in *The European*, Lady Thatcher attacked the Maastricht Treaty and warned that 'Maastricht will hand over more power to unelected bureaucrats and erode the freedoms of ordinary men and women'.

16 October. An extraordinary meeting of the European Council was convened in Birmingham in an attempt to iron out the problems that existed with the ERM. The meeting was also intended as a means of defining a suitable stance for Denmark and the UK so that their government positions could be made easier through a declaration on subsidiarity. In the end all decisions were deferred to the Edinburgh European Summit.

4 November. In a debate on the Maastricht Treaty in the House of Commons, the government won the paving debate allowing the Bill to proceed into the committee stage by 319 votes to 316. While 19 Liberal Democrats voted with the government, 26 Conservatives voted against it, along with Labour MPs. There were seven deliberate Conservative abstentions. Without Liberal Democrat votes the government would have lost the vote, despite the fact that the government commanded a 21-seat majority in the House of Commons.

5 November. The UK Prime Minister said that the European Communities (Amendment) Bill would not receive its third reading until after the second Danish referendum in May 1993.

25 November. The European Court of Justice found the UK guilty of a breach of the drinking water directive.

1993

15 February. Douglas Hurd (the Foreign Secretary) announced that fresh legal advice had suggested that Parliamentary defeat over the Labour amendment (number 27) to the Social Chapter would not stop the UK ratifying the Treaty. This information contradicted earlier statements given by the Minister of State at the Foreign Office, Tristan Garel-Jones.

22 February. Michael Morris, the Chairman of the Ways and Means Committee, accepted an application by the Labour Party for an emergency debate on the conflicting statements on the legal interpretation of amendment 27. This replaced the planned committee stage debate. Sir Nicholas Lyell, the Attorney-General, stated that even if the amendment was passed, it would make no difference to the government's ratification of the Treaty. In the event, the closure motion was passed without division due to the fact that no member would act as a teller in the government lobby.

8 March. The government was defeated by 314 votes to 292 on a Labour amendment to the Maastricht Bill concerning membership of the Council of Regions, despite the fact it had a majority in the House of Commons of 20 seats: 26 Conservative MPs voted for the Labour amendment, while 22 abstained; four Plaid Cymru and three Scottish National Party MPs voted with the government.

15 March. Michael Morris, the Chairman of the Ways and Means Committee, ruled that MPs could not vote on amendment 27. This was because it would have removed the government's ability to opt-out of the Social Chapter. However, he allowed a division on another Labour amendment which required a further debate on the Social Chapter before final ratification of the Treaty. In the event, the government accepted the amendment rather than lose the vote.

19 March. The amended Clause 1 of the European Communities (Amendment) Bill was passed by 296 votes to 96. The unamended Clause 2 was passed by 271 votes to 55, and the unamended Clause 3 was passed without division.

21 March. The ruling French Socialist Party was defeated by the right-wing RPR–UDF alliance in the first round of legislative elections.

22 March. The House of Commons rejected a call for a referendum on the Maastricht Treaty, while the committee stage was finally completed after 163 hours of debate.

4 May. At the House of Commons report stage of the Maastricht Treaty, the Speaker (Betty Boothroyd) stated that she would allow a division on a new Labour amendment which, nearly the same as amendment 27, would delete the government's opt-out from the Social Chapter from the Bill. With the prospect of defeat through an alliance of Labour, Liberal Democrat and Conservative Euro-sceptics, the Foreign Secretary announced that the government would accept the amendment as it would have no legal effect on the ability of the government to ratify the Treaty.

5 May. Completion of the report stage of the European Communities (Amendment) Bill.

20 May. The House of Commons gave a third reading to the Maastricht Treaty Bill and the government secured a majority by 292 votes to 112: 41 Conservative MPs voted against the Bill and five abstained. While the Labour Party officially abstained, five MPs voted with the government and 66 against. The Liberal Democrats voted with the government.

27 May. Norman Lamont resigned as Chancellor of the Exchequer and was replaced by Kenneth Clarke, who had been Home Secretary since April 1992.

22 June. The European Communities (Amendment) Bill reached the committee stage in the House of Lords. This was the first of six days in committee which ended without any amendment being passed.

12 July. In the House of Commons vote on VAT on domestic fuel, the majority of the government was reduced to eight. The report stage of the European Communities (Amendment) Bill in the House of Lords – the first of three days spent on report. Brussels Ecofin Council discusses the UK's report of its convergence criteria programme for EMU.

14 July. An amendment to the European Communities (Amendment) Bill was moved in the House of Lords by the Conservative Lord Blake, calling for a UK referendum. It was defeated by 445 votes to 176. The motion had been supported by Baroness Thatcher.

20 July. The third reading of the European Communities (Amendment) Bill in the House of Lords was secured by 141 votes to 29. This, therefore, completed the Parliamentary stages of the Bill and it received royal assent that evening.

21 July. In the European Communities (Amendment) Bill debate, the Speaker stated that it was her view that it would be contrary to the 1689 Bill of Rights for the courts to question the proceedings of Parliament, but that it was up to the House of Lords to provide a decision.

22 July. The House of Commons and House of Lords held identical motions on the Social Chapter. An opposition amendment in the House of Lords, suggesting that the Treaty could not take place 'until such time as the Government have given notification of the EC that it intends to adopt the agreement attached to the protocol on social policy', was defeated by 295 votes to 88. The government motion, 'noting the policy of her Majesty's Government on the adoption of the protocol on social policy', was passed by 271 votes to 85. No resolution was reached in the House of Commons with the Labour amendment defeated, and the vote was thought to be 317 votes in favour and against. The Speaker, therefore, cast her vote with the government in accordance with precedent. However, it was later highlighted that the original vote was 316 for and 317 against. The government lost its motion by 324 votes to 316. On the amendment, 15 Conservative MPs voted against the government and eight abstained; 23 Conservative MPs voted against the government on the main motion and one abstained. Although the Ulster Unionists voted with the government, both parties stated that they had not done a deal. However, as the Act stipulated that both Houses of Parliament needed to come to a resolution on the Social Chapter before the Maastricht Treaty could be ratified by the UK, the Prime Minister announced that a revised motion would be tabled the next day and that this would be made a vote of confidence in the government. Therefore, this threatened a general election if a defeat was inflicted upon the government.

23 July. The government defeated the Labour amendment, which was the same as the previous day's amendment, by 339 votes to 301. The government confidence motion was passed by 339 votes to 299 with only one Conservative MP, Rupert Allason, abstaining. He had abstained the day before and his actions resulted in him having the Conservative whip suspended.

25 July. John Major referred to three members of the Cabinet as 'bastards'.

30 July. Lord Rees-Mogg's action, which challenged the legality of the European Communities (Amendment) Bill ratification process, failed. It had been launched on 26 July.

2 August. The UK government formally ratified the Maastricht Treaty in Rome. The ERM of the EMS effectively collapsed and agreement was reached to allow currencies to fluctuate within a broad band of 15% either side of their central rates, rather than the 2.25% band for strong currencies or the 6% for the Spanish and Portuguese currencies.

2 September. The UK deposited its instrument of ratification of the Maastricht Treaty.

20 September. John Major told Conservative MPs to show loyalty to their leaders and to stop their 'stupid internecine squabbling'.

23 September. John Major issued his post-Maastricht view for the development of the European Community and rejected a corporate power structure in favour of a decentralised market solution.

25 September. John Major put forward his views of Europe in an article in *The Economist.*

1994

3 March. The House of Lords ruled that certain aspects of UK employment protection legislation relating to statutory redundancy payments and unfair dismissal were in conflict with EU directives of 1975 and 1976. This was because they discriminated against part-time workers.

15 March. Negotiations in Brussels over the size of the blocking minority broke down due to the UK's reluctance to allow an increase from three countries and 23 votes for a blocking vote to four countries and 27 votes.

26–27 March. Ioannina informal General Affairs Council (Greece). John Major told the House of Commons on 29 March that at the meeting a compromise had been reached and that the blocking minority would be increased to 27 votes, but with the ability for the existing 23-vote minority to create a delay in the implementation of EU legislation.

1 May. Michael Portillo fuelled Conservative divisions over Europe by insisting, on GMTV, that the UK should never sign up to a single currency. He, therefore, stepped out of line of UK government policy.

31 May. John Major talked of a 'multi-track' Europe.

9 June. The Conservative Party lost 14 seats in the fourth direct European Parliament elections (European elections were also held in Denmark, Ireland and the Netherlands).

24–25 June. The European Council meeting in Corfu was dominated by the failure of the Heads of State and Government to appoint a President of the European Commission. John Major vetoed the candidacy of the Belgian Prime Minister Jean-Luc Dehaene due to his 'interventionist tendencies'.

15 July. An extraordinary meeting of the European Council in Brussels agreed on the selection of Jacques Santer to succeed Jacques Delors as President of the European Commission for a five-year term from January 1995. Santer had been Prime Minister of Luxembourg since 1984. Santer was a compromise candidate following John Major's veto of the Belgian Prime Minister Jean-Luc Dehaene at the June Corfu Summit.

20 July. John Major reshuffled the government in an attempt to improve its image after the poor results in the May–June Parliamentary by-elections, and in the June local and European elections. Four members of the Cabinet were replaced: Peter Brooke (National Heritage), John Patten (Education), Lord Wakeham (Leader of the House of Lords), and John

MacGregor (Transport). David Hunt became Chancellor of the Duchy of Lancaster, Stephen Dorrell became Secretary of State for National Heritage, William Waldergrave was appointed Minister of Agriculture, Fisheries and Food, Brian Mawhinney was appointed Secretary of State for Transport, Jonathan Aitken became Chief Secretary to the Treasury, Jeremy Hanley was appointed Minister without Portfolio and Chairman of the Conservative Party Organisation, and Viscount Cranborne (Lord Cecil of Essendon) became Lord Privy Seal and Leader of the House of Lords.

21 July.   Tony Blair was elected Leader of the Labour Party, winning an outright majority of 57% in the first round vote conducted among MPs, party members and trade unions.

7 September.   The Prime Minister, John Major, gave the William and Mary Lecture at the University of Leiden, on 'Europe: A Future that Works'. In it he rejected Franco-German proposals for a two-tier Europe.

1995

1 January.   Austria, Finland and Sweden joined the EU on the basis of the terms settled in March 1994, and approved in referendum votes in June, October and November respectively. The Twelve became the Fifteen, and the EU's population increased from 345 million to 368 million. With regard to voting in the Council of Ministers, Austria and Sweden would have four votes and Finland three, out of a total of 87. A qualified majority therefore required 62 votes (except for decisions on Commission proposals), with at least ten Member States voting in favour. The accession of the three states meant that the EP increased from 567 to 625 members, with 22 from Sweden, 21 from Austria and 16 from Finland.

18 January.   The government narrowly won a vote in the House of Commons on a December agreement on the Common Fisheries Policy. This agreement allowed Spanish vessels to have access to large areas of the 'Irish box' from January 1996.

2 February.   The Bank of England raised the base lending rate by a half a percentage point to 6.75%.

12 February.   A junior member of the UK government, Charles Wardle, resigned to draw attention to what he saw as the threat of the EU imposing the removal of passport controls. He believed that this would cause an influx of economic migrants into the UK. However, John Major told the House of Commons on 14 February and 16 February that the UK would maintain its border controls.

16 February.   John Major ordered the Cabinet to cease 'speculative debate' as divisions within the Cabinet over policy to the EU became increasingly evident during February. The decision was taken by Major primarily because a vote on EU policy was scheduled for March.

1 March.   The former Chancellor, Norman Lamont, voted for an opposition motion in the House of Commons. The motion criticised the government's handling of policy related to the EU. It was defeated by 319 votes to 314.

2 June.   The IGC Reflection Group was launched. The first Ministerial meeting in Messina revealed that a large gulf existed between the UK and the majority of the other Member States over the extent of reform that was desired.

22 June.   John Major resigned as leader of the Conservative Party and stated that he would stand in the forthcoming leadership contest.

23 June.   Douglas Hurd announced that he would resign as Foreign Secretary after the leadership election.

25 June.   John Redwood stated that he would stand in the Conservative leadership contest, and resigned as Secretary of State for Wales on 26 June.

4 July.   John Major won the Conservative leadership election with 218 votes of the 329 Conservative MPs entitled to vote. John Redwood received 89 votes, while eight MPs abstained and 12 votes were spoiled. 327 out of the 329 MPs voted.

5 July.   John Major announced the reshuffled Cabinet. In the reshuffle the Department of Employment was abolished and the majority of its concerns were incorporated into the Department of Education. Michael Heseltine's position as Deputy Prime Minister had greater scope than the previous occupiers of the title, namely Sir Geoffrey Howe and William Whitelaw. Heseltine's position included chairing key Cabinet committees, while also retaining control over competition policy, which had been part of his remit as President of the Board of Trade. Douglas Hurd resigned from the Cabinet along with Jonathan Aitken, the latter's reason was due to his involvement in fighting a libel case. Jeremy Hanley and David Hunt were demoted from the Cabinet, while John Redwood had resigned from the Cabinet to fight the leadership contest and was not reinstated.

1996

12 March.   UK government White Paper on the IGC: 'A Partnership of Nations'.

20 March.   It was announced that the UK could face a major health crisis in the form of a possible link between BSE which is found in cattle, and the fatal disease found in humans known as Creutzfeldt-Jakob disease (CJD).

25 March.   The EU veterinary committee voted by 14 to one, to recommend a total ban, which was immediately implemented, on the export of beef and beef products from the UK. The only dissenter was the UK.

29 March.   The 1996 IGC was launched in Turin. The IGC process was expected to continue until mid-1997, concluding at the June 1997 Amsterdam Summit.

3 April.   The UK government announced that it would hold a referendum if it decided that the UK should join a European single currency.

21 May.   The UK adopted a policy of non-cooperation with the EU until a timetable to lift the ban on the export of beef was settled. The government established a Ministerial committee on 22 May, chaired by Prime Minister Major, to oversee the confrontational strategy.

24 May.   The UK vetoed a EU bankruptcy convention as part of its policy of non-cooperation.

4 June.   The European Commission announced that it would phase out the UK export ban on tallow, gelatine and semen over the following weeks if stricter health controls were imposed (commencing on 11 June). On the same day the UK government put forward to EU Agriculture Ministers its plans for the eradication of BSE from cattle herds, which, despite some additional safety measures, was the reiteration of its existing stance.

5 June.   The UK approved the EU–Slovenia association agreement, despite its policy of non-cooperation.

17 June.   The UK agricultural dispute dominated the Rome Foreign Ministers' meeting which was intended to prepare the agenda for the forthcoming European Council meeting in Florence. EU Transport Ministers meeting in Luxembourg produced agreement by 14 to one (the UK voted against) that future negotiations with the USA on the 'open skies' agreements, relating to the liberalisation of the aviation industry, should be negotiated by the EU as a bloc rather than by individual Member States.

21–22 June.   At the European Council meeting in Florence, Foreign Ministers reached agreement on the first day to end the confrontation between the UK and the other Member States over the EU-imposed ban on UK exports of beef and beef products. The summit was therefore able to deal with the main items on the agenda, which included an analysis of the first three months of the IGC to review the Maastricht TEU.

2 July.   The European Commissioner responsible for fisheries suggested that 1997 fish quotas should reduce the quota for North Sea herring by a half.

12 July.   The European Court of Justice rejected an appeal by the UK government to lift the ban on UK beef exports, which had been imposed by the European Commission in March 1996. The Court's ruling was based on scientific evidence of a link between BSE in cattle and Creutzfeldt-Jakob disease in humans.

22 July.   The European Commissioner with responsibility for agriculture, Franz Fischler, asked EU Agriculture Ministers to ban the spleen, brain and spinal cord of sheep and goats from entering the human food chain.

17 September. Agricultural Ministers reached agreement on the request of an increase in the intervention purchasing of beef.

24 September. Agricultural Ministers proposed the use of 500 million ECU from surplus budget funds to assist farmers affected by the loss of consumer confidence in beef products as a result of the BSE crisis. This was in addition to the 850 million ECU which was approved in June 1996.

5 October. An extraordinary Dublin European Council meeting examined the IGC negotiations, at which Member States reaffirmed June 1997 as the deadline for completing all work. The UK Prime Minister, John Major, noted his opposition to 'over-extending' the EU's competence in the field of defence cooperation. He also insisted that any treaty should remove the possibility of allowing health and safety regulations to limit the length of the working week.

14 October. The UK noted its opposition to European Commission proposals to reduce up to 50% the capacity of fishing fleets for certain types of fish.

12 November. European Court of Justice rejected UK government's challenge to the Working Time Directive.

8. A change of direction, 1997–

1997

17–19 March. In Brussels, the EU Agricultural Ministers meeting reached agreement that all beef had to be marked with its country of origin. This development was resisted by the UK because the government considered it would affect the sales of beef in the wake of the March 1996 world-wide ban on UK beef exports, which was a response to BSE fears.

1 May. Labour Party gained 44.4% of vote in UK general election and won 418 seats, a majority of 179 in the House of Commons. The Labour leader, Tony Blair, became the youngest Prime Minister since 1812.

16–17 June. The Amsterdam European Council meeting finalised the Treaty negotiated during the IGC, while the newly elected UK Labour government accepted the Social Chapter.

22 December. The Defence Ministers of Germany, Italy, Spain and the UK signed an agreement for the full production phase of the £42 billion Eurofighter aircraft, the idea for which had been initially conceived in the late 1970s.

1998

January. The EU approved a partial lifting of the 1996 export ban on UK beef, with the proposal only applying to the export of beef products from Northern Ireland. This was because it was the only part of the UK that had a complete, computerised tracking system and fewer recorded cases of BSE than elsewhere in the UK.

16–17 March. The Brussels meeting of EU Agricultural Ministers approved a partial lifting of the 1996 export ban of UK beef. This had previously been approved by the European Commission in January 1998. Eleven of the 15 Member States supported a relaxation of the ban, Belgium and Germany voting against and Luxembourg and Spain abstaining. The easing of export restrictions applied to deboned beef from cattle aged between six and 30 months which had come from herds certified to have been BSE-free for the last eight years.

8 April. The UK Court of Appeal ruled that Spanish trawlers were able to claim £100 million in compensation from the UK government for the time they had been banned from fishing in UK waters.

27 May. The European Commission agreed to lift the ban on the exportation of beef from Northern Ireland from 1 June 1998. The lifting of the ban in Ulster had been agreed in March 1998 but it was conditional on the inspection of meat plants by EU veterinary experts.

15–16 July. Cardiff European Council meeting.

6 July. UK Strategic Defence Review outlined a reduction of £915 million in British defence spending in real terms over a three-year period (to £23 million in 200–02 or 2.4% of GDP).

27–29 July. UK Cabinet reshuffle resulted in the dismissal of four members of the Cabinet. It was perceived as a means of strengthening the Blairite and pro-European representation of government as well as curbing the power of Chancellor Brown. The new appointments included Peter Mandelson as President of the Board of Trade and Secretary for Trade and Industry, Nick Brown as Minister of Agriculture, Fisheries and Food, Stephen Byers as Chief Secretary to the Treasury and Baroness Jay of Paddington as Lord Privy Seal, Leader of the House of Lords and Minister for Women.

1 October. EU Working Time Directive came into force in Britain.

2 November. Meeting in London between Tony Blair and Gerhard Schröder, prompting a new Anglo-German relationship.

Pressure Groups

In the last two decades there has been an increase in Euro-scepticism within the UK. This has taken place most visibly within the realms of the Conservative Party and is exemplified by the emergence of the Bruges Group. There are, however, many other groups with an interest in European affairs, which do not share this sceptical perspective. The following pages provide a brief resumé of the more influential of these groups which have an interest in European affairs and provides details of key personnel.

Action Centre for Europe Ltd

181 Town Lane, Whittle le Woods, Chorley, Lancashire PR6 8AG
Tel: 01257 276 992   Fax: 01257 231 254

An agency which organises working groups on EU subjects of particular interest, such as EMU.

Adam Smith Institute

50 Westminster Mansions, Little Smith Street, Westminster, London SW1P 3DJ
Tel: 0171-222 4995   Fax: 0171-222 7444

A liberal economic pressure group that is opposed to the EU because of its dirigiste tendencies.

Anti-Maastricht Alliance

72 Loftus Road, London W12 7EL
Tel: 0181-740 7194   Fax: 0181-740 7194

An anti-EU umbrella group with no individual membership.

Bruges Group

Suite 216, The Linen Hall, 162–168 Regent Street, London W1R 5TB
Tel: 0171-287 4414   Fax: 0171-287 5522

Established in February 1989 to campaign for a less centralised EU, the group was inspired by Thatcher's September 1988 Bruges speech, in which she stressed that the UK had not rolled back the frontiers of the state in order to have them re-imposed from Brussels. The group believes there have to be major reforms within the EU, for example in the field of Common Agricultural Policy, and is against economic and monetary union. It advocates withdrawal from the European Union if its objectives are not met. Its Honorary President is Lady Thatcher.

The Campaign for an Independent Britain

81 Ashmole Street, London SW8 1NF
Tel: 0181-340 0314   Fax: 0171-582 7021

Formed in 1976 as the Safeguard Britain Campaign, its name was changed to the British Anti-Common Market Campaign in 1983 and further changed in 1989 to The Campaign for an Independent Britain. A cross-party and non-sectarian organisation, it aims to repeal the 1972 European Communities Act under which EU directives take precedence over UK law. Its President is Sir Richard Body MP, the Vice-President is Leolin Price QC, the Chairman is Lord Stoddart of Swindon, and the Vice-Chairmen are Austin Mitchell MP, Professor Stephen Bush, Lionel Bell, and Lord Pearson of Rannoch.

Confederation of British Industry

Centre Point, 103 New Oxford Street, London WC1A 1DU
Tel: 0171-379 7400   Fax: 0171-240 1578

Founded in 1965 as an independent, non-party political body financed by commerce and industry, it promotes the interests of British business. It represents the interests of small and large firms from all industries and has tended to have a pro-European viewpoint, evidenced by its campaign for UK entry to the ERM in 1990.

Conservatives against a Federal Europe

PO Box 5357, Southend-on-Sea, Essex SS1 3BF
Tel: 0171-219 2083   Fax: 0171-219 2031

Launched at the Conservative Party Conference in Bournemouth in October 1996 this is a revamped pressure group backed by the 'rebel' eight Conservative MPs (Christopher Gill, Teresa Gorman, Sir Teddy Taylor, Tony Marlow, Nicholas Budgen, Sir Richard Body, John Wilkinson and Richard Shepherd). It believes that the powers of European Courts over British affairs must be revoked, that the UK must regain control of its fisheries and agricultural policies, must make its own foreign and defence policies, and that the European Parliament must be reformed. In addition, the UK must not agree to Economic and Monetary Union. If it is not possible to attain these ends by negotiation, then it believes that the UK must withdraw from the EU. Its Presidents are Lord Pearson of Rannoch and Lord McAlpine of West Green, while its Chairman is Norman Lamont.

Conservative Group for Europe

Little Swinburne, Colwell, Hexham, Northumberland NE46 4TT
Tel: 01434 681 415   Fax: 01434 681 149

A pro-European Conservative group whose objectives are to promote the importance of the EU and develop links with other European political parties of a similar viewpoint.

Conservative Way Forward

PO Box 563, Watford, London WD1 3GZ
Tel: 0171-233 2023   Fax: 01923 442519

An organisation founded to defend the achievements of the Thatcher governments and to develop further Thatcherite ideals within the British Conservative Party. While many of these issues relate to domestic politics, they also affect European politics, including a desire for small government, tax cuts, deregulation and national sovereignty. Its President is Lady Thatcher, the Vice-President is Lord Tebbit, the Chairman is Lord Parkinson, the Secretary is Mark Allatt and the Treasurer is Barry Legg MP.

European Labour Forum

Bertrand Russel House, Gamble Street, Nottingham NG7 4ET
Tel: 0115 970 8318   Fax: 0115 942 0433

An organisation which attempts to promote European economic, political and social issues through discussion groups, including the ELF journal and ELF book series.

European Movement

11 Tufton Street, London SW1P 3QB
Tel: 0171-233 1422   Fax: 0171-799 2817

A non-party political organisation which promotes the UK's membership of the EU. This consists of various public campaigns and information programmes, while there is also a Young European Movement and a Business Forum for corporate members.

Federal Trust

11 Tufton Street, London SW1P 3QB
Tel: 0171-799 2818   Fax: 0171-799 2820

Founded in 1945 as a means of studying the post-war European environment, it has conducted major studies of the UK's relationship with the EU. These have included books and other research material.

Labour Movement in Europe

11 Tufton Street, London SW1P 3QB
Tel: 0171-233 1422   Fax: 0171-779 2817

This is an organisation comprising members of the Labour Party who favour the UK's participation in the EU.

The Liberal Democrat European Group

1 The Vat House, 27 Regents Bridge Gardens, London SW8 1HD
Tel/Fax: 0171-735 0241

As the European arm of the Liberal Democrat Party, which is itself pro-European, it aims to provide information to party members on EU policy developments.

Trades Union Congress

Congress House, 23–28 Great Russell Street, London WC1B 3LS
Tel: 0171-636 4030   Fax: 0171-636 0632

Founded in 1868, it is an independent association of trade unions which promotes the rights and welfare of those in work as well as assisting the unemployed. In recent years it has advocated a pro-European viewpoint, a factor influenced by the EU's ability to influence domestic governance. This was especially noticeable in the realm of social policy, where the then Conservative government of Margaret Thatcher advocated a policy of deregulation and flexibility, marked by an increase in part-time and temporary employment. By contrast, the EU, under the Presidency of Jacques Delors, put forward a social action programme, initially in the form of the Social Charter and thereafter comprising the Social Chapter, which attempted to set minimum standards throughout Europe. Predictably, the Conservative government did not accept this.

British European Commissioners

1 January 1973	Sir Christopher Soames
1 January 1973	George Thompson
1 January 1977	Roy Jenkins (President)
1 January 1977	Christopher Tugendhat
1 January 1981	Christopher Tugendhat
1 January 1981	I. Richard
1 January 1985	Lord Cockfield
1 January 1985	S. Clinton Davies
1 January 1989	Sir Leon Brittan
1 January 1989	Bruce Millan
1 January 1993	Sir Leon Brittan
1 January 1993	Bruce Millan
1 January 1995	Sir Leon Brittan
1 January 1995	Neil Kinnock

The Tory Rebel League

R = Rebellion: a vote against the government. A = No vote.
G = Voted with the government. * shows a member of the 1992 intake.

MP	Constituency	R	A	G	Points
W. Cash	Stafford	47	13	2	107
N. Winterton	Macclesfield	46	15	1	107
Sir T. Taylor	Southend E	48	10	4	106
Mrs A. Winterton	Congleton	44	17	1	105
*R. Knapman	Stroud	44	16	2	104
C. Gill	Ludlow	43	17	2	103
Sir T. Skeet	Beds N	41	19	2	101
T. Jessel	Twickenham	42	16	4	100
Mrs T. Gorman	Billericay	40	19	3	99
B. Walker	Tayside N	39	19	4	97
Sir I. Lawrence	Burton	38	21	3	97
M. Spicer	Worcs S	37	23	2	97
T. Marlow	Northampton N	36	25	1	97
N. Budgen	Wolverhampton SE	36	24	2	96
R. Shepherd	Aldridge	34	26	2	94
M. Lord	Suffolk Central	35	23	4	93
J. Cran	Beverley	30	31	1	91
J. Wilkinson	Ruislip	31	28	3	90
Sir R. Body	Holland	30	28	4	88
J. Biffen	Shropshire N	26	35	1	87
Sir P. Tapsell	Lindsey E	24	34	4	82
J. Carlisle	Luton N	21	40	1	82
J. Butcher	Coventry SW	19	43	0	81
Sir G. Gardiner	Reigate	23	34	5	80
W. Hawksley	Stourbridge	18	44	0	80
*W. Sweeney	Vale of Glam	21	36	5	78
*B. Legg	Milton Keynes SW	18	41	3	77
M. Carttiss	Gt Yarmouth	17	41	4	75
D. Porter	Waveney	15	44	3	74
R. Allason	Torbay	12	46	4	70
I. Duncan-Smith	Chingford	11	47	4	69
V. Bendall	Ilford N	4	56	2	64

MP	Constituency	R	A	G	Points
Sir R. Boyson	Brent N	12	39	11	63
J. Pawsey	Rugby	14	34	14	62
J. Townend	Bridlington	6	50	6	62
Sir R. Moate	Faversham	4	53	5	61
Sir N. Bonsor	Upminster	3	55	4	61
*B. Jenkin	Colchester N	1	58	3	60
K. Baker	Mole Valley	1	56	5	58
P. Fry	Wellingborough	5	47	10	57
Dr M. Clark	Rochford	2	51	9	55
*J. Whittingdale	Colchester S	1	41	20	43
A. Hunter	Basingstoke	5	24	33	34
Sir G. Vaughan	Reading E	1	27	34	29
G. Walden	Buckingham	0	24	38	24
Sir M. Grylls	Surrey NW	0	17	45	17
H. Greenway	Ealing N	4	8	50	16

(Reproduced by permission of *The Guardian.*)

SECTION X

Biographies

Adenauer, Konrad (1876–1967): The first Chancellor of the Federal Republic of Germany, he remained in office from 1949 until 1963 (resigned), having been re-elected in 1953 and 1957. Between 1951 and 1955 he also held the office of Foreign Minister. He negotiated German entry into the EEC and NATO and established diplomatic relations with the USSR in 1955. His foreign policy was known as 'policy of strength' and had two main objectives: the rehabilitation and reunification of Germany. Adenauer developed a close relationship with the French President, Charles de Gaulle, which produced the 1963 Treaty of Friendship between the two nations and served as the basis for the Franco-German axis which shaped the development of the European Community. Earlier in his career he was president of the Prussian State Council between 1920 and 1933 and served as mayor of Cologne (1917–33), but was then removed by the Nazis. During the Weimer Republic he was a key member of the Catholic Centre Party and subsequently founded the Christian Democratic Union in 1945, while he led the German delegation to the Congress of Europe at The Hague in 1948.

Bangemann, Martin (b. 1934): A member of the European Commission with responsibility for industrial affairs and information and telecommunications technologies. From 1989 to 1993 he was Vice-President of the European Commission with responsibility for the internal market, industrial affairs and relations with the European Parliament. Between 1993 and 1994 he had responsibility for industrial affairs and information and telecommunications technologies. Born in Wanzleben, he obtained a Doctor of Law from Munich University in 1964. He was elected a member of the Bundestag (1972–78) and was Chairman of the Baden–Württemberg FDP (1974–78). Between 1985 and 1988 he was Chairman of the FDP, while also having been a member of the European Parliament (1973–84). During that period he was Chairman of the Liberal and Democratic Group in the European Parliament (1979–84). In 1984 he was appointed Federal Minister of Economic Affairs, a post he maintained until 1988. Between 1986 and 1989 he was a member of the Bundestag.

Bevin, Ernest (1881–1951): A prominent member of the UK Labour movement both as a trade unionist and a member of government. In his earlier career as a trade unionist he helped establish the Transport and General Workers' Union, becoming its first general secretary. However, it was within the realm of politics that he is most remembered. He was an active supporter of UK rearmament in the 1930s to counter the threat from Nazi Germany. Churchill appointed him Minister of Labour and National Service in 1940, a post he held until 1945. In the post-war Labour government of 1945–51 he was appointed Foreign Secretary, although he expected to be made Chancellor of the Exchequer. But this change did not affect him and his influence in the post-war world of international politics proved to be highly significant, with him taking the initiative in the formation of the Organisation of European Economic Cooperation in 1947. He was also an important figure behind the creation of NATO. His enthusiasm in these fields influenced his health, of which there was a marked deterioration in the latter part of the Labour government, resulting in the Prime Minister, Clement Attlee, moving him from the Foreign Office.

Bjerregaard, Ritt (b. 1941): A Danish member of the European Commission with responsibility for environment and nuclear safety. Prior to her appointment to the European Commission she entered the Danish Parliament for the Social Democratic Party in 1971, being appointed Minister for Education in 1973, a position she subsequently held between 1975 and 1978. She was Minister for Social Affairs (1979–81) and Leader of the Parliamentary Social Democratic Party (1981–82), serving as Deputy Leader (1982–87) and again as Leader (1987–92).

Blair, Anthony (b. 1953): Appointed leader of the Labour Party in 1994 after the death of John Smith. Blair entered parliament in 1983 and was elected to the shadow Cabinet in 1988. However, it was not until his appointment as opposition spokesman on Home Affairs in 1992 that he rose to prominence, thereby providing a platform for his election as leader. In 1997 the Labour Party won the general election and Blair became Prime Minister. His government has proved to be both cautious and activist. It has decided to stay within Conservative spending limits for its first two years, but has proved activist in the granting of supervisory powers to the Bank of England for the setting of interest rates. The government is more pro-European than the previous Conservative administration, and has not been hampered by a significant band of Euro-sceptics. Under Blair the UK signed up to the Social Chapter at the Amsterdam European Council of June 1997 and successfully managed to steer its chairing of the Presidency in the first six months of 1998.

Bonino, Emma (b. 1948): An Italian member of the European Commission with responsibility for fisheries, consumer policy and the European Community Humanitarian Office (ECHO). She was elected to the Italian Chamber of Deputies in 1976 and re-elected in 1979, 1983, 1987, 1992, 1994. In 1979 she was elected to the European Parliament and was re-elected in 1984.

Brandt, Willy (1913–92): A German Social Democrat who was a member of the Bundestag between 1949 and 1957 and President of the Bundesrat (1955–57). As leader of the Social Democratic–Free Democratic coalition he was Chancellor of the Federal Republic of Germany between

1969 and 1974. During this time his greatest interest was foreign policy and he produced various agreements that were collectively referred to as *Ostpolitik*. This was negotiated between the Federal Republic of Germany and the states of Eastern Europe, including the Soviet Union. The most significant agreement was with the German Democratic Republic which ensured that East German products could enter the European Community through the Federal Republic of Germany. This policy therefore emphasised a shift away from the 'policy of strength' of Konrad Adenauer, although that did not mean that the Federal Republic under Brandt was less committed to organisations such as NATO and the EC. In this context, Brandt favoured a less insular approach to the Community and along with the French President, Georges Pompidou, advocated enlargement which eventually resulted in the accession of Denmark, Ireland and the UK in 1973.

Brittan, Sir Leon (b. 1939): A British Vice-President of the European Commission with responsibility for external relations with North America, Australia, New Zealand, Japan, China, Korea, Hong Kong, Macao and Taiwan; common commercial policy; and relations with the OECD and WTO. He was appointed by Margaret Thatcher as the UK's senior European Commissioner in 1989 after her refusal to reappoint the pro-integrationist Lord Cockfield. Brittan was given the responsibility of competition, while he also served as Vice-President (1989–93). From 1993 to 1994 he was a member of the European Commission with responsibility for external economic affairs and trade policy. Prior to his European Commission appointment, Brittan was Home Secretary (1983–85) and Secretary of State for Trade and Industry (1985–86) in the UK Conservative government led by Margaret Thatcher. However, he resigned from the latter post after a disagreement with the Defence Secretary, Michael Heseltine, over the procurement of helicopters for the armed forces, of which Heseltine favoured a European bid centred on the UK firm of Westland.

Broek, Hans van den (b. 1936): A Dutch member of the European Commission with responsibility for external relations with the countries of Central and Eastern Europe, the former Soviet Union, Mongolia, Turkey, Cyprus, Malta and other European countries; common foreign and security policy and human rights (in agreement with the President); and external missions. Between 1993 and 1994 he was responsible for external political relations, common foreign and security policy and enlargement negotiations. Born in Paris, he is a lawyer by trade and was a member of the Lower House of Parliament between 1976 and 1981. In 1978 he was a member of the executive of the Christian Democratic Party and was subsequently appointed State Secretary for Foreign Affairs between 1981 and 1982. In 1982 he was appointed Minister of Foreign Affairs, a post to which he was reappointed in 1986 and 1989. During that time he had the crucial task of chairing Foreign Ministers' meetings during the 1991 Intergovernmental Conference which produced the Treaty on European Union.

Brosio, Manlio (1897–1980): An Italian national whose opposition to fascism resulted in him being forbidden from taking part in politics during the inter-war period. He was a member of the National Liberation Committee in 1943–44 and was appointed Deputy Prime Minister (1943–44) and Minister of Defence (1945–46). He subsequently held various Ambassadorial appointments, including Moscow (1947–51), London (1952–55), Washington (1955–61) and Paris (1961–64). Thereafter he was chosen in 1964 by the North Atlantic Council to succeed Dirk Stikker as Secretary-General of NATO, a position which he held until his resignation in 1971, when he was succeeded by Joseph Luns.

Brown, Gordon (b. 1951): A British Labour politician, he was appointed Chancellor of the Exchequer in May 1997 having been Shadow Chancellor since 1992. A native of Scotland, he famously obtained a 1st Class Honours degree and a Doctorate at an early age from Edinburgh University. As Chancellor, he has been responsible for giving the Bank of England responsibility for setting interest rates.

Callaghan, Lord James (b. 1912): A former Labour British Prime Minister from 1976 until 1979 (having succeeded Harold Wilson), James Callaghan was elected MP for South Cardiff in 1945 and continued to serve that geographical area until 1987, when he was made a Life Peer. (He joined the Labour Party in 1931.) During his time in Parliament he served in a number of government posts, including Chancellor of the Exchequer (1964–67), Home Secretary (1967–70) and Foreign Secretary (1974–76). During the latter period he was responsible for managing the government's renegotiation and referendum on its terms of entry to the European Economic Community. That period in the history of the Labour Party helped to sow the seeds of discord which subsequently resulted in the Party advocating withdrawal from the EEC in the early 1980s. Callaghan's rise to power came from relatively humble origins; he was educated only to secondary school level, after which he entered the Civil Service as a tax officer in 1929.

Carrington, Lord (Peter) (b. 1919): A former UK Conservative government Minister, who served as Secretary of State for Defence (1970–74), for Energy (1974) and for Foreign and Commonwealth Affairs (1979–82). His resignation from the latter post was a result of Argentina's invasion of the Falklands. Thereafter he was appointed Secretary-General of NATO (1984–88), being succeeded in July 1988 by Manfred Wörner. Carrington was subsequently appointed Chairman of the EC Conference on Yugoslavia between 1991 and 1992. His resignation from that post was primarily caused by his frustration at not being able to establish an agreement suitable to all parties, not least the USA. Indeed, his initial proposals were essentially identical to the final agreement reached at Dayton, Ohio, in the USA.

Chirac, Jacques (b. 1932): Born in Paris, he was educated at the prestigious Ecole National d'Administration and after military service in Algeria served in numerous government departments, including the position as Secretary of State for Economy and Finance (1968–71), before being appointed Prime Minister of France (1974–76). Chirac held that post again between 1986 and 1988, having headed a successful Conservative coalition in the 1986 parliamentary elections. This period in office was marked by international differences, while he was constantly challenged by President Mitterrand who retained control over foreign policy. Chirac stood as a candidate in the 1988 Presidential elections and managed to see off the challenge of the centrist Raymond Barre in the first round, though being defeated in the second round by Mitterrand. By 1995 Chirac had established a firmer base of power than in 1986 and was regarded as having been a good mayor of Paris. He was therefore able to successfully contest the 1995 Presidential elections. His early period of office was marked by international issues, including French nuclear tests. In 1997 he took a risk in dissolving the National Assembly, which proved to be a mistake with the elimination of his parliamentary majority and appointment of his opponent, Lionel Jospin. Chirac therefore faced a further period of cohabitation government, although this time as President.

Churchill, Sir Winston (1874–1965): British statesman who was both a Conservative MP (1900–4, 1908–22 and 1924–64) and a Liberal MP (1906–8). He held numerous high-profile positions, including Home Secretary (1910–11), First Lord of the Admiralty (1911–15), Chancellor of the Duchy of Lancaster (1915), Minister of munitions (1917–19), Secretary for war and air (1919–21), Secretary for air and colonies (1921), Colonial Secretary (1921–22), Chancellor of the Exchequer (1924–29), First Lord of the Admiralty (1939–40), Prime Minister and Minister of Defence (1940–45), Prime Minister (1951–55) and Minister of Defence (1951–52). As Prime Minister he inspired the nation during the Second World War. During that period he also supported policies for the future development of the country, including the Beveridge Plan for social insurance (1942) and the Butler Education Act (1944). He made a significant development to European affairs in the post-1945 period, despite having lost the premiership in that year. He urged the construction of a United States of Europe in a speech in Zürich in 1946 and provided backing to the International Committee of the Movements for European Unity. Churchill also acted as President of the sessions of the 1948 Congress of Europe, in the wake of which he became one of the patrons of the European Movement. However, he did not perceive the UK as being part of an integrated Europe, which he considered would rather be based upon the reconciliation of France and Germany. Therefore, when he returned to power as Prime Minister in 1951 he continued to advocate the policy of the previous Labour government that saw the UK as only being involved in intergovernmental cooperation. This led to the UK, under his leadership, not taking part in the developments which were pursued by the Six.

Cockfield, Lord (Arthur) (b. 1916): A British member and Vice-President of the European Commission between 1985 and 1989, he was key to the implementation of the internal market which fell under his policy portfolio. In response to the request of the Brussels European Council in March 1985, he produced in June 1985 a White Paper with a timetable for completing the internal market. This included 282 measures relating to the removal of physical, technical and fiscal barriers to trade. The report recommended the removal of frontier barriers by 1992. His tenure as a European Commissioner was stopped by Margaret Thatcher who refused to reappoint him in 1988, partly because of his pro-integrationist position.

Colombo, Emilio (b. 1920): An Italian politician who served in various posts within different governments, including Minister of Foreign Trade (1958–59), of Industry and Commerce (1959–60), of the Treasury (1963–70), and Prime Minister (1970–72). He was subsequently appointed Minister of Finance (1973–74), of the Treasury (1974–76), and of Foreign Affairs (1980–83 and 1992–93). During his period of office between 1980 and 1983, he lent his name and supported proposals for a draft European Act. This extended to supporting the draft declaration on economic integration advanced by the German Foreign Minister, Hans-Dietrich Genscher, and eventually resulted in the 1981 Genscher–Colombo Plan. He was a member of the European Parliament between 1976 and 1980 and its President in 1977–79.

Cook, Robin (b. 1946): A British Labour politician who was appointed Foreign Secretary in May 1997 with the election of the Labour government. Prior to his appointment he was the shadow Foreign Secretary (1994–97). He is generally regarded as an enthusiastic pro-European, but has had many disagreements with the Chancellor of the Exchequer, Gordon Brown, over foreign policy, including the single currency.

Cresson, Edith (b. 1934): A French member of the European Commission with responsibility for science, research and development, the joint research centre, human resources, education, training and youth. She holds a Doctorate in demography. In 1979 she was elected a member of the European Parliament, where she was a member of the Agriculture Committee. She was the French Minister of Agriculture (1981–83) and Minister of Industrial Redeployment and Foreign Trade (1984–86). In 1988 she was appointed Minister of European Affairs and served as Prime Minister of France between 1991 and 1992.

Davignon, Viscount Etienne (b. 1932): As political director of the Belgian Foreign Ministry in the early 1970s, he played a major role in the development of European Political Cooperation by chairing the committee of permanent representatives which devised the plan. He was later appointed a European Commissioner from 1977 until 1985, under the leadership of Roy Jenkins and Gaston Thorn. During that time he was responsible for industry policy and therefore was an active participant in encouraging greater competitiveness within Member States.

De Gasperi, Alcide (1881–1954): As Prime Minister of Italy from 1945 to 1954 he was the first and longest-serving Prime Minister of the post-war period, during which time he pursued a policy of the modernisation of the Italian economy. He was a member of the dominant Christian Democratic Party (Democrazia Cristani) and steered a pro-western foreign policy, being a committed supporter of greater European integration. He advocated the economic development of Italy but also suppressed extreme political challenges, particularly from the Italian Communist Party (Partito Communista Italiano).

De Gaulle, Charles (1890–1970): As the London-based leader of the Free French during the Second World War, he proved to be a key figure in French politics in the post-war period, being the first leader of the liberated nation. His retirement from office in 1946 through discontent over the Fourth Republic's constitution reduced his influence upon French politics. This marginalisation continued until he became the first leader of the Fifth Republic in 1958, serving as President until 1969. During this time he placed great emphasis in restoring France's position in international affairs. This included a move away from any reliance on the USA and the assertion of a policy which maintained national sovereignty as well as French leadership of the EC. Within the Community his aims were reflected in the 1963 Treaty of Friendship between France and Germany, while his emphasis on national sovereignty resulted in the 'empty chair' crisis in the second half of 1965 when he withdrew French participation in the Council of Ministers. This difficulty was eventually resolved by the 1966 Luxembourg Compromise which reasserted the importance of Member States and their ability to use the veto. On a wider level he personally vetoed the UK's application to the Community in 1963 and 1967, partly because he considered it would result in a large degree of US influence. He withdrew French forces from the integrated military structure of NATO in 1966, resulting in the removal of NATO's political and military headquarters from France to Belgium.

Delors, Jacques (b. 1925): As President of the European Commission between 1985 and 1995 he played a major role in the development of the Community. During his period of office the Community expanded from ten to fifteen members, while he oversaw reform through the Single European Act and the Treaty on European Union. His efforts to foster closer political integration ensured that he was the most active President since Walter Hallstein. His influence included being a prominent figure in drafting the 1989 Charter of Fundamental Rights and being the chair of the committee which examined the prospect of monetary union, producing the Delors Report in April 1989. While in office he fostered a workmanlike attitude within the Commission, where he was renowned for having a clear perception of where the Community should go. That often meant that he worked closely with immediate colleagues, including members of his own Cabinet, and prompted concern that more peripheral European Commissioners were not able to exercise the influence that their position merited. Among Member States, he had frequent clashes with Margaret Thatcher, despite the fact that she approved his appointment as President of the European Commission and as chair of the committee which examined the prospect of monetary union. Thatcher was especially vociferous in attacking the introduction of a social dimension to the Community. However, the relationship between Delors and other leaders was by no means easy; his contacts with François Mitterrand were often tense. This partly stemmed from his own experience of French politics where he had been Finance Minister between March 1983 and July 1984.

Duisenberg, Willem (b. 1935): An economist by trade, having received his PhD in economics from the University of Groningen in 1965, he served as the Netherlands Minister of Finance between 1973 and 1977. He subsequently served on the executive board of Rabobank Nederland (1978–81) before being appointed President of the Netherlands Central Bank in 1982. Since then he has been Chairman of the Board and President of the Bank for International Settlements in 1988–90 and 1994–97. Duisenberg was a Council Member of the European Monetary Institute between 1994 and 1997, and was thereafter appointed its President. In this capacity he will be responsible for ensuring the success of the Euro.

Eden, Anthony (1897–1977): A British Conservative politician who was appointed Foreign Secretary in 1938 and was Churchill's Foreign Minister between 1940 and 1945. With the return of the Conservative government in 1951, Eden was again appointed Foreign Secretary, a position he maintained until 1955. In 1955 he succeeded Churchill as Prime Minister, but his premiership was soon dominated by the Suez crisis which brought about his resignation.

Ersbøll, Niels (b. 1926): A Danish civil servant who served in various postings to international organisations (NATO, 1958–60; EFTA, 1963–64) and worked in the EFTA secretariat in Geneva (1960–63). He was appointed permanent representative to the European Community between 1973 and 1977. In 1980 he was elected Secretary-General of the EU Council, a post which he kept until 1994. During that time he was a particularly influential individual as the primary administrator of the organisation which assists Member States during negotiations.

Fischler, Franz (b. 1946): Austria's first member of the European Commission, he is responsible for agriculture and rural development. He has a background in farming and obtained a Doctorate in November 1978. From 1979 to 1984 he worked for the Tyrol Chamber of Agriculture, being responsible for culture and education, land-use planning and environmental protection, and served as Director of the Chamber of Agriculture from 1985 to 1989. Prior to his appointment to the European Commission he was a member of the National Parliament from 1990–94.

Flynn, Pádraig (b. 1939): An Irish member of the European Commission with responsibility for employment and social affairs and relations with the Economic and Social Committee. Previously he had responsibility for social affairs and employment, immigration, home affairs and justice from 1993 to 1994. Born in Castlebar, County Mayo, he was formerly a school teacher and businessman. Between 1967 and 1987 he was a member of Mayo County Council, and was elected Vice-Chairman (1975–77). In 1977 he was elected to the Dáil, being appointed Minister of State in the Department of Transport and Power between 1981 and 1982. Subsequently he was the Fianna Fáil Spokesman on Trade, Commerce and Tourism (1982–87), before being appointed Minister for the Environment in 1987, a post he retained until 1991. In 1992 he was named Minister of Justice.

Genscher, Hans-Dietrich (b. 1927): As Foreign Minister of the Federal Republic of Germany from 1974 until 1992 he proved to be a major force within his own nation where he was Chairman of the influential Free Democratic Party. In this context, his decision to switch the coalition partnership from the Social Democrats to the Christian Democrats in 1982 resulted in Helmut Schmidt being removed as Chancellor and Helmut Kohl taking his place. Genscher's later resignation as Foreign Minister in 1992 consequently weakened the political position of Kohl. As Foreign Minister he attempted to maintain the policy of developing links with Eastern Europe which had been initiated by Willy Brandt, while being committed to the EEC and NATO. But during the Cold War atmosphere of the early 1980s, this policy drew some criticism from the USA and the UK. Within the Community he was the main architect of the 1981 Genscher–Colombo Plan.

Gil-Robles, José María (b. 1935): A Spanish national who has served as a member of the European Parliament since 1989, being made Vice-President in 1994 and President in 1997. He is a barrister by trade and has taken a particular interest in employment and social affairs, being the EPP coordinator in the Committee on Social Affairs and Employment within the European Parliament between 1994 and 1996.

Giscard d'Estaing, Valéry (b. 1926): As President of France between 1974 and 1981 he played an important role within the European Community and developed a strong relationship with the German Chancellor, Helmut Schmidt, who entered office at roughly the same time. That Franco-German alliance further developed the relationship which had been grounded in the 1963 Treaty of Friendship, with both leaders meeting regularly. He played an especially key role in the institutionalisation of summit meetings of Heads of State and Government, where he argued in 1974 for their development into the European Council. He was also a strong supporter of the European Monetary System, while he did not want to accelerate Spain's accession to the Community. After the 1981 election of François Mitterrand as President, Giscard continued to be a member of the French Parliament until 1989 when he entered the European Parliament and subsequently led the Liberal group. Within the European Parliament he proved to be a regular campaigner for granting it increased powers, which he incidentally opposed when President of France.

Gradin, Anita (b. 1933): Sweden's first member of the European Commission with responsibility for immigration, home affairs and justice, relations with the Ombudsman, financial control and fraud prevention. She holds a degree in social work and public administration from the University of Stockholm and served as a journalist in the early years of her career. Between 1976 and 1968 she was an adviser in the Cabinet Office and a member of Parliament from 1968–92. During that period she was a delegate to the Council of Europe, while in 1982 she was made a Minister with responsibility for immigrant and equality affairs. In 1986 she became a Minister with responsibility for foreign trade. Immediately prior to her appointment to the European Commission she served as Sweden's Ambassador to Austria and Slovenia as well as to the IAEA and UN in Vienna.

Guigou, Elisabeth (b. 1946): French Minister of Justice in the Jospin government elected in June 1997. A graduate of Ecole Nationale d'Administration, she initially worked as a civil servant in the Ministry of the Economy. She became head of the European, American and Asian States Office at the Ministry for the Economy and Finance's Trésor Directorate between 1981 and 1982. She was an adviser in the Secretariat-General of the Presidency of the Republic (1982–88) and was a special adviser to the President of the Republic (1988–90). Between 1990 and 1993 she was a Minister Delegate, attached to the Ministre d'Etat, Minister of Foreign Affairs, with special responsibility for European Affairs. During that period she played an important role in the 1990–91 intergovernmental conference negotiations which led to the Maastricht Treaty on European Union. Thereafter she was elected a member of the European Parliament in 1994, where she joined the Party of European Socialists Group. The election of the Jospin government in 1997 resulted in her appointment as a Minister and she therefore gave up her seat in the European Parliament.

Hallstein, Walter (1901–82): He was the first, and to date the second longest-serving, President of the European Commission, having held office between 1958 and 1967. Before then he led the West German delegation to the 1950 conference that discussed the Schuman Plan, while he participated in the 1955 Messina conference which produced agreement on the establishment of a common market. His view of the Commission acting as the engine of European integration produced several clashes with the French President Charles de Gaulle, and provided a great deal of the motivation behind that government's action with respect to the 'empty chair' crisis. A reason for this was because Hallstein proposed that the completion of the CAP's financial settlement should be linked to the granting of increased budgetary power to the European Parliament, with the European Commission being given executive authority.

Heath, Edward (b. 1916): British Conservative parliamentarian who had various junior government positions before becoming Prime Minister in June 1970. These included Lord of the Treasury and Senior Government Whip (1951–52), Joint Deputy Chief Whip (1952–53), Deputy Chief Whip (1953–55), Parliamentary Secretary to the Treasury and Government Chief Whip (1955–59), Minister of Labour (1959–60), Lord Privy Seal (1960–63) and Secretary of State for Industry, Trade and Regional

Development and President of the Board of Trade (1963–64). Of these, his position as Lord Privy Seal meant he was in charge of the first application to enter the EEC under the government of Harold Macmillan. This highlighted him as a committed European, which was further emphasised when, as Prime Minister, he was responsible for the renewal of talks which eventually resulted in UK accession to the Community. During the negotiations for entry, Heath's major concern was for the Community to develop a strong regional policy. He perceived this to be a means of benefiting the UK economy and at the same time helping to offset the costs of membership which would result from participation in the Common Agricultural Policy. However, his premiership became hampered by industrial unrest which eventually resulted in electoral defeat and the coming to power of the Labour Party in March 1974.

Howe of Aberavon, Lord Geoffrey (b. 1926): A former UK Conservative politician, Howe was educated at Cambridge University where he was Chairman of the Conservative Association in 1951. He was elected Conservative MP for Bebington (1964–66), Reigate (1970–74) and Surrey East (1974–92). He held a number of Conservative Front-Bench posts and served as Chancellor of the Exchequer from 1979 until 1983, when he was appointed Foreign Secretary until 1989. His departure from that office was caused by Prime Minister Thatcher's desire to surround herself with like-minded individuals. Howe was subsequently appointed Lord President of the Council, Leader of the House of Commons and Deputy Prime Minister from 1989 to 1990. Although these were grand titles, they brought little of the power of his former position as Foreign Secretary. His frustration with government policy, and especially its anti-European content, resulted in his resignation in November 1990, with his speech of 13 November doing great harm to Thatcher's position as Prime Minister. In it he stressed that the negative tones of Thatcher seriously hampered the Chancellor and Governor of the Bank of England's attempts to sell the Hard ECU to other European Member States. Such views were subsequently highlighted in his 1994 memoirs *Conflict of Loyalty*.

Ismay, Lord (1887–1965): Born in India, he served in UK forces in Somaliland during the First World War, after which he returned to India. Upon the outbreak of the Second World War he was appointed Deputy Secretary to the UK War Cabinet and later became Chief of Staff to Winston Churchill and his successor Clement Attlee. The experience Ismay obtained from participating in negotiations at Moscow, Tehran and Yalta proved vital to his appointment in 1952 as the first Secretary-General of NATO and Vice-Chairman of the North Atlantic Council. Until 1956 the Chairmanship of the latter continued to be held by the Foreign Minister of a Member State based upon annual rotation; thereafter the

Secretary-General of NATO became the Chairman of the North Atlantic Council. Ismay's retirement in May 1957 resulted in him being succeeded by Paul-Henri Spaak, Foreign Minister of Belgium.

Jenkins, Lord Roy (b. 1920): A former UK Labour Party Home Secretary and Chancellor of the Exchequer, he was appointed President of the European Commission from 1977 to 1981. A committed European, he previously led a minority section of the Labour Party in supporting UK membership of the Community in 1971 during a vote within the House of Commons. His time as President of the European Commission was dominated by complaints from the UK about its budget contribution. He was a prime motivator behind greater European integration, where he helped to develop the European Monetary System. He also obtained the right for the President to represent the Community at one of the sessions of the annual Western Economic Summits, although this was done very much at the reluctance of France. After his period as President he proved to be a key figure in UK politics, winning the Hillhead by-election and breaking away from the Labour Party to be a founder member of the Social Democratic Party.

Jospin, Lionel (b. 1937): He was appointed Prime Minister of France on 2 June 1997 following the early general election of 25 May and 1 June 1997. A graduate of the Ecole Nationale d'Administration, he joined the Ministry of Foreign Affairs as Secrétaire des Affaires Étrangères in 1965. In October 1970 he was seconded from the Ministry of Foreign Affairs to the Paris XI University, where he was initially a senior lecturer and then professor of economics, a position he retained until June 1981 when he was elected National Assembly Deputy for a Paris constituency. From 12 May 1988 to 2 April 1992, he was Ministre d'Etat, Minister for National Education. His ministerial career initially ceased in April 1992, at which point he returned to the Ministry of Foreign Affairs until 10 May 1993.

Kinkel, Klaus (b. 1936): A law graduate who received his Doctorate in 1964, he was German Federal Minister of Foreign Affairs and Vice-Chancellor from 1992 until 1998. From 1965 to 1970 he was an employee of the Federal Office for Civilian Protection and between 1970 and 1974 was a personal assistant to the Federal Minister of the Interior and Head of the Minister's Office. He was subsequently head of the administration staff at the Foreign Office until 1979, when he was appointed head of the planning staff at the Foreign Office. From 1979 to 1982 he was President of the Federal Intelligence Service, after which he served as Under-Secretary at the Federal Ministry of Justice until 1991. In 1991 he became a member of the Free Democratic Party and served as Federal Minister of Justice (1991–92) until his appointment as Federal Minister of Foreign Affairs. His career therefore resembles that of other German, and indeed French Ministers, who have had both official and ministerial experience. Consequently it differentiates from the British tradition where there is little or no overlap between these occupations.

Kinnock, Neil (b. 1942): A British member of the European Commission with responsibility for transport (including trans-European networks). Born in Tredegar, South Wales, and educated at Cardiff University, he entered the House of Commons in 1970 as the Labour Member for Bedwellty and Islwyn in South Wales. In 1978 he was elected a member of the National Executive Committee of the Labour Party, a position he maintained until 1994. In 1980 he was elected to the Shadow Cabinet, being appointed leader of the Labour Party in 1983 until he resigned in 1992 in the wake of general election defeat. During that time he was the driving force behind the modernisation of the Labour Party, including the elimination of the Militant Tendency. That work essentially sowed the seeds for the Labour Party's victory in the 1997 general election. His wife is a member of the European Parliament.

Kohl, Helmut (b. 1930): Chancellor of the Federal Republic of Germany from 1982 to 1998. A graduate of the Universities of Frankfurt and Heidelberg (where he received his DrPhil in 1958), he became a member of the Parliament of Rhineland Palatinate in 1959. He continued in that position until 1976, during which time he was leader of the Christian Democrat Union Party (CDU) of the Rhineland Palatinate Parliament from 1963 to 1979 and Chairman from 1966 to 1974. Between 1969 and 1976 he was Minister-President of the Rhineland Palatinate Parliament and was leader of the opposition in the Bundestag from 1976 to 1982. He has been leader of the national CDU Party from 1973, and his strength within the Party was demonstrated in the 1998 election campaign when the CDU campaigned solely on Kohl's personality. His election as Chancellor of the reunified Germany in 1990 has proved to be one of the most significant aspects of his period of office. Reunification was also a significant issue in his relations with other Member States, of which the UK under Margaret Thatcher appeared to resist, while France under François Mitterrand was unequivocal, and the Prime Minister of the Netherlands, Ruud Lubbers, provided a lukewarm response. The attitude of the latter could be said to have influenced Kohl's decision to veto his nomination to succeed Jacques Delors as President of the European Commission. However, with reunification established, Kohl sought further European political integration, partly as a means of tying Germany into the EC. At the same time France sought monetary integration as a means of countering the strength of the Bundesbank. A bargain was therefore struck between the two leaders over these issues, which essentially formed the agenda for the 1990–91 intergovernmental conferences that eventually produced the Treaty on European Union.

Kok, Wim (b. 1938): 'Prime Minister of the Netherlands and Minister for General Affairs. In the earlier years of his career he served as a trade union official, being appointed secretary to the Netherlands Federation of Trade Unions in 1969 and Deputy Chairman in 1972. From 1973 to 1975 he was Chairman of the Federation of Netherlands Trade Unions (FNV). Between 1979 and 1982 he was also Chairman of the European Trade Union Confederation. Between 1986 and 1989 and after the 1994 and 1998 elections, he was a member of the Lower House of the States General and leader of the parliamentary Labour Party (PvdA). Between 1989 and 1994 he was Deputy Prime Minister and Minister of Finance in the third Lubbers government, after which he was appointed, in August 1994, Prime Minister and Minister for General Affairs, a position to which he was reappointed in August 1998.

Lamont, Lord Norman (b. 1942): A former UK Conservative politician, Lamont was educated at Cambridge University, where he was elected Chairman of the Conservative Association in 1963 and President of the Union in 1964. Prior to entering Parliament he worked in the Conservative Research Department (1966–68) and was employed as a merchant banker (1968–79). In 1979 he was elected Conservative MP for the safe seat of Kingston-upon-Thames, which he retained until 1997 when boundary changes meant that his constituency was amalgamated with others. In 1997 he unsuccessfully contested Harrogate and Knaresborough. While Lamont is now regarded as a prominent Euro-sceptic, this position was less evident in his earlier career when he served as Financial Secretary to the Treasury (1986–89), Chief Secretary to the Treasury (1989–90) and Chancellor of the Exchequer (1990–93). As Chancellor he was responsible for negotiating the monetary union part of the 1990–91 intergovernmental negotiations which led to the Maastricht Treaty, and for administering the UK's participation in the Exchange Rate Mechanism. This was a policy which he had inherited from John Major who had supervised sterling's entry to the system in October 1990. But it proved a difficult task and sterling's exit from the ERM in September 1992 was handled poorly by Lamont. Afterwards he commented that he had no regrets over the administering of exchange rates. His departure from office was influenced by John Major's view that he had outlived his period as Chancellor, although Lamont did turn down a further Cabinet post.

Lawson of Blaby, Lord Nigel (b. 1932): A former UK Conservative politician, Lawson was educated at Oxford. He subsequently worked as a journalist for the *Financial Times* and *The Sunday Telegraph*, and he was editor of *The Spectator* from 1966 to 1970. Possessing a first-class intellect, Lawson was a special assistant to Prime Minister Sir Alec Douglas-Home (1963–64) and was a special policy adviser to the Conservative Party Headquarters (1973–74). In 1974 he was appointed Conservative MP for Blaby in Leicestershire, a position he retained until his retirement in 1992. During that period he served as Secretary of State for Energy (1981–83) and Chancellor of the Exchequer (1983–89). As Chancellor he campaigned for UK participation in the Exchange Rate Mechanism, but this was contested by Thatcher, resulting in him 'unofficially' shadowing the Deutschmark in 1987–88 as a means of highlighting that sterling was ready to enter the ERM. Such efforts were lost on Thatcher, who was increasingly relying on the advice of special advisers, in particular Sir Alan Walters. Differences of opinion between the Chancellor and the Prime Minister over the conduct of economic policy therefore provoked Lawson to resign in October 1989, after which he became a loyal supporter of Geoffrey Howe. Out of office, Lawson published an extremely detailed account of the Thatcher government in his 1992 memoirs, *The View from No. 11: Memoirs of Tory Radical.*

Liikanen, Erkki Antero (b. 1950): As Finland's first member of the European Commission, he is responsible for managing the budget, personnel and administration, and translation and in-house computer services. He is widely regarded as having been an extremely effective manager of the budget. Educated at the University of Helsinki, where he obtained a Masters degree in political science, he entered Parliament in 1972 and served until 1990. During that time he held various posts, including Vice-Chairman of the Forestry Committee (1977–79), Chairman of the Foreign Affairs Committee (1983–87) and Minister of the Interior with responsibility for regional policy (1987–90). In 1990 he was appointed Finland's Ambassador to the European Union.

Luns, Joseph (b. 1911): A Dutch national who studied at the Universities of Leiden and Amsterdam, the London School of Economics and Berlin University prior to his entry into the Netherlands Foreign Service. He served as the Dutch representative to the United Nations (1949–52), resigning upon his appointment as joint Minister of Foreign Affairs of the Netherlands. He thereafter served as Foreign Minister in various administrations and in that capacity signed the 1957 Treaty of Rome. In 1971 he was appointed Secretary-General of NATO and was succeeded by Lord Carrington in 1984.

Macmillan, Harold (1894–1986): Upon becoming UK Conservative Prime Minister in January 1957 he had already held numerous government positions. These included Parliamentary Secretary in the Ministry of Supply (1940–42), Parliamentary Under Secretary for the Colonies

(February–December 1942), Minister Resident, Allied Headquarters (December 1942–May 1945), Minister for Housing and Local Government (1951–54), Minister of Defence (1954–55), Secretary of State for Foreign Affairs (April–December 1945) and Chancellor of the Exchequer (1955–57). During his tenure as Prime Minister, which lasted until October 1963, he attempted to reverse the UK's position of non-involvement with European development, which extended beyond intergovernmental cooperation when he stressed in July 1961 that the UK would seek membership of the European Community. Although unsuccessful, the UK's position had altered primarily because of the change in its own economic circumstances, with EFTA not proving to be a vigorous market. Yet, membership was also perceived by Macmillan as a means of maintaining and strengthening the nation's influence in world affairs and was therefore conducted for practical reasons. That was not lost on the French President, Charles de Gaulle, who took the opportunity of the UK obtaining the Polaris nuclear missile from the USA in December 1962 as a demonstration that London would only be acting as a Trojan Horse for Washington. In that context, as well as a desire to maintain French dominance within the Community, de Gaulle vetoed the UK's application in January 1963.

Major, John (b. 1943). Having beaten Douglas Hurd and Michael Heseltine in the November 1990 UK Conservative Party leadership election, he succeeded Margaret Thatcher as Prime Minister on 28 November. Major's appointment meant that he was the youngest Prime Minister in the twentieth century and the first Conservative to hold that office by virtue of winning a leadership election. He had risen from humble beginnings, entering Parliament in 1979, having previously worked in a number of professions, most notably for Standard Chartered Bank from 1965 to 1979. During these years he was an active member of the Lambeth Borough Council (1968–71) and was Chairman of the Housing Committee (1970–71). Major was regarded as a very capable Chairman, even among Labour members, who included Ken Livingstone. Thereafter, he obtained relatively quick promotion from Assistant Whip (1983–84), Lord Commissioner of the Treasury (1984–85), Parliamentary Under-Secretary of State, Department of Health and Social Security (1985–86), Minister of State, Department of Health and Social Security (1986–87) to Chief Secretary to the Treasury (1987–89). His appointment as Secretary of State for Foreign and Commonwealth Affairs (July–October 1989) took place after Sir (Lord) Geoffrey Howe was 'demoted' to the position of Deputy Prime Minister. He subsequently became Chancellor of the Exchequer (October 1989–November 1990) upon the resignation of Nigel Lawson. Few expected he would become Prime Minister, a position he held until the Conservative Party was defeated in the general election of May 1997. It was clear that on becoming Prime Minister he would attempt to chart a more constructive position within the Community, not least since he had been instrumental in advocating the Hard ECU plan in the summer of 1990 and in campaigning for ERM membership, resulting in entry in October 1990. This was initially signalled by the 'Heart of Europe' speech in March 1991. He also developed a closer relationship with Helmut Kohl which proved crucial to the UK obtaining a satisfactory agreement in the Treaty on European Union in December 1991. Thereafter, although he won the 1992 general election, albeit with a reduced majority, his premiership was dominated by domestic scandals and confrontation from Euro-sceptics. This worsened the UK's relationship with the Community, culminating in the debate over the reweighting of QMV in 1994, the 1995 beef crisis and the subsequent policy of non-cooperation. By the end of his tenure, his government was officially a minority one, isolated within the EU and pandering to the interests of Euro-sceptics at home.

Malfatti, Franco (b. 1927): A former Italian politician and government minister, he replaced Jean Rey as President of the European Commission in July 1970. His period in office was undistinguished, primarily because the Commission remained weak in the aftermath of the 'empty chair' crisis. His own tenure as President was relatively short, resigning two years early in March 1972 to enable him to pursue a career in Italian politics.

Mansholt, Sicco (1908–95): During his lengthy tenure as a European Commissioner from January 1958 until January 1973 he occupied the post of President from March 1972 after the resignation of Franco Malfatti. He made an especially significant contribution to European integration through implementing the CAP, while emphasising the problems of its excesses in later years. His experience in this policy arena came from a farming background and having served as Minister for Agriculture in the Netherlands. Within the European Commission he was appointed Vice-President and had specific responsibility for agriculture. In December 1964 the Council accepted the 'Mansholt Plan' which established a Community-wide fixed price for wheat and feed grains commencing from 1 July 1967.

Marín, Manuel (b. 1949): A Spanish member of the European Commission and Vice-President, he has responsibility for external relations with southern Mediterranean countries, the Middle East, Latin America and Asia (except Japan, China, South Korea, Hong Kong, Macao and Taiwan), including development aid. Born in Ciudad Real, he studied law at the Universities of Madrid and Nancy. He became a member of the Spanish Socialist Party (PSOE) in 1974 and a member of Parliament in 1977, to which he was re-elected in 1979 and 1982. From 1982 to 1985 he was

State Secretary for relations with the European Communities, which included administering the negotiations which resulted in Spain's accession to the EC. He commenced his duties with the European Commission in 1986, with his election as Vice-President with responsibility for social affairs, education and employment. In 1989 he was again re-elected Vice-President of the European Commission, but was given the portfolio of development cooperation and common fisheries policy. From 1993 to 1994 he was Vice-President of the European Commission with responsibility for development and cooperation and economic external relations with southern Mediterranean countries, Latin America, Asia, the ACP countries, and humanitarian aid.

Marjolin, Robert (1911–86): A senior member and Vice-President of the European Commission led by Walter Hallstein, he was a pragmatic individual committed to the process of European integration. A French national, he worked closely with Jean Monnet on the French Nationalisation Plan in the post-war period and was subsequently appointed Secretary-General of the OEEC until 1955. During his period as a European Commissioner he advocated a more restrained approach to integration and suggested that the Commission should not attempt to pressurise for extra powers, advice which was not accepted and ultimately provoked the 1965 'empty chair' crisis. Later in life, Marjolin proved to be an influential figure by assisting in the preparation of a report on Community reform as one of the 'three wise men', the report of which was published in 1980.

Marshall, George C. (1880–1959): A US general, Marshall was appointed Secretary of State in 1947 having previously been the Army Chief of Staff between 1939 and 1945. As Secretary of State he announced in June 1947 a plan for the economic rehabilitation of Europe, which motivated the European Recovery Programme and helped form the Organisation for European Economic Cooperation (OEEC). Later, in April 1948 President Truman signed the Foreign Assistance Act which made the Marshall Plan law.

Miert, Karel Van (b. 1942): A Belgian member of the European Commission with responsibility for competition policy who has served as a Commissioner since 1989. From 1989 to 1992 he held the portfolio of transport, credit and investment, and consumer policy, and in July 1992 was given the additional temporary responsibility for the environment. Between 1993 and 1994 he was responsible for competition policy, personnel and administration policy, translation and in-house computer services. Prior to his appointment to the European Commission, he was a member of the Private Office of Vice-President of the European Commission, Henri Simonet (1973–75). In 1977 he was given the job as head of the Private Office of Willy Claes, the Belgium Minister of Economic Affairs. He was a member of the European Parliament (1979–85) and a member of the Belgian Chamber of Representatives (1985–88).

Mitterrand, François (1916–96): As President of France between 1981 and 1995, he was an active campaigner of closer European integration, while continuing to maintain France's national interest. He played a key role in the resolution of the UK budget problem at the June 1984 Fontainebleau European Council, while he would later be a prime instigator behind moves to develop a European single currency. In that context, he provided much of the motivation behind the convening of an intergovernmental conference on EMU, which took place in 1991, while a joint letter from him and Chancellor Kohl in April 1990 provided the impetus behind the convening of a second intergovernmental conference on political union. During these negotiations, he obtained the crucial French objective that EMU would commence by 1999. However, the ratification of the Treaty on European Union proved more problematic for him when he decided to hold a referendum on its acceptance in September 1992 as a means of demonstrating support for the Treaty in the wake of the Danish 'no' vote in May 1992. The gesture nearly proved fatal as the referendum was only approved by 50.4% to 49.6%. Domestically, his period as President was marked by the initial failure of his experiment with socialism from 1981 to 1983, with the government thereafter adopting a capitalist economic strategy. Mitterrand was faced with right-wing Prime Ministers between 1986 and 1988 (Chirac) and 1993 and 1995 (Balladur) because of their victory in elections to the National Assembly. Accordingly, this reduced his influence over the wider scope of government affairs, although he continued to maintain control of foreign and defence policy.

Monnet, Jean (1888–1979): He proved to be a key figure in the European integration process after 1945, being appointed head of the French Planning Commission which was responsible for the Modernisation Plan. His analysis suggested that it was impossible for any European nation independently to plan for economic growth and prosperity. He believed in the gradual process of European integration, where he considered development in one sector would spillover into another. In that context he was an instrumental figure behind the Schuman Plan and was appointed the first President of the High Authority of the European Coal and Steel Community. He additionally provided impetus behind the Pleven Plan that led to the EDC and after the latter's collapse he resigned from the High Authority to establish the Action Committee for a United States of Europe (ACUSE). Thereafter, he helped to foster the development of a European Atomic Energy Community (Euratom).

Monti, Mario (b. 1943): An Italian member of the European Commission with responsibility for the internal market, financial services and financial integration, customs and taxation. A trained economist, with degrees from Bocconi and Yale University, he taught at Bocconi University between 1965 and 1969, at which time he moved to the University of Trento. In 1970 he was appointed Professor at the University of Turin, a position which he held until 1979. He was Chairman of the Treasury Committee on the Banking and Financial System (1981–82), Professor of Economics (1985–94), and Director of the Institute of Economics at Bocconi University (1985–94). From 1989 to 1994 he was rector of Bocconi University.

Noël, Emile (b. 1922): Appointed Executive Secretary of the Commission of the European Economic Community in 1958, he served as the first Secretary-General of the European Commission from 1968 until 1987. A committed European, he had previously been secretary of the General Affairs Committee of the Consultative Assembly of the Council of Europe between 1949 and 1952 and prior to his appointment in 1958 was the chief personal assistant to Guy Mollet when he was president of the Consultative Assembly of the Council of Europe and President of France. During his time as Secretary-General of the European Commission he served under Presidents Walter Hallstein, Jean Rey, Franco Malfatti, Sicco Mansholt, François-Xavier Ortoli, Roy Jenkins, Gaston Thorn and Jacques Delors. His position as the most senior administrator in the European Commission, combined with his length of tenure, meant that he helped to shape and consolidate the administrative machinery of the European Communities and overcome difficulties such as the 1965 'empty chair' crisis. After leaving the European Commission, where he was replaced by David Williamson, he was appointed President of the European University Institute.

Oreja Aguirre, Marcelino (b. 1935): A Spanish member of the European Commission responsible for relations with the European Parliament; relations with Member States, including transparency, communication and information; culture and audio-visual policy; the office for official publications; and institutional matters. Born in Madrid, he holds a Doctor of Law degree from the University of Madrid. A career civil servant, he entered the diplomatic service in 1960 and was head of the Foreign Minister's office from 1962 to 1970. He then entered the diplomatic service, and was appointed to the Foreign Minister's Office, at which time he was made head of international services of the Bank of Spain. In 1974 he was appointed State Secretary in the Spanish Ministry of Information and Tourism and in 1975 State Secretary in the Ministry of Foreign Affairs. He served as Minister of Foreign Affairs (1976–80) and as Secretary-

General of the Council of Europe 1984–89. In 1989 he was elected a member of the European Parliament for the European People's Party and in 1994 became a member of the European Commission with responsibility for energy, the Euratom Supply Agency and transport.

Ortoli, François-Xavier (b. 1925): As President of the European Commission between 1973 and 1977 he helped to direct the Community's progress during a period of enlargement and the economic difficulties which were principally caused by the 1973–74 oil crisis. He was, however, a largely ineffective President, despite having had considerable experience as the French Finance Minister between 1968 and 1969. The economic difficulties which helped to stifle the Community's growth were not assisted by his cautious nature, with one of his most important initiatives as President being the introduction of the New Community Instrument.

Papoutsis, Christos (b. 1953): A Greek member of the European Commission, he is responsible for energy and the Euratom Supply Agency, small business and tourism. He was a special adviser on public administration affairs to the Greek government (1981–84) and a member of the European Parliament (1984–94). During the latter period he acted as Leader of the PASOK (Pan Helenic Socialist Party) delegation and was a member of the Budget Committee and the Committee on Foreign Affairs. Between 1987 and 1994 he was Vice-Chairman of the Party of European Socialists in the European Parliament.

Pinheiro, João de Deus Rogado Salvador (b. 1945): A Portuguese member of the European Commission with responsibility for external relations with ACP countries and South Africa as well as the Lomé Convention. Born in Lisbon, he holds a PhD in Chemical Engineering from the University of Birmingham. He was the Portuguese State Secretary for Education and School Administration (1981–82) and was appointed Minister of Education and Culture (1984–86). From 1987 to 1993 he served as Minister of Foreign Affairs, at which time he was appointed a member of the European Commission with special responsibility for relations with the European Parliament and with Member States (transparency, communication and information), culture and audio-visual policy.

Pompidou, Georges (1911–74): As President of France from 1969 until his death in 1974, he provided the initiative behind the important Hague Summit of the Six in December 1969. Providing the European Community with a fresh sense of direction and purpose, it demonstrated that he was not as rigid an individual as his predecessor, Charles de Gaulle. This was particularly visible in relation to the question of UK membership, which resulted in the enlargement of the Six to the Nine in 1973, although his flexibility in this matter was rewarded with agreement on financing the Common Agricultural Policy. His own views represented certain traditional French positions, including a desire not to empower the European Commission with greater authority, while ensuring that Member States retained the ability to shape future developments. He considered summit meetings were a particularly valuable vehicle for achieving this objective.

Prodi, Romano (b. 1939): President of the Italian Council of Ministers (Prime Minister) from 1995 to October 1998. A graduate of the Catholic University of Milan, he is a trained economist and has served as Professor of Economics and Industrial Policy at the University of Bologna. From 1978 to 1979 he was Minister of Industry. Between 1982 and 1989 he was Chairman of IRI (Istituto per la Ricostruzione Industriale) in Rome, the IRI being the largest Italian and European industrial and financial holding. From 1990 to 1993 he taught Industrial Organisation and Industrial Policy at the University of Bologna. He was reappointed Chairman of IRI in 1993, a position he held until July 1994.

Rasmussen, Poul Nyrup (b. 1943): Social Democrat Prime Minister of Denmark. An economics graduate from the University of Copenhagen, he worked as an economist in the Danish Confederation of Trade Unions (1971–86), during which time he was chief economist (1980–86). Between 1986 and 1988 he was managing director of the Employees Capital Pension Fund. In 1987 he became deputy chair of the Social Democrat Party and entered Parliament in 1988. Upon his entry to Parliament he was chair of the parliamentary Trade and Industry Committee until 1992, after which he was elected chair of the parliamentary group of the Social Democrats and their leader. Since January 1993 he has been Prime Minister and led three governments, being re-elected in March 1998 for a fourth time as leader of a two-party minority government.

Rey, Jean (1902–83): His tenure as President of the European Commission between 1967 and 1970 was hampered by difficulties caused by the 1965 'empty chair' crisis, the problems of merging the three executives of the European Communities in 1967 and Charles de Gaulle's resignation as President of France in 1969. His Presidency was notably cautious, with him attempting to maintain a balance between the positions of different Member States.

Santer, Jacques (b. 1937): President of the European Commission since 1995, Prime Minister of Luxembourg (1984–95), a member of the European Parliament (1975–79) and Vice-President of the European

Parliament (1975–77). Santer's election to the Presidency of the European Commission was because of the failure of Member States to agree on the Belgian Prime Minister, Jean-Luc Dehaene, at the Corfu European Council of June 1994. A further European Council was scheduled for July 1994, at which Santer was elected as a compromise candidate. His Presidency has proved to be less interventionist than his predecessor, Jacques Delors, while his style of leadership is less confrontational. Although agreement was reached at the June 1997 Amsterdam European Council on the Treaty of Amsterdam, it failed to tackle key subject areas such as institutional reform. Much of the effort of the Santer Presidency has been directed towards the achievement of EMU and developing links with applicant members from Central and Eastern Europe.

Schmidt, Helmut (b. 1918): As Chancellor of the Federal Republic of Germany from 1974 until 1982 he was particularly influential in shaping the development of the European Community, notably with regard to being the main advocate of the European Monetary System that was proposed by the President of the European Commission, Roy Jenkins. This eventually resulted in the European Council endorsing the proposal in 1978. Although a pragmatic individual who was often sceptical about the wider development of the Community, he established a fruitful alliance with the French President, Valéry Giscard d'Estaing.

Schröder, Gerhard (b. 1944). He is Germany's first post-war leader not to have personal experience of war. When elected Federal Chancellor on 27 October 1998, Schröder was elected by more than the combined strength of the MPs in his coalition within the Bundestag. This was because while his government has a 21-seat majority in parliament, he was voted into office by a majority of 27. He is the seventh Chancellor in post-war Germany and his coalition is the third SPD-led government and is the first red–green government at national level and the first to be constructed purely of left-of-centre parties. The month between Schröder's election victory and appointment as Chancellor was spent constructing his Cabinet, in which he encountered a setback when Jorst Stollmann rejected the post of economics minister, principally because two departments within the ministry were merged with the finance portfolio given to the powerful Social Democrat Party (SPD) chairman, Oskar Lafontaine. Schröder's political career can be traced back to 1963 when he joined the SPD. Despite leaving school at 14, he subsequently studied at night-school and then studied law in Gottingen, becoming a lawyer in Hanover in 1976. Elected National Chairman of the Young Socialists between 1978 and 1980, he was elected a member of the Bundestag in 1980. In 1986 he became leader of the Opposition in the State Parliament and was Minister President of Lower Saxony from 1990 until his election as Chancellor.

Schröder's private life has been coloured by four marriages, of which his third, to Hiltrud Hampel, lasted twelve years until its break up in 1996. As Chancellor, Schröder intends to make the Cabinet a genuine forum for decision-making, although he will have the final word. It is evident that he does not as yet have a concrete position on foreign policy, although a goal is to bring the UK more closely into the running of Europe as a means of counter-balancing France. This partly reflects his origins as a Protestant from Hanover (northern Germany), whereas Kohl was a Catholic Francophile from nearby Rhineland. Most EU countries hope that Schröder will be more sympathetic than Kohl was to revamping the CAP. This would mean lower EU prices for meat, grain and butter. (Kohl resisted changes because he relied on a large Bavarian vote.)

Schuman, Robert (1886–1963): Although born in Luxembourg, he was an important European statesman in the inter-war period when he served as Foreign Minister of France. As a strong supporter of European integration, he advocated in May 1950 the pooling of coal and steel resources which resulted in the European Coal and Steel Community. This initiative helped to propel Member States to establish the European Economic Community, and he was elected President at the first meeting of the Parliamentary Assembly. His role in the advancement of European integration was emphasised in 1986 when the European Communities stated that 9 May (the day when he advocated the ECSC) would be referred to as Europe Day.

Silguy, Yves-Thibault de (b. 1948): A French member of the European Commission with responsibility for economic and financial affairs, monetary matters (in agreement with the President), credit and investments and the Statistical Office. Born in Rennes, he was educated as a lawyer and is a graduate of the Ecole Nationale d'Administration. Between 1976 and 1981 he worked for the Ministry of Foreign Affairs. From 1981 until 1984 he was an adviser and then subsequently Deputy Chef de cabinet to François-Xavier Ortoli, Vice-President of the European Commission, with responsibility for economic and monetary affairs. Thereafter, between 1985 and 1988 he served as Counsellor for economic affairs in the French Embassy in Washington and later as an adviser for European and international economic affairs in the Prime Minister's Office. Before his appointment to the European Commission he was, in 1993, Secretary-General of the Interdepartmental Committee for Questions of Economic Cooperation in Europe and advised the Prime Minister on European affairs. In 1994 he was Minister Plenipotentiary.

Spaak, Paul-Henri (1889–1972): He held the office of Prime Minister and Foreign Minister of Belgium on various occasions after 1945, during which time he acted as a driving force behind European integration. In this context, his initiatives included helping to establish Benelux, the 1948 Congress of Europe and he was a guiding light behind the European Movement. The latter provided the direction which established the Council of Europe, of which Spaak was elected the Assembly's first President. However, he resigned from that post in 1951, partly because of its lack of progress. Thereafter, he was a key figure at the 1955 Messina Conference, where he attended as the Belgian Foreign Minister and was empowered with the authority to chair a committee which would examine proposals for a European Community. The subsequent Spaak Report was accepted by the Six and resulted in the committee, which he chaired, being further entrusted with the task of drafting the EEC and Euratom Treaties.

Spinelli, Altiero (1907–86): A member of the European Commission from 1970 until 1976 who advocated a federal United States of Europe. He was later elected a Member of the European Parliament where, between 1979 and 1986, he served as an independent on the Italian Communist list. In 1980 he established the Crocodile Group that provided the motivation behind the Draft Treaty on European Union, of which he was the principal architect. He had previously been active in federalist organisations in the 1940s and 1950s where he established the European Federalist Movement in Milan in 1943. He was later the founder and director of the Institute for International Affairs in Rome during the mid-1960s.

Stikker, Dirk (1887–1979): A Dutch national who founded the Party for Freedom and Democracy in 1946, being appointed Minister for Foreign Affairs from 1948 until 1952. He was appointed Political Mediator of the Organisation for European Economic Cooperation (OEEC) in 1950, with him later being appointed its Chairman. In 1958 he was appointed the Netherlands Permanent Representative to the North Atlantic Council and to the OEEC, and was chosen in April 1961 by the North Atlantic Council to succeed Paul-Henri Spaak as Secretary-General of NATO and Chairman of the North Atlantic Council, a post which he held until 1964 when he was succeeded by Manlio Brosio.

Thatcher, Margaret (b. 1925): UK Conservative Prime Minister between May 1979 and November 1990. First woman Prime Minister, prior to which she was Joint Parliamentary Secretary, Ministry of Pensions and National Insurance (1961–64) and Secretary of State for Education and Science (1970–74). Thatcher was a particularly dominant personality in the Community during her time in office, the early period of which was shaped by the dispute over the UK's contribution to the budget. The disagreement centred on the UK being the second largest net contributor to the budget, although being one of the poorer Member States in terms of GDP per head of population, and to Thatcher's perception that the CAP was an especially wasteful policy. Agreement on a rebate was eventually reached at the June 1984 Fontainebleau European Council meeting, although by that time she was perceived by other Member States as an awkward negotiator, particularly because her forthright personality often clashed with the cosy atmosphere at European Council meetings. Nevertheless, she was not necessarily a Euro-sceptic and proved a vigorous supporter of economic integration via the SEA, but she considered that did not extend to granting the European Commission greater powers. In this context, she criticised it in 1988 for attempting to create an 'identikit' European personality, which resulted in her views clashing with a majority of other Member States and the European Commission. This was emphasised by her opposition to the 1989 proposals for the Social Charter and EMU. Domestically, this position brought her into conflict with senior Cabinet members, notably Douglas Hurd and John Major, who forced her to join the ERM in October 1990. A fear of losing the general election resulted in her losing a Conservative leadership contest the following month. Out of office, she proved to be a thorn in the side of the Conservative government led by Major, especially after the negotiation of the Treaty on European Union and her own elevation to the House of Lords in 1992.

Thorn, Gaston (b. 1928): His Presidency of the European Commission between 1981 and 1985 proved not to be as dynamic as either his predecessor, Roy Jenkins, or his successor, Jacques Delors. Prior to his appointment he had served as a Luxembourg government minister since 1969, during which time he was Prime Minister between 1974 until 1979. Thorn was therefore fully aware of the mechanics of negotiating within Brussels, but this experience proved to be of little assistance during a Presidency that was perceived to be a disappointment. But his task had not been an easy one, with the UK budget dispute dominating the agenda. It, combined with lengthy negotiations over the entry of Portugal and Spain, the question of institutional reform and the technological advancements made in Japan and the USA, proved to be difficult problems for the European Commission to manage.

Tindemans, Leo (b. 1922): As Prime Minister of Belgium from 1974 until 1978 he was an active proponent of greater European integration, as demonstrated in the 1975 Tindemans Report. It highlighted a desire to propel the Community out of a period of slow growth, but found little support from other Member States. However, as Foreign Minister of Belgium from 1981 until 1989 he took part in the economic revival of the Community, where he used the Belgian Presidencies as a means of promoting the single market and advancing the SEA. After leaving the office of Foreign Minister in 1989, he became a Member of the European Parliament.

Uri, Pierre (1911–92): He was an active participant in the European integration process during the 1940s and 1950s, along with Jean Monnet and Robert Marjolin. As financial and economic adviser to the French Planning Commission between 1947 and 1952 he was instrumental in the development of a warmer policy towards Germany within France, which eventually resulted in the ECSC Treaty. His importance to this development was emphasised by his position as a senior official within the ECSC from 1952 until 1959.

Waigel, Theodor (b. 1939): German Federal Minister of Finance from 1989 until 1998. A law and political science graduate, he received his Doctorate in law in 1967. From 1967 to 1969 he was a junior legal official at the district attorney's office, regional court, Munich and from 1969–70 was a personal assistant to the Secretary of State for Finance, Bavaria. Between 1970 and 1972 he was personal assistant to the State Minister of Economic Affairs and Transport, Bavaria. Since 1972 he has been a member of the German Bundestag and was Chairman of the CDU/CSU parliamentary group in the Economics Committee of the German Bundestag between 1978 and 1980. From 1980 to 1982 he was Chairman of the Working Group on Economics and spokesman for economics of the CDU/CSU parliamentary group in the Bundestag. Between 1982 and 1989 he served as Chairman of the CSU group and first Vice Chairman of the CDU/CSU parliamentary group in the German Bundestag. Since 1988 he has also been Chairman of the CSU.

Williamson, David (b. 1934): He was appointed Secretary-General of the European Commission in 1987 on the retirement of Emile Noël, a position in which he continued to serve until June 1997. Williamson had first had experience of working with Community policies as a former UK civil servant in the Ministry of Agriculture, and had served as the government's representative on the EC special committee on agriculture between 1976 and 1977. He was seconded to the European Commission in 1977 and was deputy director-general for Agriculture from 1977 to 1983. Upon his return to the UK he was appointed deputy secretary and head of the European Secretariat of the Cabinet Office between 1983 and 1987, a post which brought him into the frontline of UK European policy by being responsible for coordinating UK negotiating tactics. While this prepared him for the post of Secretary-General, he was never likely to wield the influence of Noël over the direction of the Community. This was both because of the length of service of the latter and Williamson having to work with an activist President in the shape of Jacques Delors, who often curtailed formal procedures by negotiating agreements among an inner core of officials.

Wilson, Harold (b. 1916): A UK Labour Prime Minister from October 1964 to June 1970 and March 1974 to April 1976, he previously held various government posts including Parliamentary Secretary in the Ministry of Works (1945–47), Secretary for Overseas Trade (March–October 1947) and President of the Board of Trade (1947–51). During his first tenure as Prime Minister he oversaw the UK's second application for UK membership of the Community, although its failure owed much to the problems associated with the first application. Upon his return to office in 1974, he applied for a renegotiation of the terms of entry which Edward Heath had obtained, accepting the new terms in January 1975. That was later followed by a referendum on Community membership in 1975, in which Wilson allowed his own Cabinet a free vote. This resulted in seven of the twenty-three Cabinet Ministers voting against the terms of entry, including the future Labour Party leader, Michael Foot.

Wörner, Manfred (1934–94): A former Minister of Defence of the Federal Republic of Germany from 1982 to 1988 who had been elected to the German Bundestag in 1965. He completed a doctorate in international law at the University of Munich in 1958, which dealt with the defence relations of allied countries his special interests centred on security policy. He chaired the Working Group on Defence of the CDU/CSU parliamentary party until 1976, was Chairman of the Defence Committee of the German Bundestag until 1980, and was Deputy Chairman of the CDU/CSU parliamentary party until 1982. After his tenure as Minister of Defence, he succeeded Lord Carrington in 1988 as Secretary-General of NATO. This proved to be an extremely turbulent period for the Alliance, caused by the collapse of Soviet-dominated Eastern Europe, the drive towards a separate European defence identity and the challenge of the 1991 Gulf War. During this period Wörner managed to ensure that NATO retained its primary European defence identity, with it proving crucial to the resolution of the conflict in the former Yugoslavia.

Wulf-Mathies, Monika (b. 1942): A German member of the European Commission with responsibility for regional policies, relations with the Committee of the Regions and the Cohesion Fund. She holds a PhD in History. From 1968 to 1971 she was Head of Division in the Federal Ministry of Economic Affairs and subsequently served in the Federal Chancellery between 1971 and 1976. Thereafter she occupied a number of positions, including that of a member of the supervisory board of Deutsche Lufthansa AG.

SECTION XI

Glossary

Accession. Refers to the act of joining the EU. The treaties which cover the conclusion of the negotiations between applicant countries and EU Member States are known as 'Treaties of Accession'.

Country	Date of application	Comments
Bulgaria	December 1995	July 1997 – European Commission to re-examine the case for membership on an annual basis.
Cyprus	July 1990	Accession negotiations started in 1998.
Czech Republic	January 1996	Accession negotiations started in 1998.
Estonia	November 1995	Accession negotiations started in 1998.
Hungary	March 1994	Accession negotiations started in 1998.
Latvia	November 1995	July 1997 – European Commission to re-examine the case for membership on an annual basis.
Lithuania	December 1995	July 1997 – European Commission to re-examine the case for membership on an annual basis.
Malta	July 1990	Following national elections in 1996, the structured dialogue within the Council has been discontinued.
Morocco	1987	Refused.
Norway (1st)	1967	Negative referendum on 24–25 September 1972.
Norway (2nd)	November 1992	Negative referendum on 28 November 1994.
Poland	April 1994	Accession negotiations started in 1998.
Romania	June 1995	July 1997 – European Commission to re-examine the case for membership on an annual basis.
Slovak Republic	June 1995	July 1997 – European Commission to re-examine the case for membership on an annual basis.

Country	Date of application	Comments
Slovenia	June 1996	Accession negotiations started in 1998.
Switzerland	May 1992	Negative referendum on European Economic Area on 6 December 1992.
Turkey	April 1987	The European Commission considered the request to be premature because of its economic and democratic problems.

ACE.   Acronym for Action by the Community relating to the Environment, being a Community programme to improve the environment.

Acquis communitaire.   Describes the body of legislation and guarantees between Member States as a result of legislative and Treaty obligations taken since 1957. All prospective members of the EU have to accept this before they can enter.

Action Committee for a United States of Europe (ACUSE).   A small pressure group formed by Jean Monnet in 1954 after his resignation as President of the ECSC. It campaigned for greater European integration, its members comprising representatives from political parties and trade unions.

Acts of the Community Institutions.   The acts which are adopted by the Council and the European Commission. They are divided into four categories: (1) regulations that have direct force of law in all Member States; (2) directives that require Member States to adopt appropriate rules, although they are left with choice as to how to achieve the objectives; (3) decisions that have direct effect in law – these refer to specific individual cases that can be addressed to firms, individuals or a Member State; and (4) recommendations and opinions that are not binding, such as resolutions of the Council.

Adoption.   The forming of a measure which has legal effect.

Advocate-General.   An officer of the European Court of Justice. There are nine and their role is to act as advisers and consultants to the Court.

African, Caribbean and Pacific States (ACP).   The term given to the developing countries that have an association agreement with the EU under Articles 131–136 of the Treaties of Rome. While the original provisions were directed towards the former colonies of the Six, and documented by the 1963 and 1969 Yaoundé Convention, the enlargement of the Community has brought new members into the agreement, which, since 1975, has fallen under the Lomé Convention. There are now some 70 states that are linked to the EU under the Fourth Lomé Convention, which was agreed in 1990, and these states are eligible for grants from the EIB and EDF.

Agenda. The EP adopts its plenary agenda at the start of each part-session, having already consulted members of the various political groups about its contents. By contrast, the Council's agenda is principally established by the Member State which holds the Presidency, though it is equally subject to consultation with other interested parties.

Agenda 2000. The President of the European Commission, Jacques Santer, presented *Agenda 2000* to the European Parliament in Strasbourg on 16 July 1997. The 1,300-page package of plans covered EU enlargement, the budget and the future of the CAP, although the European Commission warned that these plans could not be implemented until agreement was obtained on the reform of voting in the Council of Ministers, the extension of QMV and the streamlining of the European Commission, questions which the June 1997 Treaty of Amsterdam failed to tackle. The *Agenda 2000* document examined the issue of admitting ten countries of Eastern Europe to the EU by suggesting that entry negotiations should commence with five of them in 1998.

Agricultural levies. A duty charged on farm products imported into the EU from non-member countries which offsets differences between price levels inside the Community and externally lower world market prices. In this context, the actual rates change according to world market prices. The effect of this process is that EU farmers are guaranteed high prices while providing finance for the Union.

Airbus. This air industry originally began in 1965 as an Anglo-French proposal, with Airbus Industrie being founded in 1990 as a European economic interest grouping. It is now one of the most widely known collaborative projects within the EU. The most significant members of the project are France, Germany and the UK, while Belgium, the Netherlands and Spain make smaller contributions. The main assembly plant is in Toulouse, with British Aerospace being primarily engaged in the design and manufacture of the wings.

Amendment. The changing or correction of a bill.

Amendment of the Treaties.   Proposals to amend the Treaties may be submitted by any Member State to the Council via Article N of the TEU. The Council can call an intergovernmental conference of the Member States after having consulted the European Parliament and the European Commission. An amendment has to be ratified by all Member States.

Andean Pact.   A cooperation agreement for bilateral trade aid signed with Bolivia, Ecuador, Peru and Venezuela on 17 December 1983. The official name for the group is, however, the Acuerdo de Cartagena. They have benefited from the Community adopting a Generalised System of Preferences, which has equally proved of assistance to other Latin American countries.

Annual legislative programme.   This procedure is a means of establishing priorities between different items of forthcoming legislation and is published towards the end of each year by the European Commission after discussion with the EP.

Annulment.   An act that declares void an act of the Community institution.

Antici.   An informal group of assistants to Member States' permanent representatives that acts as a forum where a Presidency can coordinate work programmes. At European Council meetings the Antici group acts as a liaison between national delegations and Heads of State or Government.

Anti-dumping.   Anti-dumping duties are imposed on goods which are imported into the EU at lower prices than those in the exporter's home market.

Anti-poverty Programme.   This was highlighted as one of the primary tasks of the 1974 Social Action Programme, being adopted by the Council of Ministers in 1975.

Approximation.   This refers to the approximation of provisions to overcome the differing national provisions laid down by law, regulation and administrative action that are pertinent to the single market. The Council generally uses directives to achieve approximation.

Ariane.   A French-designed rocket launcher that has been used by ESA for the placing of satellites in space, with partial funding having come from the EIB.

Article(s).   A clause or unit of a Community Treaty that can be divided into paragraphs.

Article 6 Committee. A committee established by the European Commission that implements Financial Protocols that relate to agreements signed between the Community and Mediterranean countries.

Article 113 Committee. A Brussels-based committee of national officials which prepares the decisions of the Council of Ministers in the area of external trade policy, the Committee being sanctioned by Article 113 of the Treaties of Rome.

Article K.4 Committee. Introduced in the TEU, it acts as a coordinating committee consisting of senior officials doing preparatory work for Council deliberations on JHA.

Assembly. Previous name of the EP.

Assent procedure. The assent of the EP, by means of an absolute majority of its members, is necessary before certain important decisions can be adopted. The assent procedure provides the EP with an ability to accept or reject a proposal, but not to amend it. The procedure is applicable to decisions on the accession of new Member States, association agreements with third countries and the conclusion of international agreements. It is also required for citizenship, the specific tasks of the ECB, amendments to the statute of the ESCB and of the ECB, the structural funds and cohesion funds and the uniform procedure for elections to the EP.

Assizes. Describes consultative meetings of representatives from national parliaments who seek to support the process of European integration.

Association Agreement. Refers to the original means of establishing agreements under Article 238 between candidate Member States and the EC, of which the first was signed in 1961 with Greece. Subsequent agreements have included Turkey in 1964, Malta in 1970, Cyprus in 1972, and Poland and Hungary in 1994. The ending of the Cold War brought forth a new type of Europe Agreement for Central and Eastern European countries which seek membership of the Community.

Association of European Chambers of Commerce and Industry. Established in 1958, the Brussels-based association consists of 24 member organisations representing over 1,200 chambers of commerce and industry.

Association of South East Asian Nations (ASEAN). Since 1978 there has been a political cooperation agreement between the EU and ASEAN states (Brunei, Indonesia, Malaysia, the Philippines, Singapore, Thailand and Vietnam). This has resulted in a biennial conference of EU and

ASEAN Foreign Ministers, while a permanent bureau (ASEAN Brussels Committee) ensures that continuous contact is achieved.

Atlantic Alliance.   A common name for NATO.

Atypical worker.   An individual who does not operate in full-time permanent employment, such as a part-time, fixed term or temporary employee.

Audit board.   Established by the Treaties of Rome to examine the revenue and expenditure of the Community, it was replaced by the more dynamic Court of Auditors in 1977.

Avis.   Statement by the European Commission on the degree to which an application for membership of the EU is acceptable.

Balance of payments.   Refers to the external transactions of a country over a certain period of time.

Balladur Memorandum.   The name given to the French government's report on the reform of the EMS with respect to the completion of the internal market. It was presented by the then Finance Minister, Edouard Balladur, in January 1998. It advocated that all Member States should join the ERM in the context of the 'rapid pursuit of the monetary construction of Europe'. It was influential in providing momentum towards EMU, with the then German Foreign Minister, Hans-Dietrich Genscher, issuing a memorandum in February 1998 entitled 'A European Currency Area and a European Central Bank'.

Bank for International Settlements (BIS).   Founded in 1930 to assist cooperation between central banks and as a means of easing international financial operations.

Barcelona Conference.   EU Member States agreed to the Barcelona declaration with 12 adjoining Mediterranean states at a conference in November 1995, the aim of which was to guarantee security in the Mediterranean region. In so doing, three pillars were established. The first provided for a political and security partnership, guaranteeing human rights and basic political freedoms. The second pillar had the aim of establishing a Euro-Mediterranean free trade area by 2010. The third pillar dealt with cultural and social issues, including a mutual respect for culture and religion.

Basket of currencies.   Refers to the currencies which determined the value of the ECU, whereby each currency received a different weight in the basket depending upon its GNP, trade and quotas for short-term credits.

Beef crisis.   Refers to the health crisis encountered in the UK after the announcement on 20 March 1996 that there could be a possible link between BSE found in cattle and the fatal disease found in humans known as Creutzfeldt-Jakob disease. This resulted in the EU veterinary committee voting by 14 to 1 on 25 March to recommend a total ban of UK beef exports. The ban on the export of beef and beef products from the UK was immediately implemented, the only dissenter being the UK. As a response to the ban, the UK government of John Major adopted, on 21 May 1996, a policy of non-cooperation with the EU until a time-table to lift the ban on the export of beef was settled. The European Court of Justice rejected an appeal by the UK government on 12 July 1996 to lift the ban on UK beef exports, while on 17–19 March 1997 the Brussels EU Agricultural Ministers meeting reached agreement that all beef had to be marked with its country of origin. However, by January 1998 the EU approved a partial lifting of the 1996 export ban on UK beef, with the proposal applying only to the export of beef products from North-ern Ireland. This was because it was the only part of the UK which had a complete, computerised tracking system and fewer recorded cases of BSE than elsewhere in the UK.

Belgo-Luxembourg Economic Union (BLEU).   A customs union between Belgium and Luxembourg which was created in 1921 and subsequently expanded in 1944 with the creation of Benelux. The presence of the BLEU resulted in financial statistics for Belgium and Luxembourg being jointly documented.

Benelux.   The customs union of Belgium, the Netherlands and Luxem-bourg which was agreed to by Treaty in February 1958 and came into effect on 1 November 1960.

Berlaymont.   The name of the building which housed the Euro-pean Commission from 1969 until renovations commenced in 1992, when staff were temporarily moved to the Breydel building. The word 'Berlaymont' has, however, remained synonymous with the European Commission.

BEUC.   The European bureau of consumers' unions is an umbrella organisation of national consumer organisations, with the aim of pro-moting the interests of consumers within the EU.

Bilaterals.   Terminology for negotiations between two sides, such as meetings between Member States or a Member State and the European Commission.

Border controls.   A single market initiative for Member States to align their national rules through mutual recognition to ensure that border controls could be eliminated by 1 January 1993. While this was achieved for traffic in goods, controls on individuals were not dismantled until 26 March 1995, and even then only covered those countries which had signed the Schengen agreement.

Brussels.   General term often used to indicate the Community and its decision-makers.

Budget of the EU.   Includes revenue obtained from own resources, money spent upon common policies and the costs of running the EU institutions. The largest element of the budget has traditionally been the price support system of the CAP.

Bundesrat.   German federal council elected by members of the 16 Länder governments.

Bundestag.   German Federal Parliament established on 23 May 1949 and elected for a four-year term.

Butter mountain.   Just as with the wine lake, this popular phrase described the effect of the CAP price guarantee and intervention system in the area of dairy farming whereby overproduction resulted in large amounts of butter being accumulated in storage facilities. This problem was tackled by limits being placed on dairy farming in 1984 through the introduction of milk quotas, thereby reducing the demands made on the CAP. Butter in storage was then sold at a discounted price.

Cabinet.   Private office of a European Commissioner.

Cassis de Dijon.   Judgment of the Court of Justice in the 1979 case of *Rewe-Zentrale AG v Bundesmonopolverwaltung für Branntwein* (case 120/78), but known as 'Cassis de Dijon'. It established that it was not possible for restrictions to be imposed on a product lawfully manufactured and on sale in one Member State when it was imported into another Member State. Being based on the principle of mutual recognition, it was therefore an important landmark in the creation of the single market.

Cecchini Report.   Throughout 1986 and 1987 the Italian economist, Paolo Cecchini, led a group of researchers who considered the 'costs of non-Europe', that is, the impediments which hampered the free movement of goods, services, persons and capital within the Community. Published in 1988 at the request of the European Commission, the report examined the economic consequences of the plan to establish the single market by 1992. It suggested that the removal of frontier barriers, including those of a technical nature and frontier controls, would be likely to produce savings of some 200 billion ECU. This would in turn result in greater economic growth and increased employment. The summary of this report was also published by Cecchini in 1988 as a book entitled *The European Challenge: 1992*.

CEDEFOP.   An agency of the EU that is primarily concerned with research into mutual recognition of qualifications.

CELEX.   A constantly updated multilingual EU database containing official legislation and other documentation, including proposals from the European Commission and opinions of the Court of Auditors.

CEN/CENELEC.   Acronyms for European Committee for Standardisation (CEN) and European Committee for Electrotechnical Standardisation (CENELEC). Both organisations are based in Brussels and aim to establish joint European standardisation, embracing EU, EFTA and national standards.

Censure motion.   The EP has the ability to sack the European Commission only if a motion is tabled by more than one-tenth of its members and passed by an absolute majority.

Central and Eastern European countries.   Refers to the ten countries of Central and Eastern Europe that have applied for membership of the EU, namely Bulgaria, the Czech and Slovak Republics, Estonia, Hungary, Latvia, Lithuania, Poland, Romania and Slovenia.

Central Bank Governors.   The governors of the central banks of EU Member States have played an important role in European financial affairs through the EMS and were crucial to the shaping of the TEU provisions on EMU where the committee of central bank governors was one of the main negotiating bodies alongside the monetary committee and Finance Ministers. Central bank governors were particularly involved in writing the draft statutes for the ESCB and the EMI. They will receive greater powers with the creation of EMU, there having already been a merger in 1994 of the Committee of Central Bank Governors and the EMCF to form the EMI.

Central banks.   These are the central banks of EU Member States which play an important role in the coordination of both national and European monetary policy. The governors of the central banks are especially crucial. Some banks have been more independent than others, such as the central bank of the Federal Republic of Germany, whereas the UK Bank of England has traditionally been perceived to suffer from political influence, although reforms in 1997 by the Labour government have provided it with more independence, notably regarding the setting of interest rates. The 15 central banks are: Austria – Oesterreichische Nationalbank; Belgium – Banque Nationale de Belgique; Denmark – Danmarks Nationalbank; Finland – Suomen Pankki; France – Banque de France; Federal Republic of Germany – Deutsche Bundesbank; Greece – Bank of Greece; Ireland – Central Bank of Ireland; Italy – Banca d'Italia; Luxembourg – Institut Monétaire Luxembourgeois; the Netherlands – De Nederlandsche Bank; Portugal – Banco de Portugal; Spain – Banco de España; Sweden – Sveriges Riksbank; and the UK – Bank of England.

Centre for Industrial Development.   Covered by the Lomé Convention, it provides financial and logistic assistance for promoters of industrial projects in the ACP States, including studies of joint venture formalities, financing visits to identify partners, and staff training.

CERN.   The Geneva-based European Organisation for Nuclear Research which was established in 1954 with the aim of promoting cooperation between European nations in research on nuclear energy and related policies. The acronym comes from the previous French title of Conseil européen pour la recherche nucléaire.

Chamber.   The division in which the Court of Justice sits when not sitting in plenary session.

Chapter.   A subdivision of a Title in a Community Treaty, which can be further subdivided into sections.

Charter of Paris.   The signature by CSCE members of the Charter of Paris for a New Europe on 21 November 1990 is generally considered to be the formal end of the Cold War as a result of the collapse of the Soviet satellite states in Eastern Europe. The Charter emphasised the concepts that were established in the Helsinki Final Act. It also demonstrated the transformation of the CSCE into a permanent organisation which resulted in its name changing to OSCE.

Chef de cabinet.   The personal political adviser to a European Commissioner who heads the Cabinet of officials.

Christian democracy.   The largest grouping of centre and centre-right political parties in post-war Europe, of which the German Christian Democratic Union (CDU) has been the most influential. Christian democracy was particularly important to European integration, embracing figures such as Konrad Adenauer, Alcide de Gasperi, Walter Hallstein and Helmut Kohl. At a European level, Christian democratic political parties in the EP form the Group of the European People's Party. The leaders of Christian democratic political parties usually meet prior to a European Council where they form an important caucus in the establishment of points of consensus.

Citizenship.   Citizenship of the EU was inserted under the TEU, Article 8 noting that 'every person holding the nationality of a Member State shall be a citizen of the Union'. It is relevant in the granting of some powers to citizens, including the ability to refer points of concern to the Ombudsman.

Co-decision.   Introduced in the TEU under Article 189b EC, by which the EP was provided with greater powers. The adoption of legislation involves both the Council and the EP and if disagreement arises between the two institutions after the EP's second reading, then the Council has the ability to call a Conciliation Committee. The Committee comprises an equal number of members from the Council and the EP. If no agreement is reached, then it is not possible for an act to be adopted against the will of the EP. The procedure embraces decisions on consumer protection, culture, education, free movement, health, the right of establishment, freedom to provide services, the single market (Article 100a EC) and the adoption of guidelines or programmes covering trans-European networks, research and the environment.

Codetermination.   As a legislative framework requirement in the operation of works councils in several Member States, it stipulates the various areas where the agreement of employee representatives is essential before any action can be taken by management. This includes the monitoring of employee performance.

Cohesion fund.   Established in 1993 under Article 130d of the TEU to provide financial assistance for projects in the domains of the environment and transport infrastructure. The four poorest areas of the Community (Ireland, Greece, Spain and Portugal) receive finance from the fund with the aim of reducing differences between Member States' economies.

Cold War.   A phrase first used in the late 1940s to highlight the tension which had developed in the wake of the Second World War between the USA and the USSR, particularly in the European theatre. The reality of Soviet dominance over Eastern Europe by 1948 resulted in the freezing of relations between the two powers and their allies. As a result, a system of western collective defence was established through the signing of the

1949 Treaty of Washington which founded NATO. The 1990 Charter of Paris is generally considered to signify the formal end of the Cold War.

Collective defence.   Both the Treaty of Brussels (Article V) and the Treaty of Washington (Article 5) stress that signatory states are required to provide assistance in the event of aggression.

COM-Doc.   A European Commission document generally used for publishing proposed legislation.

COMETT.   Acronym for Community Action Programme in Education and Training for Technology. Initially established in 1987 to develop cooperation between universities and industry through exchanges and training partnerships, it was absorbed into the Leonardo programme in 1995.

Comitology.   Refers to the various committee procedures which oversee the implementation of Community law. The EC Treaty provides for the European Commission to be normally responsible for implementing decisions adopted by the Council of the European Union (Article 145). The executive activities of the European Commission are monitored by the Council via advisory, management or regulatory committees, which are composed of national experts. The power of advisory committees is limited to making non-binding recommendations to the European Commission. By contrast, management committees have the ability to refer the implementing measures of the European Commission back to the Council for a decision within a set period of time. Measures are suspended in the intervening period. If a decision is not reached by the Council in the set time, the European Commission is able to implement the measures. European Commission measures can also be suspended and referred back to the Council by regulatory committees. However, in those areas where the Council has not taken a decision within the time limit, then the European Commission is only able to adopt the measures if the Council has not rejected them. It can do this by a simple majority. The Council has tended to prefer using the regulatory procedure which it is able to choose whenever it likes, much to the aggravation of the European Commission.

Committee for a People's Europe.   The Fontainebleau 1984 European Council established a committee to 'suggest ways of strengthening the identity of the Community at the individual level and of improving the image of the Community among the national populations'. The committee, which was chaired by the Italian MEP Pietro Adonnino and comprised the personal representatives of Member States, produced an initial report in March 1985 which was followed by a more detailed report in the Milan European Council of June 1985. A central part of the report related to citizens' rights, including the right to participate in direct elections to the EP through a uniformal process and the right to live in another Member State on the same conditions as those available to national citizens.

Committee of inquiry. The TEU provided the EP with the ability to establish temporary committees of inquiry to investigate violations of EU law. These committees can be established by a request of one quarter of MEPs (Article 138c).

Committee of the Regions (CoR). A new advisory body established by the TEU to take account of the views of regional and local government in European decision-making. It comprises some 222 members (the same as the ESC) who are appointed by national governments and not directly by any regional authority. Although it sits in Brussels and must be consulted before the adoption of decisions that affect regional interests, it can also deliver opinions on its own initiative.

Common Agricultural Policy (CAP). Established in 1962, it is a price and structural support system for agricultural production within the EC.

Common Fisheries Policy. While it was established as a primary principle of the original six Member States, it was not until 1983 that it was adopted as a common policy. A central part of the Community, it was intended to promote the conservation of fish stocks, establish a similar system of price support systems as the CAP and modernise the industry, though in pursuing such objectives it has attracted much criticism.

Common foreign and security policy (CFSP). Established by Title V of the TEU, it replaced European Political Cooperation and provided for the eventual framing of a common defence policy which might in time lead to a common defence. Article J.1 secured the objectives of the second pillar of the Union.

Common market. General term that refers to the customs union established by the Treaties of Rome which aimed to provide free movement of capital, goods, persons and services, in addition to the establishment of common policies.

Common position. Refers to procedures within the intergovernmental pillars of the EU, embracing CFSP and JHA. Within these frameworks, governments inform and consult each other and are also able to adopt a common position and joint action. A common position refers to a situation whereby Member States are able to define and defend a course of action which is in line with national policies to the greatest extent (Article J.2; Article K.3).

Communitization.   The transfer of a policy from the intergovernmental arena of the second and third pillars to the Community arena of the first pillar.

Community bridge.   Often used in the context of JHA whereby Article K.9 of the TEU provided the opportunity for making certain areas of Title VI applicable to Community provisions, most notably the provision in Article 100c for QMV. The bridge, or passerelle procedure, necessitates unanimity in the Council and ratification in each Member State in line with its national constitutional requirements.

Community initiatives.   Aid or action programmes established to complement the operation of the structural fund in certain specific areas. While coordinated and implemented under national control, they are initially drawn up by the European Commission. Community initiatives embrace cross-border cooperation (Interreg, Regen II), rural development (Leader II), the most remote regions (REGIS II), human resources (NOW, Horizon, Youthstart), industrial change/employment (ADAPT), industrial change (Rechar II, coal-mining areas; Resider II, steel areas; Konver, defence industry conversion; RETEX, textile areas, Portuguese textile industry), encouraging small and medium-sized firms (SMEs), urban crisis areas (URBAN), and fisheries (PESCA).

Community law.   This embraces three forms, the first of which is the Treaties and related instruments, including the own resources decision. The second, legislation, consists of regulations, directives and decisions. The third, case-law, is materialised in decisions of the Court of Justice.

Community method.   The furthering of EU integration via usage of its institutions rather than intergovernmental processes.

Community preference.   A part of the CAP whereby Member States are expected to give preference to agricultural products from within the EU over those from outside.

Community support framework (CSF).   Coordinates the regional activities of the EU. At times this involves the structural funds (ERDF, ESF, EAGGF) and the EIB.

Competence.   The ability of the Community to undertake specific policies.

Competition policy.   The adoption of a course of action to ensure that a desired level of rivalry is maintained between commercial undertakings. It is required by the Treaties of Rome, the European Commission being entrusted with the task of ensuring both Member States and companies comply to the stipulated procedures. In this context, the European Commission has the ability to act on its own initiative without reference to the Council of Ministers if it has received complaints from Member States, companies or individuals. In general, the application of a competition policy has resulted in numerous trading agreements being outlawed, such as price-fixing, market-sharing and exclusive agreements.

Competitiveness.   Refers to the ability of Member States to compete with each other and with outside states, while also highlighting the economic strength of the EU versus other trading nations and trading blocs. The European Commission's 1994 White Paper on 'Growth, Competitiveness and Employment' contained guidelines for a policy of global competitiveness.

Concentric circles.   Refers to a situation where the process of European integration results in different groupings of Member States reflecting distinct levels of integration. In this context, Member States pursue policies where they have shared objectives, as in the field of defence.

Conciliation Committee.   This can be established under the co-decision procedure, as provided in Article 189b(4) of the TEU. It consists of members of the Council or their representatives and an equal number of representatives of the EP. It is referred to in the event of disagreement between the two institutions on the outcome of a co-decision procedure. The rationale is to ensure that a text is agreed which is acceptable to both sides. The draft of such a text must then be ratified within six weeks by a qualified majority in the Council and by an absolute majority of the members of the EP. But if one of the two institutions does not approve the proposal, then it is not adopted.

Conference on Security and Cooperation in Europe (CSCE).   Established by the signing of the Helsinki Final Act on 1 August 1975, it represented an attempt to reconcile the different interests of NATO and the Warsaw Pact, with all European countries apart from Albania taking part in the negotiations, in addition to Canada and the USA. The initial membership of 35 nations has expanded to 53, and its name has been changed to the Organisation for Security and Cooperation in Europe (OSCE), to reflect a more proactive institution. Members include: Albania, Armenia, Austria, Azerbaijan, Belarus, Belgium, Bosnia and Herzegovina, Bulgaria, Canada, Croatia, Cyprus, Czech Republic, Denmark,

Estonia, Finland, France, Georgia, Federal Republic of Germany, Greece, Holy See, Hungary, Iceland, Ireland, Italy, Kazakhstan, Kyrgyzstan, Latvia, Liechtenstein, Lithuania, Luxembourg, Malta, Moldova, Monaco, the Netherlands, Norway, Poland, Portugal, Romania, Russian Federation, San Marino, the Slovak Republic, Slovenia, Spain, Sweden, Switzerland, Tajikistan, Turkmenistan, Turkey, Ukraine, United Kingdom, United States of America, Uzbekistan, Yugoslavia (suspended from activities). The Former Yugoslav Republic of Macedonia is an observer.

Congress of Europe. A meeting of over 800 individuals held in The Hague in May 1948, including politicians and lawyers, that was organised by the International Committee of the Movements for European Union, and directly led to the foundation of the European Movement in October 1948. The President-of-Honour was Winston Churchill.

Consultation procedure. The opinion of the EP must be obtained before the Council adopts a European Commission legislative proposal. While such an opinion is intended to influence the decision of the Council, the latter is not bound by it. As a procedure it is particularly applicable to the CAP (Article 43 (2,3)), though also covering citizenship, cohesion funds, the excessive deficit procedure, the appointment of EMI president and the start of the third stage of EMU.

Consumer policy. While the Treaties of Rome did not mention consumer policy, both the EP and numerous interest groups have campaigned for such a policy, resulting in the Council of Ministers launching a consumer information and protections programme in April 1975, embracing economic justice, health and safety issues, consultation, remedy for damages, and education and information. This was later advanced when national Ministers for consumer affairs started to meet on a regular basis within the Council of Ministers, and various directives have been instigated to protect consumer interests. Indeed, DG XXIV of the European Commission specifically deals with consumer policy.

Contact Group. Refers to the meetings of representatives of France, FRG, Russia, the UK and the USA concerning the former Yugoslavia. The purpose of the meetings was to present a united front to the warring parties. The first such meeting took place in London on 26 April 1994.

Convergence criteria. The TEU established five convergence criteria which each Member State must make before it can take part in stage three of EMU: (1) the ratio of government deficit to GDP must not exceed 3%; (2) the ratio of government debt to GDP must not exceed 60%; (3) a sustainable degree of price stability and an average inflation rate have to be observed over a period of one year prior to examination – they should not exceed, by more than one and a half percentage points, that of the three best-performing Member States in terms of price stability; (4) long-term nominal interest rates should not exceed, by more than two percentage points, that of the three best-performing Member States in terms of price stability; (5) Member States' should have respected the normal fluctuation margins provided for by the ERM of the EMS for at least the last two years before examination.

Convertibility.   The degree to which one currency can be exchanged for another.

Cooperation.   Refers to the development of intergovernmental action rather than integration via the Community method.

Cooperation procedure.   Introduced in the SEA (Article 189c), it provided the EP with a greater say in the legislative process, with European Commission proposals being subjected to a 'double reading'. In this context, if the Council does not take into account the initial EP opinion in its common position, then the EP is able to reject it at the second reading. Thereafter, it is only possible for the Council to overturn the position of the EP by means of a unanimous decision. But, as it is not always possible to obtain unanimity, the Council can seek conciliation with the EP to ensure proposals are not rejected. The procedure is applicable to research, the environment, cooperation and development, trans-European networks, economic and social cohesion, and health and safety of workers (Article 118a).

COREPER.   Acronym for the Committee of Permanent Representatives which was made official in 1965. It comprises senior officials from the 15 Member States who examine draft legislation before it is examined in the Council of Ministers (Article 151). A proposal which has been agreed by COREPER becomes item A on the Council's agenda and is adopted without debate, while an issue that has not been agreed becomes item B and is debated. COREPER I consists of Deputy Permanent Representatives, while COREPER II consists of Permanent Representatives who are the Ambassadors of the Member States. Some 250 working parties report to COREPER, having examined the necessary legal instruments.

COREUR.   The system which allows the Foreign Offices of EU Member States to exchange information in the form of faxes, telex messages and telegrams. This process is supervised by political directors and their assistants, known as European correspondents, and was initially introduced as a component of EPC.

COSAC.   Acronym for Conference of European Community Affairs Committees which consists of members of the relevant national parliamentary committees and of members of the EP. The six-monthly meetings (since 1988) are important for providing a framework where views can be exchanged between national parliaments and the EP, the pertinence of which has increased with the transfer to the EU of some policies which were purely a national preserve, such as JHA.

COST.   Acronym for the Committee on European Cooperation in the Field of Scientific and Technical Research. It is a funding framework for the implementation and promotion of collaborative scientific research in the fields of agriculture, environmental protection, oceanography, telecommunications and transport.

Council for Mutual Economic Assistance (CMEA).   An organisation which is often referred to as COMECON.

Council of Europe.   Established in May 1949 'to achieve a greater unity between its members for the purpose of safeguarding and realising the ideals and principles which are their common heritage and facilitating their economic and social progress'. The primary aim of the Council is to assist the maintenance of the rules of law and democracy. It has cooperated with the EP to foster European integration, but is not part of the Community, although it has provided European symbols such as the European anthem and flag.

Council of Ministers.   The EU's main decision-making institution consisting of national Ministers and a European Commissioner. Legislating and decision-making are the most important powers of the Council of Ministers, providing Member States with ultimate control over the destiny of the EU. Decisions can be taken by unanimity, QMV or simple majority voting. The business of the Council is organised by the Member State which holds the Presidency (which rotates twice a year; January to June, July to December). The task of managing the Presidency includes the setting of agendas and drafting texts during intergovernmental conferences. In exercising these duties, the Presidency is assisted by a Council Secretariat (based in Brussels) of some 2,000 officials who assist the resolution of compromises. This includes the writing of council minutes and offering impartial legal advice. Such assistance is of greater importance to smaller Member States who do not always have the necessary resources in their Brussels Permanent Representations to fully exercise the duties of the Presidency. Representatives agree under certain circumstances to be out-voted in the decision-making process. Several Councils are organised along sectoral lines, including agriculture, finance, the internal market and transport, with the general affairs council, consisting of Foreign Ministers, being the most important. The number of Councils has grown over the years to keep pace with the expansion of the activities of the EU. This multiplication increases efficiency, but also distributes decision-making among a wider circle of Cabinet colleagues. The Brussels General Affairs Council of 8–9 November 1993 decided to rename the Council of Ministers as the Council of the EU.

Court of Auditors.   Established in 1975 by the Treaty of Brussels, its main role is to audit the accounts of the institutions of the EU and other Union bodies. Comprising 15 members (each of which has a specific area of responsibility), it examines whether revenue and expenditure have been properly handled and checks if sound financial management has taken place.

Court of First Instance.   A division of the European Court of Justice which was created under the terms of the SEA. It came into operation in 1989 as a means of reducing the burden of work on the Court of Justice. Its jurisdiction covers the ECSC, competition policy and cases affecting EU employees.

Court of Justice.   Based in Luxembourg, it is the supreme court of the EU comprising 15 judges and nine advocates-general. Although national governments put forward nominations for appointment to the Court, it is the Council of Ministers that makes formal appointments. The Court is only concerned with EC law and ensures that the Treaties are applied and respected.

Crocodile group.   Refers to a small group of MEPs in the 1979–84 Parliament who believed that the EP should accelerate the process of European integration. The crocodile initiative eventually resulted in the 1984 Draft Treaty on European Union, which assisted the momentum towards the SEA, being adopted by the EP. The crocodile initiative is also known as the Spinelli initiative, while the group's name comes from the Strasbourg restaurant where the first meeting took place.

Customs union.   Refers to the merger of several customs areas into a single whole, resulting in the lifting of duties between participating countries. In this situation, members are not allowed to levy their own duties on imports from countries outside the Union, which contrasts with a Free Trade Area (in a Customs union a common external tariff is set).

Davignon Report.   In an effort to deepen the Community at the time of the first enlargement in the early 1970s, a system of foreign policy cooperation was proposed by the French President, Georges Pompidou. In response to this, Member States appointed the senior Belgian Foreign Ministry official, Etienne Davignon, to draft a report which was submitted to Foreign Minister's in May 1970 and adopted in October. While the report was far less ambitious than Pompidou desired, it suggested that a process of European Political Cooperation would consist of biannual meetings between Foreign Ministers and more regular contact between political directors.

Decisions.　This is one of the acts adopted by the Council and the European Commission (acts of the Community institutions). Decisions have direct effect in law, referring to specific individual cases, and may be addressed to firms, individuals or a particular Member State.

Declaration.　A statement by the Community that tends to be of limited judicial importance. Declarations can also be attached to a Final Act, or be a minor part of a Treaty, whereby its signatories express certain intentions. In this context it is not as significant as a protocol.

Deepening.　A process of strengthening particular policies which may also produce certain institutional reforms that further European integration. While this process is considered by some to be necessary prior to enlargement, others, such as the UK, have traditionally perceived the enlargement of the Community as not necessitating deepening. A debate has therefore developed between widening versus deepening.

Delors I Package.　A 1987 European Commission proposal to reform Community financing, reduce agricultural spending, increase the structural funds and reconsider the budget management rules. It formed the basis for the February 1988 Brussels European Council.

Delors II Package.　In the wake of the signing of the TEU, the European Commission presented a budget package in February 1992 with the aim of securing the financing of the EU in the medium term. To allow the implementation of the decisions taken at the Maastricht European Council meeting with regard to the TEU, budget resources were increased, being particularly pertinent to ensuring cohesion between Member States. The package was subsequently approved by the Edinburgh European Council in December 1992, and provided for an increase in the own resources of the Community to 1.27% of GDP in 1999, while also establishing the cohesion fund and providing greater resources for the structural funds.

Delors Report.　Published in 1989, it proposed a three-stage transition to EMU, the first of which involved the completion of the single market.

The second provided for the creation of 'soft' monetary union whereby the ECSB would coordinate national monetary policies. Finally, a 'hard' monetary union would be established with the irrevocable locking of exchange rates and the transfer of monetary authority to the ECB. Of the three stages, the first was defined in a clear and detailed manner, while the third was relatively clearly outlined. By contrast, the second stage was only vaguely outlined.

Democratic deficit. Refers to the belief that the Community does not have sufficient democratic and parliamentary supervision. This term developed because of the lack of resources traditionally available to the EP to provide it with sufficient powers and also because the national parliaments lacked influence in examining the work of the European Commission and Council of Ministers.

Depression. Economic downturn that is of greater significance than a recession.

Deregulation. Refers to the removal of qualitative and quantitative restrictions to trade that impeded the implementation of the single market by creating barriers.

Derogation. A temporary waiver from a regulation or a directive, which is generally only granted by a unanimous agreement of the Council of Ministers.

Differentiated integration. A process of integration where Member States choose to progress at different speeds, possibly towards common objectives. This therefore contrasts with the perception of all states moving towards the same objectives at a similar speed.

Direct action. Legal proceedings of a contentious nature that commence and terminate in the Court of Justice.

Direct applicability. An EU provision that becomes law in a Member State without needing additional national enactment.

Direct elections. Refers to the direct elections to the EP as provided for in the Treaties of Rome, and agreed to by Heads of State and Government at the Paris European Council meeting of 9–10 December 1974. Taking place every five years, the first set were held on 7–10 June 1979, the second set on 14–17 June 1984, the third on 15–18 June 1989 and the fourth on 9–12 June 1994. The next election is scheduled for June 1999.

Directives.   A legal instrument by which the Council or European Commission can require Member States to amend or adopt national legislation by a specific deadline so as to achieve the aims established in the directive (acts of the Community institutions).

Directorates General (DG).   They are the principal bureaucratic ministries of the European Commission, carrying out EU policy and administering allocations from the budget to different policy areas and the structural funds.

Dooge Committee.   An *ad-hoc* committee on institutional affairs was established by Member States at the June 1984 Fontainebleau European Council to examine amendments to the Treaties of Rome, under the chairmanship of the former Irish Foreign Minister, Jim Dooge. The Committee made use of the 1981 Genscher–Colombo Plan and the European Parliament's Draft Treaty on European Union, with the report providing the basis for the decision by Member States at the June 1985 Milan European Council to establish an intergovernmental conference. That decision eventually produced the SEA.

Draft Treaty on European Union.   The name of a document which, in the wake of the first direct elections to the EP, came from Altiero Spinelli and other MEPs who formed an action group (Crocodile group) which aimed to reform the institutional dynamics of the Community. The EP appointed an institutional committee in 1981 to construct a Draft Treaty on political union under the chairmanship of Spinelli. The contents of the Draft Treaty were approved by a majority of MEPs in February 1984. It advocated enlarged powers for the European Commission, including the preparation and implementation of the budget, and that the European Commission should become the sole executive power, accountable to both the EP and the Council of Ministers. It also suggested that the use of QMV would be extended in the Council.

ECHO.   The European Community Humanitarian Office was established in 1992 and supports victims of disasters or wars, providing free assistance to countries outside the EU. Assistance has been provided to Afghanistan, Angola, Burundi, Cuba, Haiti, Rwanda, Sudan and the former Yugoslavia.

EcoFin Council.   Refers to the EU Council of Economics and Finance Ministers, which is the second most important part of the Council of Ministers after the Foreign Affairs Council. The responsibilities of the EcoFin Council were expanded by the TEU to cover the supervision of Member States' progress towards EMU, a task carried out in collaboration with the EMI.

Economic and Monetary Union (EMU).   While the objective of EMU was initially established in 1969 at a meeting of the Six and thereafter outlined in the 1970 Werner Report, it was not until the 1989 Delors Report that EMU became more of a reality. It led to the decision to convene an intergovernmental conference on EMU, the decisions of which formed a key part of the TEU. The Delors Report detailed three stages for currency union: (1) linking the currencies together through strengthening existing procedures; (2) integration between states through a new Treaty; and (3) the creation of an ECB resulting in the transfer of monetary policy from national authorities, and the irrevocable locking of currencies. Member States at the June 1989 Madrid European Council decided the Delors Report provided a basis for further work. In so deciding, the Council launched the process leading to EMU, with agreement that the first stage of the realisation of EMU should begin on 1 July 1990. The second stage began on 1 January 1994, with a coordinating role being taken on by the newly established EMI. The third stage will commence on 1 January 1999, with 11 of the 15 Member States having met the convergence criteria. The participating Member States at the start of stage three will adopt the irrevocably fixed rates at which the Euro will be substituted for national currencies. Euro banknotes will be issued by the ECB. The third stage also involves the creation of an ESCB, to be composed of the ECB, which replaces the EMI, and national central bank representatives.

Economic and Social Committee (ECOSOC or ESC).   Established in 1957 by the Treaties of Rome with the primary purpose of advising the European Commission and the Council on social and economic matters, it is composed of 222 members representing different interest groups: employers, workers and other interest groups. Members are nominated by national governments, appointed by the Council and serve a four-year term of office which is renewable.

Education policy.   Although the Treaties of Rome did not include much reference to education policy, apart from an arrangement for Member States to recognise diplomas, professional qualifications and vocational training in other Member States, there has recently been an increase in the number of programmes relevant to education. These have included ERASMUS, Socrates and TEMPUS.

Effective date.   This is the date given in an EU directive as the deadline for its incorporation into national legislation.

'Empty chair' crisis.   A development which took place between July and December 1965 when French Ministers refused to participate in meetings of the Council of Ministers under the instructions of President

Charles de Gaulle. He also withdrew the French permanent representative from Brussels. This dispute with the Community was because France was opposed to European Commission proposals relating to the financing of the CAP, introduction of own resources, the extension of budgetary powers to the EP and especially the introduction of majority voting into the Council of Ministers. The outcome of this period of tension was the January 1966 Luxembourg compromise, while policies such as the introduction of own resources were delayed until 1970.

Energy policy.   Despite the existence of Euratom, a coherent European energy policy (as first suggested in 1974) has proved problematic, partly because it is directly relevant to national interests. Nevertheless, targets were established in 1986 on levels of consumption, nuclear energy, oil imports and the development of alternative energy sources up to 1995, while a European energy charter was signed by Member States in 1991.

Enlargement.   Refers to the process whereby nations join the EU by accession, of which the TEU states that 'any European state may apply to become a member of the Union. It shall address its application to the Council, which shall act unanimously after consulting the European Commission and after receiving the assent of the European Parliament.' Since 1957 there have been four enlargements: Ireland, Denmark and the UK joined in 1973; Greece in 1981; Portugal and Spain in 1986; and Austria, Finland and Sweden in 1995. In addition, the German Democratic Republic was incorporated into the EU in 1990 as a consequence of German reunification. Other nations have applied for membership; of those which have not been accepted, some have been given association agreements – for example, the countries of Central and Eastern Europe have Europe Agreements.

Environment policy.   This has been a concern of the Community since 1972, as advanced through a series of five-year action programmes, but it was not until the SEA that energy policy was provided with competence (Article 130r). While the aim has been to foster a policy of sustainable development, with emphasis on prevention rather than cure, the policy area has been subjected to different decision-making procedures depending on the areas affected.

Equal opportunities.   The principle is a fundamental part of the EC Treaty (Article 119) and refers to the provision of equality for men and women with the intention of being applicable to all areas, but especially the economic, cultural and social fields. Equality is of cultural importance due to the many different backgrounds of EU citizens. Since 1975 directives have been aimed at employment, career progression, training and working conditions so as to reduce discrimination between men and women in the workplace. At a later stage it embraced social security.

ERASMUS (European Community action scheme for the mobility of university students). The scheme, which was established in 1987, has supported student and teacher exchanges throughout the EU.

ESPRIT. Acronym for European Strategic Programme for Research and Development in Information Technology. It was created in 1984 as a means of promoting cooperation in information technology research and development.

Euratom Supply Agency. Established in 1957 by the Treaties of Rome it administers the supply policy to the European Commission in the area of nuclear energy, with the aim of ensuring the supply of ores, source materials and special fossil materials.

EUREKA. Acronym for European Research Coordination Agency. The Agency was created under the initiative of former French President François Mitterrand as a means of coordinating research and development in new technology.

Euro. The Euro will replace national currencies on 1 January 1999 in Member States that meet the convergence criteria outlined in the TEU. At that time the Euro will become the EU's only currency. This will affect capital and foreign exchange markets and monetary and exchange rate policy. Euro coins and notes will enter into circulation from 1 January 2002, immediately being legal tender. At this point national currency coins and notes will start to be withdrawn, although remaining legal tender in the nations concerned for a further six months. Thereafter the Euro will be used. The UK and Denmark are exempt from any obligation to use the Euro under the TEU, although they may decide to join in the future.

Euro info centres. These are maintained by the EU in the capitals and other dominant cities of Member States, whereby the public can obtain information (often free of charge) on different policy areas.

Eurobarometer. The public opinion surveys conducted in EU Member States twice a year on behalf of the European Commission.

Eurocorps. Established in May 1992 at the 59th Franco-German Summit in La Rochelle, the 60,000-strong corps was subsequently joined by Belgium and Spain in 1993 and Luxembourg in 1996. It has been operational since November 1995 and reinforces the concept of a European security and defence identity. Its remit is to operate within the limits of Article V of the WEU and Article 5 of NATO, of which the former has political control. The corps can be activated for missions involving humanitarian relief, the evacuation of Member State nationals, and peacekeeping and peacemaking operations. Both the peacekeeping and peacemaking roles fall under the UN or the OSCE. The first operation of the corps took place on 23 June 1998 when 150 troops flew to Sarajevo from their Strasbourg base.

Eurocrat. A term that denotes an official who works in one of the bodies or institutions of the EU.

Eurofighter. A joint project conceived in the late 1970s by Germany, Italy, Spain and the UK to develop and construct a European fighter aircraft. The project encountered problems in the early 1990s when, in June 1992, the German government withdrew from the project, citing cost and lesser security needs in the post-Cold War environment as the reasons for withdrawal. The problems were finally resolved in December 1992 when the Defence Ministers of the four nations agreed to produce a less costly aircraft, and reduce project costs by 30%. Also in December, the Defence Ministers signed a deal for the £42 billion project, thereby launching the production phase of the project.

EUROGROUP. Refers to a grouping of European governments within the NATO framework between 1968 and 1993, after which certain functions, including training, were transferred to NATO, while publicity was transferred to the WEU. By January 1994 the EUROGROUP was disbanded.

Europe Agreements. These are the association agreements between the EU and Central and Eastern European countries concluded since 1991. Their objective is to allow these nations to participate in the economic, political and trading aspects of European integration. The first Europe Agreements were signed in December 1991 with Poland, Hungary and Czechoslovakia. The agreements with Poland and Hungary came into force on 1 February 1994. These were followed a year later by agreements with Bulgaria, Romania, the Czech Republic and Slovakia. On 12 June 1995 agreements were signed with Estonia, Latvia and Lithuania, and on 10 June 1996 with Slovenia.

Europe à la carte. A process of European integration whereby Member States are able to select certain integrationist policies (as if choosing from a restaurant menu). This strategy does not represent a uniform path of integration as some Member States will choose policies that are not adopted by others. Although there will exist a number of common objectives and policies shared by all Member States, the fact that some Member States do not share more objectives serves to undermine concepts of solidarity and the institutional framework.

European anthem.   The EU adopted from the Council of Europe the anthem of 'Ode to Joy' from Beethoven's Ninth Symphony, thereby constituting one of the European symbols.

European Agricultural Guidance and Guarantee Fund (EAGGF). Established in 1962, this fund finances the CAP, promoting structural adjustments and providing market support in agriculture. The guarantee part of the fund is specifically responsible for controlling the import prices of agricultural goods by using variable import levies, while supporting internal agricultural markets through guaranteeing minimum prices.

European Atomic Energy Community (Euratom).   Established on 1 January 1958 with the aim of conducting research and developing nuclear energy, it created a common market for nuclear fuels and supervised the nuclear industry. The institutions of the European Atomic Energy Community, the ECSC and the EEC were merged in 1967.

European Bank for Reconstruction and Development (EBRD). Established in April 1991, the London-based EBRD grants loans for private and commercial risks and infrastructure projects that aid the transition to a free market economy in Central and Eastern European countries.

European Central Bank (ECB).   An institution that replaced the EMI on transition to the third stage of EMU, resulting in a single currency. The ECB is responsible for carrying out the monetary policy of the Community, with instructions coming from the decision-making bodies of the Executive Board and Governing Council. It supervises the ESCB, which conducts foreign-exchange operations, administers money in circulation, ensures the smooth operation of the payment systems and manages the official reserves of Member States.

European Coal and Steel Community (ECSC).   Founded in 1952 by the Benelux states, the Federal Republic of Germany, France and Italy, it was the first of the European Communities and established a common market for coal and steel products. Its foundation can be traced back to the 1950 Schuman Plan. In 1967 the institutions of the ECSC, the EEC and Euratom were amalgamated.

European Commission.   Established in 1965, it comprises a group of 20 European Commissioners, one of whom is nominated by each Member State, although larger states provide an additional nominee. Initially known as the Commission of the European Communities, it was renamed on 17 November 1993. While the Council of Ministers is the EC's decision-making centre, the European Commission plays an important role as the dynamic engine of the Community's legislation and action programmes. The Council is sometimes portrayed as the blocking institution which represents national governments, while others consider that the European Commission has attempted to both centralise and take power away from the Member States. The European Commission has responsibility for initiating legislation and overseeing the implementation of common policies, decisions being taken by a simple majority. The European Commission is also the guardian of the Treaties and the *acquis communitaire*. It acts as a mediator between Member States in order to reach compromise and as the diplomatic representative of the Community in third countries and in many international organisations. Each Commissioner is assisted by a Directorate-General (DG). The EP must give its approval of appointments to the European Commission.

European Commissioner.   An individual responsible for one or more policy areas within the European Commission.

European Community (EC).   Collective term for the European Coal and Steel Community (ECSC), European Economic Community (EEC) and European Atomic Energy Community (Euratom).

European Community Investment Partners (ECIP).   A programme which supports European investment and exports to Asia, Latin America and the Mediterranean. In 1992–97 300 million ECU was devoted to this task. Aid is granted to four complementary areas: (1) the identification of projects and partners; (2) operations prior to the formation of a joint venture; (3) the financing of capital needs; and (4) the provision of management training or assistance for joint ventures.

European Convention on Human Rights (ECHR).   Signed in November 1950 by members of the Council of Europe, it established a European Commission and a European Court of Human Rights in Strasbourg to ensure the observation of human rights. The rights protected by the Convention include life, liberty and security of the person, the right to respect for private and family life, the right to a fair trial, the right to freedom of accession and assembly, the right to freedom of thought, conscience and religion, and the banning of torture, slavery and forced labour.

European Correspondent. The junior Foreign Office official who is appointed by each Member State to supervise and direct the communication of faxes and telegrams associated with EPC and who is the main assistant to the Political Director.

European Council. Meetings of Heads of State or Government of the Member States (assisted by their Foreign Ministers) and the President of the European Commission which take place at least twice a year. They provide impetus and direction for the Union by establishing broad guidelines for action, while also dealing with CFSP and cooperation in JHA. Important European Council meetings include: Bremen (1978) – decision to launch EMS; Fontainebleau (1984) – resolution of UK budget dispute; Milan (1985) – motivation for IGC which produced the SEA; Maastricht (1991) – agreement on TEU; Edinburgh (1992) – acceptance of the Danish opt-outs.

European Court of Human Rights. Not to be confused with the Court of Justice, it is a body based in Strasbourg within the Council of Europe and hears cases relating to states that have ratified the European Convention on Human Rights.

European Currency Unit (ECU). The accounting and currency unit of Europe which is made up of a basket of currencies of the European Monetary System (EMS), whose shares are fixed. As a primary element of the EMS the ECU is used for establishing the differences of fluctuation among Community currencies and supports the ERM. Beyond this it is used as a unit of account for settling trade balances between Member States' central banks, and as a reserve currency. Within the Community the ECU serves as a vehicle for establishing farm prices, customs duties and is the accounting currency of the budget. The ECU is supported by the EMCF, which is a reserve fund where countries taking part in the basket of currencies have to place 20% of their gold and dollar reserves.

European Defence Community (EDC). Created by the EDC Treaty of May 1952, it is the plan for a common European army under one commander, within which a re-armed Federal Republic of Germany could be contained. The plan emanated from the 1950 Pleven Plan. While the Treaty was ratified in the FRG, Italy and the Benelux countries, it suffered setbacks in France through fear of German dominance and loss of national sovereignty. This eventually resulted in the French National Assembly voting by 319 to 264, with 43 abstentions, to postpone discussion of the Treaty *sine die*, which essentially brought it to an end. A response to its failure was the creation of the WEU via a UK proposal.

European Development Fund. Established in 1957, it promotes economic and social development in the ACP countries and funds schemes to promote export marketing and sales, technical cooperation projects and in special cases emergency aid.

European Economic Area (EEA). Comprises the territory of EFTA and the EU after an agreement signed in 1992 and provides for the free movement of capital, goods, services and workers. To ensure compliance of rules and regulations, EFTA countries agreed to accept over 80% of the Community's rules pertaining to the single market. Nevertheless, the agreement does not include Switzerland, a decision caused by a 'no' vote in a referendum. This delayed the ratification process and therefore meant that the EEA Treaty did not come into force until 1 January 1994. But its significance was soon diminished by the entry into the EU of three EFTA countries on 1 January 1995 (Austria, Finland and Sweden).

European Economic Community (EEC). One of the founding treaties of the European Community. Established by the 1957 Treaties of Rome, providing common trade, agriculture, transport and competition policies, in addition to cooperation in economic and monetary affairs and closer political union.

European Economic Community Treaty. Refers to the Treaties establishing the European Economic Community and the European Atomic Energy Community, which were signed on 25 March 1957 in Rome by Belgium, France, the FRG, Italy, Luxembourg and the Netherlands. The EEC Treaty has been revised via the SEA and TEU. As the latter came into force on 1 January 1993, the EEC Treaty was renamed the EC Treaty.

European elections. Refers to EP elections held every five years. Prior to the first direct elections that took place in 1979, the EP comprised MEPs appointed by national parliaments. Although Article 7 of the European Elections Act states that a uniform electoral procedure will be introduced in the future, the present system is that MEPs are elected by the same electoral systems used in each individual Member State. Thus, in the 1994 elections, Denmark, Luxembourg and the Netherlands used proportional representation and national lists with preferential voting, France, Germany, Greece, Portugal and Spain used proportional representation and national lists with a strict party list, Belgium and Italy adopted proportional representation with regional lists and preferential voting, Ireland and Northern Ireland used a system of multi-member constituencies and a single transferable vote, and in Great Britain a first-past-the-post system was used.

It is evident that there exists a wide divergence of voting patterns within the EU Member States (see the table below). The UK has traditionally had the lowest turnout. In recent years, a decline in the turnout in the elections for Ireland and the Netherlands has been evident, while Portugal experienced a marked decrease from 1989–94. By contrast, other Member States have experienced a higher voter turnout, particularly Belgium, Italy and Luxembourg. There are some clear reasons for these differentials. Nations such as Belgium and Luxembourg generally have a high degree of support for the EU. This is not surprising as both countries receive large financial injections from having EU institutions based there, and accordingly concepts of public apathy and discontent are less relevant. By contrast, the high turnout in Italian elections can be explained from a public desire to support a democratic European Parliament in the face of domestic corruption. However, it is very important to note that voting is compulsory in Belgium, Greece and Luxembourg, and while not so in Italy, it is still regarded as a public duty. Where turnout is declining, it is worth considering that voting apathy is influenced by the perceived need to participate in other domestic elections, such as local and regional elections, which are often held at the same time as European elections.

But irrespective of the turnout within each Member State, European elections face the additional problem of being used as a sounding board for national policies, especially when the European election falls within a government's term of office. Thus, the Conservative Party performed badly in the 1994 European Parliament elections because voters wanted to express discontent with the UK government. By contrast, when a European Parliament election is held at the same time or a few months after a national election, the winning party can expect its candidates to do well, as was the case for the UK Conservative Party in 1979 and the Forza Italia Party in 1994.

European Energy Charter.   Established in 1991 at The Hague, it provides a set of principles and objectives for the achievement of pan-European cooperation in the field of energy.

European Environment Agency.   Its establishment in May 1990 mirrored the increasing importance attached to the protection of the environment within the EU. Its primary task is the composition of environmental data that is central to the creation of an environmental policy.

European Free Trade Association (EFTA).   Established in 1960 in response to the creation of the EEC, its primary aim is the prevention of economic discrimination. Closer contact between both organisations has taken place, resulting in the establishment of the EEA in 1984. The

Turnout in European Parliament elections, 1979–94

State	1979	1984	1989	1994	Seats
Belgium	91.4	92.1	90.7	90.7	25[1]
Denmark	47.8	52.3	46.2	52.5	16
France	60.7	56.7	48.7	52.7	87[2]
Germany	65.7	56.8	62.3	60.1	99
Greece	–	77.2	79.9	71.2	25
Ireland	63.6	47.6	68.3	44.0	15
Italy	84.9	83.4	81.5	74.8	87
Luxembourg	88.9	88.8	87.4	86.6	6
Netherlands	57.8	50.6	47.2	35.6	31[3]
Portugal	–	–	51.2	35.6	25[4]
Spain	–	–	54.6	60.0	64[5]
UK	32.3	32.6	36.2	36.4	87[6]
Average 6	74.9	71.4	69.6	66.8	–
Average 12	–	–	–	58.5	567

1 24 seats in 1989 – 14 for Flanders, 10 for Wallonia and 1 for the German-speaking region.
2 Along with Germany, Italy and the UK, France had 81 seats until 1994.
3 25 seats until 1994.
4 24 seats until 1994.
5 60 seats until 1994.
6 Northern Ireland has generally had a higher turnout in comparison to Great Britain. This is influenced by the use of proportional representation in the former. In Northern Ireland turnout was 56.9% in 1979, 64.5% in 1984, 48.8% in 1989 and 48.7% in 1994.

(*Source*: J. Lodge (ed.), *The 1994 Elections to the European Parliament* (Pinter, 1996), p. 4.)

accession of several EFTA members to the EU reduced the former's membership to Iceland, Liechtenstein, Norway and Switzerland by 1995.

European Fund.   The European Monetary Agreement (EMA) provided for a European Fund to help finance temporary deficits in the balance of payments of a country emanating from a decision to make its currency convertible into dollars.

European Investment Bank (EIB).   Established in 1957 by the Treaties of Rome it is a non-profit development bank with the primary aim of promoting long-term loans and guarantees for investment in industry and infrastructure projects in priority areas. These include less developed regions, industrial modernisation and joint industrial projects.

The activities of the EIB have expanded beyond the EU and now embrace ACP nations and other countries which have association agreements with the EU. The Bank's operations are financed by borrowing on both the international and EU capital markets. The ECU was adopted as its unit of account in 1981, replacing the EUA which had the same composition and value in relation to Member States' currencies.

European Investment Fund. It was established in June 1994 as a means of tackling economic problems, including unemployment. It helps finance trans-European infrastructure projects and supports small and medium-sized businesses by guaranteeing loans.

European Monetary Agreement. Approved by the Council of the OEEC in August 1955, the agreement demonstrated a willingness of European nations to gradually make their currencies convertible into dollars. This replaced the European Payments Union when the agreement was implemented in December 1958. The BIS became the agent for financing operations.

European Monetary Cooperation Fund (EMCF). A pool of 20% of each members' gold and dollar reserves, it acts as a credit facility.

European Monetary Institute (EMI). Based in Frankfurt, it was established under the terms of the TEU to coordinate the monetary policy of the central banks of Member States within the ESCB. It assisted the preparation of the third stage of EMU, with a European single currency introduced in 1999, at which point the EMI was renamed the ECB.

European Monetary System (EMS). Established in 1979 as a 'zone of monetary stability' (stable but adjustable exchange rates) whereby Member States coordinate exchange rates through the ERM. Currency rates were established in relation to the ECU at meetings of Finance Ministers, and in the intervening period Member States support the agreed value of the currencies within the system by drawing on the resources of the EMCF.

European Movement. A pro-European integration political lobby based in the UK which was formed in October 1948, having received impetus from the May 1948 meeting of the Congress of Europe.

European Ombudsman. Investigates complaints about maladministration by institutions and bodies of the EU and is not able to deal with complaints regarding national, regional or local administrations of the Member States.

European Parliament (EP).   The EP has 626 members and is the only democratically elected EU institution. It helps to make policy proposals and draft, amend and adopt European laws and budget.

European Parliament Bureau.   Steering group of the EP comprising the President, Vice-Presidents and Quaestors.

European passport.   Member States (Denmark, Ireland and Luxembourg) started to introduce European passports on 1 January 1985 after agreement had been reached in 1981 on the size and shape of a burgundy-coloured passport which would have European Community on the cover. In the course of 1985 the rest of the then ten-member Community introduced this style of passport, although both the FRG and the UK did not do so until 1987.

European Payments Union (EPU).   Established in 1950 by the OEEC, it replaced the intra-European payments agreements of 1948 and 1949. The EPU allowed the multilateral settlement of deficits or surpluses between European states and facilitated policies of trade liberalisation by offering automatic credit facilities to participants which encountered deficits in their balance of payments.

European Political Cooperation (EPC).   Originating in 1970, this refers to the cooperation of EC Foreign Ministers in the field of foreign policy. That process whereby Member States sought to adopt a united stance via permanent contacts between governments was incorporated into the Treaty in 1987, and was subjected to further change when it was expanded under the TEU into a CFSP. Contacts have been maintained by Foreign Ministries' Political Directors and European Correspondents.

European Regional Development Fund (ERDF).   The largest of the EU's structural funds, it was established in 1975 to provide financial assistance to development projects in poor regions so as to reduce imbalances between regions of the Community.

European security and defence identity (ESDI).   This is the concept of a European defence strategy which is designed to respond to the challenges that the EU has faced, and faces, from neighbouring conflicts, such as Bosnia-Herzegovina and Chechnya. The decline in the number of US troops based in Europe led states such as Belgium and France to suggest that the EU should fill this gap. The need to define an ESDI was stressed at the January 1994 Brussels NATO Council, a direct consequence of which was the establishment of a Combined Joint Task Force (CJTF) at the June 1996 Berlin NATO Council. However, despite the decisions taken, including the ability for NATO equipment to be used under a WEU-led operation, the majority of EU countries continue to reduce their defence budgets.

European Social Fund (ESF). Established in 1960, it is the main mechanism of Community social policy providing financial assistance for retraining, job-creation schemes and vocational training. A high proportion of the funding (75%) is targeted towards fighting youth unemployment. The Delors II budget package significantly increased the resources available to the ESF, while the focus was directed towards the reintegration of unemployed people into working life and the improvement of the functions of the labour market.

European Space Agency (ESA). Established in 1975 as a means of co-ordinating the efforts of European governments in the field of space exploration and technology and the development of cooperation with NASA (the US space agency), the 14 members of the ESA are Austria, Belgium, Denmark, the FRG, Finland, France, Ireland, Italy, the Netherlands, Norway, Spain, Sweden, Switzerland and the UK.

European symbols. These are the symbols that represent the public identity of the Union. Since 1986 the EU has been represented by the flag of twelve gold stars on a blue background used by the Council of Europe (thus, the number of stars is not related to the number of Member States) and has adopted from the Council of Europe the European anthem of 'Ode to Joy' from Beethoven's Ninth Symphony.

European System of Central Banks (ESCB). Responsible for managing EMU from the start of stage three, its primary objective is maintaining price stability, while it shares the right to propose new policies with the European Commission. Independent of national governments and EC institutions, it consists of the ECB and national banks. The Governing Council of the ECB is composed of members of the Executive Board and the governors of national central banks, with the Executive Board consisting of four members plus a president and vice-president, all of which are appointed for eight years by the European Council. By contrast, national central bank governors have to be appointed for a minimum of five years, with the ability to appeal to the Court of Justice in the event of dismissal.

European Union (EU). While the preamble of the Treaties of Rome called for 'an ever closer union' among the peoples of Europe, with the SEA thereafter naming European Union as the ultimate goal of European integration, it was the TEU which established the concept. It stated that the EU was founded upon the European Communities and was supported by JHA and CFSP. The objectives of the Union included strengthening the identity of citizenship and promoting economic and social progress.

European Unit of Account (EUA).   This was used within the Community as a means of preparing the budget and determining the price of agricultural products under the CAP. The introduction of the EMS in 1979 resulted in the EUA being replaced by the ECU.

European University Institute (EUI).   Based in Florence and established in 1975, it is a postgraduate teaching and research institute dealing with European integration. It focuses upon economics, history and civilisation, law and political and social sciences.

Europol.   A mechanism for cooperation between Member States' police forces embodied in Article K of the TEU, having been first mentioned at the Luxembourg European Council on 28 and 29 June 1991. The convention establishing Europol was eventually signed in July 1995, although a European Drugs Unit was created in January 1994 as a means of providing a practical angle to police cooperation within the paramaters established by Title VI of the TEU. Although the Unit initially focused upon drug trafficking and money laundering, its remit was widened to embrace immigration networks, trafficking in radioactive and nuclear substances, and trade in human beings.

Euro-sceptics.   These are individuals who oppose European integration, often favouring economic independence and being against the loss of national legislative sovereignty. While there are many sceptical organisations in every Member State, it is the UK that has often been perceived to harbour the greatest number of sceptics. This has been influenced by the attitudes of successive governments towards Europe and in recent years has been hardened by the negotiating position of Margaret Thatcher. Of UK Euro-sceptic groups, the Conservative Party has given birth to some of the most famous, including the Bruges Group. Other organisations have included the UK Independence Party.

Eurostat.   The Statistical Office of the EU based in Luxembourg, which publishes statistical analysis to assist the decision-making processes of EU institutions, while also providing information on EU issues to the wider public.

Excessive deficit procedure.   Introduced in the TEU as one of the convergence criteria under the provisions of EMU, the Treaty provided for Member States not to have excessive government deficits. Article 104c and the Protocol on the excessive deficit procedure stated that Member States should have a budget deficit not exceeding 3% of GDP and a public debt not exceeding 60% of GDP. An important inclusion within the procedure was the reference to 'gross errors' in Article 104c(2), which ensured that the excessive deficit procedure should only occasionally be used by taking account of cyclical developments. Emphasis on flexibility was signified by Article 104c which noted that allowance could be made if a country's deficit had 'declined substantially and continuously' or 'is only exceptional and temporary'. Hence, the convergence criteria were both tough and flexible.

Exchange Rate Mechanism (ERM).   A mechanism of coordinating the currencies of EU Member States, whereby participants followed domestic economic policies conducive to maintaining their currencies within set bands.

Exemption.   This is the field of application where a treaty, regulation or directive is not applicable.

Exclusive agreements.   Refers to market-sharing, purchasing or distribution agreements between companies and/or countries which were banned by the European Commission as they contradicted EC competition policy.

Exclusive competence.   Refers to the Community's ability to undertake specific actions, as in the field of CAP. The EC only has the explicit ability to act in the arena of commercial policy (Article 113) and association agreements (Article 238).

External relations.   A general term used to describe the trading relationships that the Community has with third countries, such as association agreements and cooperation agreements. In addition, the term external relations is used to describe the security and defence aspects of the Community.

External tariff.   The gradual establishment of a customs union within the EEC resulted in the abolition of separate national customs tariffs by 1968 and the introduction of a common external tariff. Since 1975 all revenue from the common external tariff has gone to the EU budget.

External trade.   Trade between third countries and the EU.

Federalism.   This term is often used in tandem with federation which reflects an organisation that has a division of responsibility between the states/regions and the central authority. Federalism has been a key feature in the development of the EU, with federalist ideas motivating key individuals such as Jean Monnet. In this context, a central authority has emerged through the European Commission, supported by the EP and Council of Ministers as well as the Court of Justice. These institutions and their supranational element are supported by federalists who favour European integration. In recent years, Jacques Delors' Presidency of the European Commission further advanced the remit of the community, which was perceived by individuals, such as Margaret Thatcher, to be a threat to national sovereignty. At a simplistic level, Euro-sceptics are the opposite of federalists.

Factortame.   Refers to a Spanish fishing case involving the British government which noted that national governments are vulnerable to compensation when they implement EU legal measures wrongly.

Fontainebleau agreement.   A compact reached at the Fontainebleau European Council of June 1984 which resolved the dispute over the UK's contribution to the Community's budget. The agreement gave the government an abatement on the portion of its annual contribution based on value added tax.

'Fortress Europe'.   Free trade supporters use this phrase when suggesting that the EU is too protectionist, a factor often raised in negotiations over the General Agreement on Tariffs and Trade.

Fouchet Plan.   A Draft Treaty for political union published on 2 November 1961 by a committee chaired by Christopher Fouchet, Foreign Minister of France. The plan was initiated by the French President, Charles de Gaulle, who considered that the Six should explore ways of achieving political union. In this context, it proposed the creation of a council of Heads of Government or Foreign Ministers where decisions would only be taken by unanimity; the establishment of an international secretariat composed of officials taken from national Foreign Ministries; the creation of four permanent intergovernmental committees to deal with foreign affairs, commerce, defence and cultural matters; and the development of an appointive European assembly. However, the scheme was opposed by all Member States apart from France and was essentially abandoned by 1962.

Four freedoms.   The free movement of capital, goods and persons, and the freedom to provide services across the EU, as listed in Article 3 of the Treaty of Rome.

Free movement of capital.   A situation where capital is allowed to move freely between countries with different currencies. Restrictions tend to apply on capital movements between most countries because of the effects on a nation's balance of payments and, ergo, the stability of its currency. Capital movements were fully liberalised within the EU on 1 July 1990 as the result of a 1988 Council decision.

Free movement of goods.   An essential component for the functioning of the common market, requiring the harmonisation of customs duties and taxes, uniform rules on the protection of health, consumers and the environment, and the removal of all other barriers to trade.

Free movement of persons.   Under Article 48 of the Treaty of Rome, self-employed persons and workers have the ability to live and work in any other EU Member State and are able to obtain without discrimination the welfare benefits available to local workers.

Free trade agreement.   A contract to eliminate all customs duties and prevent trade restrictions between signatory nations, as established between the EC and EFTA in 1972–73.

Free trade area.   Denotes a situation where customs duties and other restrictive trading measures have been removed between two or more customs territories. National customs duties are retained for trade with third countries and this therefore differs from a customs union which has a common external customs tariff. Examples of a free trade area include EFTA.

Freedom of establishment.   Refers to the right of EU citizens to establish themselves in other Member States under Articles 52–58 of the Treaties of Rome to run a business, farm or work in a self-employed capacity.

Freedom to provide services.   A primary freedom established within the Treaty of Rome under Article 59 which allows EU individuals to provide services across national borders.

Friends of the Presidency.   A group of officials comprising a representative from the permanent representation of each Member State to the EU, and being chaired by the official from the country which has the Presidency of the Council of Ministers. The group's primary task is to act as a clearing ground for issues before they reach permanent representative or ministerial level. It is particularly effective at coordinating policy during IGC negotiations and is similar to the Antici group.

Future financing.   An argument over the financing of the Community took place between 1986 and 1992, revolving around the Delors I Package and Delors II Package. The UK especially advocated that there should be tighter controls on the expenditure of the CAP and greater budget discipline. A final solution emerged at the Edinburgh European Council of December 1992 which included a modest increase in the budget.

General Agreement on Tariffs and Trade (GATT).   A group of some 123 trading nations which aim to dismantle national trade barriers. Discussion between participants has in recent years involved the Uruguay Round of negotiations, which commenced in 1986 and ended in December 1993 and dealt with new topics such as trade in services, investment issues of a trade-related nature and better procedures for the treatment of intellectual property. The establishment of the World Trade Organisation in 1995 meant that responsibility for trade issues passed from GATT to the WTO.

Generalised System of Preferences (GSP).   A system of preferential treatment given by the Community to non-Member States such as those covered by the Yaoundé Convention.

Genscher–Colombo Plan.   This refers to a 1981 political union initiative advanced by the German and Italian Foreign Ministers, Hans-Dietrich Genscher and Emilio Colombo. They suggested that there should be more common policies, particularly in the field of foreign affairs; that the European Council should report annually to the EP; that QMV should be increased in the Council of Ministers; and that there should be more cultural and legal cooperation. A primary aim was to make the institutions more explicit, especially the European Council which had developed outside of the Treaties of Rome. However, Denmark, the FRG, Greece and the UK objected to proposals which envisaged an extension of QMV and an expanded budget.

German reunification.   The collapse of the former Soviet Union and its satellite states in Eastern Europe throughout 1989 and 1990 provided the opportunity for the former German Democratic Republic to be incorporated into the FRG, as provided for in Article 23 of the latter's constitution. This was accepted at the Dublin European Council meeting of April 1990, with reunification being achieved on 3 October 1990 after the establishment of a State Treaty on 1 July 1990.

Green Paper.   A set of proposals advanced by the European Commission with the aim of fostering discussion by establishing a range of possible ideas in areas such as social policy, the single currency and telecommunications for example. This contrasts with a White Paper which is an official set of proposals in a given policy area.

Group of Eight (G8). The recent inclusion of Russia in the Group of Seven resulted in it being renamed the Group of Eight, of which the first meeting was hosted by the UK in Birmingham in May 1998.

Group of Seven (G7). Since 1975 the Heads of State and Government and the Finance Ministers of the seven leading western industrialised nations have held economic summits. The Group of Seven includes: Canada (since 1976), France, the FRG, Italy, Japan, the UK and the USA. Since May 1977 these meetings have been attended by the President of the European Commission. This grouping has recently been enlarged to include Russia and is now referred to as the Group of Eight.

Gulf War. Iraq's invasion of Kuwait on 2 August 1990 resulted in the massing of coalition forces from over 25 countries, of which the USA and the UK had particularly large contributions, to liberate Kuwait. The expiry on 16 January 1991 of the United Nation's deadline for Iraq's withdrawal from Kuwait led to the commencement of nearly six weeks of continuous air bombing under Operation Desert Storm. The land offensive started on 24 February 1991 and some 100 hours later on 26 February, Saddam Hussein accepted that Kuwait was not part of Iraq. The war was notable not just for its brevity, but for the reassertion of the dominant role of the USA in providing global security. It also went some way to imparting a more realistic tone to the debate over the development of an ESDI, as particularly advocated by France during the 1991 IGC negotiations which resulted in the TEU. In this connection, it was notable that Belgium refused to sell the UK ammunition during the conflict, a point which reinforced the latter's scepticism towards the development of an ESDI.

Gymnich meetings. EU Ministers tend to have few informal meetings throughout a year when a limited number of officials and interpreters are present. The intention of such fireside discussions, bearing the name of the first such meeting in April 1974 at Schloss Gymnich near Bonn, is to provide a relaxed atmosphere where compromises can be reached on outstanding issues.

Hague Congress. The Congress, which took place in May 1948, brought together 750 politicians from every European country. Its final resolutions included a call for a united and democratic Europe and provided some impetus for the establishment of the Council of Europe one year later.

Hard core.   A concept of integration embracing a small group of countries who wish to have closer cooperation with each other.

Hard ECU.   A currency proposal launched by the UK in January 1991 in an attempt to provide clarification on stage two of the Delors Report's proposals for EMU as well as providing the UK with greater influence in the 1990–91 IGC negotiations. The plan envisaged the creation of a Hard ECU, managed by the European Monetary Fund, that would float alongside existing currencies in the ERM of the EMS. However, it received little support from other Member States, except Spain, temporarily, and was effectively sunk by the summer of 1991. This was primarily because it did not envisage the creation of a single currency, as desired by a majority of Member States, and was additionally perceived to be a delaying tactic.

Harmonisation.   Coordination of Member States' economic policies and legal and administrative rules so as to prevent the single market being disrupted.

Helios II.   A programme, running from 1993 to 1996 which aimed to ensure that people with disabilities were integrated into both economic and social life.

Helsinki Final Act.   The Act was the outcome of the Conference on Security and Cooperation in Europe in Helsinki and was signed in August 1975 by the 35 states which participated in the meeting. It provided the basis for the operation of the CSCE system until further changes were made by the November 1990 Charter of Paris.

Hierarchy of Community acts (hierarchy of norms).   A declaration annexed to the TEU which stipulated that the 1996–97 IGC would examine 'to what extent it might be possible to review the classification of Community acts with a view to establishing an appropriate hierarchy between the different categories of act'. The intention was to ensure that a differentiation would be made between instruments of constitutional status, which were subject to tougher procedures, such as QMV, and legislative instruments. The latter were already subjected to tough procedures, such as co-decision.

High Authority.   An institution of the ECSC, it was the precursor of the European Commission.

Human rights.   The establishment of the Council of Europe in 1949 had as one of its basic objectives the maintenance and development of human rights. This provided the great motivation behind the signing of the European Convention on Human Rights in 1950. Although the Treaties of Rome made little reference to human rights, subsequent reforms, such as the SEA, included reference to human rights in the preamble and therefore became part of the *acquis communitaire.*

Independent European Programme Group (IEPG).   Established in 1976 to provide European members of NATO with a forum where they could formulate policies that would assist cooperation in the procurement of armaments, its functions were dissolved in December 1992 when European Defence Ministers decided to incorporate its activities into the WEU.

Institution.   A part of the Community or Union with significant status, such as the European Commission.

Integrated Mediterranean Programme.   Created in 1981 as a response to the accession of Greece, which felt that its particular needs were not reflected in its terms of membership. This was addressed in the decision by the European Council in March 1984 to establish a seven-year programme between 1986 and 1992 that would tackle the problems of the southern parts of the Community, especially the whole of Greece, the south of France and the majority of southern Italy. Funding came from structural funds, a loan from the then EIB and the budget. While the programme has not been renewed, the cohesion fund addresses the needs of Greece, Ireland, Portugal and Spain.

Integration.   Refers to the creation of unity among EU nations and is sometimes contrasted with cooperation when the Community method of integration is used.

Intergovernmental.   The process of integration whereby states choose by their own preference to cooperate. It is sometimes contrasted with supranational.

Intergovernmental conference (IGC).   A forum for negotiation comprising representatives of all Member States who aim to redefine the activities of the EU. Examples are the negotiations in the latter half of 1985 which led to agreement at the Luxembourg European Council in December 1985, resulting in the SEA, and the 1991 IGCs on EMU and European Political Union that resulted in agreement at the Maastricht European Council (December 1991), and led to the TEU. The last IGC opened on 26 March 1996 and concluded with agreement on the Treaty of Amsterdam at the June 1997 European Council.

Inter-institutional agreements.   Agreements made between two or more institutions of the Community.

Inter-institutional conference.   A formal conference between the EP, European Commission and Council, of which the latter tends to be represented by the Presidency. The conference is a means of allowing the EP to influence IGC negotiations, from which it is excluded.

Internal market.   The difference between the economic activity within EU Member States and external trade, the internal market has particular relevance to allowing the free movement of capital, goods and persons.

Interpol.   An organisation that gathers and exchanges information with other police forces, and acts as a forum for discussing issues of common interest, such as terrorism and police training. Originally named the International Criminal Police Commission, which was established in Vienna in 1923, it has been known as Interpol since 1956.

Intervention.   Represents a part of the CAP price support system whereby a product will be purchased and stored for the future if it cannot be sold at an agreed price during the year in question. Examples are the butter mountain and wine lake. The cost of this process is borne by the budget.

Intra-Community trade.   Trade between EU Member States.

Investiture.   The action whereby the European Commission is provided with the authority to act on behalf of the Community.

Inward investment.   The creation of jobs through outside investment in one Member State. Funds can either come from a source within another EU Member State or from outside. The UK has traditionally had a high level of inward investment, sustained by flexible labour laws which proved to be one of the reasons why it did not accept the Social Chapter at the Maastricht European Council in December 1991. Such action attracted criticism from other Member States of social dumping, a factor especially related to the relocation in February 1993 of the Hoover plant from Dijon in France to Cambuslang in Scotland.

Ioannina compromise.   The decision taken on QMV in a Community of 16 members at an informal Foreign Ministers' meeting in the Greek city of Ioannina on 27 March 1994. Norway's decision not to join the Community meant that the compromise was altered. The consequence of this was that the compromise stipulated that where a vote in the Council fell between 23 votes (the old blocking minority threshold) and 26 votes (the new threshold), and therefore signified opposition by certain states to a Council decision, then the Council would do everything in its power to reach a satisfactory solution that could be adopted by at least 65 votes out of total number of 87 votes.

Joint action.   The procedure established in the TEU (Article J.3) for Member States to take action in the area of CFSP. The specific process is that the Council, acting by unanimous decision, defines the scope and objectives of joint action and the means, procedures and conditions for implementing it. Member States are bound to uphold the agreed position in the actions they take and views they express.

Joint European Torus (JET).   An experimental project in thermonuclear fusion research.

Joint Interpreting and Conference Service.   A department of the European Commission which deals with the translation of written and spoken texts and the organisation of conferences.

Joint Parliamentary Committee.   Committees established with the parliaments of states that have association agreements with the EU or those states where negotiations for accession have commenced.

JOPP.   A part of the PHARE and TACIS programmes, it aims to establish joint ventures between EU economic interests and those based in Central and Eastern Europe (the countries eligible under the PHARE programme).

Justice and home affairs (JHA).   The TEU provided for this new area of closer cooperation with the general aim of providing both greater security for citizens and more freedom of movement. It is concerned with asylum policy; rules governing the crossing of the external borders of the Member States; immigration policy; combating drugs; combating international fraud; judicial cooperation in civil and criminal matters; customs cooperation; police cooperation.

Justiciable.   Under the EU Treaty it is possible for disputed issues to be submitted for decision to the Court of Justice and Court of First Instance.

Kangaroo Group.   A group of MEPs who have traditionally advocated a frontier-free Europe.

Kennedy Round.   A series of negotiations on tariff reductions held by GATT, which commenced in May 1964 and finished on 15 May 1967.

Named after President John F. Kennedy of the USA, it was the first time that the European Commission had been the sole Community spokesperson, producing agreement on reducing the common external tariff by an average of 35%.

Kirchberg Declaration. The WEU Council of Ministers' declaration of May 1994 gave nine Central and Eastern European countries the status of 'associate partners', which was a distinction from the associate membership of Iceland, Norway and Turkey. The meeting produced a system of variable geometry with there being three different levels of membership, as well as observer status: (1) WEU *members* that are also members of both the EU and NATO; (2) WEU *associate members* that are members of NATO but not the EU; and (3) WEU *associate partners* that are neither members of the EU nor NATO. WEU observers can be members of NATO and/or the EU. The product of this reform was that the forum of consultation with Central and Eastern European nations, established in 1992 by the Petersberg Declaration, was abolished.

Legal personality. The situation that allows a body to take actions in international law on an autonomous basis instead of having to allow governments to act on its behalf. In this context, the legal status of the EU is pertinent because it does not have the international legal right to conclude agreements with third countries, otherwise referred to as Treaty-making powers.

Legal service. A department of the European Commission that provides advice on legal matters, assists in the drafting of legislative proposals and initiates legal proceedings in the Court of Justice. In addition, it checks whether affairs and actions of the EU countries are in accordance with, authorised, or required by the law or EU Treaties.

Legislation. Policy decisions passed by the Council. At a national level they would be passed by Parliaments.

Leonardo. The Community programme for vocational training which replaced various programmes, including COMETT (cooperation on training and further training between universities and industry) and PETRA (initial vocational training).

Liberalisation. The process of removing restrictions placed by Member States on the free movement of goods, capital, payments and services across frontiers. Apart from the EU, other organisations which are dedicated to this process include GATT and the OECD.

Lingua. Established in 1990 as a means of improving and promoting the teaching of foreign languages within the EU, it was merged in 1995 into the Socrates and Leonardo programmes.

Linkage. The process where agreement on one particular issue is dependent on obtaining a satisfactory outcome on another. There is greater room for negotiation of this sort when decisions are taken purely by unanimity and states are therefore provided with a veto.

Lobbying. Lobbying is the process whereby groups campaign to persuade legislators to make regulations which favour their interests. There has been a vast expansion in the lobbying of both the institutions of the Community and the nationally based permanent representations. Lobbying can be undertaken by private enterprises, trade unions, pressure groups, and regional bodies such as the German Länder.

Lomé Convention. A process which began with Lomé I in 1975, followed by Lomé II in 1980, Lomé III in 1985 and Lomé IV in 1990, the last of which will run for ten years. The aim of the Conventions, which succeeded the Yaoundé Convention, has been to focus on long-term development for the 70 ACP states which it embraces, covering multi-lateral trade and development agreements between them and the EU. The ACP nations are provided with associate status to the EU, which includes financial assistance and trading advantages, while Lomé IV also embraced agreements for the protection of human rights and democratic development.

London Agreement. A guarantee made in June 1961 by EFTA countries applying for EC membership that they would not accept any terms of entry that did not make provision for non-applicant EFTA countries.

Louvre Accord. An agreement on 22 February 1987 among the Group of Seven countries to stabilise the US dollar.

Luxembourg compromise. An informal agreement established by the Six in January 1966 allowing for decisions that the Treaties of Rome perceived to be subjected to majority voting within the Council of Ministers to be delayed until a unanimous agreement was achieved. This therefore provided each nation with a veto over key policy decisions and was a response to the 'empty chair' crisis in the second half of 1965. It had a profound effect on the Community over the next two decades when it essentially limited major policy advancements.

Maastricht Treaty. A term that is generally used to describe the TEU because it was signed in the Dutch town of Maastricht in December 1991.

MacDougal Report. The 1972 decision to establish EMU by 1980 led to the publication of a report authored by Sir Donald MacDougal which examined the role of public finance if EMU was to be created. Published in 1977, it suggested that it would be necessary for public expenditure at the Community level to play a significant role in the redistribution of wealth if EMU was to have any chance of succeeding. However, because aspirations for EMU did not materialise in the 1970s, the Report was not adopted.

Majority Voting. While some decisions of the Council of the EU are taken by unanimity, others are taken by either simple or qualified majority voting. Majority voting was extended by the SEA to cover single market procedures, with a further widening of policy competences taking place under the TEU. In majority voting each Member State's vote is weighted, ranging from ten in the case of the larger Member States to two for the smallest (Luxembourg). Majority voting can either be a simple majority, for example eight out of 15 Member States in favour, or a qualified majority (which is the more usual).

Mansholt Plan. The CAP emerged out of this document which was finally published in 1968 under the authorship of Sicco Mansholt. It provided for the restructuring and modernising of agriculture as well as the provision of guaranteed prices.

Marshall Plan. The scheme announced in 1947 by US Secretary of State George Marshall to aid the rebuilding of European economies in the wake of the Second World War. It was also known as the European Recovery Programme.

MED-Campus. This programme aims to develop further the human resources of Mediterranean countries by encouraging cooperation between universities in the EU and these countries through teacher training, continuing education, training courses and temporary secondment, applied research and the purchase of small items of equipment for training projects.

MED-Invest. An EU decentralised cooperation project aimed at providing joint funding for Mediterranean countries through financing business contracts and implementing pilot projects to support small businesses.

MED-URBS. Aimed at developing cooperation between EU local authorities and Mediterranean countries so as to encourage the transfer of skills and knowledge through the establishment or consolidation of trans-Mediterranean cooperation networks and the fostering of lasting cooperation ties between network partners. Projects have to involve at least two local authorities from different Member States and at least two local authorities from a Mediterranean country.

Member of the European Parliament (MEP). An MEP is one of 626 individuals directly elected from Member States. The total number of MEPs representing each Member State relates to the size of population of that state. The first democratic election took place in 1979, and elections are held every five years. MEPs do not sit in national delegation within the EP, but rather take part in transnational political groupings.

Merger Treaty. Signed on 8 April 1965, it established the joint institutions of the European Atomic Energy Community, the European Coal and Steel Community and the European Economic Community. It came into force on 1 July 1967.

Messina conference. A conference attended by the Foreign Ministers of the six nations of the ECSC in Messina on 1–2 June 1955 to discuss further European integration. It resulted in the Spaak Report which recommended the creation of the EEC and Euratom. The UK only sent an observer to the conference, a junior Board of Trade official, Russell Bretherton.

Monetary Committee. Established in Article 109c of the Treaties of Rome, the committee (which meets monthly) advises the Council of Ministers in the arena of financial affairs and is composed of two high-level officials from each national Finance Ministry and the central bank, as well as two officials from the European Commission. The president of the committee is elected for a period of two years and during that time usually attends meetings of Finance Ministers. Agreements established within the committee generally form the basis for agreement at Finance Minister level. The work of the committee extended to the ERM where it helped to determine exchange rate parities after currency realignments, including agreeing to the temporary suspension of the Italian lira from the ERM in September 1992. The work of the Monetary Committee also included monitoring the progress of each Member State towards the convergence criteria required for stage two of EMU. Moreover, the committee was heavily involved in the EMU negotiations during the 1990–91 IGC which resulted in the TEU. Indeed, during that negotiation it was evident that a sub-group of alternates of the Monetary Committee (a group of more junior officials who met on the margins of the Monetary Committee, whose members could also take the place of national representatives) was heavily involved in technical aspects, notably what became the monetary and economic chapters of the TEU, especially the convergence criteria and excessive deficit procedure, with the full Monetary Committee generally endorsing its work. At the start of stage three, the Monetary Committee will be replaced by a new Economic and Financial Committee, which will continue the work of the Monetary Committee but will also include ECB representatives.

Monetary Compensatory Amounts (MCAs).   Introduced into the CAP as a means of temporarily easing the difficulties encountered by the decision to retain common agricultural prices at their original level of exchange.

Multi-speed Europe.   A method of differentiated integration where common objectives are pursued by a group of states, with the intention that the other states will achieve the same goal at a later date.

Mutual recognition.   The process whereby Member States are obliged to recognise each other's rules of qualification as the same if they fulfil a similar purpose. This was the principle used by the Court of Justice in the 1979 Cassis de Dijon case.

National Parliaments.   They play an important role in the process of European integration by providing the members of the Parliamentary Assembly of the Council of Europe and the North Atlantic Assembly. The members of the EP were compiled of national parliamentarians before the first direct elections in 1979.

Neo-functionalism.   A theory relevant to both politics and economics which suggests that the process of European integration is advanced by the successful development of specific community policies which would spillover into other non-integrated sectors therefore creating a process of sectoral integration. This contrasts with politically motivated desires to integrate as advanced in federalism.

Net contributor/beneficiary.   Refers to the differences between what a country pays into the budget of the EU and what it gets back. Countries which tend to benefit the most are those that are major farm producers as agricultural policy dominates a large proportion of EU finances. The largest net contributor is the FRG.

New Community Instrument (NCI).   A financial instrument used by the Community to assist structural policy objectives by raising loans in conjunction with the EIB, so as to finance investments in the fields of energy, industrial restructuring and regional development.

Non-compulsory expenditure. The section of the EU budget which refers to policies that are not directly provided for by the Treaties of Rome.

Non-discrimination principle. Discrimination on the basis of nationality is not permitted in areas covered by the EC Treaty.

Non-Governmental Organisation (NGO). Within the European context, these are interest groups, companies, consumer groups and trade unions that influence policy within the EU.

Non-paper. A draft negotiating text that may establish a compromise. It especially denotes those texts in the Council which emanate from either the Presidency or secretariat general and are particularly apparent during IGC negotiations.

North Atlantic Assembly. An inter-parliamentary forum of the 16 Alliance members that is independent of NATO. The 188-strong Assembly, which meets twice a year in plenary session, provides a link between national parliaments and the Atlantic Alliance by providing a forum where both European and North American legislators are able to discuss common concerns. Meetings take place in national capitals through a strict rotation system, while the Assembly's work is principally directed through five committees: (1) civilian affairs; (2) defence and security; (3) economic; (4) political; and (5) scientific and technical. NATO's warming to the countries of Central and Eastern Europe has resulted in 14 additional nations participating in the Assembly's activities. They are referred to as associate delegates and include Albania, Belarus, Bulgaria, Czech Republic, Estonia, Hungary, Latvia, Lithuania, Moldova, Poland, Romania, Russia, Slovakia and Ukraine.

North Atlantic Cooperation Council (NACC). The November 1991 Rome meeting of NATO resulted in agreement on the establishment of the NACC as a means of providing a forum where NATO members could discuss security issues with the nations of Central and Eastern Europe as well as those of the Baltic. The first meeting of the NACC took place in Brussels in December 1991.

North Atlantic Treaty Organisation (NATO). The North Atlantic Treaty (Treaty of Washington) was signed in April 1949 by Belgium, Canada, Denmark, France, Iceland, Luxembourg, the Netherlands, Norway, Portugal, the UK and the USA, and came into force in August of that year. Subsequent members include Greece and Turkey (1952), Federal Republic of Germany (1955) and Spain (1982). Today, there are 16 members.

Nyborg Agreements.   The decisions taken in Nyborg (Denmark) by EU Finance Ministers in November 1987, whereby they relaxed the practice of intra-marginal interventions inside the ERM. Previous adjustments had to be made with the consent of the Central Bank of the affected country, with repayment made in the currency of the creditor. However, the agreement ensured that repayments could be made in ECUs.

Official Journal of the European Communities.   Decisions adopted by the institutions are published daily in the 11 official languages in the *Official Journal of the European Communities.*

Official Languages of the EU.   The EU has 11 official languages, all having equal status: Danish, Dutch, English, Finnish, French, German, Greek, Italian, Portuguese, Spanish and Swedish. National Ministers prefer to use their own languages, but among officials the working languages are English, French and more recently German. Only French is used in the Court of Justice.

Ombudsman.   The EP appoints an ombudsman for the lifetime of the Parliament under Article 138e of the EC Treaty. The ombudsman investigates all complaints concerning maladministration in Community activities. The current ombudsman is Jacob Magnus Södermann.

Opinion.   The opinion of the EP has to be obtained before a legislative proposal from the Commission is adopted by the Council, with the opinion being a means of influencing the Council's decision. Constituting part of the consultation procedure, it applies to the agricultural price review. It is also possible for opinions to be obtained from the EP Stranding Committees on a report for the responsible committee.

Opt-out.   The decision to accord a state the ability to not take part in a specific policy area. The UK was given the right not to participate in the third stage of EMU, although this was presented by the government as an opt-in because there still existed the ability to join at a later stage.

Organisation for Economic Cooperation and Development (OECD).   Established in 1961, this intergovernmental organisation promotes international cooperation between industrialised countries with free-market economies. The primary aim is to coordinate economic, trade and development policy. The organisation has 24 members, embracing all EU Member States.

Organisation for European Economic Cooperation (OEEC).   In 1947 a 16-nation Committee of European Economic Cooperation was established to administer the European Economic Recovery Programme (initiated by the Marshall Plan). However, it soon became apparent that there was a need for a permanent coordinating agency. A convention creating the OEEC was subsequently signed in 1948. Canada and the USA became associate members in 1950 and full members in 1961, at which time the organisation was renamed the Organisation for Economic Cooperation and Development (OECD), reflecting the no longer purely European nature of the agency.

Origin.   The criterion used to describe imported goods by their place of origin, that is the country where the goods were *produced*. If goods have been produced in more than one country, they are regarded as having originated in the country where they were last *manufactured*.

Oslo Declaration.   The Heads of Government of EFTA countries issued a statement in March 1990 which reconfirmed a willingness to strengthen their relationship with the EU.

Ostpolitik.   Refers to the policy towards Eastern Europe adopted by the Chancellor of the FRG, Willy Brandt, when he came to power in 1969. This essentially replaced the previous Hallstein Doctrine which advocated the non-recognition of any western state which diplomatically recognised the German Democratic Republic. *Ostpolitik* was important to the development of EPC, while the French President, Georges Pompidou, highlighted it as a reason for the enlargement of the Community.

Own resources.   The financial resources of the EU budget that have been obtained from its own revenue and are subject to control by the EP. It includes levies, additional or compensatory amounts, duties obtained from the CAP for trade with non-member countries, duties on trade with non-member countries, custom duties on products that fall within the ECSC Treaty, premiums and VAT revenue.

Package deal.   An overall proposal, incorporating various measures, that has been drawn up for universal adoption. The package is often drawn up by a Community institution as a means of breaking an impasse which has developed out of a difference of opinions between negotiators.

Padoa–Schioppa Report.   The deputy director-general of the Bank of Italy, Tommaso Padoa–Schioppa, submitted a report to the European Commission in April 1987 entitled 'Efficiency, Stability and Equity: A Strategy for the Evolution of the Economic System of the European Community'. This was done at the request of the President of the European Commission, Jacques Delors, who wanted Padoa–Schioppa, and the six individuals who participated in the committee, to examine the implications of the accession of Portugal and Spain, and the single market, on the economic system of the Community. In this context, the report stressed four priorities, the first of which was the need to complete the single market. The second included the development of a single monetary policy. The third was the need to promote cohesion, while the last was the necessity to establish a macro-economic strategy. The significance of the report was emphasised by the decision taken at the February 1988 Brussels European Council to increase the size of the structural funds targeted at the poorer regions of the Community.

Paragraph.   Subdivision of a Treaty Article which tends to be numbered.

Parliamentary Committee.   Study groups within the EP which examine policy proposals. It includes a Committee of Inquiry.

Partnership Agreement.   Created to satisfy the demand of the former nations of the Soviet Union, they are concluded for ten years and provide political contacts at both ministerial and parliamentary level. More ambitious than Cooperation Agreements, they in fact resemble Europe Agreements, although unlike them they make no reference to eventual accession to the EU.

Partnership for Peace.   An initiative of NATO that was endorsed by the North Atlantic Council at Brussels in January 1994 when leaders announced that 'We have decided to launch an immediate and practical programme that will transform the relationship between NATO and participating states. This new programme goes beyond dialogue and cooperation to forge a real partnership – a Partnership for Peace'. Aimed at the countries of Central and Eastern Europe and the Baltic States, it is a military complement to the NACC. The agreement permits partner states to establish liaison offices with NATO headquarters as well as with the Partnership Coordination Cell at the Supreme Headquarters Allied Powers Europe (SHAPE). Cooperation with the partner states takes place in military exercises, peacekeeping exercises, joint planning, search and rescue and humanitarian operations, and in promoting democratic control of defence ministries.

Passerelle.   A Community bridge between two buildings, but it is often used to describe the linkage of JHA (Article K.9) to the first pillar via Article 100c.

Permanent Representation.   Every Member State has a permanent representation to the EU which acts as the Brussels arm of national governments, thereby advocating national policy and informing officials and Ministers at home of policy developments. Within Brussels, states which are members of the EU and NATO have a different permanent representation to each of these institutions, while the latter also acts as the permanent representation to the WEU. In addition, states not within the EU also have permanent representations to the EU, such as the individual states of the USA.

Petersberg Declaration. Issued in June 1992 by WEU Foreign and Defence Ministers, it established the guidelines for the organisation's future development as established in the TEU. Members gave their support to conflict prevention and peacekeeping efforts, while a WEU Planning Cell was established. A forum of consultation was also established with the Foreign and Defence Ministers of eight Central and Eastern European nations, namely Bulgaria, Romania, Czechoslovakia, Hungary, Poland, Estonia, Lithuania and Latvia. This was later abolished by the Kirchberg Declaration.

Petitions. Any EU citizen and any natural or legal person residing in a Member State has the ability to address a petition to the EP. It was initially a unilateral provision in the rules of the EP and is now a right guaranteed in the EC Treaty (Article 138d). The EP's Committee on Petitions determines whether such requests are admissible, and may put a question to the Ombudsman where it sees fit.

PETRA. Established in 1989, it is a Community action programme for the vocational training of young people with the purpose of improving the quality of training in tandem with the needs of the single market. It is to be replaced by the Leonardo programme.

PHARE. A programme of aid aimed at assisting the economic reconstruction of Eastern Europe that was agreed in 1989 by 24 nations comprising the EC, EFTA, Australia, Canada, Japan, New Zealand, Turkey and the USA. Of the programme's total budget, the EU and its Member States contribute 50%, with the aid being principally directed towards private enterprise. The programme is linked to the Europe Agreements and other aid operations, as agreed by the Council in November 1992.

Pillars of the EU. The first pillar includes the Treaties of Rome (revised by the SEA), democratisation of the institutions, citizenship, EMU, single currency, ECB, single monetary policy and coordination of economic policies. The second pillar includes the CFSP, common positions and joint action, and the common defence policy based on the WEU, as covered by Title V of the TEU. The third pillar includes cooperation in the field of JHA, as covered by Title VI of the TEU, which refers to asylum policy, rules on crossing the Member States' external borders, immigration policy, combating drug trafficking, combating international fraud, customs and police and judicial cooperation.

Plenary.   Describes the entire EP or one of its part-sessions, occasionally referred to as plenary sessions.

Policy.   A series of legislative decrees with the intention of fulfilling specific objectives such as in relation to the CAP.

Political Directors.   These are the senior Foreign Ministry officials who were provided with the responsibility of coordinating the EPC process in 1970. They meet every month under the chairmanship of the country that holds the Presidency of the Council of Ministers, and are assisted by a European Correspondent.

Political groups.   Members of the EP sit in political groups dependent upon their political allegiance, for example the Party of the European Socialists which includes the UK Labour Party.

Preamble.   The sentences at the start of a Treaty which establish the primary aims of the signatories. It is possible for the Court of Justice to draw on these when defining Community law.

Preferential Agreement.   Any agreement in which preferential treatment in trade is granted by one country to another.

Preliminary ruling.   A Court of Justice decision on a point of Community law that has been referred to it by a tribunal or national Court.

Presidency of the Council.   The post held by each Member State in strict rotation. The President-in-office has the task of organising the agenda for each Council meeting and acting as a mediator among the Member States.

Presidential 'Troika'.   Refers to the meetings between the preceding, present and succeeding Presidencies of the Council of Ministers to ensure continuity.

Primacy.   The primacy of Community law over national law as established in the Court of Justice ruling in the case of *Costa v ENEL*, when the Court ruled that 'the law stemming from the Treaty . . . [cannot] be overridden by domestic legal provisions'.

Proportionality.   The methods used to ensure that a given end should not exceed what is appropriate to achieve that end.

Protocol. A section of a Treaty which is attached to it but enjoys the same status. The reason for its attachment is because it often contains large amounts of material, such as the protocol on the excessive deficit procedure attached to the TEU.

Provisions. The aims and contents of a Treaty.

Quaestor. Officers who are responsible for administrative and financial matters that relate to MEPs. They work in accordance with guidelines provided by the bureau of the EP.

Qualified Majority Voting (QMV). Decisions are taken by the Council either by unanimity or by simple or qualified majority voting, the latter of which was extended by the SEA and TEU. Under Article 148(2) of the Treaty of Rome, QMV votes are divided with France, the FRG, Italy and the UK receiving 10 votes, Spain 8, Belgium, Greece, the Netherlands and Portugal 5, Austria and Sweden 4, Denmark, Finland and Ireland 3, and Luxembourg 2. A decision is adopted if it obtains 62 votes (out of the total 87). Decisions under CFSP also require the support of at least ten Member States. QMV was subjected to debate at a Foreign Ministers' meeting at Ioannina in 1994, when agreement was reached that if a narrow QMV was produced, then every effort would be made to obtain a larger majority. The effect of this was to solve the dispute surrounding QMV re-weighting in the light of enlargement.

Quantitative restrictions. Measures that impose partial or total restraints on imports.

Quotas. A restriction on the volume of trade in a particular area.

RACE. Acronym for research and development in advanced communications technologies for Europe, it being a comprehensive telecommunications programme with the aim of fostering broadband communication technologies to ensure the concurrent broadcast of data, images and sound.

Rapporteur. The EP Committee spokesperson who drafts reports on proposed legislation that is to be adopted by the Parliament.

Ratification. The Treaties of Rome require Treaty changes to be approved by signatory states, involving a parliamentary vote or a referendum. The former applied to the UK's ratification of the TEU, while the latter applied to Denmark's ratification of the TEU.

Recommendation.   A measure adopted by the Council or the European Commission that is not binding under Article 189 of the Treaties of Rome.

Referendum.   A national vote on a specific policy proposal, such as Denmark's referendum on the ratification of the TEU or the UK's 1975 referendum on Community membership.

Reflection group.   Such a group was established in June 1995 in accordance with the decision of the Corfu European Council in June 1994. The group's task was to prepare for the 1996–97 intergovernmental conference, consisting of a representative from each Member State and the European Commission and EP. The 15 members of the group were: Austria – Manfred Scheich (Permanent Representative to the EC); Belgium – Franklin Dehousse (Professor of European Law); Denmark – Niels Ersbøll (ex-Council Secretary General); Finland – Ingvar Melin (ex-Defence Minister); France – Michel Barnier (Minister for European Affairs); FRG – Werner Hoyer (Foreign Affairs Minister); Greece – Stefanos Stathatos (ex-Diplomat); Ireland – Gay Mitchell (Minister for Europe); Italy – Silvio Fagiolo (Diplomat); Luxembourg – Joseph Weyland (Ambassador to UK); the Netherlands – Michiel Patijn (Minister for Europe); Portugal – Andre Goncalves (ex-Foreign Minister); Spain – Carlos Westendorp (Minister for Europe); Sweden – Gunnar Lund (State Secretary for Foreign Affairs); UK – David Davis (Minister of State for European Affairs); European Commission – Marcelino Oreja (Commissioner); European Parliament – Elisabeth Guigou (French Socialist MEP) and Elmar Brok (German Christian Democrat MEP).

Region.   The subdivision of Member States which have been given greater influence by the creation of the Committee of the Regions, as established by the TEU.

Regulation.   The strongest form of Community legislation (acts of the Community institutions), having general application and being entirely binding and applicable directly to all Member States.

Renegotiation.   The process of challenging the sets of conditions of membership of an organisation, such as the UK's 1974 renegotiation of membership.

Representative Office.   The European Commission local office in individual states throughout the world.

Resolution.   A form of Community legislation (acts of the Community institutions) that is not binding.

Right of initiative. The European Commission has the responsibility for drafting legislative proposals, although it may have been influenced by comments from the Council of Ministers, European Council and EP.

Schengen agreement. Established in the Luxembourg town of Schengen in 1985, the agreement (which was initially formed outside the legal framework of the EU) aimed to remove border controls between EU Member States. The full removal of borders was agreed in March 1995 in the wake of the establishment of the Schengen Information System (SIS), which represented a significant delay in the initial goal of opening up borders by 1990. The initial signature countries were Belgium, France, the FRG, Luxembourg, the Netherlands, Portugal and Spain. It has been expanded to include Austria, Greece and Italy. However, Denmark, Finland, Ireland, Sweden and the UK have demonstrated reluctance to join the system. The recent Treaty of Amsterdam, which was negotiated at the Amsterdam European Council in June 1997, resulted in the Schengen agreement being incorporated within the Union's single institutional framework.

Schuman Plan. Published on 9 May 1950 by the French Foreign Minister, Robert Schuman, with the aim of fostering European integration, a process which eventually produced the ECSC in 1952. The success of the scheme and its origins in the process of European integration has resulted in 9 May being designated Europe Day.

Scrutiny. The monitoring of EU legislation by national parliaments, for example the UK House of Commons Foreign Affairs Select Committee.

Secretariat General. The central bureaucratic department of the European Commission, headed by the Secretary General of the European Commission, it acts as the primary administrative link between the President and the overall work of the Directorates General and other agencies.

Section. In terms of the EU Treaty, this refers to the subdivision of a chapter.

Security Office. A service of the EU which deals with the state of security in the EU Member States and organises the security policy in Europe.

Select Committees. House of Commons departmental Select Committees provide a means of examining important subjects, by calling for written memoranda as well as taking oral evidence. European business is primarily tackled by the Foreign Affairs departmental Select Committee, though others such as Defence, Trade and Industry and the Treasury examine pertinent questions. The most important non-departmental Select Committee is European Legislation.

Semi-detachment.   Principally, this refers to the UK's traditional hostility to closer integration, with successive governments placing emphasis on the defence of national sovereignty. It also relates to the slow adaptation of the UK to bargaining and negotiating procedures, while both the public and party system have not always shown a genuine preference for EU membership.

Set-aside.   Introduced in 1988 to limit agricultural production under the CAP, set-aside is a scheme whereby farmers would be paid compensation if they took at least one-fifth of their land out of production over a minimum five-year period.

Single currency.   Introduced with the third stage of EMU.

Single European Act (SEA).   Ratified in 1987, it emanated from an intergovernmental conference negotiation in the second half of 1985. The SEA amended and supplemented the Treaties of Rome, including the introduction of QMV decision-making under the cooperation procedure, which was perceived to be necessary for the completion of the single market.

Single market.   The single market represents the total amount of economic activity within Member States, especially in relation to trade across frontiers. The Cassis de Dijon case had an important impact on the creation of the single market, as did the report of the Kangaroo Group and the White Paper on completing the internal market. By January 1994 the majority of single market legislation also applied to the European Economic Area.

SME action programme.   A programme aimed at enhancing competitiveness, employment and growth among small and medium-sized enterprises (SMEs).

Snake in the tunnel.   An agreement in 1972 permitted Member States' currencies a narrow margin of fluctuation against the US dollar of 1.25% on either side. The tunnel was the limit to which currencies could fluctuate while the snake referred to the line that currencies created as they increased and decreased. By 1976 all of the participants had abandoned the system apart from the FRG and the Benelux nations, although currency coordination shortly re-emerged in the form of the ERM.

Soames Affair.   Refers to a Paris meeting in February 1969 between the UK Ambassador, Christopher Soames, and the French President, Charles de Gaulle, when the latter implied the possibility of UK membership in a broader and weaker Community. The political direction of such a Community would be established by France, the FRG, Italy and the UK, which would then establish a European axis independent of influence from the USA. The importance of the meeting was that it demonstrated a change in de Gaulle's attitude towards UK membership of the Community (he had vetoed two previous applications). However, the change was principally motivated by personal concerns – he had recently suffered numerous foreign policy setbacks and therefore wanted to reassert his position both domestically and internationally. In addition, he realised the value of UK participation in a Community which would increasingly be dominated by the economic and political influence of the FRG. But the initiative, which de Gaulle considered would be pursued only by France and the UK, collapsed after the UK Foreign Office informed other Member States of the proposal. De Gaulle perceived the disclosure to have been a breach of trust. In effect it meant that UK accession to the Community would be extremely unlikely as long as he remained President of France.

Social Chapter.   Initially intended to form part of the TEU, but taken out of the Draft Treaty after the then UK Prime Minister, John Major, refused to accept its inclusion despite being offered a watered-down version. One reason for Major's opposition was the role being given to the social partners in the formation of policy. Instead, the contents of the Social Chapter were included as a separate Social Policy Agreement which was signed by the other 11 Member States and annexed to the Social Policy Protocol. This was referred to as a UK opt-out. The UK's exclusion from this area of policy resulted in the other Member States and the European Commission attempting to include social policy issues under Articles 118A of the SEA which provided for QMV, notably a working-time directive which the Court of Justice determined was applicable to the UK in 1996. The arrival of the Labour government in May 1997 resulted in the UK accepting the Social Chapter at the Amsterdam European Council in June, thereby ending its exclusion.

Social Charter.   Adopted by the European Council at Strasbourg on 9 December 1989 with the purpose of emphasising the social dimension of the single market. Although the agreement was not legally binding, the UK voted against it. The fundamental 12 rights of the Social Charter are: freedom of movement; employment and remuneration; social protection; improvement of living and working conditions; freedom of association and collective bargaining; worker information, consultation and participation; vocational training; equal treatment for men and women; health and safety protection at the workplace; upon retirement, the provision of a pension that will provide a decent standard of living for the elderly; improvements in the social integration of people with disabilities, especially with regard to housing, mobility and employment; and the protection of children and adolescents.

Social dialogue.   European-level meetings between labour and management representatives, otherwise known as the social partners. The origins of this process started with meetings under the chairmanship of the European Commission in the mid-1980s between the European Trade Union Confederation (ETUC), the Union des Industries de la Communauté européenne (UNICE) and the European Centre for Public Enterprises (ECPE).

Social dumping.   This happens when a Member State attracts or retains job-creation programmes through lower labour costs or less restrictive labour practices. A way of maintaining inward investment, it was one of the reasons why the UK refused to accept the Social Chapter at the Maastricht European Council in December 1991.

Social partners.   Reflecting a corporatist strategy evident in many continental European countries, especially the FRG, this refers to meetings of the two sides of industry, namely employers and employees. The UK partly refused the Social Chapter because it included a role for the social partners in the formation of employment policy. The presence of the Economic and Social Committee does, however, provide a framework where the social partners can debate issues.

Social policy.   A term which represents employment policy, including labour law, working conditions and parts of vocational training. Articles 117–127 of the Treaties of Rome refer to social policy.

Social Policy Agreement.   An agreement annexed to the Social Policy Protocol (which in turn is annexed to the TEU) it was accepted by 11 of the then 12 Member States, with the UK having decided to opt-out. The agreement established objectives in the field of social policy and clearly built upon the momentum that had commenced with the 1989 Social Charter.

Social Policy Protocol.   Adopted in December 1991 at the Maastricht European Council and annexed to the TEU. While the then 12 Member States signed the Protocol, all but the UK noted their desire to make advances in the field of social policy on the basis of the Social Policy Agreement annexed to the Protocol. The Protocol subsequently included Austria, Finland and Sweden after the enlargement of the EU in 1995.

Socrates. This programme, from 1995–99, replaced the earlier ERASMUS and Lingua schemes in the domain of student and teacher exchanges and language training.

Solemn Declaration on European Union. Member States adopted a 'Solemn Declaration' at the June 1983 Stuttgart European Council. It stressed the international identity of the Community and expressed a desire to coordinate EPC matters more closely, and had clearly been motivated by the 1981 Genscher–Colombo Plan.

Sovereignty. EU membership is perceived by Euro-sceptics to involve a loss of sovereignty and is therefore used to challenge further integration. It is clear that Member States have agreed to cooperate in certain policy areas which involve majority voting, but they have also chosen to cooperate on an intergovernmental basis in other areas, such as CFSP.

Spaak Report. Presented to the ECSC Foreign Ministers in April 1956 with the recommendation of establishing a European Economic Community and a European Atomic Energy Community. The report's origins were based in the 1955 Messina conference, which had asked the Belgian Foreign Minister, Paul-Henri Spaak, to chair a committee of experts to examine methods of advancing further European integration.

Special Committee on Agriculture (SCA). A committee of Member State representatives responsible for preparing the work of Agriculture Ministers that meet within the Council of Ministers and for fulfilling the tasks which the Council gives it.

Special Drawing Rights (SDR). A country which is a member of the IMF has the ability to purchase an amount of currency that has been given to another member of the IMF under the SDR system and does not have any obligation to sell it back within a fixed time period.

Spillover. The development of the Community by the transfer of national policies of individual Member States to the Community. Integrated sectors would essentially spill into those sectors not integrated. This was perceived by neo-functionalists as the crucial means of furthering integration.

Spofford Proposal.   Announced on 18 December 1950, it stressed that the USA would increase its defence commitment to Europe if European NATO powers agreed to establish an integrated European force (including a West German contribution).

Spokesman's Service.   A department of the European Commission which supplies the press and other media with news of the Union and European Commission developments.

Stability and growth pact.   Member States decided at the Dublin European Council of 13–14 December 1996 to pass powers to the Council of Ministers to control those countries participating in the single currency, with agreement being reached that if a nation within the EMU broke the terms of the stability and growth pact, then large financial penalties could be imposed by the Council.

Stagiaire.   Individuals who are appointed on a short-term basis to the offices of the European Commission.

Standardisation.   National standards within Member States have been replaced by European standards in line with the requirements of the single market. The creation of common standards is a means of reducing barriers to trade. The EU standards organisations are CEN and CENELEC.

State aids.   Finance provided from public funds to commercial enterprises that bend the principles of competition within the EU must be subjected to examination by the European Commission, which has the power to block them, or determine that repayment is necessary. The final arbiter of state aids is the Court of Justice.

Stockholm Convention.   A document signed on 4 January 1960 by Austria, Denmark, Norway, Portugal, Sweden, Switzerland and the UK which established EFTA. While Finland participated in the discussions, it did not sign the Convention.

Stresa Conference.   A conference convened in 1958 by Sicco Mansholt who was Vice-President of the European Commission and responsible for the CAP. The aim of the gathering of European Commission officials, national experts and farmers' representatives was to examine means of implementing the goals of the CAP, an important conclusion of which was the decision to support agriculture through a system of guaranteed prices.

Structural funds. Administered by the European Commission with the purpose of financing Community structural aid, they embrace the Guidance Section of the EAGGF for agriculture, the Regional Fund for structural aid under the regional policy, the Social Fund for measures relating to social policy, and the new Financial Instrument for Fisheries (FIFG). Such financial support is primarily directed towards poorer regions and is based on six main objectives. The greater proportion goes to Objective 1 (to develop regions which are significantly behind the others). The cohesion fund, which was created in 1993, also assists this process. Objective 1: Promoting the development and structural adjustment of regions whose development is falling behind; Objective 2: Converting the regions, frontier regions or parts of regions (including employment areas and urban communities) badly affected by industrial decline; Objective 3: Tackling long-term unemployment and ensuring that young people excluded from the labour market are integrated into working life; promoting equal opportunities for men and women in the labour market; Objective 4: Ensuring that workers are able to adapt to industrial change and to changes in production systems; Objective 5(a): Promoting rural development by accelerating adjustment of agricultural structures in the reform of the Common Agricultural Policy and review of Common Fisheries Policy; Objective 5(b): Promoting rural development through the development and structural adjustment of rural areas; Objective 6: Promoting the development and structural adjustment of regions with an extremely low population density.

Subcontracting. Refers to the process whereby temporary labour is secured to complete projects on terms and conditions that are possibly inferior to those enjoyed by permanent employees. This practice is tackled by the 'Posting of Workers' directive, effective from 24 September 1999.

Subsidiarity. Introduced in the TEU to ensure that decisions are taken as closely as possible to the citizen and whether action at the Community level is justified in light of the possibilities available at national, regional or local level. The Union should not take action (except in the areas which fall within its exclusive competence) unless it is more effective than action taken at national, regional or local level.

Subsidiary. A company established within another company in an additional Member State.

Subsidy. Economic aids granted to businesses, such as tax concessions and financial support. Clearly, subsidies can upset European competition. For this reason subsidies which distort the market are forbidden by the EU.

Summit. Meetings of Heads of State and Government institutionalised in the European Council.

Supranational. Denotes a process of law that is superior to Member States, contrasting with intergovernmental.

Surplus. A situation where an excess has been produced, notably within the agricultural sector, with it being possible for the Community to restrict the production guarantee given to farmers.

TACIS (Technical assistance to the Commonwealth of Independent States and Georgia). Established in 1990 to provide technical assistance for the independent states of the former Soviet Union and Mongolia.

Target price. The price which producers anticipate their products will obtain.

Tariff quotas. A means of allowing limited amounts of particular goods to be imported at either reduced or duty-free rates, thereby allowing Member States to obtain particular goods of an essential nature without endangering the overall customs protection.

Tax harmonisation. The provision of Article 99 EC (as amended by Article G(20)TEU) for the harmonisation of indirect taxation, involving the removal of all tax borders within the Community.

Technical barriers to trade. Obstacles to trade that emanate from national consumer safety and environmental standards that goods have to meet.

TEMPUS. Trans-European mobility scheme for university students of Central and Eastern Europe, providing financial assistance for joint projects established by organisations from EU Member States with partners from Central and Eastern European countries. While the programme initially embraced Bulgaria, Czechoslovakia and its successor states, Hungary, Poland and the former Yugoslavia, the second stage of the programme (1994–98) included, under the TACIS programme, the nations of the former Soviet Union. It has paid particular attention to those studying applied economics, agriculture and agricultural economics, applied science, technology and engineering, business management, environmental protection, and modern European languages. The TEMPUS programme also provides grants for Central and Eastern Europe staff members going to an EU country (and vice versa) for the purpose of attending practical courses and carrying out teaching or training duties.

Terms of entry.   The conditions which applicant members achieve when they obtain membership of the EU.

The Fifteen.   The accession of Austria, Finland and Sweden as members of the Community in 1995 meant that the Twelve became the Fifteen.

The Nine.   The enlargement of the Community in 1973 to include Denmark, Ireland and the UK meant that the Six became the Nine.

The Six.   Refers to the initial six countries which formed the ECSC in 1951 and thereafter established the EEC and Euratom under the 1957 Treaties of Rome, namely Belgium, France, Italy, Luxembourg, the Netherlands and the FRG. The Six became the Nine in 1973 with the accession of Denmark, Ireland and the UK, the Ten in 1981 with the accession of Greece, the Twelve in 1986 with the accession of Portugal and Spain, and the Fifteen in 1995 with the accession of Austria, Finland and Sweden.

The Ten.   The accession of Greece to the Community in 1981 meant that the Nine became the Ten.

The Twelve.   The enlargement of the Community in 1986 to include Portugal and Spain meant that the Ten became the Twelve.

Thermie II.   Financial assistance is offered by this programme to projects that demonstrate new innovative technologies.

Third country.   A state that is not a member of the EU.

Three Wise Men.   A report commissioned by the Brussels European Council of December 1978 to examine means of making the institutions of the Community more effective, particularly with the likelihood of future enlargement. The 'Three Wise Men' who conducted the report were Darend Biesheivel (a former Prime Minister of the Netherlands), Edmund Dell (a former UK Secretary of State for Trade in the then Labour government), and Robert Marjolin (a former Vice-President of the European Commission). The 'Report on European Institutions' was published in October 1979 and formed the basis of discussions by Foreign Ministers, though its actual recommendations were hardly adopted.

Threshold price.   The minimum prices for the importation of farm products into the EU. Cheaper imports are increased to the threshold price by means of levies and customs duties, thereby protecting the European farming industry from cheaper competitors.

Tindemans Report.   The report conducted at the request of the European Council by the then Prime Minister of Belgium, Leo Tindemans, it analysed the ways in which a more integrated Europe, that was also closer to the citizen, could be achieved. Of note was the contribution by the European Commission, which included the first mention of the term subsidiarity.

Title.   The subdivision of a Treaty below a part.

Trade barriers.   While the desire to create the single market brought with it the removal of customs duties and quantitative restrictions in trade between Member States, free trade was hampered by other non-tariff barriers, including those of a technical nature due to differing laws between Member States. This was particularly evident in the arena of foodstuffs, although the process of harmonisation essentially removed all remaining barriers to trade by the commencement of the single market in 1992.

Trans European Networks (TENs).   Listed under Articles 129b–129d of the EC Treaty, they serve the purpose of developing the full potential of the single market by assisting cross-frontier infrastructures in the areas of energy, environment, transport and telecommunications.

Transitional period.   A period of time that new Member States are given to allow them to introduce and apply the rules of the EU, as determined by the process of accession.

Transparency.   The process of greater openness and attainment of access to EU documents.

Treaties of Rome.   Signed on 25 March 1957 (came into force on 1 January 1958) they established the European Economic Community (EEC) and European Atomic Energy Community (Euratom), as well as additional protocols. In conjunction with the European Coal and Steel Community (ECSC), they made up the European Community.

Treaty of Amsterdam.   Represented 15 months of negotiations after the establishment of an intergovernmental conference in Turin on 26 March 1996. The primary objectives of the Treaty, which was concluded at the June 1997 Amsterdam European Council, were: (1) to place citizen and employment rights at the heart of the Union; (2) to get rid of any remaining obstacles to free movement; (3) to provide the Union with a stronger voice in international affairs; and (4) to increase the efficiency of the Union's institutional framework, particularly with regard to the prospect of future enlargement.

Treaty of Brussels. Signed in March 1948, the Treaty demonstrated a willingness on the part of Belgium, France, Luxembourg, the Netherlands and the UK to establish a common defence system and to strengthen their relationship with each other so that they would be able to thwart ideological, military and political threats to their security. This was a realistic fear in light of threats to the sovereignty of various countries at this time, notably Greece, Norway and Turkey, while the Berlin blockade and a coup in Czechoslovakia took place in 1948. The desire to protect their own borders through a pact of collective security ultimately resulted in the April 1949 Treaty of Washington which established the North Atlantic Treaty Organisation.

Treaty of Dunkirk. France and the UK signed a 50-year Treaty of Alliance and Mutual Assistance at Dunkirk on 4 March 1947.

Treaty of Friendship. French President Charles de Gaulle and German Chancellor Konrad Adenauer signed the Franco-German Treaty of Friendship and Cooperation on 22 January 1963. It was all that was rescued from the failure of the Fouchet Plan which had aimed to create greater political integration.

Treaty of Luxembourg. An agreement signed by the Six on 22 April 1950 and came into effect on 1 January 1971. It amended the Treaties of Rome by providing the Community with its own resources and increased the power of the EP with regard to the budget.

Treaty of Paris. Signed on 18 April 1951, it established the ECSC.

Treaty of Washington. The product of formal negotiations to establish a collective security alliance which took place in Washington between December 1948 and April 1949, with the Treaty being signed on 4 April. It established a defence organisation that was known as the North Atlantic Treaty Organisation. This marked a process which had commenced with the March 1948 Treaty of Brussels when its five signatories (Belgium, France, Luxembourg, the Netherlands and the UK) demonstrated a desire to establish a common defence system. Momentum towards widening the security and defence relations of the Treaty of Brussels had been accelerated by the beginning of the Berlin blockade in the summer of 1948, which highlighted a deterioration in the relationship between the USA and Soviet Union. The Treaty came into force in August 1949, with the commitment to collective defence being embodied in Article 5.

Treaty on European Union (TEU). Otherwise known as the Maastricht Treaty after its signature in the Dutch town of Maastricht on 7 February

1992. It came into force on 1 November 1993, after ratification by the then 12 Member States. The main initiatives of the Treaty were the adoption of a single currency, the introduction of a CFSP, cooperation on JHA and new rights for European citizens.

Trevi Group.   Established in 1975 with the purpose of creating informal cooperation among EU Ministers for JHA so as to tackle drug trafficking and international terrorism. Meetings took place twice a year. It was replaced by meetings of the EU Interior and Justice Ministers from November 1993.

Troika.   The preceding, current and succeeding Presidency of the EU (Article J.5, TEU). The aim of this group is to ensure a coordinated strategy in the organisation of foreign policy. For instance, in June 1991 the troika of Community Foreign Ministers – Jacques Poos (Luxembourg), Hans van den Broek (the Netherlands) and Gianni de Michelis (Italy) – departed for the former Yugoslavia to investigate the outbreak of hostilities.

Truman Doctrine.   US President Truman said, on 12 March 1947, that 'it must be the policy of the United States to support free peoples who are resisting attempted subjugation by armed minorities or by outside pressure'.

UK budget dispute.   The dispute between the UK and the EC between 1979 and 1984 over its position as the second largest net contributor to the budget, despite being one of the poorest Member States in terms of per capita GNP. The pre-1979 and post-1979 Labour and Conservative governments considered this situation to be unjust. After temporary solutions were first established, a final settlement was agreed at the June 1984 Fontainebleau European Council meeting.

Unanimity.   Unanimity requires all Member States meeting in the Council to be in agreement before a proposal can be adopted. In the wake of the SEA it was applicable to a more limited area. Voting by QMV is now the rule within the first pillar. However, pillars two and three operate exclusively according to the intergovernmental method and unanimity requirement.

UNICE.   Acronym for the Union of Industries of the European Community which was founded in 1959. It represents the interests of member confederations from the EU and EFTA and coordinates their policies on European affairs when lobbying Member States and European institutions. It also participates in the social dialogue and comes under the social partners.

United States of Europe. The idea of a United States of Europe came from a passage in a speech by Winston Churchill at Zurich in 1949.

Validity. An act of the Community that has legal force and effect.

Value added tax. A system of value added tax was adopted by the Six in 1967. It subsequently constituted an important part of the own resources of the Community, evolving from the application of a standard rate (1% in 1999) to the VAT base which is settled in a uniform style for all Member States.

Variable geometry. A method of differentiated integration which accepts that Member States have European integration objectives that are so different that it necessitates a permanent separation between different groups of Member States, although some may choose to join policy areas at a later date. It is a similar assumption to a multi-speed Europe because the hard core is open to those states that are willing and, in time, able to join. However, the likelihood is that the hard core would establish objectives themselves, thereby shifting the goal posts for other Member States.

Veto. Provision for Member States to block a decision, such as in the Council of Ministers.

Visegrad states. Refers to the Czech Republic, Hungary, Poland and Slovakia. The leaders of Hungary, Poland and the then Czechoslovakia met at Visegrad in Hungary in February 1991 to determine their approach to European integration. All of the four countries have established Europe Agreements with the EU, and are also members of the Council of Europe and North Atlantic Cooperation Council.

Werner Report. The decision taken at the 1969 Hague Summit to achieve EMU by 1980 resulted in the then Luxembourg Prime Minister, Pierre Werner, being commissioned to detail a possible route to EMU. The subsequent 1970 Werner Report stressed that the Community should progress in an equal manner with regard to narrowing the margins of exchange rates, harmonising capital markets, creating a European central bank and developing a common currency. An additional institutional aspect included the creation of a monetary policy decision-making centre that would be supervised by the EP. However, despite the fact that EMU would be reached in stages, of which the snake would be the first stage, its very failure meant that the objectives of the Werner Report were abandoned.

Western European Union (WEU).   Established in 1954 from the ashes of the 1948 Brussels Treaty, it includes EU Member States (except Austria, Denmark, Finland, Ireland and Sweden, which have observer status). Its main role is to guarantee mutual assistance if an attack on Europe takes place, while maintaining peace and security within Europe. Although correctly viewed as a weaker organisation than NATO, it has recently encountered a revival in its fortunes, as demonstrated by the October 1987 'Platform on European Security Interests'. The TEU increased its position to that of an 'integral part of the development of the Union', while at the same time providing it with the job of elaborating and implementing decisions and actions which have defence implications.

Western European Union associate partners.   The ten Central and Eastern European countries of Bulgaria, Hungary, Poland, the Czech Republic, Romania, the Slovak Republic, Slovenia and the three Baltic States have associate partner status with the EU. This provides for them to be kept informed of developments through attendance at WEU meetings, while they also have a permanent liaison arrangement with the Planning Cell. In addition, they can participate in the decisions of Member States taken in respect of the Petersberg Declaration, that is humanitarian, peacekeeping and peacemaking efforts.

Western European Union observer status.   The TEU made provision that EU Member States that were not members of the WEU should either become members or observers. In this context, Austria, Denmark, Finland, Ireland and Sweden have observer status, providing them with the ability to attend WEU Council meetings and to be invited (with the possibility of speaking) to meetings of working parties.

White Paper.   An official set of European proposals advanced by the European Commission in a specific policy area. It contrasts with a Green Paper, which is merely a forum for discussion.

White Paper on completing the internal market.   Published by the European Commission under the authorship of the UK European Commissioner Lord Cockfield and approved by the European Council in 1985, it noted some 282 proposals which would assist the creation of the single market by eliminating both technical and practical barriers to trade, of which the majority had been completed by 1993.

White Paper on growth, competitiveness and employment.   This paper was published by the European Commission in 1994 and established a set of policy goals with the overall aim of reducing EU unemployment, including a call for market-oriented economic strategies. It acknowledged that high rates of unemployment on the continent were partly due to labour market rigidities which were not present in nations such as Japan and the USA. It proposed a 'social pact' where productivity gains produced by limited deregulation of labour markets are used to fund job creation and training. Emphasis was placed on job creation, flexibility, reduced non-wage labour costs, structural reforms of social security and taxation systems. Generally, it signalled a decline in Community activism, with attention directed towards consolidation rather than new initiatives, and in sum marked a gradual move away from traditional social welfarism to the dual goal of protection and flexibility.

Widening. The enlargement of the EU that is often used in the same breadth as deepening. Those who favour widening consider it imperative that the policies of the Union are strengthened, particularly the institutional design. By contrast, some states have traditionally advocated that widening does not necessitate deepening because such a process would make the process of enlargement more difficult, as all new Member States would not just have to accept existing competences but also those envisaged in any deepening, given the requirement for all new entrants to accept the *acquis communitaire*. The UK, especially under the leadership of Margaret Thatcher, defended that widening did not necessitate deepening.

Wine lake. A phrase synonymous with the butter mountain and equally affected by the price guarantee and intervention system of the CAP. Large amounts of wine were accumulated through overproduction. An agreement reached at the December 1984 Dublin European Council reduced wine production.

Working document. Generally a first stage in the drafting of reports in the EP. In this context a rapporteur may submit an outline of the intended report or of the policy proposals with which it is concerned.

Working Group. This is a body of officials which meets to settle details surrounding particular EU policies.

Working Time Directive. Refers to the basic hours, shift and overtime hours, rest periods and holiday entitlements applicable to employees in Member States which are covered by an EU directive. It provides a minimum rest period of 11 consecutive hours a day, a rest break where the working day is longer than six hours, a minimum rest period of one day a week, a maximum working week of 48 hours on average including overtime, four weeks annual holiday and those engaged in night work should not exceed more than eight hours a night on average. The directive does not cover workers in the transport sector – air, rails, sea, roads – as well as doctors in training. Other jobs, such as senior managers, family workers and jobs in hospitals and airports, docks and prisons, the emergency services, agriculture, electricity, gas and water are covered by special arrangements.

World Trade Organisation (WTO).   Established in 1995 in the wake of the conclusion of the GATT Uruguay Round. All GATT members now belong to the WTO, which furthers trade relations among its members and forms a basis for further multilateral trade discussions. As recently as November 1998 the US and the EU were locked in intensive negotiations at the WTO in Geneva in an attempt to resolve the row over the EU's banana import regime. The dispute arose because the US considered that the banana regime, which gives preferential access to the EU market for bananas from former French and UK colonies in Africa, the Caribbean and Pacific, does not allow US companies which distribute Latin American bananas to compete on an equal basis.

Xenophobia.   A term which denotes the hatred of foreigners. Such discrimination is outlawed under Article 48 of the Treaty of Rome.

Yaoundé Convention.   A trade agreement between the Six and the 18 nations of the Associated African States and Madagascar which was signed in 1963 in Yaoundé, Cameroon. Coming into force in 1964, the Convention was renegotiated in 1969 and thereafter was superseded by the Lomé Convention.

SECTION XII

Bibliography

This bibliography is intended to provide a sample of the best books written in English on the European Union. Some pertinent academic journal articles are also listed. There has, in recent years, been a dramatic increase in the number of books devoted to the study of the EU, reflecting both its expansion in membership and a widening of policy areas, and it would be impossible to list them all. However, I have attempted to cover the full range of the EU's impact, while highlighting different types of sources, including introductory texts, analysis of major policies, the impact of Member States and memoirs by those who took part in events. The place of publication is London unless otherwise stated.

Official documentation

Those who wish to examine official documentation should consult the *Official Journal of the European Communities* (Office for Official Publications of the European Communities, Luxembourg). As the official gazette of the EU, it contains the texts of secondary legislation and draft legislation. Of the main institutions, a factual account of the work of the Council is supplied in *A Review of the Council's Work* (Office for Official Publications of the European Communities, Luxembourg), while a list of the national representatives who negotiate on behalf of Member States is detailed at frequent intervals in the *Guide to the Council of the European Communities* (Office for Official Publications of the European Communities, Luxembourg). The officials who work in the European Commission are named in the annual *Directory of the Commission of the European Communities* (Office for Official Publications of the European Communities, Luxembourg). Its activities can be found in the *Working Documents of the Commission* (Office for Official Publications of the European Communities, Luxembourg). A great deal of the extensive material produced consists of reports, communications and proposals for legislation. Papers are named by document number, involving the prefix COM or SEC, a date code and running number, i.e. COM (85) 768 final. The inclusion of 'final' shows that the document has reached its final state of draft.

Information regarding the European Parliament is likewise an important aspect of the EU, especially the *Debates of the European Parliament* (Office for Official Publications of the European Communities, Luxembourg). They have been published as an annex to the *Official Journal* and provide a verbatim record of plenary sessions of the European Parliament. Despite the merits of this information, the major work of the European Parliament is carried out in committees which prepare reports to be considered in plenary session. This material can be found in the *Working Documents of the European Parliament* (Office for Official Publications of the European Communities, Luxembourg), which, like the European Commission, is identifiable by a specific number. Each number comprises a running number and a date code, such as European Parliament Doc.243/75. Other important documentation is that concerning the cases brought before the Court of Justice of the European Communities, published as *Reports of Cases before the Court* (Office for Official Publications of the European Communities, Luxembourg). These are also identifiable by a specific number within the current year.

Outside the main institutions, it is worth examining the annual *General Report of the Activities of the European Community* which provides a guide to events and policies in the European Union (Office for Official Publications of the European Communities, Luxembourg). The use of footnote references also ensures that it guides the reader to detailed policy areas. Another wide-ranging account of recent developments is the monthly *Bulletin of the European Community* (Office for Official Publications of the European Communities, Luxembourg). The first part of the *Bulletin* details topics of current interest, while the second part constitutes the main section. It provides in-depth information of events in each of the major policy areas of the EU, an account of documentation that has been prepared or is being considered as well as an analysis of the work of the main institutions. Those engaged in detailed research will find the separately published supplements to be a great benefit. They provide information on studies undertaken by independent experts on behalf of the European Commission along with important European Commission proposals and reports. The UK government also provides a twice-yearly review of EU activities, *Developments in the European Union* (HMSO). Less official, but nonetheless accurate, information is provided in the daily press bulletin *Agence Europe* (Brussels).

The present importance attached to Economic and Monetary Union necessitates the consultation of data on the current economic situation in the EU. This can be found in the quarterly publication *European Economy* (Office for Official Publications of the European Communities, Luxembourg). The European Commission's annual report on the EU's economic situation is published in the November issue. Statistical information can be found in various publications, including *Basic Statistics of the Community* (Office for Official Publications of the European Communities, Luxembourg). Although it is relatively small, it nevertheless provides a very good introduction to the major statistics. On social policy it is worth consulting *Social Europe* (Office for Official Publications of the European Communities, Luxembourg) which provides a review of current trends, and *Employment in Europe* (Office for Official Publications of the European Communities, Luxembourg), which is published annually, is aimed at a local readership in Member States, and covers business, trade unions and interest groups. On agriculture one should see *Agriculture: Statistical Yearbook* (Office for Official Publications of the European Communities, Luxembourg), which covers the major statistical information. Other important subjects include foreign trade, of which the *External Trade Monthly Bulletin* (Office for Official Publications of the European Communities, Luxembourg) provides information on the short-term development of EU foreign trade, trade between Member States as well as EU trade with third countries. Coverage of external affairs can be found in the *Annual Report of the ACP–EEC Council of Ministers* (Office for Official Publications of the European Communities, Luxembourg), which details the cooperation between the African, Caribbean and Pacific nations and the EU.

General and historical texts

Of the general works on the development of the European Community, one of the most comprehensive and accessible is Dinan, Desmond, *Ever Closer Union? An Introduction to the European Community* (Macmillan, Houndmills, 1994). But Urwin, Derek, *The European Community. A History of European Integration since 1945* (2nd edn, Longman, 1995) also serves this purpose well, as does Archer, Clive and Butler, Fiona, *The European Community: Structure and Process* (2nd edn, Pinter, 1994), and a first-class account is Barnes, Ian and Barnes, Pamela, *The Enlarged European Union* (Longman, 1995). A highly readable analysis is given by Pinder, John, *The European Community. The Building of a Union* (Opus, Oxford, 1991). The introduction to the history of European integration is covered by Dedman, Martin J., *The Origins and Development of the European Union 1945–95* (Routledge, 1996) and Henig, S., *The Uniting of Europe* (Routledge, 1997). Also of use is Nicoll, William and Salmon, Trevor, *Understanding the New European Community* (Harvester Wheatsheaf, Hemel Hempstead, 1994) and a clear review of the Community is provided in Williams, Alan M., *The European Community* (2nd edn, Blackwell, Oxford, 1994). Those wanting an easy introduction to the subject should consult Barbour, Philippe (ed.) *The European Union Handbook* (Fitzroy Dearborn, 1996) and Church, C. and Phinnemore, D., *European Union and European Community: A Handbook and Commentary on the post-Maastricht Treaties* (Harvester Wheatsheaf, Hemel Hempstead, 1994).

Excellent coverage of European developments in the post-war period is provided by Milward, A.S., *The Reconstruction of Western Europe 1945–51* (Methuen, 1984), Lipgens, W., *A History of European Integration, Vol. 1, 1945–47* (Clarendon Press, Oxford, 1982), Young, J.W., *Britain, France and the Unity of Europe 1945–1951* (Leicester University Press, Leicester, 1984), and Vaughan, Richard, *Post-War Integration in Europe* (Edward Arnold, 1976). Additionally, see Beloff, M., *Europe and the Europeans* (Chatto and Windus, 1957) and for a personal account, Acheson, Dean, *Present at the Creation* (Hamish Hamilton, 1970). Primary evidence can be uncovered from *Statements and Declarations of the Action Committee for the*

United States of Europe, 1955–67 (Chatham House/PEP, 1969 – European Series No. 9). In the early years of the Community much emphasis was attached to the importance of the institutions in propelling integration. One should see Haas, E., *The Uniting of Europe: Political, Social and Economic Forces, 1950–1957* (Stanford University Press, Stanford, CA, 1968). Also of use is Pinder, John, *Federal Union: The Pioneers* (Macmillan, Houndmills, 1990).

De Gaulle, Britain and the Common Market

By the mid-1960s it was the case that Member States proved to be central to the achievement of progress, as demonstrated by General de Gaulle's veto of the UK's application for membership and France's 1965 boycott of Community activities. These developments are well documented by Camps, Miriam, *European Unification in the Sixties. From the Veto to the Crisis* (McGraw Hill, 1966), which also serves as an excellent demonstration of research based upon contemporary history. The 1965 crisis is examined in detail by Newhouse, John, *Collision in Brussels: The Common Market Crisis of 30 June 1965* (Norton and Company, New York, 1967). One should also explore the short account provided by Knapp, Wilfrid, *Unity and Nationalism in Europe since 1945* (Pergamon Press, 1969). De Gaulle is further investigated by Newhouse, John, *De Gaulle and the Anglo-Saxons* (André Deutsch, 1970). Much material has been devoted to the personalities who helped shape the European Community in its formative years and one should consult Duchene, F., *Jean Monnet: The First Statesman of Interdependence* (Norton and Company, New York, 1994) and Spaak, Paul-Henri, *The Continuing Battle: Memoirs of a European 1936–1966* (Weidenfeld and Nicolson, 1971).

That the 1960s were partly dominated by the question of UK membership is represented in the literature devoted to this topic. It is worth reading three books by Kitzinger, U.W., namely *The Challenge of the Common Market* (Basil Blackwell, Oxford, 1961), *The European Common Market and Community* (Routledge and Kegan Paul, 1967) and *The Second Try: Labour and the EEC* (Pergamon Press, 1968). Other analysis is provided by Jay, Douglas, *After the Common Market* (Penguin, Harmondsworth, 1968), Jebb, G., *The European Idea* (Weidenfeld and Nicolson, 1966) and Wilkes, Georges (ed.), *Britain's Failure to Enter the European Community 1961–63* (Frank Cass, 1997). For a review of the debate in the early post-war years, see Nutting, Anthony, *Europe Will Not Wait. A Warning and a Way Out* (Hollis and Carter, 1960) and Gladwyn, Lord, *The European Idea* (Weidenfeld and Nicolson, 1966). The debate surrounding the 1975 referendum is explored in Evans, D., *While Britain Slept: The Selling of the Common Market* (Victor Gollancz, 1975). The shift from Commonwealth ties to Europe is analysed in Uri, Pierre (ed.), *From Commonwealth to*

Common Market (Penguin, Harmondsworth, 1968). The concept of Europe being the only realistic choice for the UK is explored in Northledge, F.S., *Descent from Power: British Foreign Policy, 1945–73* (Allen and Unwin, 1974).

The replacement of de Gaulle with Pompidou in 1969 paved the way for an expansion of Community membership, and the UK, Denmark and Ireland joined in January 1973. One should consult Lord, C., *British Entry to the European Community under the Heath Government 1970–1974* (Dartmouth, Aldershot, 1993). For an account of the issues facing the European Community in the 1970s, see Shonfield, Andrew, *Europe: Journey to an Unknown Destination* (Penguin, Harmondsworth, 1973). The increase in the members of the Community was subsequently followed by Greece in 1981 and Portugal and Spain in 1986. These developments are well documented in Nicholson, Frances and East, Roger, *From the Six to the Twelve: The Enlargement of the European Communities* (Longman, 1987). But despite the expansion of membership in the 1970s, the decade was primarily dominated by the sluggish growth of the Community, partly through a lack of institutional leadership and partly through the general economic downturn caused by the major oil shocks in 1973 and later in 1979. That the Community made progress towards the end of the decade, with plans for the creation of the European Monetary System, owes much to the leadership of Roy Jenkins during his Presidency of the European Commission (1977–81). A detailed and informative account of this period can be found in Jenkins, Roy, *European Diary 1977–1981* (Collins, 1989). This period also witnessed the introduction of direct elections to the European Parliament, for the first time in 1979. On this topic, one should consult Butler, David, and Marquand, David *European Elections and British Politics* (Longman, 1981), Butler, David and Jowett, Paul, *Party Strategies in Britain: A Study of the 1984 European Parliament Elections* (Macmillan, Houndmills, 1985), Lodge, Juliet (ed.), *Direct Elections to the European Parliament 1984* (Macmillan, Houndmills, 1985), Lodge, Juliet (ed.), *The 1989 Election of the European Parliament* (Macmillan, Houndmills, 1990), and Lodge, Juliet (ed.), *The 1994 Elections to the European Parliament* (Pinter, 1996). A good review of the challenges which the Community faced in the early 1980s is provided by Tsoukalis, Loukas (ed.), *The European Community: Past, Present and Future* (Blackwell, Oxford, 1983), while fine personal opinions from those on the 'inside' can be found in Butler, Michael, *Europe: More than a Continent* (Heinemann, 1986) and Tugendhat, Christopher, *Making Sense of Europe* (Penguin, Harmondsworth, 1986).

The reform of the 1980s

The 1980s heralded renewed optimism in the Community, especially with the appointment in 1985 of Jacques Delors as President of the

European Commission: he remained in the position until 1995. During that time he was an important motivator behind greater European integration and one should consult Grant, Charles, *Delors: Inside the House that Jacques Built* (Nicholas Brealey Publishing, 1994) for a fair assessment of his period in office. A more biased account in favour of Delors, but nonetheless useful, can be found in Ross, George, *Jacques Delors and European Integration* (Polity Press, Cambridge, 1995). The significant development of the 1980s was the intergovernmental conference in the second half of 1985 which led to the Single European Act. It provided the momentum for the single market programme and sparked debate as to where power lay within the Community. In this context, some academics considered that the reform had been motivated by the leadership of the European Commission, a view advocated by Sandholtz, W. and Zysman, J., '1992: Recasting the European Bargain, *World Politics*, Vol. 42, No. 1, 1989, pp. 95–128. By contrast, Moravcsik, Andrew, 'Negotiating the Single European Act: National Interests and Conventional Statecraft in the European Community', *International Organization*, Vol. 45, No. 1, 1991, pp. 19–56, considered change had been essentially shaped by the three most powerful nations: the UK, France and Germany, a view which he later refined in Moravcsik, Andrew, 'Preferences and Power in the European Community: A Liberal Intergovernmentalist Approach', *Journal of Common Market Studies*, Vol. 31, No. 4, December 1993, pp. 473–524. One should also consult Cameron, David, 'The 1992 Initiative: Causes and Consequences', in Sbragia, Albert M. (ed.), *Euro-Politics: Institutions and Policymaking in the New European Community* (Brookings, Washington, 1992). These, and other relevant theories in European integration, can be found in Nelsen, Brent and Stubb, Alexander (eds), *The European Union: Readings on the Theory and Practice of European Integration* (Lynne Reinner, Boulder, CO, 1994).

An important aspect of the Single European Act was the focus attached to the single market, and readers should consult Cecchini, P., *The European Challenge, 1992: The Benefits of a Single Market* (Wildwood House, Aldershot, 1988) and Albert, M. and Ball, J., *Towards European Economic Recovery in the 1980s* (European Parliament Working Documents, 1983/84, Luxembourg). One should similarly examine Crouch, Colin, *The Politics of 1992: Beyond the Single European Market* (Basil Blackwell, Oxford, 1990) and Grahl, John and Teague, Paul, *The Big Market: The Future of the European Community* (Lawrence and Wishart, 1990). A particularly easy read is Palmer, John, *1992 and Beyond* (Office for Official Publications of the European Communities, Luxembourg, 1989). The Single European Act also brought with it a strengthening in the powers of the European Parliament through the cooperation procedure.

From Maastricht to Amsterdam

It was not until the 1990–91 intergovernmental conferences on political union and monetary union that significant reform of the European Parliament's powers took place, it being granted the co-decision procedure. The Single European Act also called for a commitment towards monetary union, a goal established in the 1992 Treaty on European Union. The momentum towards this process is examined in De Grauwe, P. and Papademos, L. (eds), *The European Monetary System in the 1990s* (Longman, 1990). One should also see Gros, D. and Thygesen, N., *European Monetary Integration* (Longman, 1992), and Marsh, D., *The Bundesbank: The Bank that Rules Europe* (Mandarin, 1993). In 1990–91 the UK government was reluctant to proceed to a single currency but did consider that the existing ECU could be strengthened to become a common currency. This plan proved unacceptable to the other Member States and its details can be found in Grice, J., 'The UK Proposal for a European Monetary Fund and a "Hard ECU": Making Progress towards Economic and Monetary Union in Europe', *Treasury Bulletin* (HMSO, Autumn 1990, pp. 1–9). On the issue of monetary union, a fine and balanced account is that of Dyson, K., *Elusive Union: The Process of Economic and Monetary Union in Europe* (Longman, 1994). An anti-monetary union and biased opinion is that of Connolly, B., *The Rotten Heart of Europe* (Faber and Faber, 1995), which is a colourful inside view by a former European Commission employee. An analysis of European economic affairs can also be found in Tsoukalis, Loukas, *The New European Economy: The Politics and Economics of Integration* (Oxford University Press, Oxford, 1993) and Healey, Nigel (ed.), *The Economics of the New Europe: From Community to Union* (Routledge, 1995).

For a review of the 1990–91 intergovernmental conference, see Laursen, F. and Vanhoonacker, S. (eds), *The Intergovernmental Conference on Political Union: Institutional Reforms, New Policies and International Identity of the European Community* (Martinus Nijhoff, Dordrecht, 1992) and O'Keefe, David and Twomey, Patrick (eds), *Legal Issues of the Maastricht Treaty* (Wiley Chancery, Chichester, 1995). Other useful accounts are Noel, Emile, 'Reflections on the Maastricht Treaty', *Government and Opposition*, Vol. 27, 1992, and Corbett, Richard, 'The Intergovernmental Conference on Political Union', *Journal of Common Market Studies*, Vol. 30, No. 3, September 1992, pp. 271–98. A detailed account of the UK's involvement in the Maastricht Treaty negotiations can be found in Blair, Alasdair, *Dealing with Europe: Britain and the Negotiation of the Maastricht Treaty* (Ashgate, Aldershot, 1999). An aspect of this Treaty was the inclusion of citizenship. A useful text on this subject is Rosas, Allan and Antola, Esko (eds), *A Citizen's Europe: In Search of a New Order* (Sage, 1995), while an understanding of social policy can be obtained in Wise, Mark and Gibb, Richard, *Single Market to Social Europe* (Longman, 1993). A further important aspect of the Maastricht Treaty was the creation of a Committee of the Regions. This, and the growing importance of regional and federal government within EU Member States, has increased the role of regional government within the EU, provoking a shift to a further level of decision-making – a third (regional) level. Such changes are examined in Jeffery, Charlie (ed.), *The Regional Dimension of the European Union: Towards a Third Level in Europe* (Frank Cass, Ilford, 1997).

The Treaty on European Union and the end of the Cold War brought with it further emphasis on the question of future developments in the 1990s, and these challenges are tackled in Lodge, Juliet (ed.), *The European Community and the Challenge of the Future* (Pinter, 1993) and Duff, A., Pinder, J. and Pryce, A., *Maastricht and Beyond: Building the European Union* (Routledge, 1994). A comprehensive review of the post-Cold War development of the European Union is Hayward, J. and Page, E. (eds), *Governing the New Europe* (Polity Press, Cambridge, 1995). A far shorter, but nonetheless useful, analysis of Europe is Miall, Hugh, *Shaping the New Europe* (Pinter, 1993), with a wider emphasis on the security as well as political challenges.

The possibility of a review conference was built into the Treaty on European Union, resulting in the 1996–97 intergovernmental conference to amend the Treaties. Time has not yet allowed for comprehensive analysis of this negotiation and the 1997 Treaty of Amsterdam, but it is worth examining Xuereb, Peter G. and Pace, Roderick, *The European Union, The IGC and the Mediterranean* (European Documentation and Research Centre, University of Malta, 1996). Although published before the completion of the conference, it nonetheless provides an insight to national positions. A more substantial contribution is that of Westlake, Martin, *The European Union beyond Amsterdam: New Concepts of Integration* (Routledge, 1998), which outlines possible future developments, while Rees, W., Neuwahl, N. and Lynch, P., *Reforming the European Union* (Longman, 1999) provides a more in-depth analysis of Amsterdam and its aftermath. Possible future reform of the EU is analysed by Dehousse, Renaud, *Europe: The Impossible Status Quo* (Macmillan, Houndmills, 1997) for the Club of Florence, a group consisting of former senior European Commission officials.

Policy dynamics

The changes to the European Community since its creation in 1957 have produced some fine literature which has focused upon concepts of integration and policy dynamics, including Ionescu, Ghita, *The New*

Politics of European Integration (Macmillan, Houndmills, 1972), Holland, Martin, *European Community Integration* (Pinter, 1993) and Wallace, William, *The Dynamics of European Integration* (Pinter, 1990). A particularly good study is that of Keohane, R. and Hoffman, S., *The New European Community: Decision Making and Institutional Change* (Westview Press, Boulder, CO, 1991), while one of the best is George, Stephen, *Politics and Policy in the European Community* (3rd edn, Oxford University Press, Oxford, 1996). Lafflan, Brigid, *Integration and Cooperation in Europe* (Routledge, 1992) also provides a clear, thematic account. Readers should equally consult O'Neill, Michael (ed.), *The Politics of European Integration: A Reader* (Routledge, 1996) and Nugent, N., *The Government and Politics of the European Union* (3rd edn, Macmillan, Houndmills, 1994).

Regarding policy-making within the EU, see Cram, Laura, *Policy-making in the EU* (Routledge, 1997), which analyses the EU policy process through social policy and information technology policy. One should also consult Richardson, Jeremy (ed.), *European Union: Power and Policy-Making* (Routledge, 1996), while Marks, G., Scharpf, F., Schmitter, P. and Streek, W., *Governance in the European Union* (Sage, 1996) is also worthy. A comprehensive survey is that of Wallace, H. and Wallace, W. (eds), *Policy-Making in the European Union* (Oxford University Press, Oxford, 1996).

Institutions

An important aspect of policy-making within the EU is the roles played by the institutional actors, which have undergone rapid periods of change in recent years. This is especially true for the European Parliament which obtained the co-decision power in the Treaty on European Union. An insider account of its work is provided by Westlake, Martin, *A Modern Guide to the European Parliament* (Pinter, 1994). Also see Corbett, R., Jacobs, F. and Shackleton, M., *The European Parliament* (3rd edn, Cartermill, 1995). As the initiator of policy, the European Commission has played an important role in the development of the Community and it is worth consulting the highly readable and detailed account by Cini, Michelle, *The European Commission* (Manchester University Press, Manchester, 1996). One should also see Edwards, G. and Spence, D. (eds), *The European Commission* (Longman, 1994) and Nugent, Neil (ed.), *At the Heart of the Union: Studies of the European Commission* (Macmillan, Houndmills, 1997). The complex relationship between the European Commission and European Parliament is covered by Westlake, M., *The Commission and the Parliament: Partners and Rivals in the European Policy-Making Process* (Butterworth, 1994). But the policy-making process does not just involve the main institutions and national governments. A great number of interest groups are also actively involved in this process. For the best account, see Greenwood, Justin, *Representing Interests in the European Union* (Macmillan, Houndmills, 1997).

Member States have clearly been central to Community policy procedures, and in recent years the European Council has taken on a significant role as an initiator and resolver of disputes. A useful study of the creation of the European Council is that of Morgan, Annette, *From Summit to Council: Evolution in the EEC* (Chatham House, 1976), while a highly readable, if somewhat dated, study is Bulmer, S. and Wessels, W., *The European Council* (Macmillan, Houndmills, 1987). A comprehensive review of the European Council's work can be found in Werts, Jan, *The European Council* (North Holland, Amsterdam, 1992). It is also worth consulting Johnston, Mary, *The European Council. Gatekeeper of the European Community* (Westview Press, Boulder, CO, 1994). One should equally see Westlake, Martin and Trumpf, Jürgen, *The Council of the European Union* (Catermill, 1995). An important duty of Member States is chairing the Presidency of the Council of Ministers, an early account of which is Edwards, Geoffrey and Wallace, Helen, *The Council of Ministers of the European Community and the President in-Office* (Federal Trust, 1977). Also see O'Nuallain, C., *The Presidency of the European Council of Ministers* (Croom Helm, 1987), and Kirchner, Emil, *Decision-Making in the European Community, the Council Presidency and European Integration* (Manchester University Press, Manchester, 1992). A highly readable account is provided by de Bassompierre, Guy, *Changing the Guard in Brussels: An Insider's View of the EC Presidency* (Praeger, New York, 1988). Analysis of the work of the Presidency during an intergovernmental conference is outlined in Kirchner, Emil and Tsagkari, Anastassia, *The EC Council Presidency. The Dutch and Luxembourg Presidencies* (UACES, 1993). On this topic it is also worth consulting the views of the former UK Foreign Minister, Garel-Jones, Tristan, 'The UK Presidency: An Inside View', *Journal of Common Market Studies*, Vol. 31, No. 2, June 1993, pp. 261–7. An excellent and highly readable text on the Council of Ministers is Hayes-Renshaw, F. and Wallace, H., *The Council of Ministers* (Macmillan, Houndmills, 1997).

As a lot of the work of the EU is legalistic, it is worthwhile to examining some relevant texts, especially Weatherill, Stephen and Beaumont, Paul, *EC Law. The Essential Guide to the Legal Workings of the European Community* (Penguin, Harmondsworth, 1993) and Wyatt, Derek, *European Community Law* (3rd edn, Sweet and Maxwell, 1993). Also see Kent, Penelope, *Law of the European Union* (2nd edn, Pitman, 1996), Charlesworth, Andrew and Cullen, Holly, *European Community Law* (Pitman, 1994), and Foster, Nigel, *Blackstone's EC Legislation* (4th edn, Blackstone Press, 1993). On the Court of Justice the most recent text is Dehousse, Renaud, *The European Court of Justice: The Politics of Judicial Integration* (Macmillan, Houndmills, 1998).

Foreign policy

Since the 1970s an important aspect of European affairs has been cooperation between Member States in the realms of foreign policy. Texts
worthy of examination include Allen, D., Rummel, R. and Wessels, W.,
European Political Co-operation: Towards a Foreign Policy for Western Europe
(Butterworth Scientific, 1982) and Hill, Christopher (ed.), *National Foreign Policies and European Political Cooperation* (George Allen and Unwin,
Hemel Hempstead, 1983). The process of European Political Cooperation was incorporated by the SEA Treaty in 1987, developments of which
in the 1980s can be charted in Pijpers, A., Regelsberger, E. and Wessels,
W. (eds), *European Political Cooperation in the 1980s: A Common Foreign
Policy for Western Europe?* (Martinus Nijhoff, Dordrecht, 1988). More
recent changes took place in the Treaty on European Union with its
expansion into a common foreign and security policy. One should examine
Rummel, R. (ed.), *Toward Political Union: Planning a Common Foreign and
Security Policy in the European Community* (Westview Press, Boulder, CO,
1992) and Carlsnaes, W. and Smith, S. (eds), *European Foreign Policy: The
EC and Changing Perspectives in Europe* (London, 1994). A broader focus
can be found in Petersen, N. (ed.), *The European Community in World
Politics* (Pinter, 1993) and Regelsberger, E. et al. (eds), *Foreign Policy of
the European Union* (Lynne Reinner, Boulder, CO, 1997). Those who
wish to examine the influence of Member States on European foreign
policy should consult Hill, Christopher (ed.), *The Actors in Europe's Foreign Policy* (Routledge, 1996).

Member States

Coverage of the impact of the EU on Member States is provided by
Mény, Y., Muller, P. and Quermonne, J.L., *Adjusting to Europe: The Impact
of the European Union on National Institutions and Policies* (Routledge, 1996).
Other general studies on politics and government in Europe include the
excellent Smith, Gordon, *Politics in Western Europe* (5th edn, Dartmouth,
Aldershot, 1990) and Campbell, C., Feigenbaum, H., Linden, R. and
Norpoth, H., *Politics and Government in Europe Today* (Houghton Miffin
Company, Boston, 1995). Clearly, an important aspect of the impact of
the EU upon Member States has been its implication for political parties
and the construction and development of transnational links. But the
importance of party politics to the functioning of the EU is an often
underestimated issue and this is a point stressed by Hix, Simon and
Lord, Christopher, *Political Parties in the European Union* (Macmillan,
Houndmills, 1997).

Turning to national studies, on Germany one should see Bulmer,
S. and Paterson, W., *The Federal Republic of Germany and the European*

Community (Allen and Unwin, 1987), and Schweitzer, C.-C. and Karsten, D. (eds), *The Federal Republic of Germany and EC Membership Evaluated* (Pinter, 1990). A very useful text is that of Padgett, Stephen (ed.), *Adenauer to Kohl: The Development of the German Chancellorship* (Hurst and Company, 1994), while the Schmidt Chancellorship is explored by Carr, Jonathan, *Helmut Schmidt: Helmsman of Germany* (Weidenfeld and Nicolson, 1995). The difficulties surrounding German unification are examined by Fritsch-Bournazel, Renata, *Europe and German Unification* (Berg, Oxford, 1992) as well as Marsh, David, *Germany and Europe: The Crisis of Unity* (Heinemann, 1994), while the post-unification period is examined by Larres, Klaus *Germany since Unification: The Domestic and External Consequences* (Macmillan, Houndmills, 1997). The relationship between Germany and the EU is outlined in Lankowski, Carl, *Germany and the European Community* (Macmillan, Houndmills, 1994). For an informative and up-to-date account of French politics, consult Stevens, Anne, *The Government and Politics of France* (2nd edn, Macmillan, Houndmills, 1996). Regarding its relationship with Europe, see Wadia, K. and Williams, W., *France and Europe* (School of Languages and European Studies, University of Wolverhampton, Wolverhampton, 1993) and Guyomarch, A., Machin, H. and Ritchie, E., *France in the European Union* (Macmillan, Houndmills, 1998). The latter focuses on the impact of EU policies on France and how they have transformed many aspects of the domestic, economic and political environment. On Italy, one should see Francioni, Francesco (ed.), *Italy and EC Membership Evaluated* (Pinter, 1992), while for Spain, consult Barbado, A.A. (ed.), *Spain and EC Membership Evaluated* (Pinter, 1993). The best account of Spanish domestic politics is Heywood, Paul, *The Government and Politics of Spain* (Macmillan, Houndmills, 1995). The question of the accession of new Member States is tackled by Redmond, John (ed.), *Prospective Europeans: New Members for the European Union* (Harvester Wheatsheaf, Hemel Hempstead, 1994), while the EU's policies towards those Member States is examined in Mayhew, Alan, *Recreating Europe: The European Union's Policy Towards Central and Eastern Europe* (Cambridge University Press, Cambridge, 1998). It is also worth consulting Maresceau, Marc, *Enlarging the European Union: Relations between the EU and Central and Eastern Europe* (Longman, 1997).

The UK and Europe

The 1990s have witnessed both a development in the progress of the EU and a growing unrest among the national public, demonstrated by such events as the May 1992 Danish negative vote on the Treaty on European Union. However, it has been within the UK that Euro-scepticism has been particularly apparent, with the last Conservative government dividing over the issue of Europe. It is therefore worth consulting Holmes,

Martin (ed.), *The Eurosceptical Reader* (Macmillan, Houndmills, 1996). Other sceptical accounts include Spicer, Michael, *A Treaty Too Far: A New Policy for Europe* (Fourth Estate, 1992), Gorman, T., *The Bastards: Dirty Tricks and the Challenge to Europe* (Pan Books, 1993), and Goldsmith, James, *The Trap* (Macmillan, Houndmills, 1994).

General introductory texts on the UK and Europe (apart from those listed above) are Pilkington, Colin, *Britain in the European Union Today* (Manchester University Press, Manchester, 1995) and Greenwood, Sean, *Britain and European Integration since 1945* (Blackwell, Oxford, 1992). An extremely good text is George, S., *An Awkward Partner* (2nd edn, Oxford University Press, Oxford, 1994), and one should also consult Young, J.W., *Britain and European Unity, 1945–1992* (Macmillan, Houndmills, 1993). A short chronological, rather than thematic, review is May, Alex, *Britain and Europe since 1945* (Longman, 1998). Comprehensive analysis of specific policy areas can be found in Bulmer, S., George, S. and Scott, A. (eds), *The United Kingdom and EC Membership Evaluated* (Pinter, 1992). Those who wish to consult documentation should see Greenwood, Sean (ed.), *Britain and European Integration since the Second World War* (Manchester University Press, Manchester, 1996).

The options available to the UK in the post-war years are examined in Ovendale, R. (ed.), *The Foreign Policy of the British Labour Governments 1945–51* (Leicester University Press, Leicester, 1984) and Becker, J. and Knipping, F. (eds), *Power in Europe? France, Great Britain, Germany and Italy in a Post-war World, 1945–50* (New York, 1986). The best account of the UK's first application to the EEC is Ludlow, N. Piers, *Dealing with Europe: The Six and the First UK Application to the EEC* (Cambridge University Press, Cambridge, 1997).

It is important for anyone engaging in detailed research on the UK to consult memoirs. These include Brown, George, *In My Way* (Penguin, Harmondsworth, 1972), who highlights his views on Europe in Chapter 11. The specific tension of the Thatcher governments in the 1980s can be seen from many perspectives. A sympathetic view towards Europe is provided by Howe, Geoffrey, *Conflict of Loyalty* (Macmillan, Houndmills, 1994), who skilfully details his years as Foreign Secretary. The duties of that job are also examined in Dickie, J., *Inside the Foreign Office* (Chapmans, 1992) and Edwards, R.D., *True Brits: Inside the Foreign Office* (BBC Books, 1994). An extremely detailed study is Lawson, Nigel, *The View From No. 11* (Bantam Press, 1992), who, as a former Chancellor, injects an economic viewpoint into the debate. On many crucial points, both Howe and Lawson differ from the account of Thatcher, Margaret, *The Downing Street Years* (HarperCollins, 1993). This is particularly true for the later period of her administration. The recent publication of the memoirs of Thatcher's predecessor as leader of the Conservative Party, Sir Edward Heath, have provided a valuable source of information beyond his period as Prime Minister in the early 1970s. See Edward Heath, *The Course of My Life* (Hodder and Stoughton, 1998).

The decline of Margaret Thatcher and the appointment of John Major as Prime Minister in November 1990 brought with it a shift in the UK's relationship with its European partners. Although Major suggested in March 1991 that the country could be at the 'heart of Europe', this proved not to be the case. On the early years of the Major government it is worth consulting Hogg, S. and Hill, J., *Too Close To Call: Power and Politics – John Major in No. 10* (Little, Brown and Company, Boston, MA, 1995). With both of the writers being employed in No. 10, this is not a critical evaluation of the Major premiership, but Chapters 5 and 9 do provide good insight on European affairs. Another memoir to consult is Baker, Kenneth, *The Turbulent Years: My Life in Politics* (Faber and Faber, 1993). He was, however, frozen out of much of the crucial policy-making on European affairs in 1991, and as Home Secretary did not inject much influence on the justice and home affairs debate prior to Maastricht, a factor which is apparent by his comments in Chapters 17 and 19.

A more wide-ranging survey of the Major government is that of Kavanagh, Dennis and Seldon, Anthony (eds), *The Major Effect* (Macmillan, Houndmills, 1994). The chapter on foreign policy by William Wallace is especially worth consulting. The most detailed biography of Major is Seldon, Anthony, *Major: A Political Life* (Weidenfeld and Nicolson, 1997), while a broad view of the Thatcher and Major governments can be found in Cradock, Percy, *In Pursuit of British Interests: Reflections on Foreign Policy under Margaret Thatcher and John Major* (John Murray, 1997). As a former adviser to both Prime Ministers, this is a particularly authoritative study. Readers can also consult Ludlam, S. and Smith, S. (eds), *Contemporary British Conservatism* (Macmillan, Houndmills, 1996).

SECTION XIII

Maps and Diagram

Map 1   The Six (1957)

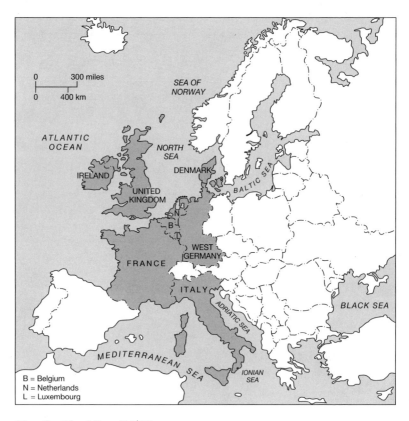

Map 2   The Nine (1973)

Map 3   The Ten (1981)

Map 4   The Twelve (1986)

Map 5   The Fifteen and enlargement (1995)

		EUROPEAN UNION (15)

	EUROPEAN UNION (12)		
WESTERN EUROPEAN UNION (9)	France, Germany, the Netherlands, Belgium, Luxembourg, Italy, the UK, Spain, Portugal	Ireland	Austria, Finland, Sweden
	Denmark, Greece		

NORTH ATLANTIC TREATY ORGANISATION (16)   Canada, USA, Iceland, Turkey, Norway

European institutional dimensions

APPENDIX

Useful Addresses

Member States

Austria

Federal Government: http://www.austria.gv.at/

Permanent Representation to the EU
Avenue de Cortenbergh 30, B–1040 Brussels, Belgium
Tel: (32–2) 282 11 11   Fax: (32–2) 230 79 30

European Commission Representation
Kärtner Ring 5–7, A–1010 Vienna, Austria
Tel: (43–1) 516 18   Fax: (43–1) 513 4225

Belgium

Federal Government: http://belgium.fgov.be/

Permanent Representation to the EU
Rue Belliard 62, B–1040, Brussels, Belgium
Tel: (32–2) 233 21 11   Fax: (32–2) 233 10 75

European Commission Representation
Rue Archiméde 73, B–1000 Brussels, Belgium
Tel: (32–2) 295 38 44   Fax: (32–2) 295 01 66

Denmark

Government: http://www.sdn.dk/sdn/jump/minstyr.htm

Permanent Representation to the EU
Rue d'Arlon 73, B–1040, Brussels, Belgium
Tel: (32–2) 233 08 11   Fax: (32–2) 230 93 84

European Commission Representation
Østergade 61, Postbox 144, DK–1004, Copenhagen, Denmark
Tel: (45–33) 14 41 40   Fax: (45–33) 11 12 03

Finland

Government: http://www.vn.fi/

Permanent Representation to the EU
Rue de Trèves 100, B–1040 Brussels, Belgium
Tel: (32–2) 287 84 11   Fax: (32–2) 287 84 00

European Commission Representation
Pohjoisesplanadi 31, FIN–00100 Helsinki, Finland
Tel: (358–9) 62 65 44   Fax: (358–9) 65 67 28

France

Government: http://www.france.diplomatie.fr/

Permanent Representation to the EU
Place de Louvain 14, B–1000 Brussels, Belgium
Tel: (32–2) 229 82 11   Fax: (32–2) 229 82 82

European Commission Representation
Bld St Germanin 288, F–75007 Paris, France
Tel: (33–1) 40 63 38 00   Fax: (33–1) 45 56 94 17/19

Germany

Government: http://www.bundesregierung.de/

Permanent Representation to the EU
Rue Jacques de Lalaing 19–21, B–1040 Brussels, Belgium
Tel: (32–2) 238 18 11   Fax: (32–2) 238 19 78

European Commission Representation
Kurfürstendam 102, D–10711 Berlin, Germany
Tel: (49–30) 896 09 30   Fax: (49–30) 892 290 59

Greece

Government: http://www.mfa.gr/

Permanent Representation to the EU
Rue Montoyer 25, B–1040 Brussels, Belgium
Tel: (32–2) 551 56 11   Fax: (32–2) 551 56 51

European Commission Representation
2 Vassilissis Sofias, Athens GR–106 74, Greece
Tel: (30–1) 725 10 00   Fax: (30–1) 724 46 20

Ireland

Government: http://www.irlgov.ie/

Permanent Representation to the EU
Rue Froissart 89–93, B–1040 Brussels, Belgium
Tel: (32–2) 230 85 80   Fax: (32–2) 230 32 03

European Commission Representation
18 Dawson Street, Dublin 2, Ireland
Tel: (353–1) 662 51 13   Fax: (353–1) 662 51 18

Italy

Government: http://www.aipa.it/

Permanent Representation to the EU
Rue du Marteau 9, B–1040 Brussels, Belgium
Tel: (32–2) 220 04 01   Fax: (32–2) 219 34 49

European Commission Representation
Via Poli 29, I–00187 Rome, Italy
Tel: (39–6) 69 99 91   Fax: (39–6) 679 16 58/679 36 52

Luxembourg

Government: http://www.restena.lu/gover/

Permanent Representation to the EU
Avenue de Cortenbergh 75, B–1000 Brussels, Belgium
Tel: (32–2) 737 56 00   Fax: (32–2) 737 56 10

European Commission Representation
Bâtiment Jean Monnet, Rue Alcide de Gasperi, L–2920 Luxembourg
Tel: (352) 4301 34925   Fax: (352) 4301 34433

The Netherlands

Government: http://www.postbus51.nl/

Permanent Representation to the EU
Avenue Herman Debroux 48, B–1160 Brussels, Belgium
Tel: (32–2) 679 15 11   Fax: (32–2) 679 17 15

European Commission Representation
Korte Vijverberg 5, 2513 AB The Hague, The Netherlands
Postal address: Postbus 30465, 2500GL The Hague, The Netherlands
Tel: (31–70) 346 93 26   Fax: (31–70) 364 66 19

Portugal

Government: http://www.infocid.pt/

Permanent Representation to the EU
Rue Marie-Thérèse 11–13, B–1040 Brussels, Belgium
Tel: (32–2) 227 42 00   Fax: (32–2) 218 15 42

European Commission Representation
Largo Jean Monnet 1–10, P–1200 Lisbon, Portugal
Tel: (351–1) 350 98 00   Fax: (351–1) 350 98 01

Spain

Government: http://www.la-moncloa.es/

Permanent Representation to the EU
Boulevard du Régent 52–54, B–1000 Brussels, Belgium
Tel: (32–2) 509 86 11   Fax: (32–2) 511 19 40

European Commission Representation
Paseo de la Castellana 46, E–28046 Madrid, Spain
Tel: (34–1) 431 57 11   Fax: (34–1) 432 17 64

Sweden

Government: http://www.regeringen.se/

Permanent Representation to the EU
Squar de Meeûss 30, B–1000, Brussels, Belgium
Tel: (32–2) 289 56 11   Fax: (32–2) 289 56 00

European Commission Representation
Nybrogatan 11, Box 7323, S–10390 Stockholm, Sweden
Tel: (46–8) 562 444 11   Fax: (46–8) 562 444 12

The United Kingdom

Government: http://www.fco.gov.uk/

Permanent Representation to the EU
Avenue d'Auderghem 10, B–1040 Brussels, Belgium
Tel: (32–2) 287 82 11   Fax: (32–2) 287 83 98
http://ukrep.fco.gov.uk/

European Commission Representation
8 Storey's Gate, London SW1P 3AT, UK
Tel: 0171–973 1992   Fax: 0171–973 1900

European Union

Commission of the European Communities
Rue de la Loi 200, B–1049 Brussels, Belgium
Tel: (32–2) 299 11 11   Fax: (32–2) 295 01 38
http://europa.eu.int/comm/index_en.htm

Bâtiment Jean Monnet, Rue Alcide De Gasperi, L–2920 Luxembourg
Tel: (352) 43 011   Fax: (352) 43 61 24
http://europa.eu.int/comm/index_en.htm

Committee of the Regions
Rue Belieard 79, B–1049 Brussels, Belgium
Tel: (32–2) 282 22 11   Fax: (32–2) 282 23 25
http://www.cor.eu.int/

Council of Europe
Palais de l'Europe, 67006 Strasbourg, Cedex, France
Tel: (33–3) 88 41 20 33   Fax: (33–3) 88 41 27 80
http://www.coe.fr/index.asp

Council of the European Union
Centre de Conférences, Plateau du Kirchberg, L–2929 Luxembourg
Tel: (352) 43 00–1
http://ue.eu.int/

Council of the European Union General Secretariat
Rue de la Loi 175, B–1048 Brussels, Belgium
Tel: (32–2) 285 61 11   Fax: (32–2) 285 73 97
http://ue.eu.int/

Court of Auditors
Rue Alcide de Gasperi 12, L–1615 Luxembourg
Tel: (352) 439 81   Fax: (352) 439 342
http://www.eca.eu.int/

Court of Auditors (sub-office)
Rue de la Loi 83–85, B–1040 Brussels, Belgium
Tel: (32–2) 230 50 90   Fax: (32–2) 230 64 83
http://www.eca.eu.int/

Court of Justice of the European Communities
Palais de la Cour de Justice, L–2925 Luxembourg
Tel: (352) 430 31   Fax: (352) 4303 2600
http://europa.eu.int/cj/

Economic and Social Committee (EcoSoc)
Rue Ravenstein 2, 1000 Brussels, Belgium
Tel: (32–2) 546 90 11   Fax: (32–2) 513 48 93
http://www.esc.eu.int/

European Agency for Safety and Health at Work
Gran Via 33, E–48009 Bilbao, Spain
Tel: (34–4) 479 43 60   Fax: (34–4) 479 43 83
http://www.eu-osha.es/

European Central Bank
Postfach 16 03 19, D–60066 Frankfurt am Main, Germany
Tel: (49–69) 13 44 0   Fax: (49–69) 13 44 6000
http://ecb.int/

European Centre for the Development of Vocational Training (CEDEFOP)
12 Marinou Antipa, GR–57001, Thessaloniki, Greece
Tel: (30) 31 490 111   Fax: (30) 31 490 102
http://www.cedefob.gr

European Court of Human Rights
http://www.dhcour.coe.fr/

European Environment Agency
Kongens Nytorv 6, DK–1050 Copenhagen, Denmark
Tel: (45) 33 36 71 00   Fax: (45) 33 36 71 99
http://www.eea.dk/

European Investment Bank
Boulevard Konrad Adenauer 100, L–2950 Luxembourg
Tel: (352) 43791   Fax: (352) 43 77 04
http://www.eib.org/

European Monetary Institute
Eurotower, Kaiserstraße 29, D–60311, Frankfurt am Main, Germany
Tel: (49–69) 27 2270   Fax: (49–69) 27 227 227
http://www.ecb.int/

European Ombudsman
Avenue du Président Robert Schuman 1, B.P. 403, F–67001 Strasbourg,
France
Tel: (33–3) 88 17 2313   Fax: (33–3) 88 17 90 62
http://www.euro-ombudsman.eu.int

European Parliament (Main Secretariat)
Centre Européen, Plateau du Kirchberg, L–2929 Luxembourg
Tel: (352) 430 01   Fax: (352) 43 00 4842
http://www.europarl.eu.int/

European Parliament (Plenary Sessions)
Palais de l'Europe, F–67006 Strasbourg, Cedex, France
Tel: (33–3) 88 17 40 01   Fax: (33–3) 88 17 48 60
http://www.europarl.eu.int/

European Police Office and Europol Drugs Unit
PO Box 90850, NL–2509, The Hague, The Netherlands
Tel: (31–70) 3025 302   Fax: (31–70) 3455 896

European Training Foundation
Villa Gualino, I–10133 Torino, Viale Settimio Severo, 65, Italy
Tel: (39–11) 630 22 22   Fax: (39–11) 630 22 00
http://www.etf.eu.int/etfweb.nsf

European University Institute
Badia Fiesolana, Via dei Roccettini 5, 50016 San Domenico di Fiesole, Florence, Italy

Office for Official Publications of the European Communities
Rue Mercier 2, L–2985 Luxembourg
Tel: (352) 2929–1   Fax: (352) 49 57 19
http://eur-op.eu.int/

Statistical Office of the European Communities
Bâtiment Jean Monnet, Rue Alcide De Gasperi, L–2920 Luxembourg
Tel: (352) 4301–34567   Fax: (352) 4301–32594
http://europa.eu.int/eurostat.html

Other

North Atlantic Assembly
Place du Petit Sablon 3, B–1000 Brussels, Belgium
Tel: (32–2) 513 28 65   Fax: (32–2) 514 18 47

North Atlantic Treaty Organisation
Office of Information and Press, B–1110, Brussels, Belgium
Fax: (32–2) 707–4579

OSCE Secretariat
Kärtner Ring 5–7, A–1010 Vienna, Austria
Tel: (43–1) 514 360   Fax: (43–1) 514 3699

Western European Union
Rue de la Régence 4, B–1000 Brussels, Belgium
Tel: (32–2) 511 19 16   Fax: (32–2) 513 30 98

Western European Union Assembly
Avenue du Président Wilson 43, 75775 Paris, Cedex 16, France
Tel: (33–1) 47 23 54 32   Fax: (33–1) 47 20 45 43

Western European Union Institute for Security Studies
Avenue du Président Wilson 43, 75775, Paris, Cedex 16, France
Tel: (33–1) 53 67 22 00   Fax: (33–1) 47 20 81 78

Afterword

The dramatic resignation of the European Commission in the early hours of 16 March 1999 has come at a particularly important time. One week earlier, Germany lost its finance minister, Oskar Lafontaine; the Bundesbank did not always share his views on financial matters and a lack of agreement and symmetry affected the stability of the newly born Euro. In more general terms, the EU faces difficult challenges, including the reform of its finances, farm and regional policies to make enlargement to the east possible (these policies are referred to as Agenda 2000.) And while one may expect the resignation of the executive to affect these policies, it is also evident that this development may lead to a long-term strengthening of the EU.

The Commission is just one of the EU institutions, it is unlikely that all commissioners will leave Brussels; those who are not directly criticised in the fraud report by the Committee of Independent Experts are likely to be reappointed by their member states. This is, however, a fate that will not fall on Edith Cresson, the former French Prime Minister, of whom the MEPs fraud report was particularly critical. It is also unlikely that the President of the Commission, Jacques Santer, will be reappointed. Although he is regarded as a decent man, he fundamentally failed to manage the Commission in a coherent manner, as individual Commissioners were given freedom to pursue policies. This leeway contrasted with the tight control that Jacques Delors had exercised upon the Commission, although a policy of domination did not necessarily produce consensus. The fraud report specifically noted that 'The committee did not encounter cases where a commissioner was directly and personally involved in fraudulent activities. It found, however, instances where commissioners, or the Commission as a whole, bear responsibility for instances of fraud, irregularity or mismanagement in their services or areas of special responsibility'. The decision by the Commission to resign was taken in the face of the threat by the leaders of two of the four largest political groupings to resign or face dismissal. A network of officials does, however, support the 20-strong Commission, and it is they who will assist in keeping the ship running in the interim period. The major policies of reform will therefore continue.

Alasdair Blair
17 March 1999

This book went to press just as the events described above were unfolding.

Index